Childhood Bullying, Teasing, and Violence:

What School Personnel, Other Professionals, and Parents Can Do

Second Edition

Dorothea M. Ross, PhD
Research Psychologist
Department of Pediatrics
University of California, San Francisco

5999 Stevenson Avenue
Alexandria, VA 22304-3300
www.counseling.org

Childhood Bullying, Teasing, and Violence:

What School Personnel, Other Professionals, and Parents Can Do

Second Edition

10 9 8 7 6 5 4 3 2 1

American Counseling Association
5999 Stevenson Avenue
Alexandria, VA 22304

Director of Publications
Carolyn C. Baker

Production Manager
Bonny Gaston

Copy Editor
Elaine Dunn

Cover Design
Brian Gallagher

Library of Congress Cataloging-in-Publication Data

Ross, Dorothea M.
Childhood bullying, teasing, and violence: what school personnel, other professionals, and parents can do / Dorothea M. Ross.—2nd ed.
p. cm.
Rev. ed. of: Childhood bullying and teasing. c1996.
Includes bibliographical references and index.
ISBN 1-55620-196-6 (alk. paper)
1. Bullying—United States. 2. School discipline—United States.
I. Ross, Dorothea M. Childhood bullying and teasing. II. Title.
LB3011.5 .R67 2003
371.5′8—dc21

2002151997

Tomorrow is another day. And I wonder what it will bring. But deep down inside I already know that it will be another day of trying to find a safe route home from school, . . . seeing some old person walking in fear, seeing the police cars with . . . their sirens on, seeing the ambulance coming and going, and seeing the youth of America being shot down, and killed, before they even had a chance to live (17-year-old girl in low-income neighborhood). (Prothrow-Stith, 1991, p. 80)

Bullies "don't know how much they're hurting the people they're putting down," one middle school boy told us. A girl in Delaware said, "Some of the bullies don't know what they are doing. You have to educate them." "It starts with us," said one boy. "It's too late for our age group," said a 15-year-old girl at another high school, ". . . I don't know how you do this, but we need to make acceptance cool." (Horn, 2000, p. 38)

There has never . . . been a cohort of kids that is so little affected by adult guidance and so attuned to a peer world. . . . We have removed grown-up wisdom and allowed (children) to drift into a self-constructed, highly relativistic world of friendship and peers. (Damon, 1999, p. A3)

Contents

Preface

The 6 years since the publication of the first edition of this text, *Childhood Bullying and Teasing,* have been a most productive and exciting period for increasing our understanding of the problem of childhood bullying. Much of the progress that has occurred can be attributed to the exponential increase in productive collaboration across disciplinary lines with a resultant improvement in the quality and diversity of the research.

The status of bullying has undergone marked changes. It was formerly and irrationally viewed by many as a normal, if trying, part of childhood and adolescence that might even benefit the victim by making him or her stronger for the experience. This view elicited unhelpful comments such as "we all go through it," "fight back," and "boys will be boys." Bullying has now become so cruel and costly that it often leads its victims to kill their tormentors and make other violent responses such as trying to blow up the setting where much of it occurs (usually a school). A survey in March 2002 by the Henry J. Kaiser Family Foundation showed conclusively that bullying has become the primary problem of school children, far surpassing drugs and discrimination problems. The heightened national interest and concern about bullying has its roots in the spate of school killings directly linked to children tormented by long-term bullying. It has served to focus investigative interest on a far broader range of potential causes, effects, and populations. The result has been a number of advances in our theoretical approaches as well as our applied procedures.

The purpose of this second edition is to provide a comprehensive picture of the current status of our knowledge of bullying. To do this, a number of additions have been introduced. Two new chapters have been added, one on counseling and the other on violence. In the first edition of *Childhood Bullying and Teasing* (1996), counseling for bullies and victims was not discussed because of the paucity of available material: There were no texts and few journal articles focusing specifically on counseling bullies and victims. Richard J. Hazler has rectified this gap with *Breaking the Cycle of Violence: Interventions for Bullying and Victimization* (1996a).

Another notable advance has occurred with the realization that bullying, far from being solely a problem for children, extends into the adult realm. The plight of adults who are bullied at work has long been a matter of concern to worker protection organizations, but it is only recently that this problem has achieved prominence by becoming a topic of interest to behavioral scientists. The impetus for their interest was Randall's (1997) book, *Adult Bullying: Perpetrators and Victims,* that shows a close parallel between child victims in school and adult victims at work.

Many topics that merited only brief mention in the first edition or were the subject of speculation have now become part of the mainstream of bullying, with commensurate space in this text. Bullying has now achieved the status of being a crime, which makes available the use of legal deterrents and police attention for parents of victims to fall back on when attempting to halt attacks on their children. There is heightened awareness now of the importance of parental behavior in the prenatal and early years of life in the genesis of bullying. Telling schools—schools in which children are required to report bullying—at one time strongly rejected, are now encouraged, a change possibly related to an increased concern about school violence as well as hazing. In bullying episodes attention is no longer focused solely on the bully and victim. We now know the roles that bystanders can play in encouraging or discouraging ongoing bullying. A new book edited by Smith, Morita, et al. (1999) titled *The Nature of School Bullying: A Cross-National Perspective* describes what goes on about bullying in other countries and shows clearly that bullying is a global problem and that abuse can happen in any human group.

Unchanged in this second edition, *Childhood Bullying, Teasing, and Violence,* is the strong commitment to striking a balance between the need for rigorous methodology and the value of new ideas and concepts of a more speculative nature that may provide a link to innovative approaches to investigation and management. Also unchanged is the concern about the failure to date to develop one widely accepted definition of bullying. Definitions play a vital role in interpreting research findings: If exchanges of prevalence data and other findings are to have validity, it is essential that they meet the criteria described in the definition. The lack of consensus has been a continuing problem, although some progress has been made since the publication of the first edition of *Childhood Bullying and Teasing.* The three top researchers in bullying, Dan Olweus, David Perry, and Peter K. Smith, are using Olweus's definition. It is time for other investigators to accept it and move on.

Acknowledgments

The most important contribution to this book came from Sheila Ross, who gave generously of her expertise, creativity, time, and patience throughout the writing of it. Her commitment and interest in the topic never waned. The quality of the book has been greatly enhanced by her cogent comments and expertise in writing and editing.

I wish to express my deep thanks to Mark Roberts, MBE, of Orpington, Kent, England, for his continuing interest in the book and for his sustained contributions about childhood bullying that I could not otherwise have obtained.

A number of professionals took the time to respond generously to my questions and, in some cases, went back to their original data to do so. In this group are Kaj Björkqvist, Richard Hazler, Keith McBurnett, John J. Murphy, Herbert Needleman, Dan Olweus, Kenneth Rigby, Ronald Slaby, Philip Slee, Peter K. Smith, Keith Sullivan, Richard Tremblay, and Mary Woodward. They made a major contribution to the book.

In addition to their other contributions, some of my colleagues sent me their prepublication materials and I greatly appreciate their willingness to share them with me: Kaj Björkqvist, Michael Boulton, David Finkelhor, Susan Folkman, Edward Gaughan, J. David Hawkins, Todd Herrenkohl, Nadine Hoover, Becky Kochenderfer-Ladd, Dan Olweus, David Perry, David Schwartz, Peter K. Smith, Jon Sutton, Stuart Twemlow, and Dieter Wolke.

The material in this book was greatly enhanced by the inclusion of case studies, responses to informal interviews, and the verbatim comments of a number of American children and adolescents who talked freely and cooperatively. Warmest thanks are extended to them, their parents, and the professionals who permitted me to reproduce these otherwise unobtainable materials. Brendan Byrne of Ireland and Mary McLeod and Sally Morris of ChildLine in England provided me with verbatim comments from Irish and English children about the problem of being bullied that I could not have otherwise obtained.

Special thanks are due to the reference departments of the Bainbridge Island and Seattle Public Libraries, the Seattle Law Library, the

University of Washington Library, and the staff at Eagle Harbor Books for their help in locating relevant books. Richard Walker of the Document Supply Centre of the British Library went to great lengths to get me material that was not available in the United States.

Several colleagues' suggestions and constructive criticisms for the final version of the book helped immeasurably, especially those of Carolyn Baker and John Murphy. Also appreciated was the helpful interest of Kathy Abbott, Gail Christensen, and Phyllis Leighton. It was particularly helpful to have Carol Hiltner Lindahl put the manuscript on disk so efficiently, intelligently, and cheerfully. Dr. Mary Crittenden was also a great help at crucial points.

It has been a great pleasure to work with Carolyn Baker, Director of Publications of the American Counseling Association, whose enthusiasm and belief in the importance of the problems of bullying and teasing have never wavered.

About the Author

Dorothea M. Ross was awarded a PhD in Developmental Psychology at Stanford University. During her appointment as a Research Psychologist in the Department of Pediatrics in the Stanford Medical School, she, along with Logan Wright, PhD, and Lee Salk, PhD, founded the Society of Pediatric Psychology. The Society has been successful in establishing a national and an international network of pediatric psychologists. Dr. Ross is well known for her research on children with special learning needs. Her honors and awards include the 1979 Distinguished Contribution Award of the Society of Pediatric Psychology. She is the coauthor of two books on hyperactivity and one book on childhood pain. Part of the work on the latter book involved conducting a major research project on pain in children. She was appalled to discover that children with leukemia rated as their greatest pain not the excruciatingly painful medical procedures that they had undergone, but the teasing about their baldness and illness-related pallor on their return to school. What should have been a cause for celebration instead became a nightmare. At the conclusion of the pain project, she joined the Division of Behavioral and Developmental Pediatrics of the University of California Medical School, San Francisco. At this time, she developed the Ross Teasing Program to help children with leukemia and others whose lives were made miserable by being teased. The success of this teasing program provided the impetus for the first edition of *Childhood Bullying and Teasing* (1996). This second edition captures the author's enthusiasm for this burgeoning field.

Address correspondence to Dr. Ross at P.O. Box 10846, Bainbridge Island, WA, U.S.A. 98110-0846. Telephone Number: (206) 842-8234.

1 Childhood Stress and Coping Strategies

Children in our society typically are confronted over time with a diversity of stressors ranging from daily hassles, such as the ubiquitous book report, to major life events, such as parental death or divorce (Lazarus, 1966). Mild stressors generally do not pose more than a temporary threat to the child's well-being, but more severe stressors have the potential to cause lasting damage. How children respond to stressors is important for their immediate well-being and psychological growth. Some tend to fall apart in the face of stress, and the resultant loss of confidence often makes it more difficult for them to cope with subsequent stressors. If a general pattern of failure to cope persists, their confidence may be severely diminished. Others are more resilient. They generally handle stress competently, with a resultant increase in confidence in later stress situations (Rutter, 1981).

One group of children who encounter severe stressors are those who are subjected to continual cruel bullying and teasing. Such stressful experiences do not invariably have a negative impact: Some children rise to the challenge posed by severe stressors with coping strategies and other tactics that enable them to master the threat from bullying or teasing and at the same time enjoy a satisfying feeling of competence.

Because it is neither possible nor in the child's best interest for parents or other adults to continually intervene in eliminating stress from the child's life, it is essential to help the child to cope effectively with such stressors. To accomplish this goal, the adult must understand how the child appraises stressors such as cruel bullying; the cognitive and behavioral attempts that he or she may make to cope with stressors or, at least, to modify their impact; and the quality of social support available from family and/or peers. Lazarus's (1966) theory of stress and coping incorporates such a conceptual framework. A critical component of his model of stress is that it places the child's responses to a stressor in a transactional context that allows for bidirectional influences between the child's response to a stressor and other aspects of the environment. This chapter first describes the problem of childhood stress and then continues with Lazarus's (1966) theory and its potential for understanding the stress that results from cruel bullying and teasing.

The fundamental rule in helping a child cope with an event that he or she perceives as threatening is to accept the child's appraisal of the event as fact no matter how unreasonable it may appear to the adult. Nothing is harmless if the child perceives it as a threat and believes that his or her resources are inadequate for dealing effectively with it. It is often very difficult for adults to accept a child's appraisal of an event as stressful when they, themselves, do not perceive it in that way. Typically, the adults are convinced that their assessment is the correct one. Consequently, it is logical then for them to contend that either there is no problem or it is minimal at best:

> Karina, age 8, suddenly began to complain of not feeling well and pleaded to be allowed to stay home from school. Her mother said: "I've taken her to the doctor. Nothing. Yet, every morning for the past four days, stomach aches, headaches. I finally said to her, 'Karina, this is enough. You've missed so much school.' She burst into tears. 'Mom, please, I can't go on the school bus. I just can't.' I drove her to school myself. 'It's my stupid haircut, Mom. They all laughed.'" (Lynch-Fraser, 1994, p. 46)

In a series of studies on differences between adults' and children's views of stressors, Yamamoto and his colleagues at the University of Colorado found that even professionals may not realize how stressful some apparently harmless events are for children. After identifying 20 common childhood stressors (Yamamoto, 1979; Yamamoto & Byrnes, 1984), fourth- through sixth-grade children ($N = 367$) rated the stressfulness of each one on a 7-point scale, with a rank of 1 = *least upsetting* to 7 = *most upsetting*. The stressors fell into four categories:

- *School-related events:* giving class report (2); losing in game (4); picked last on team (5); not making 100 (6); ridiculed in class (9); a poor report card (13); wetting in class (17); academic retainment (18).
- *Fear-arousing events:* going to dentist (3); scary dream (7); getting lost (10); having an operation (11); parental fights (16); going blind (19); losing parent (20).
- *Misbehavior:* sent to principal (12); suspected of lying (14); caught in theft (15).
- *Change events:* new baby sibling (1); moving to new school (8).

There were no differences associated with grade, gender, or personal experience with the 20 events either in this study or in a repetition of it (Yamamoto & Byrnes, 1984), which reported similar ratings. Note that two major sources of potential stress, bullying and teasing, were not included. In the United States during the 1970s, there was virtually no clinical or research interest in these topics.

In a third study, Yamamoto and Felsenthal (1982) asked three groups of 197 men and women (39 clinicians, 97 teachers, and 61 teacher training students) first to make *professional judgments* of how upsetting the events were for children, and then to *infer the judgments that children would make*. The three sets of adults' ratings were in close agreement with each other (correlations across the 20 events were all above .90) regardless of the adults' specialty, experience, or gender, and these professional ratings considerably overlapped the inferred ratings. However, there were some striking discrepancies between the children's ratings (Yamamoto, 1979) and the adults' ratings (Yamamoto & Felsenthal, 1982) for both the professional (r = .70) and inferred (r = .68) judgments. Consider, for example, the differences in the ratings of school-related events and having an operation (Table 1.1). All but one of the school-related events (inferred judgment of academic retainment) were seen by the adults as *less* stressful than having an operation and by the children as *more* stressful. Particularly disconcerting was the fact that increased training was not associated with greater skill in seeing events from the child's point of view: The professionals were only slightly better on inferring judgments of the

Table 1.1. Ranks and Scale Values by 197 Professionals and 367 Children

	Professional Judgment		Inferred Judgment		Children	
Life Event	Rank	Scale Value	Rank	Scale Value	Rank	Scale Value
Academic retainment	11	5.51	14	5.73	18	6.82
Sent to principal	7	4.51	6	4.64	12	5.75
Poor report card	5	4.36	4	4.32	13	6.23
Having an operation	15	5.79	13	5.63	11	5.51

Source: Reproduced with permission of the authors and publisher from Yamamoto, K., & Felsenthal, H. M. (1982). Stressful experiences of children: Professional judgments. *Psychological Reports, 50,* 1087–1093. © Psychological Reports.

20 events than the teacher training students. The disparities between these adult and child ratings, as well as the similarities between the professional and student teacher ratings, suggest that from the beginning of professional training, there should be a strong emphasis on the child's viewpoint, a focus that is clearly lacking in most traditional medical and education training programs.

Taken together, this series of studies provides strong support for Anthony's (1974) contention that "stress as experienced by the child and stress as estimated by the adult observing the impact of the stress on the child are frequently of very different orders of magnitude" (p. 106). It follows that stress event scales and checklists should not be developed on the basis of adults' views in the absence of validation by children.

Determinants of the Child's Perception of Stress

A major reason for the difficulty that adults have in evaluating the degree of stress experienced by the child in a specific situation is the fact that the child's reaction cannot be predicted accurately solely from the apparent degree of threat in that situation. This is true even for events such as parental death or impending hospitalization of the child that on the surface would appear to be highly stressful. Instead, as Sorensen (1993) has pointed out, the child's reaction partly depends on the complex interplay of a cluster of *dispositional factors* such as developmental level, temperament, and personality; social relationships and experiences; previous stressful experiences and the child's success or difficulty in dealing with them; and the interpersonal context in which the event occurs. Should an adult ignore these factors when listening to a child's account of a stressor, it is almost certain that the adult will disagree with the child's assessment of the problem and likely will be ineffective in helping the child cope with future stressors. Consider in the following example how essential it would be to consider the dispositional factors:

> I was 7 years old and I'd been playing the piano for more than 2 years when there was a piano competition for 7 and under children. I was confident that I would win—people had told me for as far back as I could remember how good I was. Then the first contestant played her piece, she was only 6 and right away I knew she was better than I was. I got panicky. When it was my turn I played badly, really badly. I refused ever to go in another piano competition. I was totally devastated. (J. A. Harris, personal communication, July 7, 1963)

Lazarus's Theory of Stress and Coping

Children who are subjected to bullying and teasing often experience moderate to severe stress over fairly long periods. Experienced investigators consider them to be the largest and also the most neglected group of special needs children in both the United States (Greenbaum, 1989) and the United Kingdom (Smith, 1991). Lazarus's (1966) theory provides a perspective on the problems that confront these children and also a theoretical basis for the kinds of intervention that should be beneficial to them.

Lazarus (1966) has assigned the elements of the stress process to three categories that are constantly in transition, with potentially overlapping boundaries and variations in complexity. *Daily hassles* are the relatively minor irritating and distressing demands of daily living that are characteristic of everyday transactions with the social environment. Included in this category are events such as a stern reprimand from a teacher for not completing a homework assignment, getting out at recess too late to join an ongoing game of baseball, having to go to the dentist, and not being allowed to watch a television program. *Chronic life strains* are demands that impose day-in and day-out long-term irritants on the child, such as having to go several times a week for physical therapy, being on a juvenile diabetic regime, and being a latch-key child after school with chores to perform. *Major life events* are the most dramatic of the three categories and often have a severe impact on the child. Included here are a sibling with a long-term illness, being partly to blame for the death of a close same-age friend as a result of carelessness, and parents who are abusive to each other and who fight all the time. There is no question that the last situation can qualify as a major life event. A 7-year-old boy gave the following description:

> The scariest is when they fight. Dad hits her and shouts a lot of words that I'm not supposed to say *ever*. And then Mom throws things at him like his baseball cup that he got when his team won. He says he's going to leave forever and ever and she screams, "Good. Get out now." On Sunday at church I pray they'll never fight again and I ask God, "Who'll look after us if Dad leaves? Will Mom leave too? Will we go to an orphan place?" The best was when Jenny (younger sister) was really, really sick, they were nice then. Sometimes at night I wake up and I think *he's already gone* and I get really scared all over. (Ross, 1977–1979)

Although some of the foregoing stressors are relatively uncomplicated short-term transactions that fall into only one of the three categories, other stressors may be characterized by a set of changing conditions with a consequent shifting in status over time from one category to another. Having to go to the dentist, for example, may shift from the level of daily hassles (a routine examination twice a year) to a regular series of visits over more than 2 years because of wearing bands. Bullying often starts as a daily hassle while the bully is assessing the victim's suitability for long-term bullying with tentative and sporadic probes. When the victim proves to be a "satisfactory" target, that is, shows visible upset and does not counterattack or report the bully, bullying becomes a chronic life strain as it increases steadily in frequency per week and sharply in intensity. Escalation to the status of a major life event, as feelings of hopelessness and helplessness increase over time with a concomitant increase in anticipatory terror, is well documented in the bullying literature (Besag, 1989; Fiennes, 1988; Smith, 1991).

APPRAISAL

Children constantly judge the quality of ongoing events and their significance for their own well-being. Within Lazarus's (1966) theory, two major sequential forms of appraisal converge to shape the meaning of events for children (Folkman, 1984). The first is *primary appraisal,* in which children assess the importance of the events in respect to their well-being. If the events are perceived as threatening, which is often the case even when the bully is assessing a potential victim, children typically resort to *secondary appraisal.* They first consider the pros and cons of the options available for managing the demands of the situation, and then they assess their competence for handling the situation. At this point the children must ask themselves, Can something be done to improve the situation, and, if so, am I capable of doing it?

COPING RESOURCES

These are the cognitive and behavioral tactics that children may call on to effectively manage or change a stressful or threatening event or mediate its impact. Note that, in this definition, coping refers to efforts to manage a situation regardless of how successful these efforts are. Coping is defined independently of both the quality of the coping efforts and their outcome. The coping resources available to the child fall into two groups: The first, called *personal resources,* are the efforts that the child makes without help from others; the second, *social support resources,* are those in which help is sought from others.

Although these are described separately, they may be used independently of each other, sequentially, or concurrently.

Personal Resources

These coping efforts have a dual function. *Problem-solving coping* is used with stressors that the child believes are controllable. It includes attempts by the child to change the threatening situation itself with direct actions such as deliberately avoiding a bully or thinking of a workable solution to the problem. For example, a boy who is being bullied in the school setting may prevent or delay the bullying by attaching himself to a protective group of peers and older siblings when in school. *Emotion-focused coping* is falling back on stressors believed to be uncontrollable. It consists of reappraising the stressor and viewing it as being less threatening than previously thought. As a result, negative emotions such as anxiety and acute embarrassment are lessened. Emotion-focused coping was used successfully by an 11-year-old girl whose early signs of breast development far ahead of her peers led to merciless teasing from them. She was upset at first and thought she could eliminate the problem by hiding her breast development (problem-solving coping):

> I had this whole routine. I actually took adhesive tape and wrapped it around my chest. Then, I put on a T-shirt, then my regular shirt—until Mom caught me and accused me of cutting off my circulation. I just couldn't stand it. "Boobers," they called me. "Boobers!" I was eleven and a half. (Lynch-Fraser, 1994, p. 171)

However, later she reappraised the stressful teasing and came to think of her tormentors as "backward" in terms of understanding incipient adolescence. She no longer felt embarrassed by their teasing.

Both forms of coping are used even by young children. In a study by Band and Weisz (1988), children ages 6, 9, and 12 were asked to try to remember stressful events within six general categories: loss/separation, medical procedures, conflicts with authority figures, peer difficulties, school failure, and physical accidents. Next, the children were asked to describe their responses to each stressor. These responses were then coded as *primary control* (taking direct action—identical to Lazarus's problem-solving category); *secondary control* (trying to adapt to the stressor—Lazarus's emotion-focused category); or *relinquished control* (failing to cope). Styles of coping varied as a function of the perceived controllability of the stressor. School failure, for example, elicited high levels of primary control probably because the children thought that they could do something about their grades, whereas medical stressors evoked secondary control, such as self-distraction, possibly because the children knew from experience that resistance was pointless. Self-reports of primary control tended to decrease with increasing age, whereas secondary control increased. With increasing maturity, children apparently are better able to judge when to resist actively and when to try to adapt to stress situations.

Direct actions may not be adaptive or even realistic in terms of probable outcome, particularly when young children resort to them. A 7-year-old girl who had to undergo weekly painful procedures at the hospital told her mother that she was going to the bathroom but instead took an elevator down to the main floor, where she was intercepted by an alert hospital employee. When asked where she was going, she pointed confidently to a nearby waiting room and said, "To see my doctor in there." It was the maternity waiting room (Ross, 1977–1979).

With older children, the direct action approach often consists of trying one coping tactic after another, without success. When this happens, flexibility is needed. The child must see that a radical change of tactics is called for rather than pursuing the failure route. As Folkman (1984, p. 843) noted, a time-honored principle of effective coping is to accept that a stress situation is uncontrollable and abandon direct attempts at altering the situation, and then turn to emotion-focused coping to adapt to the situation or tolerate it. Emotion-focused coping can be used to change the meaning of a stress situation and, in the process, increase the child's feeling of control, with a consequent lessening of distress (Silver & Wortman, 1980). Consider, for example, the girl who has been subjected to a prolonged period of vicious racial teasing and has tried unsuccessfully a variety of direct actions. She finally accepts that there is nothing she can do to prevent it and turns to a reappraisal of the situation: She places the blame for the teasing squarely on herself by deciding that it is her own fault for being the color that she is. Although this conclusion is irrational, she is likely to experience some relief because now she feels that she has some control over the situation because she is to blame for it; a substantial part of her distress has been due to her feeling that she had no control whatsoever over the teasing. An adult's reaction to this strategy may be that the relief it provides is only temporary. To the child, however, it offers a solution to the problem and, consequently, it is stress reducing.

In this example, failure led to intentional reappraisal, but successful direct action also may trigger it off spontaneously. When children use direct action in a stressful situation with some success, there may be a concomitant, almost automatic, shift in their original appraisal of the stressor. The stressor may not seem nearly so formidable when they are able to gain some control over it.

Social Support Resources

Children who are faced with stressors that they see as insurmountable (e.g., continuous bullying) can sometimes, but not always, obtain social support from their network of family, friends, and school personnel. It should be emphasized that the existence of a social network does not guarantee support from it in times of stress. The outcome will be determined by the quality of the child's social network, the extent to which the network believes in the child's need for help, and whether or not the members are able to help.

In the following example, an 11-year-old girl sought but did not obtain social support from her mother, then used a variety of direct actions before changing her appraisal of the situation and acting on it. The girl was given a dress by her grandmother that was "so totally weird it was awesome." The girl hated the dress the minute she saw it. She complained bitterly to her mother when she was teased mercilessly about it at school. When her mother insisted that she continue to wear the dress to school, the girl next tried avoidance by wearing another dress but leaving for school before her mother woke up. This gambit only served to increase her mother's determination that she wear the dress. The girl then tried unsuccessfully to negotiate an agreement with her mother that she would always wear it to her grandmother's house but not to school. Although knowing that punishment was inevitable, she finally decided that her only option was to destroy the dress: "There was no way I could get out of wearing it to school so I got my Mom's big scissors and I chopped it up" (Ross, 1977–1979).

The most common reason for children not getting help with the problems of teasing and bullying is that the members of their social networks, particularly their parents, siblings, and teachers, refuse outright to give it. They may brush the children's complaints aside with such platitudes as "It happens to everyone" or "It's part of growing up," or they may tell them to fight their own battles, coupled with derogatory comments such as "Don't be such a wimp." Typical of this attitude is a quote about Hillary Clinton:

> Not so tough at age 4, the first lady . . . came running home, scared of a bully. Rodham (her mother) blocked her path and said, "There is no room for cowards in this house. You have to go back outside and deal with problems like this." (Fournier, 1994, p. A20)

Sometimes parents mask their unwillingness to help children by blaming them. They suggest or imply that it is the children's fault, thus further eroding their confidence and increasing their vulnerability to further problems in social relationships.

When a child who is being bullied is unable to obtain support from the social network, it can be particularly damaging because often the child has explored other options first and only seeks social support as a last resort. When this final option fails, the child is likely to be overwhelmed with a feeling of hopelessness that, in turn, can put the child at risk for depression and suicide (Kashani, Reid, & Rosenberg, 1989):

> This 15-year-old boy lived with his mother, his father having left the family. . . . During the school year which ended in his death he had been continually bullied by other boys and had confided this to his principal, his mother, and the truant officer following inquiries into his frequent absences. His note said: "Day after day it's the same with no way out. I can't stop them; I ought to be able to stand up for myself but I can't. Nobody will stand up for me because nobody really cares about me and I can see why." (Leach, 1986, p. 654)

Age may be a factor, too, in the failure to seek social support for the problem of bullying. Many children, especially boys in Grade 6 or higher, are reluctant to seek help from either their parents or school personnel because they feel it is inappropriate to have to do so at their age. Often they are deeply embarrassed by their own failure to cope effectively with the bullying even when the odds against them are overwhelming. Consider the reasoning of this 12-year-old boy, small for his age, who was being bullied by a trio of 10-year-olds, all of whom were bigger than he was:

> Listen, I'm practically a *teenager!* How can I report some little 10-year-olds who lie in wait for me after school and knock me around? *Everyone* would hear about it. The guys would say, "Back in the fifth grade with the little kids, Davey, you aren't ready for junior high." (J. J. Cooper, personal communication, December 1, 1983)

It is essential, then, for children to know not only when direct action should or should not be attempted before seeking social support, but also when they are justified in seeking this support and when it is mandatory to make use of its availability.

In an interesting study of the relationship between peer-nominated sociometric status and the extent of support from the child's social network, Munsch and Kinchen (1995) began by asking students in Grades 7 and 8 ($N = 247$) to describe their attempts to get social support for help with a recent stressful event. To assess sociometric status, Munsch and Kinchen asked the students to name their classmates who fitted specific behavioral descriptors such as popular, socially isolated, and rejected. Parents and nonparental adults provided support regardless of the children's social status. However, peers were strongly influenced by sociometric status in deciding whether to provide social support. Contrary to the investigators' predictions, rejected adolescents did not receive the lowest levels of support. Instead, it was the popular adolescents who received the lowest ratings. Munsch and Kinchen speculated that this finding might be due to popular students being perceived as socially competent and consequently less in need of social support when confronted with stressors. An alternative explanation could be envy on the part of the less-popular students, leading to a decision to withhold help in situations where providing help is optional.

In discussing the positive effects of social support, Cohen and Wills (1985) offered their *buffering model* as one explanation for positive effects. According to this model, children seek social support from their allies who can protect them from the impact of the stress by eliminating it. Some children are so confident of the availability of social support that they make no attempt to use their personal resources. An 8-year-old girl with leukemia said that she never tried to stop children who teased her about being bald:

> I don't even tell them to stop it or get lost or anything, I just tell my brothers (both older) and they march up to the kid who's teasing me and they say, "We know *something about you* and if you *ever* tease Anne Marie again or do anything to her we'll tell everybody!" And then they march off and that kid never teases me again or even comes near me. (J. Porter, personal communication, September 11, 1992)

In their *direct social support model,* Cohen and Wills (1985) posited an increase in well-being on the part of the child regardless of the actual amount of concrete support given. They believed that just the presence of family and friends increases the child's ability to cope with the stressor. Support for this explanation comes from a study of childhood pain (Ross & Ross, 1988). The children were asked, "What do you think would have helped most when you were (child's report of worst pain ever)?" Over 99% of the group felt that the "thing that helped most" regardless of the type of pain was to have one or both parents present. More often than not, they freely acknowledged that usually there was nothing the parents could actually do, but they emphasized how much it helped to have them there. Merely having an empathic parent present can serve to attenuate stress:

> Six-year-old Joshua went to the hospital to have tubes put in his ears. "I was a little bit scared . . . 'cause this was my first time. I wanted to know if it hurt. . . . But it didn't."
>
> Note how much social support his mother gave him. The day before the operation he and his mother shopped for things to take and packed his suitcase together. All the while his mother answered endless questions about the procedures involved. When asked, "What made you feel better?" Joshua said, "My Mom was there and she spent the whole night with me." (Dibrell & Yamamoto, 1988, p. 19)

An integral part of the secondary appraisal process concerns the child's judgment about whether controlling the stressful event is possible. Knowing that specific personal and/or social coping resources are available that can lessen the impact of a stressor (Bandura's [1977] "outcome expectancy") is only the first step toward control. The child also must have confidence in his or her ability to implement the coping resources needed to mediate the impact of the stressor (Bandura's "efficacy expectancy").

The relationship between being in control and stress is an interesting one. Being in control does not always lead to stress reduction, nor does believing an event to be uncontrollable always result in increased stress (Folkman, 1984). Sometimes this belief results in a kind of passive resignation, a relaxing about the problem. An 8-year-old girl who was all alone in the hospital said:

> I thought there's nothing I can do, the hospital's got me now. So I thought I'd read a book so I wouldn't be dead without finding out what happened in the end to Jolly Jenny. And then I guess I must have gone to sleep because when I woke up my Mom and Dad were there and I asked them when was I going to have the operation and they said, "You've already had it and in half an hour you're coming home with us." It was the best thing in my whole life. (R. P. Atkins, personal communication, June 3, 1981)

Appraisals of control are transitory rather than static phenomena. In Lazarus's (1966) theory, the child and the environment are in a bidirectional relationship in which new information from the environment or coping efforts can result in changes in the child's appraisal. Consider, for example, the case of an 11-year-old boy who initially was pessimistic about his ability to combat cruel teasing and who was then taught how to react to the teaser, using Ross's (1996) teasing program. When he first put what he learned into action, he immediately saw that the teaser was disconcerted by the new tactics. The boy then realized that, for the first time, he had a coping resource that could appreciably influence and perhaps even eliminate the misery of being teased. His appraisal of control then shifted sharply in his favor:

> I just get there (to school) and I see Greg—waiting. And he goes, my terrible fumble in the playoff, my funny accent, my weirdo brother—you name it. And I'm *really* zeroing in on him so as to report back, but I yawn *real wide* and I look *real interested*—like you know, at the guys shooting baskets? And all of a sudden Greg grabs my arm and he goes, "Parker! Hey, Parker! You hear me?" He sounds kinda different, like more sort of worried than nasty, you know? So I turn my head real slow and I give him my Zombie look and I say, "What?" And he doesn't say nothing. And right then *I* know it's (teasing program) starting to work on him! And I jerk my arm away and I go, "See ya, Greg," and I leave him still talking. I *never* done that before. (Ross, 1977–1979)

Of relevance here is an article by Folkman and Moskowitz (2000), who contended that one of the reasons why more progress has not been made about the factors that can influence coping is that the emphasis has been almost exclusively on negative outcomes in stressful situations. Further, they stated that both positive and negative affect can occur during a stressful period of time, and they cited empirical evidence of this co-occurrence with intense stress in adults.

Evidence of co-occurrence of positive and negative affect during stress in children was apparent in a program (Ross, 1996) that was designed to teach children how to cope effectively with cruel teasing. The children were taught verbal strategies and facial expressions to use when they were teased in the school setting and were asked after each encounter with the teaser to report back to the adult who was teaching them. In the early stages of the teasing program, they generally did not have much success, presumably because it was difficult for them to stand their ground when teased and accost the teaser in a convincing manner. However, after much encouragement and role-play practice, they became very competent. In the foregoing case, and in most cases with this program, there comes a teasing interaction that starts out on a *negative note* and then the child realizes that the tactics that he has been taught to use are having an effect on the teaser. In the face of the resultant *positive affect,* the child's appraisal of the teasing situation changes abruptly, his confidence soars, and for the first time he feels in total control of the teaser.

The reciprocal influence between the child and the environment does not always operate in the child's favor. Long-term bullying, for example, often results in depressed affect (Kashani et al., 1989), leaving the child increasingly sad and irritable. This behavior pattern may then adversely influence the responses of others, particularly the child's peers, who could provide valuable social support. Instead, an all-too-common downward spiral leads to more negative interactions with previously friendly peers and a concomitant increase in the social isolation of the child.

Within this transactional framework (Lazarus & Folkman, 1984), stress can be viewed as an imbalance or poor fit between the child's personal and/or social coping resources on the one hand and the demands of a threatening event on the other. The poorer the fit between the coping resources and the threatening event, the greater the stress. It follows that stress is not a property of the child, as is a response such as poor self-esteem. Nor is it a property of the environment, as school examinations or noxious medical procedures are. Instead, stress is "a particular relationship between the person and the environment that is appraised by the person as taxing or exceeding his or her resources and endangering his or her well-being" (Lazarus & Folkman, 1984, p. 19).

COMMENT

To help a child cope effectively with a stressor such as bullying, the adult must accept the child's appraisal of the stressor as fact and work from that position. Often a stressor that the adult sees as a daily hassle seems like a major life event to the child. Initial efforts should focus on helping the child to cope by means of direct actions (problem-focused coping) because success by this route engenders a feeling of mastery and of being in control. However, if the stressor is clearly uncontrollable, adaptation in the form of emotion-focused coping could be the best solution. Most stressful situations lend themselves to a combination of the two forms of coping. It should be noted that being in control of the stressor does not invariably lead to stress reduction, nor does perceiving a stressor as uncontrollable always result in increased stress. If the stressor is one that makes help in the form of social support from parents or school personnel imperative (as many bullying problems do), it is essential that the child see this step as mandatory rather than optional. When help is given, the degree of fit between the coping resource and the stressor is of prime importance. The adult should eliminate the stressor for the child only if a good coping resource–stressor fit is not a viable alternative.

In a worst-case scenario in which all the sources of support rebuff the child and fail to help in any way, he or she usually sees suicide as the only option left. There are other options, but the child is usually unaware of their existence. Personnel in schools and other group settings for children would be making a real contribution to the welfare of children by routinely publicizing local and national sources of help for children with problems.

For children in the United States, Canada, and England who do not see seeking support from individuals in their own social network as a feasible alternative, there is another option: the telephone hotline. This includes a widely publicized, toll-free national telephone counseling service called Girls and Boys Town National Hotline (1-800-448-3000 or 1-800-448-1833 for the hearing impaired) (U.S.A. and Canada), ChildLine (0-800-1111) (England), and Kidscape (0171-730-3300) (England) that offer advice, comfort, and protection to any child up to the age of 18 for 24 hours a day, 7 days a week. Children can talk to trained professional counselors as often as they choose without saying who or where they are. They are guaranteed complete confidentiality. Often the effect of this anonymity results in their revealing information that face-to-face discussion might never elicit. Telephone helplines are also available for children in Scotland, Ireland, Scandinavia, Belgium, the Netherlands, Germany, and Australia (Smith, Morita, et al., 1999).

2 Bullying: An Overview

Childhood bullying is not a recent problem, although the widespread media coverage of the 20th and 21st centuries could lead to the belief that it is. This chapter focuses on the findings and effects of empirical studies of childhood bullying that were conducted in Japan by Morita and colleagues, and especially in Norway and Sweden in the 1970s and 1980s under the highly effective leadership of Dan Olweus. Some of the most important findings from these groundbreaking studies include the prevalence of childhood bullying, dissent about the definition of bullying, and the empirical evidence that succeeded in discounting some common myths about bullying. Of particular importance was the catalytic effect in many parts of the world that the efficacy of a school intervention program developed by Olweus had on actions against childhood bullying.

Childhood bullying has had a long, unhappy history in much of the Western world. The classical literature of the past few centuries (Dickens, 1838; Hughes, 1857) coupled with historical accounts (Ariès, 1962; Rose, 1991; Zinn, 1995) attests to the fact that two groups of children and adolescents have been cruelly bullied for centuries. One group were those in schools, particularly English boarding schools. For many generations, upper-class British boys have been sent away to boarding schools at the age of 8 (Harris, 1995). Rose (1991) described English public schoolboy society of the mid-Victorian period as barbaric. Glynn (1970, p. 129) described his experiences as a newcomer to Eton in the early 1900s:

> A boy's first week at his preparatory school is likely to be the most traumatic experience of his life, one for which he is, at the age of eight, totally unprepared. Until that moment, he has not realized that there are so many people in the world who wish to hit him and hurt him and that they will be given ample opportunity to do so, both by day and by night.

A second group of children who were cruelly bullied were those in settings from which there was little chance of escape: bondage in private homes, orphanages, factories and coal mines that children were apprenticed to at an early age, and other industrial settings. Besag (1989, p. x) described such bullying as "one of the dark, hidden areas of social interaction along with child physical and sexual abuse which has thrived on a bed of secrecy and which has been neglected by professional investigation." Present-day equivalents are the sweat shops in major American cities where illegal alien adolescents are forced, under the threat of deportation, to work long hours in substandard conditions for minimal wages (Featherstone & Henwood, 2001; Greider, 2001).

Japan

In the last century, Japan and Scandinavia were among the few countries showing active concern about school bullying. In Japan, their concern was not so much about the actual bullying but rather about the disruptive effect it had on the social order. The term for bullying, *ijime,* has been used for more than a century. Ijime has been described by Smith, Morita, et al. (1999, p. 2) as "a concept similar (though not identical) to bullying." One Japanese–English dictionary defines it in general terms as treating someone harshly, being hard on another person, being cruel, annoying, or teasing.

In the 1970s, school personnel in Japan focused on *Kounai Bouryoku,* which included school violence against teachers and other students as well as vandalism. At this time school violence attracted most of the attention of both the news media and school personnel, but by the end of the 1970s a small but very vocal number of teachers expressed concern about a new behavior problem called *Yowaimono Ijime,* or bullying. These teachers contended that it differed from the more commonly occurring type of ijime in that it involved characteristics such as duration, cunning, and numbers. However, this newly observed form of ijime was overshadowed by school violence that had become severe and blatant.

In the early 1980s, the occurrence of school violence appeared to have gradually decreased, possibly as a result of media attention to the problem of school violence combined with preventive efforts by school personnel. However, in the mid-1980s, 16 pupils committed suicide, reportedly because of being victims of ijime. An ijime case that shocked Japanese society concerned the suicide of an adolescent boy (Morita, Soeda, Soeda, & Taki, 1999, p. 311):

> In December 1986, a 13-year-old boy committed suicide that he attributed to mental and physical ijime (that is, Yowaimono

> Ijime) from two of his classmates. Once they treated him as if he was dead and staged a mock funeral for him in their classroom. Some of the teachers joined in and wrote letters of condolence with students: "Goodbye and have a peaceful sleep." The victim wrote that it was hell on earth for him.

When the boy's parents took the case to the Tokyo District Court, judgment was passed only on the bullies' violent physical actions and excluded the ijime, a defeat for the victim's parents. However, 3 years later, in May 1994, the Tokyo High Court overturned the ruling and imposed a fine of 11,500,000 yen (in U.S. dollars, $93,450.00) for the victim's death. This ruling was the first judicial recognition of mental ijime in Japanese history.

The Monbusho, Japan's Ministry of Education, Science and Culture, attempted to cope with the problem of bullying but without much success. Although reform of the rigid severity of the school system clearly was needed, the Monbusho was reluctant to modify one of the world's most admired educational systems (White, 1987). In the meantime, other educators resorted to other means of protecting children from bullying. Keiko Okuchi, the director of Tokyo Shure, an alternative school for children who refused to attend regular schools because of the bullying problem, founded the school after her own son was bullied at age 8. His classmates trampled on his eyeglasses, dumped his homework into dirty water, and repeatedly poked the back of his head with a pencil. Bullying in Japan typically involves an entire group that ostracizes a child who is somehow different. In the case of Okuchi's son, the family had just moved into the district—his problem was that he was a newcomer (Jordan, 1994).

In a culture that in some respects represents a high degree of civility, it seems incongruous that the ugly behavior that defines bullying should be a major problem in Japan. Ryoko Uchida, an authority on bullying, believes that it stems from the severe control that is exerted over students. Every moment of the day and every move are regulated to a ridiculous degree: For example, the length of girls' bangs and the number of times sock cuffs may be rolled over are specified. Okuchi pointed out that, unlike American schools, which reward particular talents in children, Japanese schools reward sameness as noted in the Japanese saying, "The nail that sticks up is hammered down" (Jordan, 1994, p. 21). Many educators feel that the extreme pressure for top academic performance puts excessive demands on children and is a causal factor in their angry reactions to others. Okuchi described the pressure as unnatural.

Teachers are often role models for bullies in that they frequently behave brutally to students who fail to conform to every rule. In 1990 two girls were killed, one by a teacher who slammed the school's iron gate on her when she was seconds late for class, and the other by a teacher who flung her repeatedly against a concrete wall for wearing a short skirt and replying in a disobedient manner. Despite the public outcry over these incidents, little has changed in the schools (Jordan, 1994). Many teachers adhere to the Japanese belief that, in a quarrel, both sides are at fault. It took extreme pressure from angry parents before the Education Ministry only recently acknowledged that bullying may not be the fault of the victim (Jordan, 1994).

It is interesting to note that changes have also occurred in the definition of bullying most frequently used today in Japanese government documents and research papers. Morita (1985) and his colleagues defined bullying in more specific terms than was the case for ijime in the 1970s: "A type of aggressive behavior by which someone who holds a dominant position in a group-interaction process, by intentional or collective acts, causes mental and/or physical suffering to others in the group" (p. 311). This definition is similar to those used in Europe (see, e.g., Olweus, 1993b; Whitney & Smith, 1993). Note, however, that Morita's definition includes the phrase "who holds a dominant position in a group-interaction process" and that the word "mental" comes before "physical."

Scandinavia

Prior to 1970, investigative interest in childhood bullying was at best sporadic (see Farrington, 1993). The first significant contribution came from a Swedish physician who was appalled by schoolyard bullying (Heinemann, 1973). His book focused attention on a still ongoing longitudinal study of childhood bullying in boys that Olweus had begun in the 1970s. This study is remarkable for the quality of information about bullying that Olweus is continuing to report. Of particular relevance to intervention was his finding (Olweus, 1978) that instead of the well-entrenched dichotomy of bullies and victims, distinct subgroups exist in both populations—which means, for example, that a single form of intervention for bullies would not fit *all* bullies. Olweus was also the first to make the distinction between *direct* (physical aggression) and *indirect* (isolation and rumor spreading) bullying. In 1980 Olweus used measures of these two aspects in discounting the assumption that bullies are characterized by an underlying anxiety and insecurity.

In 1982 the status of the bullying problem in Norway changed abruptly with the report that three boys ages 10 to 14 years had committed suicide as a result of severe, long-term bullying. These tragedies led to a widespread demand by school administrators and the public for government action. A group of experienced investigators headed by Dan Olweus and Erling Roland were then charged with the task of mounting an attack on the problem of school bullying. The work of this group was to have an enormous effect on concern about bullying not only in Scandinavia but also in other countries worldwide (Smith, Morita, et al., 1999).

THE CAMPAIGN AGAINST BULLYING

The Campaign Against Bullying was launched in Norway in 1983. The primary goals of the campaign were to sharply reduce bullying in Norwegian schools while fostering the active involvement of teachers and parents in the change process. The school programs used in the campaign were noteworthy for their simplicity. In his book, *Bullying at School: What We Know and What We Can Do,* Olweus (1993a) described in detail the surveys and intervention program used in the campaign. The data provide interesting factual information about bullies and victims but also destroy some strongly ingrained beliefs about these two groups. The empirical findings and the procedures that are described provide valuable information for school personnel and parents who are trying to put an end to bullying.

To assess the problem of bullying in the campaign, Olweus (1983) developed the Bully/Victim Questionnaire,[1] which covers multiple aspects of the bullying problem. In empirical investigations (Ahmad & Smith, 1990), the questionnaire has proved to be reliable and valid. There is now a Revised Bully/Victim Questionnaire[2] (Olweus, 1996) that is being used in the United Kingdom, a number of countries in Europe including Spain, Italy, Portugal, Belgium, and the Netherlands, as well as in the United States, Canada, and Japan (Smith, Morita, et al., 1999).

RESULTS OF THE CAMPAIGN AGAINST BULLYING

Olweus's (1993a) school-based intervention program produced excellent results. After the first year, bully/victim problems decreased by

[1] An English version of this questionnaire (Olweus & Smith, 1995) is available. For information, contact Dr. P. K. Smith, Department of Psychology, Goldsmiths College, New Cross, London SE 146 NW, United Kingdom.

[2] Contact Dr. D. Olweus, Research Center for Health Promotion, University of Bergen, Oisteinsgate 3, N-5007 Bergen, Norway.

50% or more, and there were fewer new victims. These improvements were even greater after the second year. A marked improvement in the social climate of the school was coupled with an increase in satisfaction with school life. Reductions also occurred in the amount of bullying and of general antisocial behaviors outside the schools' jurisdiction. Given these excellent results, it is commendable that Olweus regards the plan for school intervention as in transition and subject to change pending further research and increased experience with it in the school setting. Such caution is exemplary and rare. It reflects a concern for excellence that in general is characteristic of the European researchers in this field. The school-based intervention program is discussed in detail in chapter 9. The Core Program Against Bullying and Antisocial Behavior (Olweus, 1999a, Part IV; Olweus & Limber, 1999) is being implemented in a large number of schools in the United States.

Problem of Definition in Research

The results of studies on bullying are influenced to a considerable extent by the way in which bullying is defined. If a definition specifies that there must be several attacks before the behavior can be regarded as bullying, then the respondents' answers concerning frequency will be considerably lower than would be the case if single instances of attacks were also regarded as bullying. This disparity is important because the findings of studies on bullying provide a basis for developing prevention and intervention programs. Ideally, research findings would be based on one definition acceptable to the research and clinical communities but, to date, there has been little progress toward this goal.

Defining even an apparently uncomplicated behavior such as bullying can create dissension. It can be seen from Table 2.1 that in terms of definitional accord the field was in a state of disarray by the early 1990s.

Olweus (1993a, p. 9) defined bullying as follows: "A student is being bullied or victimized when he or she is exposed, repeatedly and over time, to negative actions on the part of one or more other students." The criterion of "repeatedly and over time" was intended to exclude "nonserious" events. For Olweus, the negative actions must have occurred at least once a week for a month or more. *At the same time, he concedes that a single instance of more serious harassment can be regarded as bullying under certain (unspecified) circumstances.* The problem with the repeated occurrence requirement is that interventions would not be introduced at the earliest point in the bully/victim interactions when it is probably easiest to stop the bullying and contain the damage that has been done to the victim.

Table 2.1. Definitions of Bullying

- *Askew* (1989). Bullying is a continuum of behavior that involves the attempt to gain power and dominance over another.
- *Besag* (1989). Bullying is the repeated attack—physical, psychological, social, or verbal—by those in a position of power on those who are powerless to resist, with the intention of causing distress for their own gain or gratification.
- *Farrington* (1993). Bullying is repeated oppression, psychological or physical, of a less powerful person by a more powerful person or group of persons.
- *Johnstone, Munn, and Edwards* (1991). Bullying is the willful, conscious desire to hurt or threaten or frighten someone else.
- *Lane* (1989). Bullying includes any action or implied action, such as threats, intended to cause fear and distress. This behavior has to be repeated on more than one occasion. The definition must include evidence that those involved intended or felt fear.
- *Olweus* (1993a). A student is being bullied or victimized when he or she is exposed, repeatedly and over time, to negative actions[a] on the part of one or more other students. A single instance of more serious harassment can be regarded as bullying under certain (unspecified) circumstances.
- *Smith and Thompson* (1991). Bullying intentionally causes hurt to the recipient. This hurt can be either physical or psychological. In addition, three further criteria particularly distinguish bullying: It is unprovoked, it occurs repeatedly, and the bully is stronger than the victim or is perceived to be stronger.
- *Tattum* (1989). Bullying is a willful, conscious desire to hurt another person. It can be occasional and short-lived, or it can be regular and long-standing.

[a]Included under the rubric of negative actions is a broad spectrum of behaviors ranging from low-level nonverbal harassment such as stares and glares, through cruel teasing, social ostracism, malicious gossip, sex harassment, ethnic slurs, unreasonable territorial bans, destruction of another's property, extortion, and serious physical assault (Besag, 1989; Olweus, 1993a).

POINTS OF DISPUTE

Long-Standing Bullying

Some investigators are in agreement with Olweus's (1993a) criterion of "repeatedly and over time." Smith and Thompson (1991, p. 1), for example, stated explicitly that "something that just happens once or twice would not be called bullying." A compelling argument for the inclusion of the "repeated attacks" component in the definition is offered by other investigators (Besag, 1989; Greenbaum, 1989; Mellor, 1991). They suggested that bullying usually results in two kinds of severe distress. One is the *immediate upset* that results from the physical or psychological sequelae of bullying, such as physical pain, reaction to loss or damage of one's possessions, and humiliation, particularly when bystanders are present. The other is the *anticipatory fear* that often occurs from the spoken or implied threat of future attacks, a fear that usually increases in severity over time. Support for the anticipation aspect comes from a 14-year-old boy who said: "Pain is not the worst thing in bullying. It's the fear, fear of meeting the bully again" (Byrne, 1994, p. 14). It is the combination of these two kinds of distress that largely accounts for the misery of being bullied.

At the other end of the continuum are those investigators (e.g., Askew, 1989; Stephenson & Smith, 1989; Tattum, 1989; White, 1987) who contend that attacks should not have to be of long-standing duration to be classified as bullying. In an unpublished survey of children's and young adults' attitudes (O'Connor, 1995), the respondents, who ranged in age from 5 to 20 years, did not think that negative actions had to be repeated to constitute bullying. La Fontaine (1991, p. 5) concurred:

> . . . bullying as long-standing violence . . . implies that short-lived incidents victimizing children are excluded. Yet many of the children who telephoned the Bullying Line were referring to quite recent incidents . . . the children clearly thought that (these incidents) already qualified to be counted as bullying.

Imbalance of Power

Most investigators, including the leading Scandinavian researchers, Olweus (1993a) and Roland (1989), agree that there may be one or more bullies and one or more victims. Most also concur that bullying involves an imbalance of physical or psychological power, with the bully, or bullies, being either stronger or perceived to be stronger than the victim. Casting doubt on this assumption is the statement by Thompson and Smith (1991) that in "talking to children their perceptions (of bullying) easily shade over into including any situations involving unprovoked aggression, whether or not the odds are . . . uneven" (p. 141).

In their chapter in *The Nature of School Bullying*, Smith, Morita, et al. (1999) stated that in the United States there is seldom a standard definition of bullying in either the research literature or the mass media. Many publications refer to Olweus's research; however, few include a specific definition incorporating Olweus's (1993a) three critical elements. These are that bullying is aggressive behavior or intentional "harm doing," it is carried out repeatedly and over time, and it is an interpersonal relationship characterized by an imbalance of power. Arriving at a universally accepted definition of bullying is not just a matter of academic interest. To expand our understanding of the problem of bullying, it is of critical importance for researchers to develop and agree on a common definition of bullying. Among other things, this task would include distinguishing between bullies and other aggressive children, as well as differentiating between victims of bullies and victims of other forms of aggression. This important step should precede further research on the incidence and prevalence of bullying at least in the United States and preferably within the international research community.

Harachi, Catalano, and Hawkins (1999a), in their chapter on bullying in Canada, described a similar definition problem. Although there is not as yet a large body of research on bullying in Canada, the work that has been done is, for the most part, excellent (see, e.g., the studies by Craig, Pepler, Tremblay, Ziegler, and their associates). Adopting a common definition of bullying for research in both Canada and the United States could increase the likelihood of a similar development at the international level.

The Child's Concept of Bullying

The real weakness in the whole discussion of definition lies in the fact that an essential component has been completely overlooked, namely, the child's concept of bullying. The requirement that negative actions must occur over a period of time to qualify as bullying is a good example of an adult interpretation being superimposed on the child. It should be the child's view of a stressor that defines it as bullying; whether or not it is the first occurrence or a series is irrelevant. The provision of a definition by an adult implies that the adult's concept of bullying concurs with that of the child. This assumption has little empirically established basis. If the two concepts differ, the child's responses will have little or no validity. Questions should be phrased according to the child's concept of the topic, and this can only be done if an exploration of the child's concept precedes questionnaire development.

The developmental pattern that concept formation follows must also be considered. Many of the studies on bullying have participants ranging in age from older preschool to adolescence, which, in terms of the development of any concept, would indicate a great disparity in responses. Clearly, the 5-year-old child's view of bullying will be quite different from that of the 18-year-old respondent. As would be expected, some young children included a large number of nonbullying behaviors in their definitions, a finding that has made comparisons of frequency of bullying at different age levels invalid.

CHILDLINE: THE BULLYING LINE

An excellent source of information on the child's concept of bullying is the short-term satellite line of ChildLine, the Bullying Line. With the exception that the descriptor, *bullying*, was used to indicate the problem that this line was intended for, there was no definition of bullying and no guidelines for how the child caller should talk about the problem. In the interviews with children about bullying (MacLeod & Morris, 1996), they were asked, "What would you call bullying?" The children described a more complex experience than most adult investigators do, and their accounts challenged the basis of many adult definitions of bullying. Their descriptions were not only more straightforward but also more subtle than adult definitions suggest. A 10-year-old boy said, "If it is bullying, it'll be like a cut then go away; if you're called names it stays with you, you can't really put it out of your mind" (MacLeod & Morris, 1996, p. 41). Many of the respondents thought bullying could be unintentional as well as intentional, indiscriminate and random as well as systematic, and the target could be any child in addition to those who are less able to defend themselves. Most children do not describe bullying as repeated or long-standing, and those being interviewed, as well as children calling the Bullying Line (MacLeod & Morris, 1996), concurred: Neither duration nor frequency was seen as central to defining bullying. The children more often described instances of a single episode in which feelings of helplessness, fear, and anxiety were triggered that are characteristic of many children who are bullied.

Children respond differently to the same act of bullying. These responses have an impact on the course of subsequent acts by the bully or bullies as well as on the victims' feelings about themselves. Although the children interviewed clearly were aware of the role of intention in cases of physical attack, they also recognized that sometimes bullies were unaware of the effects of their actions. A 14-year-old girl said in her interview:

> If say you're mucking around you can make comments but not really mean to hurt them, like if you're joking around and you think they'll find it funny, but they might not, they might take it to heart. (MacLeod & Morris, 1996, p. 35)

A particularly distinctive feature of the children's responses was their perception of the spiraling nature of bullying behavior. Children in this interview study consistently described the first instance of bullying as representative of a threat of worse to come that might culminate in a physical attack: What begins as teasing that may or may not be negative shifts to verbal taunts that are more unpleasant, possibly escalating into a series of bullying episodes that become increasingly physical. This perception of the course that bullying may take apparently arises from the children's observations of others being bullied. It accounts for the level of fear that one bullying experience can generate. During the interviews (MacLeod & Morris, 1996), a 15-year-old boy described this sequence:

> It started off with name-calling and that sort of thing and in the end it got more unpleasant, a bit physical and that. You know that if you're called names you sort of wait and see if it's the usual sort of thing that happens but it didn't, it got worse. (p. 35)

Whether a single act of bullying follows this path seems to be a function of the motivation of the bully, response of the victim and bystanders, and quality of supervision in the environment in which the bullying occurs. Children appear to experience bullying as a random and unpredictable event that consequently increases their uncertainty and fear.

DEFINITION IN THIS TEXT

Bullying refers to intentional and generally unprovoked attempts by one or more individuals to inflict physical hurt and/or psychological distress on one or more victims. There must be an imbalance of physical or psychological power, with the bully actually being stronger or perceived to be stronger than the victim. The bullying may be *direct,* with face-to-face physical or verbal confrontations, or *indirect,* with less visible actions such as spreading rumors or social exclusion. Although a single attack on a victim if severe enough can be accurately described as bullying, the term more often refers to a series of negative actions that occur frequently over time. This definition includes the qualifier "generally unprovoked," because it allows for the behavior of the provocative victim (see chapter 4).

The Norwegian National Survey

From the schools participating in the Campaign Against Bullying, Olweus (1985) selected a representative sample of 715 schools, with 130,000 children ranging in age from 8 to 16 years, for the Norwegian

National Survey. The pretest data from this sample provided information about prevalence and grade-level differences in bullying.

PREVALENCE

Olweus (1985) estimated that 15% of the students in the Norwegian comprehensive schools were actively involved in the bullying sequence. To be considered a bully, a child had to have bullied others one or more times per week. Five percent of the school population were involved in more serious bully behaviors. Although Norwegians were reportedly shocked by the prevalence of bullying (Olweus, 1985), they had no grounds for hoping that the findings were exaggerations of the problem. With most investigators using slight modifications of Olweus's (1983) Bully/Victim Questionnaire, subsequent studies of prevalence in England (Smith & Sharp, 1994), Ireland (O'Moore & Hillery, 1989), the Netherlands (Haeselager & van Lieshout, 1992), Australia (Rigby & Slee, 1991), Japan (Hirano, 1992), and Canada (Ziegler & Rosenstein-Manner, 1991) have reported even higher prevalence figures than those found in Norway.

Olweus's (1985) report on the prevalence of bullying in Norway proved to have a catalytic effect: From a minor problem requiring minimal attention, bullying became a serious one demanding immediate action. The effects spread beyond the Nordic countries to other continental European countries, the United Kingdom, the United States, Canada, and Japan. Multidisciplinary meetings on childhood bullying were convened in the United States (Greenbaum, 1989) and Europe (O'Moore, 1988).

The conclusions of the two principal investigators, Olweus and Roland, about the prevalence data were notable for their restraint. Olweus (1984) stated that bullying was a considerable problem in Norwegian and Swedish comprehensive schools and one that must be taken seriously. Roland (1989, p. 27) merely pointed out that the 1983 findings were generally consistent with previous Scandinavian prevalence data and said, "It became obvious that there was work to be done!" Their restraint is commendable because there are potential pitfalls in collecting prevalence data on bullying that limit the confidence one can have in exact prevalence figures while not detracting from the established fact that bullying is a serious problem. The following two pitfalls are considered briefly here.

Teacher Nominations of Bullies and Victims

On the basis of teacher–peer agreement, Olweus (1985) expressed confidence in the accuracy of teacher nominations. However, investigators from non-Nordic countries do not share this confidence. Smith and Sharp (1994, p. 11) contended that "most teachers are only aware of a fraction of the bullying which may be going on," and O'Moore (Nash, 1989) found that teachers seriously underestimated the amount of bullying in that they were able to identify only 4 in 10 of the persistent bullies. It should be noted, however, that in Scandinavia the classes are small, and for the first 6 years children have the same teacher (Munthe, 1989), so the teacher really knows every child well.

Distortions

The characteristics of the respondents may distort responses. Bullies may minimize the frequency or severity of their bullying because they perceive these episodes differently from how their victims and uninvolved observers do (Besag, 1989). Quite cruel bullying may be viewed as "just messing around a bit." Victims, however, may consciously exaggerate aspects of the bullying to put themselves in a better light, or they may underreport if they lack confidence in the promised anonymity of the questionnaire and fear reprisal.

GRADE-LEVEL DIFFERENCES IN BULLYING

In the prevalence data (Olweus, 1985, 1993a), the percentage of victims decreased with increasing age and grade level, with the incidence of victims being twice as high in the primary grades than in the secondary grades (see Figure 2.1). In contrast to the steady decline in victims, the number of bullies remained fairly stable (see Figure 2.2). Olweus (1993a, p. 16) stated that "the most remarkable result from these analyses is that bully and victim problems in primary schools were considerably more marked than previously assumed." Certainly the finding that one third of the boys and girls in the second grade reported being bullied is surprisingly high, and this figure is even more disconcerting in view of Smith and Levan's (1995) speculation that if the age trends in the Whitney and Smith (1993) data were extrapolated backward, one could predict an even greater incidence of being bullied in 5- to 7-year-olds. The latter hypothetical prevalence figures suggest that the child entering kindergarten could be at high risk for being bullied.

Cognitive development may influence prevalence figures. Smith and Levan (1995) demonstrated that 6- and 7-year-old children interpret bullying more broadly than older children do; that is, they interpret more events as bullying. For example, the children in their study included occasional aggressive behavior and fighting in which there was

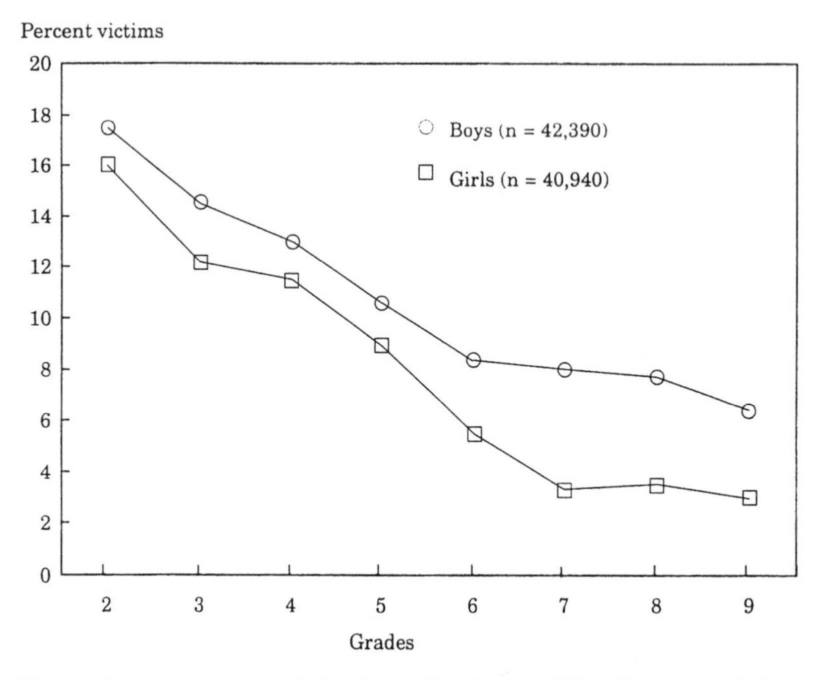

Figure 2.1. Percentage of Students, by Grade, Who Reported Being Bullied by Other Students

Adapted with permission of the author and publisher from Olweus, D. (1993a). *Bullying at School: What We Know and What We Can Do* (p. 15). © Blackwell.

no imbalance of power, and often omitted any mention of intent to hurt (a critical feature of many definitions). In the Sheffield study of attitudes toward bullying (O'Connor, 1995), there was evidence that young children tend to exaggerate the incidence of bullying. The younger children in ChildLine (La Fontaine, 1991) and the 5-year-olds in Madsen and Smith's (1993) study exhibited the same patterns in their responses.

School Characteristics and Bullying

The Norwegian prevalence data (Olweus, 1993a) show unequivocally that bullying is not evenly distributed over any school district, specific school, or class. Other investigators have confirmed this finding with junior (Smith & Sharp, 1994) and secondary schools (Arora & Thompson, 1987; Siann, Callaghan, Glissov, Lockhart, & Rawson, 1994). In addition, Stephenson and Smith (1989) have reported that within one cluster of schools the probability of being bullied was four

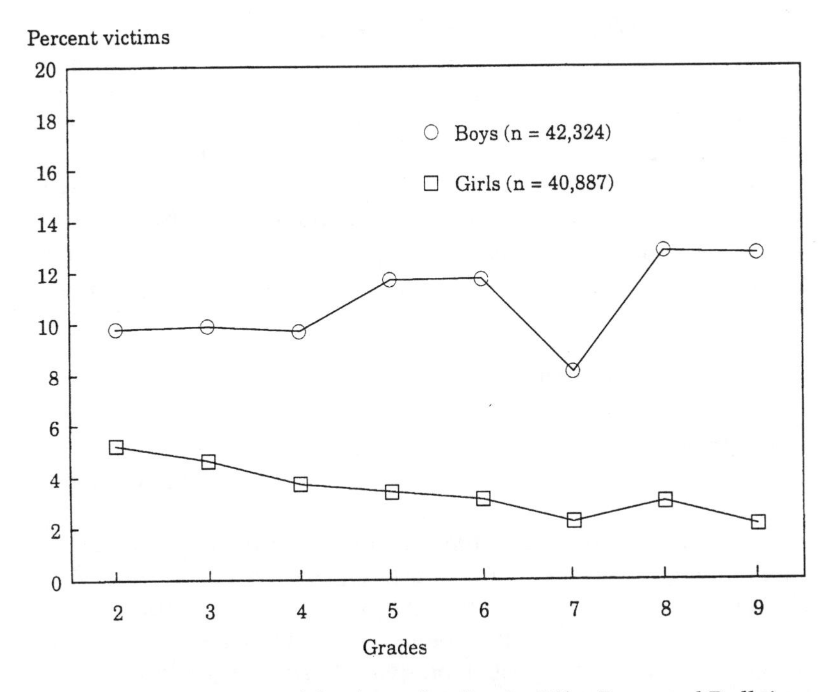

Figure 2.2. Percentage of Students, by Grade, Who Reported Bullying Other Students

Adapted with permission of the author and publisher from Olweus, D. (1993a). *Bullying at School: What We Know and What We Can Do* (p. 16). © Blackwell.

to five times greater in some schools than in others. The question then is, What characteristics of a school are associated with higher or lower prevalence of bullying?

SCHOOL AND CLASS SIZE

Commonsense reasoning would suggest that the sheer numbers of students in big-city high schools with large classes would be associated with higher rates of bullying, but this is not the case. Neither school nor class size was a significant factor in the prevalence of bullying in the Norwegian National Survey (Olweus, 1993a), the earlier Swedish data (Olweus, 1978), or the Finnish studies (Ekman, 1977; Lagerspetz, Björkqvist, Berts, & King, 1982). International research also discounts size within the range of size variations that are generally found (Rutter, 1983).

COMPETITIVENESS FOR HIGH GRADES

Another reasonable hypothesis attributes bullying to competition for top grades. This is essentially a frustration–aggression model in which the aggressive behavior of the bully can be attributed to the frustration of failure in school. However, a detailed causal analysis of the longitudinal data from the Swedish study (Olweus, 1993a, 1993b) gave no support for this idea. Although there was a moderate association between poor grades and bullying behavior, there was no evidence of a causal relationship.

GENDER DIFFERENCES

One of the most consistent findings throughout the bullying literature concerns the higher incidence of bullying in general in boys than in girls (Ahmad & Smith, 1994). This finding, reported in 1989 by Roland and in 1985 by Olweus, is in agreement with studies of gender differences in aggression (Maccoby & Jacklin, 1974; Parke & Slaby, 1983). However, when bullying is broken down into its direct (physical attack) and indirect (verbal attack) components, there are no gender differences for direct bullying (Björkqvist, Lagerspetz, & Kaukiainen, 1992; Lagerspetz, Björkqvist, & Peltonen, 1988; Rivers & Smith, 1994). Girls report more indirect bullying, a consistent finding in all studies from Olweus (1985) to the more recent Lagerspetz and Björkqvist (1994) study.

Age is a factor in gender differences in bullying behavior. The percentage of boy bullies is quite stable at different age levels, but in girls it drops slightly with age (Olweus, 1993a). Boys who bully tend to be 1 to 2 years older than their victims (who may be boys but quite often are girls), whereas girl bullies are more likely to be the same age as their victims, who generally are other girls.

COEDUCATIONAL VERSUS SAME-SEX SCHOOLS

In 1971 Dale published the results of a survey showing that, in England, coeducational schools are one variable that can have a powerful effect in reducing bullying, whereas single-sex schools lack this advantage and that, in fact, bullying thrives in them. The participants were 175 men and 620 women in English colleges of education who had each attended at least one coeducational and one single-sex school. Dale (1971) made within-sex comparisons of respondents who had been in coeducational schools prior to entering a same-sex school and those who had attended same-sex schools first and then coeducational schools. Both men and women strongly believed that disapproval of bullying engaged in by the opposite sex was a contributor to the reduction of bullying. This study is methodologically excellent, and the findings are important. To the best of my knowledge, it is the only study of the effects of the opposite sex on bullying in adolescents and young adults. A three-volume text, it was one of the earliest reports on bullying in the schools. Dale's (1971) work has been unfairly overlooked, to the detriment of progress in the field.

VARIABLES IN HIGH-BULLYING SCHOOLS

Although social disadvantage in the form of poor housing and low socioeconomic status plays a part in making a school into a high-bullying school, it is not one of the important variables. Instead, one of the most important contributors is a school climate of opportunity for bullying (Olweus, 1993a). Poor supervision during periods of free play, recess, and the noon hour sends a clear message to bullies. The failure of school personnel to address the problem of bullying in a decisive way was noted by Olweus (1984): 40% of primary students and 60% of junior high school students surveyed reported that teachers tried to stop bullying only "once in a while" or "almost never." This reluctance to act also is a recurring theme in the United States. In a survey of middle school and high school students in a rural midwestern community (Hazler, Hoover, & Oliver, 1993, p. 16), the respondents were clearly troubled by the fact that school personnel did nothing about the bullying: "They knew about it and did nothing. Our school is lazy in that way" (boy, age 15). "They know; they just don't care. They sit in the teachers' lounge and gossip" (boy, age 18).

Bullying combined with teacher indifference or contempt for the victims virtually ensures that the victims will receive no help. If the teacher is a bully, and there is one in most schools (Pyke, 1994; Smith & Sharp, 1994), the combination becomes even more a cause for concern. When inadequate supervision is combined with crowded conditions in halls or playground areas, an unusually high amount of physical contact results, with much pushing, shoving, and grabbing (Opie, 1993; Opie & Opie, 1959), again, an open invitation to the bully contingent.

Although many parents think that most bullying occurs on the way to and from school, this is not the case. In fact, most of it occurs in the school environment (La Fontaine, 1991; Olweus, 1993a; Smith & Sharp, 1994). Olweus (1991) reported that there were twice as many students bullied at school, with this ratio rising to three times as many at the junior high school level, than was the case for going to and from school. However, anxious parents have grounds for concern because victims get significantly less help from others to and from school than they get when bullied at school (Olweus, 1993a). Consider these examples of problems on the school bus. The first two are from the United States, the third from England.

> An American newspaper columnist said that she did not take her 11-year-old brother's complaints about riding the school bus seriously until she saw the imprint. It was the shape of a man-sized foot below his left shoulder, with the treads looking like tennis shoes. The lines from the rubber floor mat of the bus were imprinted in his cheek. She wrote, "Why was my brother sitting in the aisle where some high school student . . . knocked him down and stepped on him? Why didn't the bus driver do something?" (Hutchison, 1993, p. A6)
>
> When another mother lodged a complaint to the same school district about high school students circling the school bus on their bicycles, shouting obscenities, banging on the door, and taunting the grade school students as they were let off the bus, the Director of Transportation said, "To be perfectly honest with you, we regard this as minor. We have things like this that go on all the time. Kids fighting and jostling each other at the bus stop . . . kids' stuff." (Hutchison, 1993, p. A6)
>
> Sophie, age 11, called ChildLine about being bullied by Julie, another girl in her class. . . . Sophie said, "She doesn't do it at school; she waits till we're on the school bus, then she hits me." Sophie had recently received a black eye from one of these attacks and had told her teacher. The teacher had advised her to try to sort it out herself. (MacLeod & Morris, 1996, pp. 44–45)

It is incomprehensible that school personnel should implicitly condone bullying on school buses by brushing aside legitimate complaints. Such a situation clearly calls for decisive action. One solution would be to place a monitor on each bus to note details about each bullying incident. Any child who is reported would automatically be off the bus for 1 month; two reports for the same child would mean no bus privileges for the remainder of the school year. It would then be the parents' responsibility to see that the bully got to school. There would be *no* exceptions under *any* circumstances, and this would be made clear to the student body at school and to the parents in the form of a letter sent to them explaining the rule and requiring one parent to sign the letter and return it to the school.

Severe School Bullying—Is It a Crime?

In the last two decades, a major development has been the important approach to the effective management of bullying advocated by Furniss (2000), a Lecturer in Law at Leeds University. In an article titled "Bullying in Schools: It's Not a Crime—Is It?" Furniss contended that the fact that schools have rules and regulations to deal with school bullying does not make it irrelevant to treat severe bullying as a crime necessitating involvement with the criminal justice system. Under the law, schools must maintain discipline and protect the safety of their pupils (Fortin, 1998). Of relevance to the safety requirement is the fact that schools must take reasonable precautions to prevent bullying, and they can be sued for negligence if they fail to do so. Increasing numbers of parents are pursuing their complaints in the courts, but the costs of doing so are prohibitive for many parents, a deterrent that would be eliminated by removing a case from the school's jurisdiction and placing it in the criminal justice system. When schools do not or cannot take effective action, police action would be essential to show that bullying would not be ignored, tolerated, or condoned.

Lawrence (1998) agreed and in his text, *School Crime and Juvenile Justice,* further asserted that treating school crime as an internal problem is not only incomplete but also inaccurate. Of relevance here is the view of bullying that was voiced in May 1987 by a group of scholars from many parts of the world, who met at Harvard University to discuss the problems of school bullying and victimization. The fact that school bullying merited the descriptor *crime* was evident:

> Under the euphemism of "bullying," we see a much broader, more serious affair. We see instances of assault and battery, gang activity, threat of bodily harm, weapons possession, extortion, civil rights violations, attempted murder and murder.
>
> Everybody knows these are crimes. The fact that they were committed by minors upon minors does not make them less than crimes. The fact that they were committed on school grounds by students does not make them less than crimes. (Greenbaum, 1989, p. 11)

VICTIMOLOGY OF CHILDHOOD

Of relevance to the issue of whether some bullying actions should be classified as a criminal offense is the proposal from Finkelhor and Dziuba-Leatherman (1994) for the development of a potentially important field clearly relevant to violence—the victimology of childhood: "A field called the victimology of childhood should be defined that adopts a developmental approach to understanding children's vulnerability to different types of victimization and their different effects" (p. 173).

Further, Finkelhor and Dziuba-Leatherman (1994) stated that the types of child victimization should be categorized according to their order of magnitude, namely, pandemic, acute, and extraordinary victimizations. These are discussed briefly below.

Pandemic Victimizations

These victimizations are those that most children experience while growing up, such as sibling assault and peer assault. The following account describes an example:

> I was a fringe member of a popular clique and allowed to sit at their lunch table, and for a stretch of time one spring, they basically tormented Mick . . . every day at lunch. . . . Mick had very red, wiry hair. That was enough to make him a target. The leaders of this pack made it a point to give him a new derogatory nickname each day—"Brillo" and "Helmet" were two—making fun of his hair. . . . Sometimes they'd start to chant—"Don't let Mick eat," and it was like a rallying cry. They would blow snot on his sandwich or simply steal his food. One day they stole a bee from the biology lab and put it in his tuna sandwich. I didn't join in, but looking back on it, I can't believe I just sat there and let it happen around me. (Graham & Juvonen, 2001, p. 49)

Acute Victimizations

These occur to a sizable minority of children and include verbal persecution, physical abuse, and rape. The following is an account of a student whose parents had emigrated from another country. She had been harassed daily by her peers for years.

> She reported the bullying to school officials, who did nothing. She told her parents, who "listened but did not hear." One day her classmates threw tampons at her on the school bus and told her they were going to beat her up. She reported the threats to the bus driver, who laughed it off. The other girls then followed her off the school bus and beat her as the bus driver watched approvingly, giving a "*Rocky Five* victory sign" when they had finished battering the girl. "One of (them) held me from behind while the other pummeled me, while 20 of my classmates watched, and no one did anything," the girl said. "I didn't hit her once. It went on for three or four minutes." Finally a woman driving by, a neighbor of

> the girl, got out of her car and made them stop. "My shirt was covered with blood. . . . My life changed, I was in counseling for a while. I depended on the adult to protect me, and I made a mistake by doing that." (Horn, 2000, p. 25)

Extraordinary Victimizations

A very small number of children experience extraordinary victimization, but their plight attracts a great deal of media attention. Included here are gun-related homicide, child abuse homicide, and nonfamily abduction. The following example occurred in 1997 in Victoria, a small city in British Columbia, Canada.

> Reena Virk, a 14-year-old girl, had a phone call from one of the teenage girls in her school from whom she most wanted acceptance, urging her to come to a party. The party was a ruse. Two girls planned to beat her up because she had used another girl's address book and called up some boys. Reena went to the "party" behind a school and then walked to a nearby bridge with 15 teenagers (male and female). They went under the bridge where it was dark and, as planned, two girls began hurling accusations at Reena and one of them extinguished a cigarette on her forehead. She tried to run but a group of girls blocked her escape. Then seven girls swarmed over her and began beating her with kicks and punches. A boy joined the fight and kicked her in the head five times. Reena was pleading with them to stop. One girl dragged her to the water's edge and gave her another kick, another one tried to set fire to her hair. Dazed and bloodied, Reena staggered up to the bridge and started home but a boy and girl followed her across the bridge and stomped on her for almost 15 minutes before dragging her unconscious body into the water, where she drowned. (Hall, 1999, pp. A1–A2)

Bullying actions in the pandemic category would rarely merit the descriptor *criminal behavior,* but most of those in the acute category and all of those in the extraordinary category would be classed as criminal behavior. Note how well these three categories fit the variation and range in victimizations that are generally subsumed under the heading, school bullying.

Obstacles to the Construction of Bullying as a Crime

When Furniss's (2000) criteria justify qualifying a severe school bullying incident as a crime, the next step is to identify the obstacles that currently prevent the construction of bullying as a crime. Of relevance here is the distinction between two approaches to the problem of bullying: one is practical criminality and the other is formal criminality.

In *practical criminality,* the level of bullying is conceived more as a disciplinary matter than as a crime. This is the concept that most school personnel have of effective intervention in cases of school bullying. Note that advocates of this approach, as well as those of the formal criminality approach, are equally concerned with enforcement.

Formal criminality refers to the legal categorization of behavior as a crime. There is no legal definition of school bullying and no references to the crime of "bullying" in any legislation or case law in the United Kingdom. It follows that to determine whether or not a criminal offense has been committed, bullying activities must be categorized differently, for example, as assault, robbery, or extortion, rather than as bullying. Recent developments in the law have expanded the classifications of bullying activities that can be classified as criminal offenses. Psychological harm now qualifies as grounds for prosecution, and it is accepted as fact that it can be as serious as some types of physical harm. The Protection From Harassment Act of 1997 held that even indirect aggression (Björkqvist, Österman, & Kaukiainen, 1992), such as spreading defamatory rumors, could amount to an assault if psychological harm resulted. In a recent test case in England, a 12-year-old girl who suffered verbal aggression had her claim upheld in court; a boy who sued his school for failing to protect him from racist taunts was awarded significant damages (Wainwright, 1999). Although the increased scope of the criminal law has infuriated some experts, for the victim of bullying the recent legal developments are extremely important. The tools now exist to prosecute most cases of bullying using the criminal law. Furniss (2000, pp. 19–21) commented that "it will be interesting to see whether the Protection from Harassment Act will be used to protect victims of bullying where school law is not effective. This will depend largely upon the social construction of bullying as a crime."

For prosecution to occur, the views of those who have to treat such activities as criminal are of critical importance. Lacey (1995) used the metaphor of a set of lenses to illustrate this potential problem. The nature of the lens determines the appearance of what is let through about the case under investigation, as well as what is screened out. If the victim is a child, for example, the adult may not see a long-time persecution with indirect aggression as criminal at all, or may see it as criminal but not worth the time and effort needed to proceed against the bully or altogether just too problematic. Bullying must pass through several sets of lenses to be categorized as criminal. Morgan and Zedner (1992, p. 32) pointed out:

> In the case of younger children, particularly, many crimes are subject to a triple filtering process. First, the child has to disclose that he or she has been victimized to an adult; secondly, the adult has to decide whether or not to report it to the police; and, thirdly, the police make the decision whether or not to record the offence.

In some cases teachers are unable or unwilling to take action against bullying even in the face of pupils' and parents' complaints. Morgan and Zedner (1992) found that the majority of complainants did not feel that the school took them seriously. However, if police action is seen as a possibility, a threat to call the police may be enough to prevent further bullying or to motivate action on the part of the school (Children's Legal Centre, 1996). In other cases in which school internal mechanisms are ineffective, the pupil persists in bullying others, despite the school taking action to prevent this. One possible action then is to transfer the case to the criminal justice system, with expulsion used only as a last resort. The Crime and Disorder Act (1998) represents a major step forward with its new reintegrative approach to youth crime, with rehabilitation as the main goal, in combination with a mix of punishment, acceptance of responsibility, reparation, and restoration.

How serious does an incident have to be in order to be taken out of the school's jurisdiction? Seriousness depends on the nature of the act, extent of harm done, and intention of the offender. Dingwall and Harding (1998) contended that the choice between criminal justice intervention, school intervention, or both is largely a matter of common sense. The Department of Education rules are that all assault offenses causing actual bodily harm should be reported to the police and that the police should deal with any incident involving a weapon (Furniss, 2000). If an assault causes grievous bodily harm or worse, the police should be notified immediately. Criminal justice agencies should be called when internal school disciplinary actions have been ineffective and the bullying persists or escalates.

Most of the political support for legal action against school bullying has come from the Nordic countries. In 1981 Olweus had proposed the introduction of a law against bullying at school. Although his proposal was not immediately acted on, Olweus did not give up, probably because of the strong possibility that his research findings would have an effect. In 1994, the Swedish Parliament passed a new school law against school bullying (Olweus, 1999c), and in 1995 school bullying was made a penal offense in Finland (Björkqvist & Österman, 1999). In 1997 the Children's Ombudsman in Sweden proposed that the legislation against school bullying be extended and sharpened (Olweus, 1999c).

Ananiadou and Smith (in press) have obtained information on the legal situation regarding bullying and violence from all 15 European member states and the 4 associated and candidate states: Iceland, Malta, Norway, and Switzerland. To obtain this information, they wrote to the Ministries of Education or their equivalent in each country, requesting copies of any legal requirement or guidelines on school bullying and/or violence and any antibullying materials that might have been distributed on a large scale to schools in each country. Their findings are disappointing. Of the 19 countries contacted, fewer than half ($n = 9$) have any legal requirements for schools to tackle bullying or violence, and even fewer ($n = 6$) specifically mention bullying.

In the last decade there has been increased legal attention in the United States to the problem of school bullying, but no laws have been passed (Harachi, Catalano, & Hawkins, 1999b). Nonetheless, there is strong support for Furniss's (2000) approach from several sources. Perhaps legal action against school bullying will be formally enacted in view of the fact that current approaches to the problem of school bullying in the United States have not been effective in reducing the incidence of such antisocial behavior.

COMMENT

In the many studies reported throughout this text, the predominant view is that the problem of bullying is handled inadequately by the schools. The findings from these studies should not be viewed as a blanket indictment of all schools. Many make little or no systematic effort to confront the problem of bullying, but there is an encouraging number of other schools working diligently on this problem. In addition, some teachers are making largely unheralded, heroic efforts in their own classrooms to counteract the indifference of their school administrators. Later chapters describe some of these positive attacks (see, e.g., the discussions later in the text on bully courts, student watch groups, and conflict resolution programs).

3 Bullies

Bullying is a complex problem that, to date, has not been managed effectively. One reason for this failure may be that the predominant view is overly simplistic: The stereotype of bullies as louts from broken homes in high-crime, lower-class neighborhoods conveys a picture of a not-too-bright individual whose strong point is brute strength. Recent research, however, shows that those bullies who are ringleaders may be characterized as having good theory of mind abilities and as being skilled manipulators (Sutton, Smith, & Swettenham, 1999). Another simplistic view sees bullying as a normal part of growing up and, consequently, just a transient problem. These grossly inaccurate perceptions are supported by the euphemistic use of "bullying" to describe actions such as assault and extortion that would be a criminal matter if the perpetrators were adults (Finkelhor, 1995; La Fontaine, 1991).

A common misconception among some psychologists and psychiatrists is that bullies are outwardly tough but inwardly anxious and insecure. To test this belief, Olweus (1999b) used direct and indirect methods, such as stress hormones and projective techniques. There was no evidence of heightened insecurity. In fact, the results showed that the bullies either had unusually little anxiety and insecurity or were approximately average on these dimensions (Olweus, 1981; Pulkkinen & Tremblay, 1992) and were not characterized by poor self-esteem.

If efforts at intervention and prevention are to have any success, it is essential that the complexity of the bullying phenomenon be acknowledged. For example, there are distinct subgroups of bullies and victims—a sphere of perpetrators, victims, peers, parents, and school personnel all directly or indirectly involved in the immediate problem—and the serious long-term effects on the bully, which are often severe enough to justify the descriptor "lifelong losers." Bullies are not born, they are created. A cluster of contributory causes helps to set the child on the path to bullying. These include attributes of the parents that are reflected in their patterns of child rearing and characteristics of the child that elicit negative reactions from caregivers and peers. Although adults in the home and school are clearly part of the bullying problem, they can also be part of the solution *if* they know how to react when bullying occurs. To this end, this chapter discusses the failure of many parents and school personnel to take appropriate action about the problem of bullying. It begins with the distinction between bullying, aggression, and violence (Olweus, 1999b) and then goes on to the subgroups that Olweus (1978) identified within the population of bullies, followed by the prevalence findings, how children become bullies, the characteristics that experts agree are most descriptive of bullies and victims, an innovative approach for helping bullies avoid some of the long-term negative outcomes, some unexpected problems that bullies have, types of bullies, the issue of self-reports versus peer nominations, gender differences in bullying behavior, and indirect aggression in girls.

The fact that bullying is often treated as synonymous with aggression and violence in the literature has caused Olweus (1999b) to emphasize the importance of distinguishing between these three related antisocial behaviors. *Bullying* is a subcategory of aggression with two special characteristics: It usually consists of repetitive attacks on victims with low self-defense capabilities, and it generally occurs without provocation. A substantial number of other forms of aggression are not bullying, for example, conflict and aggressive exchanges between children of similar physical and psychological strength, vandalism of the homes of total strangers, or random attacks on strangers for trivial reasons such as, "I didn't like the way he looked at me."

Olweus (1999c) pointed out that violence and violent behavior are *not* more or less synonymous with aggressive behavior. He used a Venn diagram (see Figure 3.1) to clarify the relationship between violence, bullying, and aggression, with the following comment (Olweus, 1999c, p. 12):

> Aggression/aggressive behavior is the general and overarching term . . . whereas both bullying and violence/violent behavior are subcategories of aggressive behavior . . . there is also a certain overlap between violence and bullying. . . . This (overlap) area denotes situations in which . . . physical means are used in the context of bullying (e.g., hitting, kicking, shoving, etc. in situations where the general criteria of bullying are met). The diagram also makes it clear that there is a good deal of bullying without violence . . . and . . . a good deal of violence that cannot be characterized as bullying.

Prevalence

Figures regarding the prevalence of bullying during the school years vary greatly. Comparisons across studies may be largely invalidated by marked differences in definitions of bullying, whether teasing is

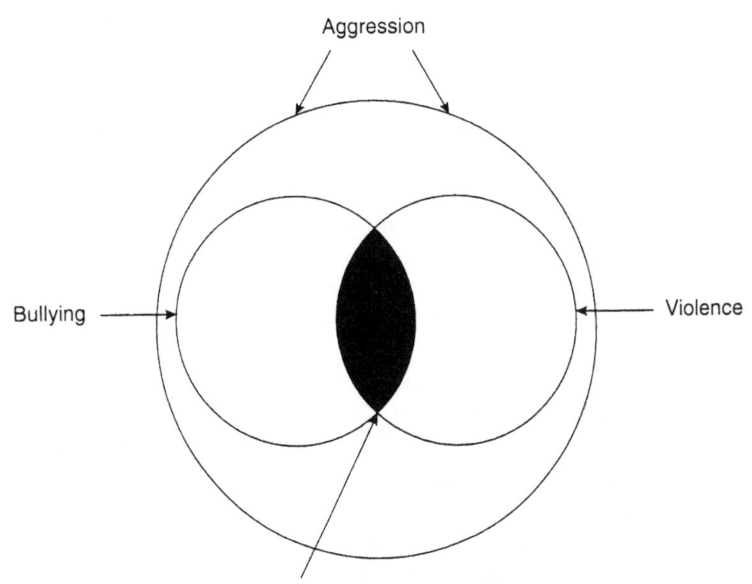

Figure 3.1. Venn Diagram Showing Relationships Among Concepts of Aggression, Violence, and Bullying

Reproduced with permission of the author and publisher from Olweus, D. (1999c). In P. K. Smith et al. (Eds.), *The Nature of School Bullying: A Cross-National Perspective* (p. 13). © Routledge.

included, types of questionnaire, wording of items, sampling, and other methodological differences. Keeping these caveats in mind, the literature clearly supports the following statements: 15% to 20% of all students will experience some form of bullying during their school years (Olweus, 1993a; Ross, 1996; Smith & Sharp, 1994); between 10% and 20% of children are bullied often enough for them to consider it a serious problem (Boulton & Smith, 1994; Perry, Kusel, & Perry, 1988); and bullying in the 1990s is more lethal and occurs more frequently than it did in the previous two decades (Olweus & Alsaker, 1991). It follows that bullying may be the most prevalent form of violence in American schools and one that is likely to affect the greatest number of students.

Following Olweus's (1985) estimate that 15% of the students in Norwegian schools were actively involved in the bullying sequence, investigators in other countries became interested. Their findings show clearly that the problem of bullying exists in many countries representing a wide spectrum of cultures, including England (Smith

& Sharp, 1994), Ireland (O'Moore & Hillery, 1989), Canada (Bentley & Li, 1995), and Australia (Rigby & Slee, 1991).

The prevalence of school bullying and its usually serious impact on its victims have caused international concern for more than a quarter of a century, first in Norway and Sweden (Olweus, 1978), and later almost worldwide (Smith, Morita, et al., 1999). Despite pockets of intensive efforts to sharply reduce it, recent research (Wolke, 1999) and sources such as ChildLine (MacLeod & Morris, 1996) suggest that school bullying is as prevalent today as it was a decade ago. The question then is, What is sustaining it and why is this the case? Attitudes toward bullying range along a continuum from complete rejection to complete acceptance, with the majority of adults falling toward the latter end. School administrators, teaching staff, and many parents often see it as a normal event in the school years, an experience that will toughen victims up and altogether one not justifying any action on their part. Buttressing this view is an underlying contempt for most victims. Given this permissiveness, there is little reason to expect any change in bullies' behavior. A more widespread permissiveness extends to other areas of antisocial actions. In a number of states in the United States, children under 18 years are protected from the consequences of many of their lesser antisocial actions (Lawrence, 1998), a protection that also applies to their parents in that they are not held responsible for their children's behavior. Although increasingly, children who commit more serious crimes are being tried as adults, for the majority, no serious consequences follow behaviors such as bullying. With many schools abdicating responsibility for eliminating school bullying and parents not held liable for their children's bullying behaviors, Furniss (2000) has raised the question of who should be responsible for coping with this problem.

SELF-REPORTS VERSUS PEER NOMINATIONS

Harassment by peers typically is assessed with self-ratings or peer nominations. The assumption underlying researcher confidence in self-reports is that children themselves are certain to know whether or not they have been victimized. At the same time, peers are assumed to be accurate informants because they are in a position to either directly witness or hear about harassment in situations when there are no adult observers. Even in the classroom, peers witness events and behavior that teachers do not see. Although both assessment procedures have adequate face validity, that is, they do measure what they appear to measure, the correlation coefficients between the two are low, typically ranging from .2 to .4 (Graham & Juvonen, 1998; Pellegrini, 2001) so that, at most, they share only 16% of the variance. The validity of the data obtained with these two procedures has also been questioned. Self-ratings appear to provide inflated estimates of harassment and so are often considered to be less valid than peer nominations (see, e.g., Österman et al., 1994).

Juvonen, Nishina, and Graham (2001) have proposed that instead of continuing attempts to prove the superiority of one procedure over the other, they should be considered complementary. Juvonen et al. reasoned that self-ratings and peer perceptions represent distinct constructs, namely, subjective experiences and social reputations, and different norms, that is, private *versus* public. This reasoning makes the low correlations between the two quite predictable and to be expected. Furthermore, they stated that "if self-views and peer perceptions of victim status represent distinct constructs (subjective experiences and peer social reputation), then they should each have unique correlates" (Juvonen et al., 2001, p. 106). In pursuit of this possibility, they used preliminary data from their own research to demonstrate examples of distinct correlates and antecedents to self-reports and peer nominations among early adolescents. In addition, they presented a conceptual model in which self-ratings of victim status and peer nominations of victim reputation were used to predict middle school students' school functioning. This model emphasizes the complementary contribution of self-perceptions and peer perception. Their work represents a major contribution to the assessment field.

Self-Report Measures

These procedures can be used to assess how often a child is bullied as well as how often he or she bullies others. The identity of the child can be either confidential or anonymous. When the identity is known, it is likely that both victimization and bullying will be underreported compared with the information that would be given when an anonymous format is used. The child may be concerned about his or her reputation and also the possibility of retaliation for naming a bully. Although self-report records could be presented as anonymous, but marked in a way that identifies the informant, no ethical investigator would stoop to such a tactic.

The most frequently used self-report procedures in the assessment of bullying and victimization are Olweus's (1983, 1996) Bully/Victim Questionnaires for Children and Adolescents. These can be used with a confidential or anonymous format. The respondents are asked to rate themselves on a number of straightforward questions such as, "How often have you been bullied?"

Peer Nominations

Some procedures here provide the child with the names of the peers in the target group or, when young children are the informants, with their pictures. Usually the peers are all in the same classroom as the child. In some procedures, only same-gender peers are in the target group, whereas in others, both genders are included. Children are first asked to name each child in the class and then to nominate one or more classmates who fit a specified criterion such as, "Tell me the names of some children who get picked on a lot." Sometimes the number of children is specified, for example, "three children." The difficulty in being specific raises the possibility that a respondent who can only think of two children who are picked on a lot may add a third name to conform to the instructions, thus making the data invalid. Note that victims identified by self-report procedures and those nominated by peers are not likely to be equivalent lists (Schwartz, Proctor, & Chien, 2001).

Peer Nomination Inventory

Perry, Kusel, & Perry (1988) developed a modified version of the Peer Nomination Inventory (Wiggins & Winder, 1961) for use in assessing children's victimization and aggressive bullying behavior. Called the Modified Peer Nomination Inventory (see Table 3.1), it asks children to nominate classmates who fit specific behavioral descriptors such as "He has lots of friends" or "Kids make fun of him." There are two forms, one for boys and one for girls, each consisting of 26 items. Seven items describe victimization, for example, "He gets beat up"; 7 items describe the aggressive behavior that bullies often exhibit, "He's just plain mean"; and the remaining 12 items are filler items, such as "He's good at sports." This last group masks the purpose of the inventory. The 26 items are listed down the left-hand margin of a legal-size sheet of paper, and the names of all the same-gender children in the class are listed across the top at right angles to the test items. Each child's task is to place an *X* beneath the name of any classmate(s) whose behavior fits an item. Any number of nominations can be made for each item. The children are asked to cross their own names off the list to prevent them from nominating themselves. Administration time is 30 minutes.

The victim score is determined by calculating the percentage of same-gender classmates who checked the child's name for each victim item and then totaling these percentages. The same procedure is used to determine the aggressive bullying score. Because there are seven items on each scale, a child's score could range from 0 to 700.

Table 3.1. Items on the Modified Peer Nomination Inventory (Boys' Form)

1. He's always losing things. (F)
2. He's a fast runner. (F)
3. Kids make fun of him. (V)
4. He is the kind of kid I like. (F)
5. When he doesn't get his way he gets real mad. (A)
6. He gets beat up. (V)
7. He has lots of friends. (F)
8. He's just plain mean. (A)
9. He shares his things with others. (F)
10. He gets called names by other kids. (V)
11. He's a real smart kid. (F)
12. He makes fun of people. (A)
13. He says he can beat everybody up. (A)
14. He's a good-looking kid. (F)
15. Kids do mean things to him. (V)
16. He tries to get other people in trouble. (A)
17. He's a good friend of mine. (F)
18. He hits and pushes other people around. (A)
19. He likes to help the teacher. (F)
20. He gets picked on by other kids. (V)
21. He's good at sports. (F)
22. He gets hit and pushed by other kids. (V)
23. All the kids like him. (F)
24. He tries to pick fights with people. (A)
25. Kids try to hurt his feelings. (V)
26. He's a real nice kid. (F)

Note: F = filler item; V = victimization item; A = aggression item.
Source: Reproduced with permission of the authors and publisher from Perry, D. G., Kusel, S. J., & Perry, L. C. (1988). Victims of peer aggression. *Developmental Psychology, 24,* 807–814. © American Psychological Association, Inc.

Methodologically sound investigations of the Modified Peer Nomination Inventory have established its reliability and validity. It is a scale that children find interesting and enjoyable to complete. As would be expected with a statistically sound instrument, the participating children's victim scores did not correlate with their aggression scores, were positively correlated with peer rejection, and were negatively correlated with peer acceptance (Perry et al., 1988).

Olweus's Typology of Bullies

In a 1978 study of boys, Olweus distinguished among the aggressive bully (regarded by Olweus and others as the prototypical bully), the passive bully, the bully-victim, and a small but intriguing group, the provocative victim. The last group is both immensely interesting and something of an enigma: Although clearly characterized by a cluster of bully characteristics, their victim qualities appear to predominate. For this reason, they are discussed later, in chapter 4.

AGGRESSIVE BULLIES

Most bullies belong in this group (Olweus, 1978). They are impulsive, hot-tempered, belligerent, fearless, coercive, confident to the point of being overconfident, and singularly lacking in empathy for their victims. Their salient characteristics are a potent combination of physical strength, a stable but aggressive personality pattern, a concern for power fueled by a compulsive need to dominate others, and an unfortunate tendency to overreact aggressively in ambiguous confrontations. Slights or hostilities are seen where neither exists. As Dodge (Greenbaum, 1989) noted, aggressive bullies see the world with a paranoid eye. In the school situation, they conform reluctantly to rules, and when compelled to conform they exhibit low frustration tolerance.

Olweus reported that aggressive bullies often are popular in the early school years, a finding that has some support from the Sheffield Bullying Project (Smith & Sharp, 1994). But their popularity generally diminishes in the upper grades, along with academic performance (Olweus, 1993a). It is likely that younger children admire or are drawn to the macho image but then draw away as their own critical faculties concerning friends and leaders become more discerning. A 17-year-old boy, for example, offered this perceptive description of the aggressive bully:

> The bully is a highly strategic person. Using his/her tactical methods he/she is able to locate the victim's Achilles heel and hammer home on this. In the case of mental bullying, the bully lowers the self-esteem of the victim, and that makes him/her feel worthless. Speaking from personal experience, even if the bullying stops, the victim still carries the mark of being extremely self-aware and self-critical. (Byrne, 1994, p. 12)

Theory of mind or mindreading is the ability of individuals to attribute mental states to themselves and others to explain and predict behavior. The popular stereotype of a bully that is supported by theories (Crick & Dodge, 1994) based on the social skills deficit model is usually of a male, a physically powerful "oafish" person, intellectually simple or backward who resorts to violence in his interactions with others because it is the only way he knows to handle the demands of daily life. Sutton et al. (1999) presented an alternative view. They contended that the social skills of a bully have been underestimated, that some bullies, such as ringleader bullies, must need good social cognition and theory of mind skills if they are to successfully manipulate and organize others to engage in antisocial behavior while avoiding being caught themselves. Although these skills are likely to be used to some extent in all bullying activities, they should prove to be particularly useful for ringleader bullies and for the instigators of indirect aggression (Björkqvist, 1994) that is common among girls. The skills involved would be useful in physical bullying when the aggressive bully must choose the optimum time and method for bullying, the goal being to maximize the victim's vulnerability and, at the same time, minimize the probability of being caught by school personnel.

The term *bullying* implies that the victim is part of the process. Confirmation of this pairing is evident in Floyd's (1985) intensive studies of bully and victim interactions:

> Bullies seem to need a victim and may work hard to create one. . . . It is striking to see a sort of choreographed victimization, a dance goes on. It is as though they court each other and often it seems as if neither can leave the other alone. (p. 11)

There is a tendency among school personnel to view bullying and aggression as interchangeable. Although bullying is a subset of aggression (Smith, 1991), boys who bully differ in some respects from chronically aggressive boys. Consider, for example, popularity with peers. In a comparison between bullies and a randomly selected group of same-age boys, Olweus (1991) found that the two groups did not differ in popularity, whereas Foster, DeLawyer, and Guevremont (1986) found chronically aggressive boys to be less popular than their peers. One possible reason for this difference may be that aggressive children tend to strike out at many children so there would be a larger group of victims with good reason to dislike them, whereas bullies do not indiscriminately abuse any peer. Instead, they reportedly assess peers carefully and try out aggressive behavior on possible victims such as those who do not seem to have a circle of friends. If a victim proves to be satisfactory, a specific dyadic relationship forms between the bully and victim (Dodge & Coie, 1989). It would be helpful to identify the qualities in a bully that combine with specific attributes of a victim to lead to the formation of a dyadic relationship (Perry et al., 1992; Pierce & Cohen, 1995).

Coie and Christopoulos (1989) have identified two types of dyadic relationships. One is the common *asymmetrical* relationship in which one member is clearly the aggressor and the other is the victim. Its development follows an orderly course. The bully tries out aggressive behaviors on victims until he or she finds one who does not resist. The bully pursues this relationship, and if the victim puts up little or no resistance, the asymmetrical relationship is soon established (Dodge & Coie, 1989; Olweus, 1978). It is not unusual for a bully to subsequently refer to the victim as "one of mine." The second type of dyadic relationship is a *symmetrical* one in which each member aggresses against and is victimized by the other. How it develops is puzzling. Coie and Christopoulos (1989) speculated that there is a quality in certain bully/victim interactions that alerts each member to the possibility of hostile intentions on the part of the other, and this causes a flow of aggression in both directions, thus forming the symmetrical dyad. It is possible that the victims in this type of dyad are primarily provocative victims, whereas those in the asymmetrical dyads are generally passive victims.

The credo of the aggressive bully is that of the macho aggressor who believes that there are two kinds of people—those who dominate and those who submit (Miedzian, 1992). Aggressive bullies do not feel remorse when they inflict pain. Although they perceive physical force as an effective means of domination, harassment with nonphysical means, such as words, gestures, or looks, is a common and often very frightening form of intimidation in this group (Olweus, 1993a). In fact, they often perceive this tactic as a higher level of bullying. There is no question that a nonphysical approach can strike terror in the victim:

> I try hard not to catch his eye in class but it's like he's pulling me, it's an awful feeling. I'm helpless and when I do look at him he gives me this look and I know what it'll be like at recess and what's going to happen to my lunch money. (J. Carmichael, personal communication, December 4, 1991)

The bullies' perception of bullying incidents is significantly less severe than that of their victims, for example, "just messing around." They view their own behavior from an egocentric stance and have little empathy and no remorse for their victims: Often they feel that the victim deserved the bullying, claiming he or she "asked for it." In place of empathy is a cold, calculated attitude that leads to premeditated and heartless attacks. When they are caught, they are noted for their skillful avoidance of any blame: Exasperated school personnel often describe them as "slippery and resistant to school efforts to intervene." Typically they exhibit a gradually decreasing interest in school achievement and rarely participate in extracurricular events at school (Mahoney, 2000).

Mahoney (2000) has focused on the antecedents of antisocial behavior and moderators affecting the development of patterns of such behavior. The fact that most antisocial youths do not become antisocial adults (Magnusson, 1996) raises the question of what developmental experiences are available that have the capability for interrupting an ongoing pattern of antisocial behavior. In pursuing an answer to this question, Mahoney (2000) conducted a longitudinal study of boys and girls (N = 695) who were in Grade 4 or 7, tracked them annually until the end of high school, and then followed up with interviews at ages 20 and 24 years. At the beginning of the study, four mixed-gender configurations were identified, each of which was reasonably homogeneous in terms of behavior and academic performance. Over time, those in the multiple-risk configuration were more likely to exhibit long-term antisocial behaviors. One particularly interesting finding in the data from the longitudinal study (Mahoney & Cairns, 1997) is that participation of one or more years in school extracurricular activities during Grades 6 to 10 was associated with a reduction in early school dropout, particularly for high-risk students, *if* the individual's social network had also participated in those activities. These results suggest that beginning in Grade 6 a concerted effort by school personnel to provide a range of extracurricular activities and encourage participation in them would be a relatively low-cost way to tackle the dropout problem and its associated negative offshoots.

In considering the question as to why such participation in the school years should be linked to more positive patterns later on for high-risk youths, Mahoney (2000, pp. 513–514) stated:

> Prevention studies have traditionally targeted specific problem behaviors for amelioration or elimination (e.g., aggression . . .). But the behaviors targeted for prevention often represent effective, functional strategies for the individual who employs them (Clarke-McLean, 1996). As a result, efforts to reduce or change antisocial patterns sometimes show limited effectiveness (Mrazek & Haggerty, 1994; Tremblay & Craig, 1995). An alternative strategy suggested by this research is not to focus upon an in-

> dividual's presumed deficits but to consider the individual's entire range of competencies and interests (Cowen, 1994). Participation in school activities provides an opportunity for high risk youths and similarly ineffective peers to form a positive connection to its faculty and values that might be otherwise unavailable. The activity represents an attractive steppingstone leading towards conventional behavior. Once involved, newly emerged constraints may render previous experience of antisocial behavior ineffective or unnecessary.

In the past 2 years, there have been encouraging signs of researcher attention directed to the accuracy of firmly established beliefs about bullies as well as to unexpected new characteristics of this group. The first of these was the finding by Forero, McLellan, Rissel, and Bauman (1999) in a study of 3,918 Australian school children in years 6, 8, and 10 that bullying was significantly associated with psychological and psychosomatic problems such as headache, stomachache, backache, and feeling irritable, nervous, or dizzy. Bully-victims had the most psychological and psychosomatic symptoms and liked school; aggressive bullies also had very high scores on psychosomatic problems and disliked school. To my knowledge, psychosomatic problems are rarely mentioned in descriptions of bullies. Health practitioners should consider being a bully and the school environment as possible causes of common physiological and psychological symptoms (Williams, Chambers, Logan, & Robinson, 1996).

Another unexpected finding came from a study of 410 Finnish adolescents ages 14 to 16 years (Kaltiala-Heino, Rimpelä, Marttunen, Rimpelä, & Rantanen, 1999). Both bullies and victims were found to be at increased risk for depression and suicide, which led Kaltiala-Heino et al. to conclude that bullies were more like victims than is commonly thought. When symptoms of depression were controlled for, suicidal ideation occurred most often among bullies. Yet in the literature and the mass media, it is almost always the victims who commit suicide.

Implications of Lazarus's (1966) Theory for Intervention

Consider the aggressive bully's behavior within the framework of Lazarus's (1966) theory. Dodge's contention (Greenbaum, 1989) that the bully views his or her world with a paranoid eye is an accurate assessment of one aspect of the bully's problem. Stressors that alert the bully to the need for action are everywhere, and particularly so in the school environment. One 10-year-old bully's defense for attacking a much younger child who apparently was just walking toward him was:

> He gave me that look, you know? Like, "Hey Mac, who do you think *you* are?" I thought this upstart needs to find out *right now* who's in charge around here. (M. M. Cunningham, personal communication, February 6, 1982)

Similar ambiguous actions by others, which to most children would be inconsequential, are often likely to be instantly appraised by the bully as threatening and therefore requiring immediate aggressive action. Usually there are no deterrents to the bully's aggression. The bully has had many previous successes with his or her immediate use of power, has the unqualified support of his or her loyal group of followers, and is totally lacking in empathy for his or her victims.

For this category of bullies, the focus should be on changing both the speed and content of their appraisal of ambiguous events. Role play would be the safest way to start an intervention, with two people acting out behavior sequences while the bully remains seated, his task being to state what actions the one playing the bully role should take in each sequence. In the early sessions, the sequences would be minimally ambiguous and clearly justifying some nonaggressive response by the role-play bully. Later sessions would have sequences in which even moderately aggressive action would be inappropriate. Inappropriate aggression could be further discouraged by having the bully's teachers make daily reports of inappropriate aggression and consequent punishment in the form of deprivation of privileges. Suitable rewards would be given for appropriate responses. It is essential that the bully learn to look at events as controllable by the use of strategies other than force. The goal here is to shift the bully's well-established aggression-based appraisals of events and everyday interactions to appropriate assertive appraisals of them. This shift may well be a difficult one to achieve.

PURE BULLIES

Within the bully group, a minority whom Wolke (1999, p. 3) referred to as "pure" bullies were children who have never been victimized, who enjoy their school days, and are rarely absent because of illness. The parents of this group reported that their children had significantly fewer stomachaches, colds, and coughs than most children and were less likely to invent illnesses, presumably because they enjoyed what went on at school. Wolke (1999) commented: "It appears that pure bullies are healthy individuals, who enjoy school and use bullying to obtain dominance" (p. 3). He described these pure bullies as "cool operators." It would be interesting to investigate this subgroup further. For example, how well would they perform on the stories designed to assess the theory of mind ability (Taylor, 1996) that were used by Sutton, Smith, and Swettenham (1999) with 7- to 10-year-old children? Do they belong in the same group that Sutton et al. described as cold, manipulative, and highly skilled in social situations?

PASSIVE BULLIES

Olweus (1978, 1993a) viewed the passive bullies as "fairly mixed," with some insecure members. Stephenson and Smith (1989) identified a group with many of the same characteristics as the passive bullies and labeled them as *anxious bullies*. These bullies are a rather sad group. They are not nearly so popular as the aggressive bullies and have low self-esteem, few likable qualities, and often unhappy home situations. They appear to have poor attention spans in the school situation coupled with great difficulty concentrating. They often have violent temper outbursts that lead to problems with their peers.

Passive bullies rarely provoke others or take the initiative in a bullying incident. Instead, they tend to hang back, but once bullying is under way (usually at the instigation of an aggressive bully), they enter the fray with enthusiasm. The behavior of the aggressive bully appears to have a disinhibitory effect on the passive bullies that is strengthened by seeing the aggressive bully rewarded (Bandura, 1969). The fact that the passive bullies are quick to align themselves with the more powerful aggressive bully has resulted in them being described as "camp followers." Their intense loyalty to the aggressive bully is remarkable. For example, if adults intervene in bullying that is initiated by the aggressive bully and impose severe sanctions, the passive bullies are often blamed and accept the punishment, making no attempt to implicate the aggressive bully.

Implications for Intervention With Passive Bullies

The first and most difficult step for the passive bullies involves changing their appraisal of the aggressive bully and their subservient obedience to that bully's demands. This is a painful and very hard change to make despite the fact that by striving to imitate the aggressive bully and cater to his or her demands, the passive bullies are doing themselves a great disservice. They must be helped to see that the aggressive bully is basically a destructive influence and that the advantages of their association with the aggressive bully are far outweighed by the negative consequences of it. If this change can be accomplished, it opens the door for initiating other changes that would lead to peer acceptance, increased confidence and self-esteem, social skills, improved academic and athletic skills, and a more assertive attitude. The probability of achieving these major changes would be greater with cooperation from the passive bully's family. In reality, it is most likely that the therapist will have no help whatsoever from that source.

COMMENT

The trend of assigning new descriptors to groups of bullies who have already been identified and labeled creates confusion and muddies our understanding of the bully problem. The anxious bullies that Stephenson and Smith (1989) have described and O'Moore's (1988) neurotic bullies are basically the same as Olweus's (1978) passive bullies.

Another aspect of this problem involves adding and labeling new subgroups of bullies without adequate empirical documentation. Elliott (1991) has reported two new typologies in the Kidscape study. One was the spoiled brats who had been overindulged and overprotected from censure: These children hit out at anyone who got in their way, a classical frustration–aggression sequence rather than bully behavior. The second group was children who were the victims of abuse or neglect and had been made to feel grossly inadequate. According to Elliott, these children then attacked other children with visible weaknesses to destroy this reminder of their own weakness. Of the two groups, this one would appear to have more potential as a new subgroup of bullies, but supporting evidence is clearly indicated. New typologies should be added only if there is strong support that the children involved really are bullies or victims and if there is no significant overlap with any of the established groups of bullies.

BULLY-VICTIMS

One small group of children, the bully-victims, overlaps passive bullies and provocative victims. Olweus (1985) reported that 6% of those who were seriously bullied in turn bullied others, a finding that Stephenson and Smith (1989) confirmed in a 1988 survey. Bully-victims often are physically weaker than those who bully them but are almost always physically stronger than their own victims. They have some of the characteristics of the provocative victims in that they sometimes provoke others who are clearly weaker than they are and also are relatively easily aroused themselves (Stephenson & Smith, 1989). Generally the bully-victims are not popular with their peers, which is unfortunate because if they could become part of a congenial network the need to be aggressive might be weakened.

Intervention With Bully-Victims

The appropriate intervention for the bully-victim is problematic. Treatment should focus first on the behaviors of the child that resemble those of provocative victims. Some thought should then be given to modifying the bully-victim's social behavior and to considering which of his or her areas of nonacademic competence, such as sports, could be strengthened to the point that might lead to acceptance by peers. If a careful assessment of the bully-victim's home environment rules out bully- and victim-related etiological factors, the final step would be to devise an individual treatment protocol.

What Parents Should Not Do If a Child Is Bullied

To help children deal with bullies, parents need to stay calm while complaining firmly to school personnel and, if necessary, going further up in the school administration system. The following account illuminates one extreme in attempting to cope with an indifferent school administration.

Two mothers with children at an elementary school in the Queens Borough of New York became angry because school personnel did not protect their children from schoolyard bullies who repeatedly punched, kicked, chased, and threatened them. Both mothers decided to take matters into their own hands. One went to the school with her 8-year-old daughter, confronted the bully, screamed at her, and reportedly scratched the child. The other mother, who had complained a number of times to her son's teacher and the principal without results, went to the school and shouted at the principal in front of school personnel. The first mother was arrested and detained by the local police; both women have been barred temporarily from the school grounds and buildings (McCarthy, 2001).

No parent should put up with repeated bullying of a child, and school personnel are greatly remiss when they allow bullying to continue. But parents are not helping their children respond to bullying when they are themselves aggressive. In the above instance, the two mothers were commendable in that they were not passively accepting the school's indifference, but they became part of the problem instead of part of the solution. At the other extreme are instances in which parents recognize the bullying problems that their children are experiencing, attempt to get help from the schools, but fail to pursue change in the face of inaction by school personnel.

What Parents Should Do When a Child Is Bullied

1. The immediate need is to offer unqualified social support, which means no criticism, blame, or shame. Talk about your own bullying experiences; let the child see that it happens to many people; and give examples, if possible, of well-known people who were bullied as children. Victims of bullying often think that they are the only ones being bullied.
2. Do not promise to keep the bullying a secret. Discuss the "code of silence" (not telling). Distinguish between tattling and telling. Point out that the code of silence protects the bully (and other wrongdoers) and that the bully is counting on it.
3. Help the child to give you full information about the bully and make written notes of the following: name, class, what the bully did or said, and names of any witnesses if the child knows any of the bystanders. Find out if this is the first time your child has been bullied by this particular child, as well as whether any children or adults tried to help your child. Get their names.
4. If there is any evidence of bullying, such as swelling, cuts, torn clothes, or damaged books and other equipment, take Polaroid photos (labeled and dated).
5. Write out a brief summary of the problem including the information from No. 3. *Note:* From this point on, keep careful records of *all* your interactions with others. Included here would be the date, whom you talked to on the phone or in person, your complaint, and their response.
6. Contact the bully's parents and tell them what has happened. One person in 20 will be shocked and will put an end to the bullying; the rest will deny or otherwise indicate that you are making a fuss about nothing. The advantage of taking this step, which is almost certain to fail, is that when you go to the school this is the first thing that the school will tell you to do. The disadvantage is that now the bully will know. Consequently, you should warn the bully's parents that if there is any more bullying they will hear from your lawyer. Do not threaten the bully.
7. Make an appointment for the next day with the principal. (The reason for this haste is that the bully knows that your child has "told," so it is essential that visible and rapid actions follow immediately.) State your case to the principal and give him or her a typed copy of the information you have collected.

8. Ask the principal exactly *what* will be done about the bully and *when* appropriate action will be taken. Tell the principal that you will expect the bullying problem to be taken care of completely within 3 school days. Remain calm no matter what the principal's response.
9. At the end of 3 school days, if you are not satisfied by the principal's actions or if the bullying continues, go to the school superintendent, again with a typed account of the steps that you have followed and their outcome.

Children's Attitudes to Victims of School Bullying

What children think about bullies and victims has a number of ramifications, particularly in relation to optimum procedures for introducing intervention programs into the school curriculum. If the majority of children in a school support the interventions and rules designed to combat bullying and protect victims, a markedly different approach would be indicated than would be the case if the majority despise victims or look down on them.

In studying children's attitudes toward the bullying and teasing problem, Rigby and Slee (1993) tackled the first step: the development of a reliable and valid scale that would be appropriate for school children. On the basis of previous research (Olweus, 1984; Rigby & Slee, 1991), it would appear that some students would be sympathetic to the plight of victims, whereas others would endorse the belief that this is a "just world" (Lerner, 1980) and would feel that the victims had it coming to them.

STUDY 1

To avoid the tendency of participants to respond indiscriminately with "yes" to items, regardless of content (Cloud & Vaughan, 1970), a balanced set of items is essential. With half of the items worded in such a way that agreement indicates a positive attitude to the topic of interest, and the second half worded so that agreement signifies a negative attitude, it is possible to counteract the "yes" to every question tendency. With this goal in mind, Rigby and Slee (1993) developed 20 items. Half expressed a provictim attitude (e.g., "weak kids need help") and half an antivictim one (e.g., "nobody likes a wimp"). Children responded by circling one of three responses: agree, unsure, or disagree. As a validity check, the following question was asked: "What do you think is the right thing for teachers and children to do about bullying: Try to stop it or just ignore it?" The assumption was that if the scale was valid, those who believed that teachers and children should try to stop bullying would also have significantly higher scores on the Pro-Victim Scale.

The 685 students (325 boys and 360 girls) ranged in age from 6 to 16 years and attended primary and state high schools in areas of similar socioeconomic status in Adelaide, Australia. To check on the validity of each item, correlations were computed between item scores and the sum of the scores for the remaining items. Each correlation was positive and significant. The scale was also reliable; the value of the alpha coefficient statistic was .78. Only 10% of the children thought bullying should be ignored, and these children also had significantly lower provictim scores than the other children. It follows that the Pro-Victim Scale is both reliable and valid as a measure of children's attitudes toward victims of school bullying.

Rigby and Slee (1993) were able to distinguish among three components of the Pro-Victim Scale:

1. *Rejection of "weak" children* was indicated by agreement with the following types of items:
   - Kids who are weak are just asking for trouble.
   - Nobody likes a wimp.
2. *Approval of bullying* was a more positive evil as is indicated by agreement with these types of items:
   - It's funny to see kids get upset when they are teased.
   - Kids who get picked on a lot usually deserve it.
3. *Support for victims* was indicated by agreement with items such as these:
   - I like it when someone stands up for kids who are being bullied.
   - It makes me angry when a kid is picked on without reason.

Rigby and Slee (1993) had expected that the participants' capacity for empathy would increase with age and, with it, a corresponding concern for the victims. Instead, the trend for both genders was a decreasing support for victims on the part of respondents between the ages of 8 and 15. One explanation offered by Rigby and Slee for the decreasing support with age is that, with age, children are increasingly exposed to normative pressures that result in less sympathy for the victims of bullying. A second possibility is that complaining about being bullied is seen as not age appropriate for older students.

STUDY 2

A second study (Rigby & Slee, 1993) with older children (ages 11 to 16) failed to support that possibility. Instead, the relationship between age and attitudes to victims was curvilinear for boys: Up to age 15 or 16, boys became less sympathetic and thereafter became more sympathetic. For girls, attitudes to victims remained more or less the same throughout the age range. In both studies girls were significantly more positive in their attitudes to victims than boys were.

STUDY 3

In a study in South Australia (Rigby & Slee, 1993), 280 school children (49% boys, 51% girls) ages 11 to 16 years were asked what they would do if they were being bullied every day by someone bigger and stronger than themselves. Although in this school a policy had recently been established to encourage children to tell if they were being bullied, only a minority (33%) said that they would inform the school authorities, and a majority (60%) would call on friends for help.

Typical Characteristics Attributed to Bullies and Victims

One problem in studying bullies and victims is the variation across studies in the typical characteristics attributed to the two groups. Hazler and his associates (Hazler, Carney, Green, Powell, & Jolly, 1997) have taken a first step toward clearing up some of the confusion by quantifying the degree of agreement among a worldwide group of experts in this field. The purpose of their study was to determine which of a list of 70 potential characteristics were seen by these experts as being the most applicable to bullies and victims and also which were the best differentiators between the two groups. The results demonstrated strong agreement among 14 experts on 19 characteristics for bullies and 21 characteristics for victims. Ten characteristics were seen as the best differentiators between bullies and victims. The 19 significant identifying characteristics for bullies are shown in Table 3.2 and those for victims are in Table 3.3. Table 3.4 shows the 10 characteristics that represent the extreme contrasts between bullies and victims. The results identify the characteristics that should be viewed as most important by counselors, psychologists, teachers, and other professionals working with children. Researchers who construct questionnaires and rating scales should also find them invaluable. Hazler et al. (1997) have made a major contribution with this research report. It is one that

Table 3.2. Significant Identifying Characteristics for Bullies as Rated by Experts

No. of bullies	Characteristic
13	Control others through verbal threats and physical actions
13	Quicker to anger and sooner to use force than others
13	Tend to have little empathy for the problems of the other person in the victim/bully relationship
13	Have often been exposed to models of aggressive behaviors
13	Chronically repeat aggressive behaviors
13	Inappropriately perceive hostile intent in the actions of others
12	Are angry, revengeful
11	Parents are poor role models for getting along with others
11	Are likely to have contact with aggressive groups
11	Parents are poor role models for constructively solving problems
11	See only aggression as a way to preserve their self-image
11	Inconsistent discipline procedures at home
11	Perceived physical image is important for maintaining a feeling of power and control
11	Focus on angry thoughts
11	Have many more family problems than usual
10	Parents often do not know child's whereabouts
10	Suffer physical and emotional abuse at home
10	Create resentment and frustration in peer group
10	Exhibit obsessive or rigid actions

Source: Reproduced with permission of the authors and publisher from Hazler, R. J., Carney, J. V., Green, S., Powell, R., & Jolly, L. S. (1997). Areas of expert agreement on identification of school bullies and victims. *School Psychology International, 18,* 3–12. © Sage Publications.

should be mandatory reading for all those who are interested in the problems of bullying and victimization.

How Do Children Become Bullies?

No single factor causes children to become bullies. Instead, a cluster of environmental conditions and personal characteristics interact and, if unchecked, cause children to become bullies.

Table 3.3. Significant Identifying Characteristics for Victims as Rated by Experts

No. of victims	Characteristic
14	Believe that they cannot control their environment
14	Have ineffective social skills
14	Have poor interpersonal skills
13	Less popular than others
13	Have underlying fears of personal inadequacy
13	Blame themselves for their problems
13	Given labels suggesting inadequacy
13	Isolated socially
13	Afraid of going to school
13	Are physically younger, smaller, and weaker than peers
12	Have limited skills for gaining success and acceptance
12	Run out of communication capabilities during high-stress incidents
12	Have a poor self-concept
12	Show physical mannerism associated with depression
11	Have frequent feelings of personal inadequacy
11	Perform self-destructive actions
11	Believe others are more capable of handling various situations
11	Have difficulty relating to peers
11	Have family members who are overinvolved in the student's decisions and activities
10	Perceived progressive failures cause this person to put forth less effort with each presenting opportunity
10	Feel external factors have more of an impact on them than internal control

Source: Reproduced with permission of the authors and publisher from Hazler, R. J., Carney, J. V., Green, S., Powell, R., & Jolly, L. S. (1997). Areas of expert agreement on identification of school bullies and victims. *School Psychology International, 18,* 3–12. © Sage Publications.

A major factor centers around *family conditions,* particularly those related to child rearing. A negative attitude toward parenting on the part of both parents, usually the mother as main caretaker during the child's early years, exerts a tremendous negative influence. A notable lack of warmth as well as indifferent caring for the child is associated with a failure on the child's part to bond with the parents or feel loved by them, the result being what Bowlby (1973) has called an *attachment*

Table 3.4. Ten Characteristics Showing Extreme Contrasts Between Bullies and Victims as Rated by Experts

Rating	Characteristic
LB/HV	Believe that others are more capable of handling various situations
HB/LV	Control others through verbal threats and physical actions
HB/LV	Quicker to anger and sooner to use force than others
HB/LV	See only aggression as the way to preserve their self-image
HB/LV	Are angry, revengeful
HB/LV	Chronically repeat aggressive behaviors
HB/LV	Inconsistent discipline procedures at home
HB/LV	Perceived physical image is important for maintaining a feeling of power and control
HB/LV	Parents often do not know child's whereabouts
HB/LV	Exhibit obsessive or rigid actions

LB = Rated as "nonsignificant" characteristic for bullies
HV = Rated as "significant" characteristic for victims
HB = Rated as "significant" characteristic for bullies
LV = Rated as "nonsignificant" characteristic for victims

Source: Reproduced with permission of the authors and publisher from Hazler, R. J., Carney, J. V., Green, S., Powell, R., & Jolly, L. S. (1997). Areas of expert agreement on identification of school bullies and victims. *School Psychology International, 18,* 3–12. © Sage Publications.

disorder. Failure to bond, in turn, is likely to be associated with a lack of empathy for other children and a tendency to behave in a coercive manner toward them.

An offshoot of the parental indifference is a failure to set and enforce adequate limits for the child's behavior. The parents, again usually the mother, often show unusual tolerance for inappropriate aggression toward themselves, other members of the family, and the child's peers. When discipline is administered, it usually involves power-assertive procedures, such as violent emotional outbursts for minor infractions and severe corporal punishment, that focus on control and coercion. Adding to the effect of this disciplinary pattern is parental inconsistency: Misbehavior that is punished on one occasion may be ignored the next time that it occurs. As a result of this uncertainty, the child comes to expect the worst in interactions with powerful others. Often this negative expectancy generalizes to interactions with peers and leads to unjustified attacks on them. The child learns that might is right. It is not uncommon for such parents to deliberately teach their children to be aggressive (Bandura & Walters, 1959) and encourage or demand that their sons settle interactions with others with physical aggression. Seldom are there consequences for complaints of bullying; instead, these parents often see bullying as evidence that their sons are "all boy" and disregard reports of bullying. The combination of parental aggression and attitudes to aggression, the child's cognitions that might is right, and the failure of the parents to teach the child more appropriate behavior is likely to further the development of the aggressive personality pattern characteristic of boys who bully (Smith & Myron-Wilson, 1998).

CONSTITUTIONAL FACTORS

A second major influence concerns *characteristics of the child* that may predispose him or her to the antisocial aggression that is typical of the aggressive bully. There is evidence that simply being male predisposes a child to aggressive behavior (Maccoby & Jacklin, 1974). The Y chromosome may be directly involved in aggressive behavior or indirectly through the production of testosterone. However, evidence for the testosterone effect is not unanimous. Olweus (Blanchard & Blanchard, 1988) suggested that testosterone may be linked to characteristics that are precursors of aggression rather than directly to aggression. Tremblay (Marano, 1995) believes that although testosterone levels in animal studies of dominance are an index of aggression, direct extrapolations of these findings to humans are in error. In his longitudinal studies with bullies and other aggressive children, he found that testosterone levels in boys who had reached puberty were negatively correlated with aggression. Humans' testosterone levels signify social success; for example, boys whom he described as *tough leaders* scored high on aggression and had the highest testosterone levels of all, but they had well-developed social skills and they established dominance in a group with verbal fluency rather than aggressive tactics. These tough leaders were the most socially successful and the most popular in Tremblay's sample.

Activity level may predispose a boy to antisocial aggression. There is unequivocal evidence that, as a group, boys are more often overactive and hyperactive than girls (Ross & Ross, 1982). Increased activity is linked to the subsequent development of antisocial aggression (Richman, Stevenson, & Graham, 1982). Temperament is also relevant to antisocial aggression. The child's temperament represents the interaction between biologically anchored predispositions and environmental demands. Temperament in the early months of life is associated with the child's later behavior. Temperament characteristics such as irregular sleeping and eating habits, difficulty adapting to new situations, negative moods and strong moods, and unpredictable behavior have been found to be associated with a number of difficult behaviors, including aggression, poor impulse control, and irritability (Thomas & Chess, 1977). These findings were consistent with those of Graham, Rutter, and George (1973), who used those three characteristics to identify a temperamental adversity index for use in predicting which children would have problems a year later. Olweus (1993a) cautioned that the effect of the temperament factor on bullying tendencies is not as powerful as parental negativity and lack of warmth on the part of the parents as well as too much "freedom" particularly in relation to aggressive behavior.

An unexpected constitutional factor that was etiologically related to bullying was the bully's level of salivary cortisol. A study by McBurnett, Lahey, Rathouz, and Loeber (2000) on the role of salivary cortisol in bully behavior provides support for the consensus among school personnel that there is a hard core of bullies who are highly resistant to the forms of intervention currently in use. In this 4-year study, McBurnett et al. found that extreme antisocial behaviors, including bullying, were strongly associated with lower than expected levels of salivary cortisol in 7- to 12-year-old boys ($N = 38$). Cortisol typically is released in response to fears, such as fear of punishment for misbehavior. Its low level in antisocial boys suggests that they do not fear negative consequences for misbehavior. Consequently, the usual deterrents to misbehavior are ineffective. Because their misbehavior may be biologically based, current treatment regimens may be of little use. K. McBurnett (personal communication, January 10, 2000) has speculated that the drug programs used with hyperactive children might prove effective.

Another substance that has been implicated in bullying is lead, a trace element that has no known essential role in the human body. Its toxic significance for adults has been recognized for centuries (Ross & Ross, 1982), and it is known to interfere with the development of the central nervous system. A research team headed by Herbert L. Needleman of the University of Pittsburgh using a new test that identifies lead deposits in the bones has reported (Needleman, 1973, 2000) that lead exposure may contribute to crime and a cluster of other antisocial behaviors in children. The researchers tracked 301 public school students from ages 7 to 11 years and found that boys with high lead levels in their bones were more likely to engage in bullying, vandalism, arson, and shoplifting than those with low lead levels. None of the boys had been diagnosed with lead poisoning, and some had normal blood-lead levels, which has been the usual method for determining exposure. In this study the researchers measured cumulative exposure by a new form of X-ray that examines the shinbones. Evaluations filled out by teachers, parents, and the children confirmed that those with high bone-lead levels had committed more antisocial and delinquent acts than those with low levels. The researchers adjusted for other known links to delinquent behavior, such as poverty and single-parent families, and concluded that limiting children's exposure to lead could prevent forms of antisocial behavior in later years. Kim Dietrich, a lead expert at the University of Cincinnati, said, "This is the first rigorous study to demonstrate a significant association between lead and antisocial behavior. It's very new and groundbreaking" (Tanner, 1996, p. A3). A paper reporting these findings was presented at the joint meeting of the American Academy of Pediatrics and the Pediatric Academic Society in May 2000. An up-to-date report on this important research is in press.

AGE DECLINE IN BULLYING

Large-scale studies of pupils in the 8- to 16-year-old range repeatedly show fairly steady and substantial year-by-year age declines in self-reports of being bullied at school. This decline has been documented in many countries, including Norway and Sweden (Olweus, 1993a), England (Whitney & Smith, 1993), Australia (Rigby, 1996, 1997), and Ireland (O'Moore, Kirkham, & Smith, 1997). Although the amount of reported victimization in these countries varies, the downward trend in age of being bullied is very consistent.

In 1999, Smith, Madsen, and Moody further investigated the reason for the age decline. The questions they raised were: Why do reports of being bullied decrease with age? Is this a *real* decrease? Both questions also have relevance for understanding the risk factors in being a victim as well as for designing interventions that target bullying. Four possible explanations (Smith & Levan, 1995) for the age decline were examined:

Hypothesis 1: Younger children have more children older than them in school who are in a position to bully them.

Hypothesis 2: Younger children have not yet been socialized into understanding that they should not bully others.

Hypothesis 3: Younger children have not yet acquired the social skills and assertiveness skills to deal effectively with bullying incidents and discourage further bullying.

Hypothesis 4: Younger children have a different definition of what bullying is, which changes as they get older.

To assess each hypothesis, Smith, Madsen, and Moody (1999) reviewed existing data (Whitney & Smith, 1993) and conducted new analyses of them. They also conducted two studies to obtain new data. In their evaluation of the hypotheses in relation to the data, Smith et al. regarded Hypotheses 1 and 3 as the two major explanations for the age decline in bullying and Hypotheses 2 and 4 as minor explanations. Although they commented that "each hypothesis may have something to offer in explaining the decrease in reports of being bullied with age" (p. 281), they clearly did not regard any of them as providing a definitive answer.

GENDER DIFFERENCES IN BULLYING BEHAVIOR

Although boys are more often identified as bullies, girls also bully. They are more likely to engage in verbal (malicious gossip) and psychological (social ostracism) forms of bullying, but they are not exempt from physical harassment (Besag, 1989).

Roland (Besag, 1989) concluded that the prime goal of girls is to be affiliated with other girls, so that by using alienation tactics they are "in" and their victims are "out." Bullying in girls has been greatly underestimated because it is a more indirect, covert, subtle, and complex form of bullying (Besag, 1989; Forero et al., 1999; Olweus, 1993a) than the overt physical aggression typical of boys. When the frequency of this indirect aggression in girls is compared with overt aggression in boys, the difference is insignificant. Contrary to what Olweus (1978) first thought, girls are just as capable of bullying as boys are.

A common misconception about bullying is that it is a transient problem of childhood and early adolescence that disappears with increasing age. Nothing could be farther from the truth: Olweus (1979) reported a remarkable persistence into adulthood of the aggressive behavior that manifests itself in childhood as bullying. Although many children who bully do outgrow this behavior (Olweus, 1993a), many others do not. Of interest here are the findings of Moffit (1993) on another antisocial behavior, delinquency. She distinguished between two categories of delinquents: a small group in her study who engaged in *life-course-persistent delinquency* (delinquency of one kind or another at every life stage) and a larger group who did so only in late middle childhood and adolescence (*adolescent-limited delinquency*).

At first glance, a similar pattern appears to be characteristic of children who bully. However, following an outstanding critique of misconceptions and controversies concerning the development of aggression and violence (Loeber & Stouthamer-Loeber, 1998), it is apparent that Moffit's (1993) life-course-persistent category for children who bully should be expanded to accommodate two age-of-onset groups: a preschool-onset and a childhood/adolescence-onset group with the behavior of some children in both groups worsening in severity from childhood to adulthood. Loeber and Stouthamer-Loeber (1998) added a *limited-duration type* that is consistent with Moffit's (1993) adolescent-limited delinquency, and also a *late-onset type* that accounts for the emergence of aggression in individuals during adulthood who do not have an earlier history of aggression. It would be interesting to know more about the late-onset bullying group. For example, are some of the school principals, military personnel, and prison guards who are bullies individuals who secretly envied aggressive bullies in childhood and adolescence but were deterred from exhibiting bullying behavior until they found themselves in positions of power, coupled with low supervision and subordinates who were in no position to complain?

For children who do not outgrow their bullying behavior, the outlook is bleak. In 1960 Eron and Huesmann began a longitudinal study of an entire group of third-grade children ($N = 870$) in the Midwest. In 1990 they reported that children who bullied others at age 8 had a 1:4 chance of ending up with a criminal record by age 30 as compared with the 1:20 chance that most children have. In addition, the childhood bullies were more likely to have been convicted of crimes, including a higher number of more serious crimes, more moving traffic violations, and more convictions for drunken driving. They had not achieved well educationally and were more often high school dropouts. Professionally and socially, they were below the nonbully group. They were more abusive to their wives and children, and, perhaps most serious of all the problems, their children were often bullies; so, in effect, they were raising a whole new generation of bullies. Contrary to common expectation, the results for the bullies in adulthood were independent of their IQs and social class at age 8 years (Eron & Huesmann, 1987, 1990).

Indirect Aggression

The first studies on this more subtle form of aggression began to appear in the late 1950s. From the beginning, the problem of defining it produced a number of descriptors amounting to a circling of the topic without coming up with one definition. It may very well be impossible to do this, making it imperative that researchers define in concrete behavioral terms the aspects of indirect aggression that they are investigating. Even this step is not a straightforward one. The Buss–Durkee Hostility and Guilt Inventory (Buss & Durkee, 1957) included a subscale on indirect aggression, with behavioral descriptors such as slamming doors, breaking things, having temper tantrums, and gossiping. When a factor analysis was carried out on the subscale (Björkqvist, Österman, & Kaukiainen, 1992), only gossiping seemed to fit the concept of indirect aggression, and most of the other items appeared to belong on the irritability scale.

In an observational study of girls' and boys' behavior toward newcomers (Feshbach, 1969), indirect aggression was coded as "ignoring," "avoidance," "refusal," and "excluding." When Frodi, Macaulay, and Thome (1977) published their careful review of gender differences in aggression, they commented that the idea of indirect aggression presented a problem. They defined it as occurring either with a substitute target person or no concrete target at all, a definition that could readily be applied to other concepts.

In 1973 Wachtel proposed that boys generally bully for power, which is consistent with the fact that they tend to bully younger or weaker boys and girls. Girls, however, strive for close affiliation with others and affirmation that they are "in" and their victims are "out" and, consequently, are more likely to engage in behavior such as social expulsion (Owens, Shute, & Slee, 2000; Roland, 1989), the often unexplained withdrawal of acceptance, spreading of rumors, and malicious gossip. The targets of this indirect aggression are almost exclusively other girls within their own age range and social environment (Roland, 1989). A 14-year-old girl said:

> These girls were my friends last year. I thought. Now they ignore me like I'm a total stranger and they spread horrible rumors like Dad's in jail (father was on military duty) and I got expelled from my last school because I've got sex disease. (Adlam, 1991, p. 20)

The first systematic investigation of indirect aggression was carried out by a Finnish team of researchers (for a review, see Björkqvist, 1994). Lagerspetz, Björkqvist, and Peltonen (1988) defined indirect aggression as social manipulation, attacking the target circuitously. They perceived indirect aggression as a kind of social manipulation in which the aggressor either persuades other children to attack the victim or makes use of the social structure to harm the target child (Owens, Slee, & Shute, 2000). In either case the aggressor is not personally involved in the attack, escapes blame for it, and avoids any possibility of retaliation. Björkqvist, Österman, and Kaukiainen (1992) have investigated three types of aggression—direct physical, direct verbal, and indirect aggression—and have developed scales over a number of studies with different age groups. In the latest version of the scales, the following items were used (Björkqvist, Österman, & Kaukiainen, 1992, p. 55):

1. *Physical Aggression.* This scale consists of seven items: "hits," "kicks," "trips," "shoves," "takes things," "pushes," and "pulls." Cronbach's alpha of this scale is .93.
2. *Direct Verbal Aggression.* The scale consists of five items: "yells," "insults," "says (s)he is going to hurt the other," "calls the other names," and "teases." Cronbach's alpha is .92.
3. *Indirect Aggression.* The scale consists of nine items: "gossips," "tells bad or false stories," "becomes friend with another as revenge," "plans secretly to bother the other," "says bad things behind the other's back," "says to others: 'let's not be with him/her,'" "tells the other one's secrets to a third person," "writes nasty notes about the other," and "tries to get others to dislike the person." Cronbach's alpha is .93.

The fact that girls exhibit direct physical and verbal aggression to a lesser degree than boys has conveyed the impression that girls are less aggressive than boys. This conclusion is no longer a valid one, following the series of studies begun in 1992 by a team of Finnish researchers headed by Kaj Björkqvist. They focused on one kind of aggression, indirect aggression, in girls. In this case the aggressor manipulates others to attack the victim and makes use of the social structure to harm the victim without being personally involved in the attack. The victim experiences social exclusion and unexplained withdrawal of acceptance and is the target of malicious gossip. The Finnish team developed a scale to measure direct aggression, that is, physical and verbal forms of it, and indirect aggression. Their results showed that although boys used more direct physical aggression than girls, the two groups did not differ on verbal aggression, and girls used more indirect aggression and at an earlier age. These results make it essential that school programs be developed to curb indirect aggression, an extremely difficult task, even to identify the participants. Indirect aggression is a very covert activity, and school personnel often are unaware of it. The first step, however, is to know that it does exist.

For each of the three scales, there is an aggressor and a victim version to allow the assessment of both aggressive behavior and victimization. On a 5-point scale from 0 to 4, the respondents are asked to estimate how each of the children in the class behaves when he or she is angry with another child or gets into a fight with the other child. They also estimate their own behavior in such situations, a procedure that allows comparisons between peer nominations and self-estimates of behavior. Results from such comparisons have never produced significant correlations between peer-nominated indirect aggression and self-rated indirect aggression, possibly because children may be reluctant to admit to socially undesirable behavior. However, the same comparisons for physical aggression and verbal aggression were all significant (Björkqvist, Österman, & Kaukiainen, 1992; Lagerspetz & Björkqvist, 1992; Lagerspetz et al., 1988).

This team has gathered data from Finnish children ages 8, 11, 15, and 18. Their results show that boys are consistently more physically aggressive than girls; the two groups do not differ on direct verbal aggression; and on peer estimates, girls use indirect aggression significantly more than do boys in all age groups except for the 8-year-olds. Lagerspetz et al. (1988) speculated that girls beyond the 8-year-old level may exhibit more indirect aggression possibly as a result of some experience in their socialization that facilitates the acquisition of such strategies. The social structure of peer groups in middle childhood and adolescence might be a factor: The small, intimate groups and pairs that girls form might have a different effect from the bigger, less-defined groups that boys form.

If social support is available, indirect aggression is not necessarily harmful. If the target child has someone to confide in, she may, with help, devise a strategy that makes her former friends' behavior pointless. I knew of one 13-year-old girl who was suddenly dropped by four other girls in her year at school for no apparent reason. Her family rallied behind her and together they drew up a plan covering a number of aspects, such as her appearance, all of which were directed at helping her have a very active social life. She had two older brothers who entered into the scheme with enthusiasm, and within a month she was clearly a very popular girl with a respectable amount of heterosexual activity. Her former friends, attracted by her social success, made overtures, which she ignored. When I asked her what advice she would give to other girls who were subjected to this antisocial experience, she grinned and said she would tell them that once they were certain that their former friends were ignoring them and trying to harm them, they should *never* look back. Instead, they should work at building up a new peer group.

There is no question that indirect aggression is a major form of harassment for girls in middle childhood and adolescence. If the victim struggles to regain her former standing with her "friends," she is almost certain to lose from the experience. She will be much stronger psychologically if she crosses her former friends off and pursues friendship with other peers.

STUDY OF INDIRECT AGGRESSION IN GIRLS

Owens and his colleagues (Owens, 1996; Owens, Slee, & Shute, 2001) have done a qualitative study of the nature of adolescent girls' indirect aggression. In their work they followed the definition used by Finnish researchers (Björkqvist, Österman, & Kaukiainen, 1992, p. 52), who defined indirect aggression as

> . . . a kind of social manipulation: the aggressor manipulates others to attack the victim, or, by other means, makes use of the social structure in order to harm the target person without being personally involved in the attack.

The Finnish team developed a Direct and Indirect Aggression Scale (DIAS) that included physical, verbal, and indirect items. They consistently found that, except for the youngest age group (in which no gender differences were found), girls used more indirect aggression than boys. Owens et al. (2001) selected adolescent girls for an investigation of the nature of indirect aggression. They used a qualitative approach because it allowed them to go beyond peer nominations to girls' own stories about their experiences with indirect aggression in their daily lives.

The method consisted first of a pilot study with six 16-year-old girls, the purpose being to assess trial questions. In the main study, focus groups, pair, and individual interviews were conducted with fifty-four 15-year-old girls who were randomly selected from 10th-grade classes and their key teachers. In addition to the focus groups, pairs of girls who were not in the focus groups were interviewed, having volunteered to take part. The following vignette was used to stimulate discussion:

> Jo is a 15-year-old Grade 10 girl, attending Wyfield (or Lockwood) College. She is average at her schoolwork, and she is involved in school tennis in summer and netball in winter. In the past, she was well accepted, having a close group of friends and getting along well with most of her peers. After a day off with illness, she returns to school to find that things have changed.
>
> She walks over to her usual group, but when she tries to talk to any of them, their responses are abrupt and unfriendly. She tries to catch the eye of her friend Brooke, but Brooke avoids her gaze.
>
> In first lesson, she sits in her usual seat only to find that Brooke is sitting with someone else. At recess time, she joins the group late but just in time to overhear one of the girls bitching about her.

After reading the vignette, the 6 to 8 girls in the focus groups were asked a series of questions about what kind of indirect aggression was happening in the school, why this kind of situation happens, what the effects are of this kind of behavior, and what can be done about it. After the students had discussed these questions, they were asked, "Does this sort of thing happen at this school?" All the discussions were taped, and confidentiality and anonymity were guaranteed. The pair interviews that followed were designed to seek further information about particular incidents that had been discussed during the focus groups.

To ensure the credibility of the study, Owens et al. (2001) asked six randomly selected girls to comment on a summary of the research findings. A second set of girls and five of the teachers were asked to judge the accuracy of the research account. Teachers and girls who had not participated in the study agreed that the indirect aggression described in the study was consistent with their own experiences. Interrater agreement on the coding of the responses was assessed. Using Cohen's kappas, it varied from a low of .83 to a high of 1.0.

Results and Discussion

There were reports of a range of exclusionary behaviors from being ignored by one girl, exclusion from the group, up to full-scale ostracism by the whole class. A particularly vicious response was first to persecute a girl so severely that she left school, then to spread defamatory information about her at the new school so that the victimization started again. Another strategy was for the girls to talk just loudly enough so that the target girl heard her name but could not hear what else was being said. Teachers were unaware of the full range of indirect harassments used, but they did report that being the victim of indirect aggression could lead to suicidal behavior.

There appeared to be two main descriptions of the characteristics of victims that elicited this vicious behavior. One was that it was the victim's own fault for having done something that merited reprisal; the other was that the victims were vulnerable or easy targets. When the girls were asked the reason for their indirect aggression, their responses fell into three categories. (a) *Alleviating boredom/creating excitement:* The girls explained that much of their behavior such as spreading rumors and breaking confidences was simply "for something to do." (b) *Attention seeking:* Spreading false stories, for example, was the girls' attempt to make themselves look as if they knew all the gossip. (c) *Group inclusion:* Reasons in this category emphasized how important it was for the girls to be included in the group. Their attacks served as a form of self-protection by conforming to the demands that members uphold the group view. The following two girls clearly put membership in the group ahead of their own feelings:

> *Student 1:* You just say it because you don't want to be left out. You don't want to disagree with the group.
> *Student 2:* I didn't really mind her, but I went along with the group . . . and, in the end, she left the school.

Interventions

When the girls were asked what, if anything, was done about indirect aggression in their schools and what could be done, they were quite derogatory about school personnel and parents' efforts. One girl said, "Teachers make it worse." Another stated, "I don't think that the teachers and counselors are very well educated about how to handle the problem." The girls generally saw parental help as ineffective.

Implications of the Study

The girls were generally pessimistic about intervention. One teacher was very enthusiastic about involving older girls in helping younger ones. This seems to have potential, particularly if the older girls are high status, such as top athletes or outstanding in some way.

The girls claimed that parents either advocated forgetting any problems, real or imaginary, or overreacted by threatening to contact the school or the abusing girls' parents. The girls regarded the idea of curriculum interventions as a "joke" that, at worst, would single out rejected girls even more. One teenage girl clearly thought that not intervening in this type of situation would be wrong:

> I don't think that not interfering is the right answer either, because sometimes it gets really bad and people . . . I mean if you get put down so much, and that, some people, like, that leads people to suicide sometimes. So I mean sometimes they must need to be educated to pick up the signs, you know. (Owens, 1998, p. 274)

Owens et al. (2001) suggested that some intervention approaches used to combat bullying might be used to reduce harassment. These approaches are summarized in Table 3.5.

In 1995, Crick and her colleagues began a series of studies of indirect aggression in girls, using the label *relational aggression*. Because social aggression, whether direct or indirect, involves others, it is hard to see what this label contributes to the field. Also inexplicable is the omission throughout Crick's work of *any* mention of the work of the

Table 3.5. A Sample of Intervention Approaches to Reduce Harassment

Intervention	Features
School-based interventions	"Whole school approach" (e.g., involvement of students, teachers, parents, and outside agencies)
No-blame approach (Maines & Robinson, 1992)	Individual/group counseling by teachers
Method of shared concern (Pikas, 1989)	Individual/group counseling by teachers
Peer counseling	Individual counseling by a trained peer
Peer mediation	Mediation by one or more trained peers with groups/individuals in conflict
Systemic thinking	Individual/group/whole school approaches

Source: Reproduced with permission of the authors and publisher from Owens, L., Slee, P., & Shute, R. (2001). Victimization among teenage girls: What can be done about indirect harassment? In J. Juvonen & S. Graham (Eds.), *Peer Harassment in School: The Plight of the Vulnerable and Victimized* (pp. 215–241). © Guilford Press.

forerunners in the field, Björkqvist and his team. Note that the terms *relational aggression* (Crick & Grotpeter, 1995, 1996), *indirect aggression* (Björkqvist, Österman, & Kaukiainen, 1992), and *social aggression* (Galen & Underwood, 1997) all refer to attempts, more often by girls than boys (Crick & Bigbee, 1998), to harm others by damaging friendships or by exclusion from the peer group.

Research on relational aggression stemmed from an interest in studying peer victimization experiences that are noticeable in girls. Relational aggression is characteristic of the peer victimization of the majority of girls (Crick & Grotpeter, 1996). It is a particularly vicious kind of behavior that focuses on a basic need of girls—the need to feel accepted, particularly by same-age, same-sex peers. The salient characteristic of it is that it is covert in nature and is probably the most subtle of the victimization procedures. The victim is not directly confronted but instead gradually becomes aware that she is no longer an accepted member of a certain group. No reason is given so it is difficult for a girl to grapple with it and painful to accept it.

Relational aggression has been observed in preschool children, although it is more direct in these years than is the case later (Crick, Casas, & Ku, 1999). In middle childhood, it becomes slightly more subtle: The peer group that is ousting the target child may tell lies about her, spread rumors, walk past her chattering enthusiastically but avoiding eye contact, and write very unpleasant notes about her. In adolescence, as peer interactions become refined to the point of artificiality, relational victimization also becomes more subtle. Efforts are directed at damaging the victim's relationship with peers, she is completely ignored while friendly overtures are made to girls who are with her at that moment, gossip about her sexual activities is rampant, and the whole victimization procedure becomes extraordinarily complex.

A report of recent research on relational victimization (Crick et al., 2001) addresses a number of topics, including the question of whether relational victimization is harmful and the association between relational victimization and aggression. Most of the discussion is organized around three developmental periods: preschool and early childhood, middle childhood, and adolescence. The need for longitudinal studies is addressed, but apparently no such action has been taken.

Immediate Effects of Bullying on Victims

Repeated bullying takes a severe toll on victims: Fear permeates their everyday life and, for many children, becomes an ingrained response. One victim told his parents that Friday afternoon was the best day of the week because there were two whole days ahead when no one would bully him, but he added sadly, "Sunday afternoon is not so good because it's almost Monday" (J. Cunningham, personal communication, December 4, 1981). Many victims adopt fugitivelike routines on their way to school and also in school in an effort to avoid the bully. While avoidance can be an effective strategy, it deprives the victim of formal and informal experiences that are essential to social development and also removes a potential buffer against the bully's attacks, that is, friends. Friends usually drop away because they often confuse the victim's avoidance of the bully with avoidance of themselves. Some of the former friends are afraid of being bullied if they associate with victims, but a substantial number come to despise the victim for not being able to cope with the bully (Besag, 1989). Many victims are disconcerted by the active rejection of peers who formerly were friends or at least were friendly (Perry et al., 1988).

Bullying occurs when children first enter school. A study of 5- and 6-year-old children ($N = 200$) by Kochenderfer and Ladd (1996) focused on victimization and its relationship on two indices of school adjustment: feelings of loneliness and school avoidance. Some children were victimized only in the fall or spring of the school year, but for 8.5% of the children the bullying persisted throughout the school year. This latter finding was consistent with that of Boulton and Underwood (1992) with 8- and 9-year-old children. Even when the bullying had stopped, feelings of loneliness persisted. In commenting on the plight of the victim, Floyd (1987, p. 24) said:

> . . . not only is the victim scorned, humiliated or attacked by the bully, but he [she] also often is rejected by others as a sort of pariah, one damaged, tainted, infected. The stigma of being victimized casts a long shadow and leaves a dark pall.

The situation worsens as the bullying continues, often intensifying, because the victims begin to see themselves as unworthy and, in some cases, deserving of the punishment. Academic performance usually plummets, a negative effect of bullying on school performance that is well documented in the clinical literature (Hazler et al., 1993). Many victims are caught in a downward spiral leading to low morale and the acute despair that leads to truancy (Reid, 1990), chronic illnesses such as recurrent abdominal pain of unknown physical origin (Ross & Ross, 1988), running away, and in extreme cases, suicide (Beck, 1986; Besag, 1989; Elliott, 1991).

Long-Term Effects of Bullying on Victims

Besag (1989) believes that while being bullied may be character building for some victims, for others the loss of self-confidence and self-esteem is so severe that even as adults, their social interactions are adversely affected. Some support for this view comes from Gilmartin (1987), who found that 80% of heterosexual men who experienced considerable difficulty in progressing beyond casual interactions with women had been bullied at school. Similarly, Parker and Asher (1987) felt that the peer rejection that often accompanies victimization in the school years is a strong predictor of disturbances in adulthood.

Further evidence of serious consequences of intense long-term bullying in the school years is contained in the following account from a 28-year-old woman, engaged to be married, whose bullying experiences had left her with anxiety about having children:

> To the question: "Do you feel that's left a residue with you . . . what do you feel the effects are?" the respondent continued:
>
> I'm quite insecure, even now . . . I won't believe that people like me . . . and also I'm afraid of children . . . and this is a problem.

> He (fiancé) would like a family, I would not and I don't want a family because I'm frightened of children and suppose they don't like me . . . those are things that have stayed with me. It's a very unreasonable fear but it is there and it's very real. (Smith & Thompson, 1991, p. 7)

In a follow-up study of two groups of Swedish boys who either were or were not victimized by their peers during the period from sixth to ninth grade, Olweus (1993a) found that the former victims were "normal" in many respects. He attributed this positive outcome to the fact that, as adults, they had much more freedom in choosing their social and physical environments than is the case for most children. As Finkelhor and Dziuba-Leatherman (1994) noted, school children probably have less choice about their companions and surroundings than any other segment of the population with the exception of prison inmates. One negative outcome in the study was that men who had been victimized at school had poorer self-esteem as adults and were also more likely to have a problem with depression than were their nonvictimized peers (Olweus, 1993a).

COMMENT

For almost two decades, Peter K. Smith has been a catalyst in research on the problem of school bullying. To my knowledge, he is the only researcher to explicitly advocate the benefits that could ensue if those in one major area of bullying research would look closely at other areas for approaches potentially applicable to their own topic of research. One example is his demonstration that research findings on workplace harassment clearly have relevance to school bullying and vice versa. In a similar vein, several years ago he and Yohji Morita saw the value of a volume that for the first time would provide detailed information from knowledgeable sources in 21 countries on how their country was tackling the problem of school bullying. The result was the book, *The Nature of School Bullying; A Cross-National Perspective* (Smith, Morita, et al., 1999), an impressive contribution. Since then, there has been increased research interest in the topic of school bullying in other countries and language groups. One problem that researchers face is finding terms in other languages that correspond to the English word *bullying*. The definition of corresponding terms is essential for the interpretation of cross-national findings. To remedy this problem, Smith, Cowie, Olafsson, and Liefooghe (2002) developed an ingenious procedure and a variety of terms related to bullying to examine the meaning children attach to the term *bullying*. In studies in 14 countries and 13 major languages (10 Indo-European and 3 Asian), they used stick figure cartoons in pictures depicting different situations that might or might not be bullying. Smith et al. discussed the findings in relation to developmental trends in children's understanding of bullying, the inferences that can be made from cross-national studies of bullying, and the design of such studies.

4 Victims

Bullies do not randomly attack any available peer target. Instead, they selectively focus on a stable and accessible subgroup of peers who often serve as victims over a period of years. Victims are a heterogeneous group: Olweus (1993a) distinguished between the passive or submissive victim, the provocative victim, and the bully-victim. Passive victims are usually the optimum choice for the aggressive bully. Although they do not intentionally provoke bullies, their generally negative demeanor alerts the bully that here is a potentially satisfactory target. The three categories provide an essential framework for planning intervention programs for victims. They also cast light on our understanding of the type of bullying that each category of victim elicits.

In some cases the genesis of victimization is linked to the prenatal period (Karr-Morse & Wiley, 1997). In others it begins in the preschool or early school years. The serious short- and long-term adjustment problems that frequently result from being bullied are described. The procedures that parents and schools should follow when a child is being victimized are outlined. Of particular importance to progress in dealing effectively with the problem of victimization is the new social–cognitive model of the psychological mechanisms linking family experience with victimization by peers that David Perry and his associates have developed (Perry, Hodges, & Egan, 2001). This model has markedly expanded our understanding of victimization and will serve as a stimulus for new investigative approaches to this problem. Perry is the leading world authority on victims.

When Does Victimization Start?

For some children, victimization is present in infancy when siblings are jealous of the amount of attention the infant receives from the mother. Many mothers refuse to accept the fact that the older children may purposely hurt the infant and, instead, insist that the older ones do love the baby. This stance merely forces the older ones to become more devious in their attacks, and there have been cases in which young infants have been severely injured by their older siblings (Karr-Morse & Wiley, 1997).

Victimization occurs early in the preschool years for some toddlers, especially in day-care and preschool settings (Alsaker & Valkanover, 2001). In many such settings, staff training and staff–child ratios are grossly out of line with acceptable practice, which means that 2- and 3-year-old children who give way when others push them or take toys away from them are neither given immediate protection nor taught how to handle such situations in the future. In most preschool settings, there is a well-established power hierarchy with children who give in to others' demands, crying and cowering away from bullies (Patterson, Littman, & Bricker, 1967). Clearly, this is very destructive for all the participants as well as the bystanders. In some cases this submissiveness is temporary, but those who continue in this pattern of response are headed toward the victim role (Schwartz, Dodge, & Coie, 1993).

Why Is Victimization of Children a Common Occurrence?

Children of small physical stature, who are less strong than normal, and who are lacking in confidence are at risk for victimization *unless* their parents have taught them to cope verbally and unhesitantly with situations that could escalate to their disadvantage. A good example of such parental foresight was provided by a 4-year-old boy who was significantly shorter than most others of the same age. On his first day at a nursery school, I asked him what he would like to do first. He wanted to get on the teeter-totter that was stalled because there were too many children at one end. As we approached, he said firmly, "Just tell them Willie-Boy is here," and to the children, "You need a little guy like me on that end so it'll go up and down." He then scrambled on very agilely and was immediately warmly accepted by the group. To my knowledge, his small stature caused no problems for him.

Children in our society have little control over their environment. In fact, as Finkelhor and Dziuba-Leatherman (1994) have pointed out, they probably have less choice about their surroundings than any other segment of the population, with the exception of prison inmates. They are limited in their choice of whom they will associate with at home, in school, and in their neighborhood. They are not free to leave abusive parents. If their school is overpopulated with bullies and other delinquents, it would be difficult to transfer to another school, and, in any case, they would still have to traverse the same neighborhood. These restrictions increase vulnerability to victimization by bullies.

Until recently, many adults in the child's environment generally accepted bullying as an inevitable hurdle of school life; some parents and school personnel actually believed that it benefited the victims, a misguided idea whose remnants still exist. This disregard for the child victim extends beyond the child's immediate environment to the police and criminal justice systems, which enforce laws against many kinds of assault and other criminal behaviors but often are not concerned with much of the victimization of children in the form of bullying. Note the double standard here: When the victim is a child, adults often tolerate forms of bullying such as theft of belongings and unprovoked bodily assault with resultant injuries. However, when the victim is an adult, these abuses are seen as grounds for legal action. With the combination of few choices and limited support from adults, children who have potential victim attributes such as a lack of confidence, small physical stature, and poor coordination are dangerously vulnerable to attack by those who are bigger, stronger, and eager to demonstrate their power at little or no risk to themselves.

A major breakthrough and compelling contribution has recently been made by Karr-Morse and Wiley (1997) in their work on *prenatal* influences. They have established that, in the case of unwanted pregnancies, the roots of victimization and other forms of antisocial behavior are present in the prenatal period. Whatever affects the pregnant mother emotionally also affects the fetus. Prenatal negative stress, for example, also has negative effects on the fetus. The most damaging combination for the fetus is prenatal alcohol exposure in conjunction with maternal stress. The earlier the stress occurs in the pregnancy period, the more intense are the effects on the fetus.

Unwanted babies are often at risk for social problems. When the unwanted baby is rejected by the mother, the probability is low that mother–infant attachment will be established in the optimum period, that is, the first 2 years of life. Failure to establish this attachment is often the first step in reducing the child's capacity for empathic connections within other subsequent relationships. Empathy is a strong protective factor against antisocial inclinations. It is shaped by early sensitive and loving responses to the subtle emotional cues from the baby and young child. The unwanted baby whose cries go unheeded may never learn what it feels like to regain balance through well-timed and loving soothing. Rage may often overwhelm a very young child who has not learned emotional regulation skills. In early childhood the ability to regulate emotion functions as a protective factor against one's own aggressive behavior. Although this ability can be taught in later childhood, it is much more difficult to do so because the basic patterns for handling strong negative emotions should have been established in the first 2 years of life. By the late preschool years, the inability to handle strong negative emotions such as rage is likely to have a negative effect on the child's social relationships, and by the school years, children who lack this skill are often labeled as bullies or troublemakers (Karr-Morse & Wiley, 1997).

Forming friendships with peers is a major developmental task of childhood (Hartup, 1996). The importance for the child of having friends and being liked by peers cannot be overestimated. When Pellegrini, Bartini, and Brooks (1999) investigated the occurrence of victimization in a total population of fifth-grade children, they found that having friends and being liked by peers were protective factors against victimization. Being liked by peers was the more powerful of the two factors.

A second study that emphasizes the importance for the child of having friends, particularly those that he or she can count on for social support, has been conducted by Hodges, Malone, and Perry (1997). Their goal was to determine whether the behavior problems that place third- through seventh-grade children at risk for peer victimization are associated with such victimization when children are also at social risk for victimization. *Social risk* was defined as being rejected by the peer group and lacking supportive friends. They reported that internalizing problems, externalizing problems, and physical weakness were more strongly related to victimization when children had few friends, or had friends who were incapable of providing protection, or were rejected by peers, than when they had more friends, or had friends capable of offering protection, or were better liked by peers.

Parent–child relationships have an enormous influence on whether the child masters the task of forming friendships with peers. Positive parental nurturing is a significant help to the child, whereas well-intentioned but misguided parenting or parental maltreatment can result in behavior by the child that makes it likely that he or she will be unpopular with other children and rejected by them (Bolger, Patterson, & Kupersmidt, 1998). It is a short step from social rejection to victimization. Should the failure to form friendships occur, the negative result is that the child is likely to have adjustment problems not only in childhood but also in adolescence and adulthood (Parker & Asher, 1987).

What Are the Effects of Negative Parenting on the Child That Make Other Children Dislike or Reject Him or Her?

Consider maternal overprotection. There is general agreement that it leads to victimization, particularly in the case of boys (Olweus, 1978).

The reasoning for this view focuses on the effects that a deficit in social experience in the preschool years can have. The preschool child who has experienced only limited, and often carefully supervised, social contacts and play opportunities is singularly unprepared to cope with the public school situation. Children who have been overprotected often exhibit patterns of inappropriate behaviors that deviate sharply from the preschool norm and establish them immediately as different in a negative way from their peers. As a result, they become targets for exploratory bullying and teasing. When conflicts with peers arise, they tend to seek adult help and protection rather than coping with the situation themselves. They tend to react even to minor slights by showing upset and, unfortunately, they cry easily.

Because overprotected children have had few interaction experiences with peers, they generally lack the social skills that are habitual for more experienced children. They often want to be first in games, for example, and they are poor losers. There is no question that maternal overprotection has the potential to seriously inhibit the young child's social development. Consider the following case of maternal infantilization and discouragement of autonomy in a preschool boy who was an only child:

> This 42-year-old mother was an extreme example of overprotection. She breast-fed her son until he was 3 and from then until he went to preschool at 5 he drank out of a baby's bottle. When he was 4½ he was toilet trained. His mother did everything for him—dressed him, fed him at the table, helped him up and down stairs. At the park he was only allowed in the sandbox, never on the swings or slides. He was never reprimanded. He thought his name was "Mummy's boy." At 5, his father and the pediatrician insisted that he go to preschool. His mother stayed all morning for the first three mornings and then the teacher insisted that she leave. The child wept inconsolably until she returned at lunch time. Socially, he was a disaster. He had never played with other children and did not have any idea how to interact with them. The staff worked intensely on him and his father. After a year he was greatly improved but in many respects well below the level of a 6-year-old boy. (Ross, 1977–1979)

A study by Finnegan and Perry (1995) has added considerably to our understanding of the role of maternal overprotection in the victimization of the child. In this research, two sets of mother–child interactions were examined: The first focused on the way the mother behaved toward the child, particularly during control and conflict situations; the second set was concerned with the child's responses during these dyadic interactions. The participants in this study were 184 fourth- through seventh-grade boys and girls who provided verbal reports about their mothers' and their own behavior at home during conflict and control episodes. Peer nominations were used to assess victimization; physical strength; internalizing behaviors such as withdrawal, anxiety, and depression; and externalizing behaviors such as aggression and disruptiveness in the school setting.

The results showed gender differences in the patterns of mother–child interaction associated with victimization. Maternal overprotectiveness was associated with victimization only for boys who reported that they felt afraid and compelled to submit to their mothers during conflicts. For girls, victimization was predicted by maternal hostility and particularly so for girls whose peers assessed them as lacking in physical strength. Finnegan and Perry (1995) suggested that hostility in the mother could create anxiety or depression in the daughter that is evident in peer interactions and attracts negative attention from aggressive peers. Despite the divergent gender results, Finnegan and Perry suggested a single principle for the influence of maternal behavior on victimization: Peer victimization may occur when maternal behavior impedes the child's progress toward the developmental goals and tasks that are salient for the child's gender. For boys, what is impeded is their progress toward autonomy and self-assertion, whereas for girls, maternal hostility may threaten their sense of connectedness in their primary relationship.

Another maternal-related behavior that has been associated with victimization in preschool (Troy & Sroufe, 1987) and school-age children (Finnegan, Hodges, & Perry, 1998) is an anxious/resistant attachment to the caregiver, usually the mother. Children with such an attachment typically have a marked need for a parent to be with them in a new situation and exhibit an unusual degree of distress when the parent leaves. On the first day of school, these children often have great difficulty coping: They tend to be visibly anxious, cry much more easily than most other children of their age, and have poor self-esteem (Bowlby, 1973). In peer-group settings these behavior patterns mark these unhappy children as potential targets for bullying. Because they are markedly incompetent in managing aggression from peers, their inept attempts to fend off exploratory bullying are dismal failures that facilitate their assumption of the victim role.

A third maternal or parental behavior that may lead to victimization is harsh maltreatment by one or both parents or very neglectful parenting. Either could cause a child to be very aggressive and coercive (Strassberg, Dodge, Pettit, & Bates, 1994; Taussig & Litrownik,

1997). There is unequivocal evidence from a substantial body of developmental research that aggressive behavior is associated with unpopularity and peer rejection, particularly among boys (see, e.g., Pope & Bierman, 1999; Ray, Cohen, Secrist, & Duncan, 1997). Even when a child's previous reputation as being aggressive is not a factor, the link between aggression and unpopularity remains firm. Research with previously unacquainted children, mostly boys, showed that highly aggressive boys tended to be rejected from the newly formed groups (Schwartz et al., 1993). Unusually close parenting is associated with victimization for boys, whereas harsh parenting is likely to lead to victimization of girls (Perry et al., 2001).

All of the above studies suggest the possibility that a pathway exists from inept parenting or parental maltreatment to an inability to function effectively in the peer group, followed by rejection by peers and the peer victimization of the child. A study by Bierman and Smoot (1991) has confirmed that this sequence does occur.

More recently, Bolger and Patterson (2001) have conducted a prospective longitudinal study of chronically maltreated children from second to seventh grade. One purpose was to further study the role of aggression in the parental maltreatment, aggression, peer rejection sequence. Aggression ratings were based on reports by the children's peers, their teachers, and themselves. The results supported previous research on the role of aggression as an intermediate step between parental maltreatment and peer rejection and indicated that this sequence was already well established by early school age. Not surprisingly, interventions aimed at counteracting the effects of parental maltreatment on the child's social development would be most effective if started at preschool level.

A second purpose was to determine the role that social withdrawal (rather than aggression) might have in the sequence. Here, the results were equivocal. Although social withdrawal was associated with peer rejection, it did not account for the association between chronic maltreatment and peer rejection.

Behavioral Characteristics Conducive to Victimization

Children who have poor motor coordination and are lacking in the motor skills in which other children in their age group are fairly proficient are at risk for victimization, as are those who have difficulty with academic tasks and, with implicit teacher support, elicit negative peer reactions such as amusement. Other possible targets are those who are abused at home and, as a result, suffer a loss of confidence and fall into the victim role. Although a victim at home is sometimes a bully at school, more often the victim demeanor generalizes to the school setting and identifies the child as a possible target for teasing and bullying. Whatever the cause(s), very few children confronted by personal verbal attacks from peers can generate the quick retort that is essential in quelling the attack. (It should be noted, however, that with training many children acquire this skill; see chapter 7.) One of the best statements on becoming a victim comes from Thompson and Smith (1991, p. 141):

> Some children and adolescents find themselves pushed into playing the role of victim in the emerging social pattern. Like the children who . . . learn to behave in a bullying manner in social groups, so many victims enter social life as children with a lesser tendency to behave aggressively or even assertively and what seems to be a slightly greater difficulty in making effective social relationships with peers . . . and find that the patterns of social interaction leave them on the margins of groups, waiting to be "picked on" by children interested in demonstrating dominance at very little cost to themselves.

Other children find themselves pushed into the role of victim by their teachers. In *Children First,* Leach (1994) wrote about the child's unremitting experience of adult power. Teachers have extraordinary power over children and in most cases use it appropriately (Rogers, 1993). However, when they abuse the power, the consequences can be exceedingly painful for the child:

> A 9-year-old girl, new to the school, poorly dressed, and quite shy was brought by the principal midway through November for placement in a fifth-grade class. The teacher had just completed a complicated survey questionnaire required by the school district and the addition of one more pupil to her class meant that parts would have to be redone. The class had been helping by adding long columns, computing averages, and other tedious tasks. The teacher made it clear to the class that the new set of tasks were "because of the new girl," and that they would not be able to have a movie that had been scheduled because of the extra work that must now be done "because of the new girl." By the end of the school day the teacher had made a number of derogatory comments about the new girl, who was never addressed by name, and the class was understandably negative about her. Three girls in the class who saw her going home beat her up. (Ross, 1977–1979)

An important question concerns why one child is selected as a target for bullying rather than another. One view, the *victim hypothesis* (Olweus, 1978), holds that certain qualities in the victim invite and sustain bullying, that the child has a victimlike demeanor. An anxious expression and body language that suggests fear, for example, are cues that guide a bully. Troy and Sroufe (1987) described this demeanor as radiating anxious vulnerability; in elementary school children it appears as an appeasing shrinking posture (Ginsburg, Pollman, & Wauson, 1977). Another explanation, the *difference hypothesis*, has been proposed as often by investigators as by victims (Pearce, 1989; Phillips, 1989). Here the bullying is attributed to external negative deviations such as physical defects like protruding teeth, speech problems such as stuttering or an unusual accent, extremes of stature, clumsiness, and obesity.

Both the difference and the victim hypotheses generally have been accepted by laymen despite the fact that there is no empirical evidence to suggest that either one is the exclusive causal link identifying a child as a victim. Valid objections to both have been raised by investigators. La Fontaine (1991) contended that the victim hypothesis is undermined by the fact that unless victims are observed or tested before the onset of bullying, it is impossible to determine whether the characteristic demeanor of the victim has preceded or followed the bullying. If it occurs or develops after the bullying begins, then it has no causal relationship to the bullying. La Fontaine also questioned the difference hypothesis: References to the victim's features and behavioral deviations are the *means* of causing distress but are not necessarily the *cause* of the bullying.

The difference hypothesis led Olweus (1978) to compare two groups of boys to determine whether victims were more externally deviant than a group of control boys who were not bullied. The only external deviation occurred in physical strength. The victims were weaker than boys in general, and this difference was even more pronounced when victims and bullies were compared (Olweus, 1993a). Further evidence of the importance of physical weakness comes from a study by Hodges and Perry (1999a) of third- through seventh-grade children to determine whether the personal and interpersonal difficulties characteristic of the victimized children are antecedents of victimization, consequences of it, or both. The children were assessed on victimization, personal variables (internalizing problems, externalizing problems, and physical strength), and interpersonal variables (number of friends and peer rejection). One year later they were assessed again on all variables. Physical weakness and peer rejection contributed uniquely to increases in victimization over time. Also, initial victimization predicted increases in later internalization of symptoms and peer rejection. These reciprocal influences suggest the existence of a vicious cycle that supports the strong temporal stability of peer victimization.

Both the victim and the difference hypotheses fail to consider the well-documented complexity of bullying (Besag, 1989; Olweus, 1993a; Smith, 1991). Multiple contributors to the selection of victims should be sought along with intensive study of the various motivations of bullies and their interaction with the characteristics of the victims. If the bully, for example, wants to enhance his or her status with peers, then the basis for selecting a victim may simply be availability, whereas if payoff is the desired outcome, the bully might choose a passive target known to have money and known to be submissive. When the motive is a need to show that the bully is in the power spot, the ideal selection would be a provocative victim (one who is noted for inviting attack and then fighting back ineffectively). As Bandura (1986) has pointed out in cognitive social learning theory, outcome expectations are considered to be causal influences on behavior.

Both the difference and victim hypotheses focus solely on the victim. Another possibility concerns factors that might be operative in the victim's social environment. To investigate this idea, Hodges et al. (1997) started from the fact that some or all of the triad of externalizing, internalizing, and physical weakness are factors likely to be implicated in victimization, but not all children who have some or all of these behavioral attributes are victimized. They speculated that certain social factors, if present, might *decrease* the risk of victimization in vulnerable children and, if absent, might *increase* it. To test the hypothesis that children with the foregoing cluster of problems would be at lower risk for victimization given social support (a supportive group of friends and acceptance by peers) but at higher risk if lacking in social support, Hodges et al. selected 119 children in Grades 3 through 7, an age group for whom social support from peers is usually of prime importance. There was strong support for the hypothesis that social risk conditions increased the probability of victimization of vulnerable children, whereas the absence of social risk served a protective function. These findings underline the need for early intervention designed to facilitate entry into the peer group and the acquisition of the social skills required for subsequent peer acceptance.

What effect does a change in victim status have on a child? To investigate this question, Kochenderfer-Ladd and Wardrop (2001) used a longitudinal research design to predict children's loneliness and social satisfaction growth curves from changes in their peer victimization status. Children (193 boys and 195 girls) were interviewed for 40 minutes at the time of entry into kindergarten and again in the spring of that year, followed by an interview in each of their first-, second-, and third-grade years. At each interview point, data were collected on the frequency of the child's peer victimization experiences and the degree of loneliness and social satisfaction experienced by the child. Several hypotheses regarding the nature of victimized children's growth curves were tested using hierarchical linear modeling. For example, the trajectories that emerged for children who moved from nonvictim to victim status showed increasing levels of loneliness and decreasing social satisfaction over time, a finding that is consistent with the *onset hypothesis*. However, findings for those moving from victim to nonvictim status (the *cessation hypothesis*) were mixed: These children did not necessarily experience significant improvement in loneliness or social satisfaction. Only two of the three groups who were formed to examine the cessation hypothesis showed evidence of decreasing loneliness as they achieved nonvictim status.

It is my opinion that many school-age children who are victimized can move from victim to nonvictim status with parental help. Victims tend to catastrophize about being bullied and teased. The effect of this tendency is to arouse anxiety about what might happen next even when the child is safe at home. One 10-year-old girl told me that she did it all the time. The victim first needs to understand the effect of catastrophizing and then must learn how to use thought-stopping. The procedure for teaching it is described later in the chapter. It is readily taught by any interested parent or other adult.

The Link Between Peer Victimization and Psychosocial Dysfunction

In a study by Hoover, Oliver, and Hazler (1992), 76.8% of a group of middle and high school students did not believe that being bullied had had a serious negative effect on their social, emotional, or academic adjustment, whereas 14% of the sample believed that such peer harassment had negatively affected some aspects of their development. In an excellent chapter that should be mandatory reading for investigators who are interested in the effects of peer victimization, Ladd and Ladd (2001) set out to investigate the specific features of peer harassment that might increase or decrease the risk of psychosocial dysfunction. To this end, they proposed three situational aspects of peer harassment that might account for the differences reported by Hoover et al. (1992), namely, the frequency of peer harassment during relatively brief time periods, the duration of it over extended developmental periods, and the type of peer harassment that occurred. They advanced the following four primary hypotheses:

1. Harassment that is more frequent, that is, higher rates of harassment per unit of time, is likely to be more stressful for children and be more likely to induce psychosocial dysfunction.
2. Harassment that is of longer rather than shorter duration acts as a chronic stressor and may result in more serious forms of maladjustment such as lasting cumulative forms of dysfunction.
3. The effects of the frequency or duration of harassment may be moderated by child factors such as the quality of the child's internal and external resources for coping. However, if long-term harassment is experienced as a chronic stressor, it may over time exhaust the quality of children's coping resources.
4. The form or specificity of ongoing harassment of children may determine the severity of its effects on their adjustment and the domains in which dysfunction is most likely to develop. (Ladd & Ladd, 2001, p. 45)

In addition to the foregoing main effects of frequency, duration, and type of harassment, the possibility of secondary effects should also be considered. The frequency of peer victimization, for example, may interact with the type or duration of harassment in ways that change the effects on children's adjustment. One possible result may be that frequent harassment has a less serious effect on a child's adjustment when it consistently takes only one form, such as a verbal form (racial taunting), than when it takes multiple forms, such as racial taunting and physical aggression. Altogether, Ladd and Ladd (2001) have made an important contribution to our understanding of the differential effects of peer victimization on children's adjustment and development.

Passive Victims

Olweus (1978) has described the largest group of victimized children as *passive victims* partly because they do not directly provoke their attacker. Instead, they are socially withdrawn and, to their peers, often appear to be anxious, depressed, or fearful. This cluster of internalizing symptoms is likely to identify them to aggressive children as attractive targets. In fact, these aggressive children seem to be unusually competent in detecting such vulnerability, particularly in boys, one reason being that a fearful, withdrawn demeanor is perceived as being more sex inappropriate for boys than for girls

(Boulton, 1999; Finnegan, Hodges, & Perry, 1996). Their vulnerability arouses intense contempt and dislike in aggressive children. The passive victims' demeanor sends signals to bullies that these targets are unlikely to retaliate: Their typical initial responses to exploratory bullying in the lower grades are crying, withdrawal, and futile anger; as the bullying progresses in the upper grades, their responses are avoidance and escape tactics, being absent from school, and running away from home (Perry et al., 1988). Suicide attempts are rare (Batsch & Knoff, 1994), although there is evidence that passive boy victims tend to bring guns to school more often than boys in general, probably because they feel safer. They seldom strike back either physically or psychologically, and if they do, their efforts are notably ineffective. One reason for this ineffectiveness may be that in boys the anxious personality is more often combined with lower physical strength than is the case for boys in general (Björkqvist, Lagerspetz, & Kaukiainen, 1992).

There is some evidence supporting Olweus's (1978) description of passive victims as often being depressed (Neary & Joseph, 1994). They also characteristically have poor self-concepts and such low self-esteem that they see themselves as unattractive, stupid, and failures (Olweus, 1993b; Rigby & Slee, 1991). They score higher on internalizing behavior and psychosomatic symptoms (Kumpulainen et al., 1998) as well as on the Eysenck Introversion factor (Slee & Rigby, 1993). It is not surprising, then, that when compared with their nonvictimized peers, they have fewer if any friends, are lonely and sad, and are more nervous about new situations (Byrne, 1994).

Passive victims are generally not capable of the relaxed give-and-take of informal peer interactions. There is some evidence that this inability precedes the child's assumption of the victim role. In an observational study of 6- to 8-year-old boys in contrived play group settings (Schwartz et al., 1993), boys who later became passive victims were more submissive in peer interactions than those who did not subsequently become victimized. Moreover, the more submissive boys were notably nonassertive in that they did not initiate social interactions. Consequently, they spent more time in passive play than in interaction with peers. Intervention at that point might have halted the trend to victimization. In a Kidscape study (Elliott, 1991), victims were described as both intelligent and creative, but lacking in those qualities that ease everyday social interactions. Particularly unfortunate is the fact that their demeanor is generally serious, and they often have no sense of humor. As McGhee (1989) has pointed out, children who are capable of the timely use of humor in peer interactions are more likely to be popular with their peers and to make friends easily. A good example of the level of social interaction of an elementary school-age boy is contained in the following fictionalized description based on observations by David Schwartz (Schwartz et al., 2001, p. 160):

> Paul would most likely meet criteria for classification as a passive victim. Paul seems to be viewed as an "easy mark" by his play group peers. During initial interactions of the newly formed peer group, Paul demonstrates a tendency to reward nonaggressive coercive overtures. For example, during a "get acquainted" ball throwing game, he gives up the ball quickly whenever asked. When the boys are taking turns using a small portable video game, Paul frequently yields his turn. Later, as the boys begin to engage in playful rough-and-tumble play bouts, Paul usually adopts a submissive role. When another child challenges him to a mock "kung fu" fight, Paul drops to the floor and covers his head. Eventually, the other boys begin to target Paul for bullying. Paul responds to these overtures passively or with overt signs of pain. By the last play session (45 minutes on 5 consecutive days), Paul has emerged as a persistently harassed child.

The kind of experiences described above tend to further lower the passive victim's confidence in the ability to interact with peers. Many passive victims do not have a single good friend in their age group; in effect, they become social isolates in the school setting. One 15-year-old girl commented that "the bullied person is always sad and depressed and doesn't have any popular friends" (Hazler et al., 1993, p. 19). The effect of this isolation and rejection is to deprive these children of the social support that could protect them from being bullied. They also miss out on the peer interactions that are critical for the development of the requisite social skills of middle childhood and early adolescence. The effect is to set the passive victim on a downward spiral of decreasing social competence. If no attempt is made to help the passive victim cope more competently, the downward spiral is likely to continue unchecked.

Implication of Lazarus's Theory for Intervention With Passive Victims

To the passive victims, their bully-related problems must seem insurmountable. Their initial appraisal of the bully as threatening rapidly shifts to omnipotent. Boys who bully are generally far more confident and psychologically intimidating than their victims. Despite these formidable differences, victims sometimes make a brave but unrealistic attempt at self-defense. When this tactic fails, the only other option is to seek social support. Choices here are limited because passive victims seldom have any close friends, and parents and siblings often have no interest in the victims' problems. In either case, victims are often reluctant to pursue this help. At this low point, they engage in reappraisal, a step that Lazarus (1966) called *emotion-focused coping*, and tell themselves that they are worthless and deserving of the punishment administered by the bully. (It is interesting to note here that this interpretation is also common to victims of wife abuse.) Curiously, the effect of self-blame may result in their feeling that they do have some control of the bullying and this, in turn, leads to a tenuous feeling of comfort that there is a rational basis for the bullying (Hodges & Perry, 1999b).

The flaw in the passive victims' attempts to cope lies in their failure to seek social support or to have such support available to them in their social environment. Some form of social support is crucial to successful intervention. These victims desperately need someone to take charge of their rehabilitation. Professional help in designing an intervention program for the family would be mandatory. Included in it should be training in assertiveness, a basic prerequisite for gaining a foothold in the peer group. Assertiveness training coupled with training in friendship skills could help children to control submissive behavior such as crying and looking downcast. Given training, most children can learn to respond in an active, but never aggressive, way. Although passive victims reported having fewer friends than other children and not being well-liked in the earlier school years, there is no evidence of an increase with age for these problems. With increasing peer-group experience in school as passive victims move to the higher grades, coupled with continuing training in social skills, they might have little or no peer harassment problems by the time they are well along in secondary school (Boulton, Trueman, Chau, Whitehand, & Amatya, 1999). When long-term follow-up assessments are made on young adults who had had peer problems in school, the results often show that they are getting along well in their work and social lives (Olweus, 1993b). This finding is usually attributed to their being able to choose their place and type of work and their friends, although, in fact, it could be due to effective intervention at a critical point in their school years.

Other Categories of Victims

Besag (1989) has described several subgroups of victims most likely to be present within the main group of passive victims, a refinement that facilitates more effective treatment.

VICARIOUS VICTIMS

These are children, sometimes called *surrogate victims*, who either witness bullying incidents or hear reports of them. They are good examples of the widespread negative impact of bullying on a school or neighborhood. They become victims of the climate of fear in the school and perceive their own vulnerability as potential targets. As a result, they suppress any tendency to help the victim or report the incident. Although they often feel sympathetic, at the same time they are wary of a contagion effect or direct retribution. Feelings of guilt about their failure to help the victim plus awareness of their own vulnerability combine to create considerable upset, which may take psychologically damaging forms.

FALSE VICTIMS

Besag (1989) hypothesized that there is a group of children who complain frequently and without justification to their teachers about being bullied by their classmates. Some empirical support for this false-victim subgroup comes from Perry et al. (1988). When they developed their Modified Peer Nomination Inventory, they identified a small group of children who reported being "extremely victimized," that is, in the top 10% of the sample. Neither their teachers nor their same-gender peers perceived them as victims, a finding that led Perry et al. to caution that it is unwise to rely solely on self-report measures to identify victimization.

The behavior of the false victims is not victim behavior but rather a dependency bid for teacher attention and sympathy. It is a destructive pattern of behavior that should be stopped: The child needs to learn that there are legitimate ways of getting the attention of teachers and others. In addition, teachers who are unsympathetic about the problem of bullying should not be handed an alibi for ignoring all complaints about bullying.

PERPETUAL VICTIMS

Elliott (1993) proposed a subgroup of victims who are bullied all their lives. *Perpetual*, however, refers to the duration of bullying rather than to a separate subgroup and clearly is not a valid descriptor. It is included here because Elliott (1993) suggested the interesting idea that such a child might have developed a *victim mentality*. The victim role could become a permanent part of the child's psyche either as a result of reward in the form of attention from others when the child was bullied or from a tendency to brood about being bullied and to constantly replay the script. In either case, a child or adult with this attitude should have therapeutic help.

PROVOCATIVE VICTIMS

In 1978 Olweus asked Swedish school teachers to provide open-ended descriptions of the social behavior of a group of sixth-grade children who were persistently bullied. Although most of the descriptions were consistent with the view of the often victimized child as passive or oversubmissive, a small distinct subgroup of children were described as irritable, restless, and hostile. Olweus named this group of children *provocative victims,* a very apt descriptor because these children often behaved in ways intended to arouse negative responses in others, such as anger, irritation, and exasperation. In the last two decades, this subgroup has been studied by a cluster of researchers, some of whom have used their own descriptors, such as *ineffectual aggressors* (Perry, Perry, & Kennedy, 1992), *bully/victims* (Boulton & Smith, 1994), or *aggressive victims* (Schwartz, Dodge, Pettit, & Bates, 1997). The term *provocative* is the most accurate descriptor of the quality of reactions that this subgroup of victims elicits in peers and adults. They are referred to as *provocative victims* throughout this text.

Prevalence

Very little empirical research on the prevalence of provocative victims has been reported, and the estimates that are available vary widely, partly because of the influence of design-specific factors but also because arbitrary classification criteria that are not necessarily comparable have been used across studies (Schwartz, Proctor, & Chien, 2001). In a large group of prevalence studies identified by Schwartz et al. (1997), provocative victims were consistently the smallest subgroup identified. Data from studies using peer nomination, teacher report, or multi-informant procedures tended to be higher: The percentage of provocative victims generally varied from 4% to 8%. In the most recent Bergen project (Olweus, 1993a, p. 13), which defined provocative victims as those scoring above a commonly used cutting point on both victim and bully self-report dimensions, there were 78 provocative victims out of approximately 4,000 students in 30 schools. There was also a marked gender imbalance of a 3:1 ratio of boys to girls, which could have been a function of the failure to include indirect aggression (Björkqvist, Österman, & Kaukiainen, 1992) as one of the dimensions.

Characteristics

Provocative victims are at once the most interesting and exasperating of the victim population. They possess a cluster of characteristics that can be virtually guaranteed to disrupt a classroom. Consider the following despairing comment by a teacher (Randall, 1997, p. 94):

> Nathan, aged 10 . . . was described by his class teacher as a child who lived "on the edge of his nerves," never still and with "his brain disconnected from his mouth." The latter trait made it likely that he would make loud remarks about other children's appearance or their work that would make them angry. He would then say to them, "What are you going to do about it then?" whereupon two or three of them might show him, violently.
>
> Nathan was described as the most unpopular child in the school, as the one "everybody loves to hate." Even pleasant, kind children egged on the bullies to "smack him one."

The irritating off-task behavior of provocative victims leads to social rejection by peers as well as other negative peer-group reactions. Although there is no question that they are a distinct subgroup, they also show behaviors characteristic of other groups of children. Olweus (2001) stated that provocative victims have clear elements of both "pure bullies" and "pure victims" in their makeup. They resemble pure bullies in that they have elevated levels of dominant, aggressive, and antisocial behavior and low levels of tolerance for frustration; consequently, they are prone to hostile behaviors. They also show behaviors of hyperactive children: They are irritable, disruptive, overreactive, impulsive, and have difficulty concentrating. In common with passive victims, they are socially anxious, with poor global self-esteem and feel disliked by peers. Altogether, they present a dispiriting picture.

The best explanatory statement for the behavior of the provocative victim comes from the leading world authority on victims, David Perry, and his associates (Perry et al., 1992). They viewed the provocative victim as an emotionally dysregulated child who can be described as an "ineffectual aggressor" or a "high-conflict victim." They hypothesized that provocative victims often become involved in extended and emotionally charged conflicts with their peers, possibly because it is difficult for them to modulate their affect during conflicts. They become overaroused and escalate relatively harmless peer-group interactions into far more aggressive exchanges. When they lose these self-initiated conflicts, they erupt with displays of uncontrolled anger, emotional upset, and frustration. At the slightest provocation, they will strike back no matter how unfavorable the odds.

One highly skilled special education teacher said, "They go wild and are right out of control and disrupt the whole class." In describing the effect of the chaos caused by provocative victims, she said she would rather have 10 additional passive victims in her class than 1 provocative victim (J. M. Allan, personal communication, summer 1963). Provocative victims generally also experience many more rebuffs from the peer group than do bullies and passive victims (Schwartz et al., 2001).

Hazler (1996a, p. 9) presented an interesting case of a 9-year-old girl whose inappropriate and provocative behavior contributed to the bullying she received. Ann was a model student who always knew the right answers and willingly accepted favors and privileges from her teachers and parents. However, she had some specific behaviors that provoked bullying. She made a point of making sure that her less fortunate peers knew about the favors she received in school. Her teachers frequently told the other students that Ann was a model that they should emulate.

Ann was picked on constantly at school by two other girls. They cornered her in the bathroom and verbally abused her, tore her clothes, and pulled her hair. Ann always complained immediately to her teacher and later to her mother. Ann let the other students know that she could get them in trouble whenever she wanted to, and she always told them when she did. She got revenge for the bullying, and the bullies resented it, striking back even more forcefully. Hazler (1996a, p. 9) commented:

> A victim being provocative does not excuse tormentors' abusive actions in any way; however, it does partly explain where their motivations originated. . . . A vicious cycle was forming between Ann and her adversaries that is common in relationships between bullies and provocative victims.

Comment

Provocative victims are clearly a distinct group. Their dysregulated aggressive behavior is qualitatively different from the goal-oriented and effective aggressive strategies that characterize bullies' behavior and from the submissive, tentative behavior of passive bullies. Very little is known about the etiology and predictors of the behavior patterns of provocative victims, but there is some preliminary evidence that they come from harsh and stressful home environments (Schwartz et al., 2001).

Implications of Lazarus's Theory for Intervention

The focus of intervention for these rather puzzling victims should be on teaching them not to pick fights. One facet of this task would be to determine how the provocative victims see the adversaries that they select and then use this information to develop an intervention program to change their perceptions. The victims' assessment of their own social status and their motivation to effect changes in it should be considered. They may need a special program to improve or eliminate their academic and cognitive shortcomings and to develop social skills. The management problems that they create in the classroom often repel peers and antagonize teachers. These victims often are more active, assertive, and confident than other categories of victims. It would be important to consider how these positive attributes could be used to the advantage of provocative victims, who, although often exasperating, are at the same time the most interesting of the bullies and victims.

Provocative Victims in Different Countries and Cultures

There is some initial evidence that provocative victims are present in diverse national and cultural settings. They have been identified in North American, Scandinavian, and Western European peer groups (Smith, Morita, et al., 1999). Patterns of findings similar to those reported by Schwartz et al. (2001) have been reported with regard to prevalence, gender distribution, social behavior, and psychosocial adjustment (see Table 6.1 in Schwartz et al., 2001, pp. 150–153). Research conducted in Japan (Morita et al., 1999) has provided some information on children who were provocative victims. In Japanese terms, they were both perpetrators and victims of *ijime*, a behavior often described as bullying that involves harassment of peers by dominant members of a group.

As part of a larger collaborative effort with international colleagues, Schwartz, Chang, and Farver (2000) have begun an investigation of the correlates of peer harassment in several Asian countries. Preliminary analysis of data collected in the People's Republic of China indicates that provocative victims are a distinct subgroup in that cultural setting, with prevalence of victim subgroups being similar to that reported in other countries. Of particular interest was the marked overrepresentation of boys even when the scales used included indirect aggression items. In addition, provocative victims were socially rejected to a far greater extent than bullies and passive victims.

A Social–Cognitive Model of Family Influences on Victimization

In their review of the determinants of chronic victimization by peers, Perry et al. (2001) focused on important proximal attractions of peer abuse, namely, the personal qualities of the victim. In the case of both passive and provocative victims, these qualities include an impaired sense of self, coupled with affective problems such as anxiety and emotional dysregulation. During peer conflicts, these characteristics together will impede effective functioning by the victim. Among the more distal influences of peer victimization that may seriously threaten the child's sense of self are two inauspicious areas of family relationships: insecure attachments and inept patterns of child rearing. Although other investigators have been interested in the problem of victimization, what distinguishes Perry et al.'s approach to this topic is that, following a comprehensive review of the relevant research on it, they have developed a social–cognitive model of the psychological mechanisms linking qualities in the victim that attract peer abuse with family experiences. Not only is this model testable but, in addition, Perry et al. have provided explicit suggestions of topics and procedures for testing their proposed model.

Central to this social–cognitive model is the concept of relational schemas—cognitive structures representing regularities in interpersonal relations that serve as guides for action (Baldwin, 1992; Bugental & Goodnow, 1998). Perry et al. (2001) proposed that on the basis of repeated observations of the parent and self by the child during critical kinds of interactions such as those involving conflict and control as well as those relevant to the child's emotional needs, children form *family-relational schemas* that involve representations of typical parent and self behavior. Of particular relevance here is the *victim schema* with its two components: a perception-of-the-parent as threatening and controlling coupled with a perception-of-the-self as helpless and defeated. This latter component may contain a feeling of incompetence and be characterized by negative emotions such as anxiety and guilt. If the victim schema is sufficiently strong, threatening peer behavior could activate it with the consequent helplessness and associated affect on the child's part. These victimlike behaviors may elicit further aggressive behavior from the peer and, at the same time, preempt cognitive activity that could lead to an assertive stand by the victim.

Perry et al. (2001) expected that the two components of the victim schema would interact synergistically, with each providing additional meaning to the other. When the self is seen as helpless, perceiving another child as threatening increases fear arousal, and this helplessness is even more destructive when the peer is clearly ready to attack. Given this set of circumstances, a chain of events is likely to be set in motion that will result in peer harassment.

VARIATIONS IN THE VICTIM SCHEMA

In the victim schema, the child's perception of the parent as sufficiently controlling and threatening to qualify as a component of the schema requires that the parent be seen as overprotective, coercive, or psychologically controlling. These three forms of parental control are associated with peer harassment. The child's perception of the self as helpless can complement a perception of the parent as controlling and threatening. First, the child must perceive himself or herself as powerless and subordinated in parent–child conflicts, and second, this perception must strongly suggest an anxious, overly dependent emotional attachment to the parent. Close relationships involve the negotiation of issues dealing with power and issues dealing with emotional attachment (Emery, 1992). Perry et al. (2001) suggested that the child can experience the self as a victim in either domain, that is, conflict or attachment, and in either domain a victim schema puts the child at risk for peer victimization.

Children also differ in their need for emotional connection with their parents. Some use their parents as a source of emotional comfort, whereas others frequently are inappropriately clinging in the face of even minor separations. Of relevance here is a study by Finnegan, Hodges, and Perry (1996) in which school children were asked the degree to which they characteristically experienced a variety of affective, behavioral, and cognitive reactions during mother–child conflicts. Factor analysis yielded a dimension labeled *debilitative coping* that was defined by high scores on fear, compulsive compliance, and self-blame and low scores on self-efficacy for assertion. A perception of the self as a debilitative coper should qualify for the perception-of-self part of the victim schema. Finnegan et al. (1996) also assessed children's perceptions of preoccupied and avoidant relating to a parent. On the preoccupied scale, high scores were associated with a strong need for the parent in novel and stressful situations, difficulty in separating from the parent, excessive concern over the parent's whereabouts, prolonged upset following reunion, and trouble meeting challenges owing to an excessive need for the parent. Because preoccupied coping entails self-perceptions of helpless, ineffective relations with the parent, a preoccupied self-construal should qualify for the perception-of-self part of the victim schema. However, Perry et al. (2001) pointed out that although preoccupied coping is directly related to victimization (Finnegan et al., 1996; Troy & Sroufe, 1987), their prediction would be that it would interact with perceptions of inept parental control to yield maximal victimization.

When the three main parent forms in the victim schema (perceiving the parent as overprotective, as psychologically controlling, or as coercive) and the two main alternative forms of perception-of-self (as helpless, i.e., debilitative coping, and as defeated, i.e., preoccupied coping) are crossed, six forms of the victim schema prototype are defined. Perry et al. (2001) believed that all six forms of the victim schema increase children's risk for peer harassment. Each of the six victim schemas is composed of a perception of the parent as psychologically controlling in a way that is likely to threaten the child's sense of self and a perception of the self as helpless and subordinated in the face of the perceived parental control. It follows that some functional equivalence among the six victim schemas can be assumed. However, Perry et al. (2001, p. 90) cautioned:

> The particular motivational systems underlying the victim schema may vary. For example, the schema in which the parent is perceived as overprotective and the self is viewed as preoccupied may represent an "enmeshed" parent–child system driven by separation anxiety in the parent (Hock, McBride, & Gnezda, 1989; Hock & Schirtzinger, 1992) and reciprocated by fear of separation and sacrifice of autonomy in the child.

Another example is a schema in which the child perceives the parent as coercive and the self as debilitative (compulsively compliant) during parent–child conflict. This set of circumstances may reflect the child's way of adapting to a fear of more dire consequences, such as abuse, that might result if the child were to be more self-assertive (Crittenden & DiLalla, 1988). At present, Perry et al. (2001) cautioned that there is no theoretical basis for assuming significant differences in the contribution to peer victimization by the six variants of the victim schema.

COMMENT

What is particularly sad about victims is that in most cases the tendency to become a victim is apparent as early as the preschool years, a period during which preventive measures could have been initiated. A beginning point might be the child's appearance: If there is anything about it, such as obesity or unusual clothing, that might elicit negative reactions from other children and could be changed, every effort should be made to do so. The child should have experience in relatively brief social interactions with other children in low-demand situations such as a playground, during slack periods, with swings and slides that do not require participation with others. The simple vocabulary of basic social exchanges should become habitual: saying "please," "thank you," "hello," and "good-bye" and addressing other children by name are essential skills. Beginning game skills should be practiced at home. These include taking turns, taking just one turn at a time, and losing (or winning) with reasonable grace. Sometimes in a game the parent or other player should deliberately play out of turn, take two turns, or break a rule. The question here for the child is, How should this be handled? The other players should show disapproval verbally and help the child to object strongly. If the infractions continue, the child should say something like, "I'm not playing with you anymore, because you don't know how to play."

Children who lack basic social skills may draw back from other children or friendly adults and cling to their mothers or hide behind them. All too often at this point the mothers smile and say, "She's shy," as though this is a positive attribute. In fact, being shy is destructive behavior that is not at all in the child's best interests; adults in the child's environment should make great efforts to teach the child social interaction skills and provide opportunities to practice them so that meeting others becomes enjoyable rather than threatening. One of the many unfortunate aspects of shyness is that other children see it as rejection of their overtures, or dislike of them, and accordingly act negatively toward the shy child. Almost all children including those who are slow academically can be taught the rudiments of social interactions. The question then is, Are parents or others willing to make the effort needed to do so?

The foregoing section focuses on the actions that a concerned parent can take to help the child who either has acquired victim status or is in the process of doing so. Most school-age victims are catastrophizers. They typically are unable to think positively about themselves. One procedure a parent can use to help a child stop this negative thought pattern is to teach the child first how to recognize his or her catastrophic thought pattern and then how to use thought-stopping (Ross, 1984) to break this self-destructive habit.

CATASTROPHIZING

Catastrophizing refers to the habitual response pattern of focusing on previous stressors or impending ones. Research by Brown, O'Keefe, Sanders, and Baker (1986) has shown that this occurs from middle childhood through adolescence at a rate they describe as "alarming." It takes many forms, including mental images, self-statements, and thoughts, *all of which are negative and usually exaggerated*. The effect of this cognitive activity is to arouse anxiety and fearful fantasies about what might happen next. An underlying theme of helplessness (Seligman, 1975) permeates it.

The tendency to catastrophize is learned through negative socialization experiences, which lead to the perception of a lack of control in major areas such as the school setting. Often the effect of this perception is a generalized apprehensiveness reflected in chronic catastrophizing. Many children who are exposed to stressors such as bullying and teasing catastrophize about the experience. Usually they exaggerate the painful aspects and in the process berate themselves for not coping more effectively with the victimization. At the same time, the exaggeration aspect becomes a kind of justification for their ineffectiveness, thus eliminating any element of positive thinking or the need for planning a strategy for coping with the stressor should it occur again.

Catastrophizing is a self-destructive response pattern that parents who listen to their children can readily identify and then modify. Any potentially negative experience can be exacerbated by catastrophizing ideation. It is a habit that must be stopped in childhood; otherwise it becomes entrenched and will persist into adulthood. The child must learn, first, to be alert for the onset of self-defeating thoughts and images characteristic of catastrophizing and, second, how to use a procedure called thought-stopping (Ross, 1984) when they next occur. The parent or other adult listens to the child's account of what is causing anxiety, then tells the child that he or she had the same kind of problem (in the same grade as the child is in) that the child is having. Then a friend told the adult how to stop worrying about it and it worked, so now the adult will teach the child so that he or she will not be worried. Tell the child it is called thought-stopping.

THOUGHT-STOPPING

This is a coping technique designed to help adults and children who have persistent and unpleasant thoughts about impending events to reduce the frequency and intensity of these thought sequences. It is training in the self-monitoring of thoughts and, once acquired, is a skill of benefit in later life. The parent or adult who teaches thought-stopping should keep in mind that habitual ways of thinking, such as catastrophizing, do not change abruptly, nor is the first sign of change likely to indicate a permanent change. Time, practice, and encouragement are needed to execute these new ways of responding consistently, smoothly, and eventually automatically.

In Wolpe and Lazarus's (1966) thought-stopping technique, the client's task is first to relax as much as possible and, while relaxed, think about the impending event, and then to say loudly and firmly, "Stop!" if the client is alone or subvocally if others are present. At this point he or she must stop thinking about the impending unpleasant event and start actively thinking about some previously identified pleasant topic. This procedure must be followed *every* time the unpleasant thought surfaces.

Although this procedure has been used successfully, it has two important disadvantages. The quality of thoughts that the client had does not change, and no information in the course of learning the procedure would facilitate coping with the negative aspects of the feared event when it next occurs.

Ross (1984) developed a thought-stopping procedure that eliminates both of these disadvantages. With an adult's help, the child is required to think of positive aspects about the unpleasant event and select the best four of these aspects. Whenever the child thinks about the event, he or she must say to himself or herself (if not alone) or out loud (if by himself or herself) all four of the positive aspects. The list can be printed on a small card or it could be memorized. In the course of learning the procedure, the input of positive information surrounding the selection of the final four positive aspects should facilitate coping with the event when it does occur. In a short time, the quality of the thoughts is likely to change from a markedly negative attitude to a neutral or mildly positive one.

Consider the following application of Ross's (1984) thought-stopping procedure for a hypothetical case in which a bright 14-year-old girl who is small for her age and overweight enough to elicit teasing is intimidated by the fact that the high school she will enter in September has had for several years serious and widely publicized bullying problems. This school emphasized athletic prowess rather than grades. With an adult's help, the girl's first task is to list four facts about the situation that are all true and are all positive. For example, *Four girls that I like a lot are going there, too. I can lose a lot of weight and be much fitter in September. They have two after-school clubs I'd like to join. I'll work real hard on tennis and swimming this summer.* She then prints them on a small card and memorizes them. *Every time* that she thinks about the impending event, she must stop what she is doing and recite the four facts subvocally if others are present, aloud if she is alone. She then returns to her previous activity but must go through the whole procedure again when she thinks about the event.

Although empirical data are lacking on the efficacy of Ross's (1984) procedure, unsolicited clinical, teacher, and parental reports indicate that it is effective in reducing the anticipatory anxiety and upset and also in increasing the serenity level during the treatment or event. Originally designed for children who experienced high levels of anxiety about dental appointments, it has since been used in a wide range of anxiety situations from minor ones (fear of shots) to major ones (children with leukemia who were extremely anxious about spinal taps).

In considering why this apparently simple technique is effective, one explanation concerns the change that occurs from the child's feeling of helplessness about the impending event (Seligman, 1975) to one of confidence that there is some action that the child can take. Also, instead of experiencing persistent and unpleasant thought sequences about the event, positive responses are consistently being substituted for the fear responses. As a result, the fear responses are gradually being weakened. Having material to recite over and over again is often inconvenient and boring, so much so that children frequently reported a feeling of exasperation at "having to say all that stuff again." The overall effect of such monotony is to further weaken the fear responses. Meanwhile, with each repetition, the child is actively presenting himself or herself with a set of positive information, all of which the child knows is true and relates specifically to him or her. The child's cognitions are changed, and his or her fears diminish to a considerable extent.

Thought-stopping can also be used effectively by adults worried about an impending feared event, provided that they adhere to the requirement that the positive aspects be verbalized *every* time they think of the event. Children seem more readily accepting of this "rule" and consequently benefit from the procedure.

5 Harassment

Although bullying and teasing qualify as harassment, there are categories of harassment with specific aspects that justify separate discussion here. Included in this chapter are racist bullying, sexual harassment, homosexuality as a special case, and bullying of adults in particular settings. As is the case with any categories of complex behaviors, some overlap frequently occurs between categories. At the same time, a category can have distinctive characteristics justifying its treatment as a unique descriptor.

Racial Bullying

Although the complexity and seriousness of racism justify its treatment as a problem in its own right, it is included here because in the school setting it frequently manifests itself as bullying. Racial bullying is often regarded as a recent variant of bullying in general, but this is not the case. In much of the American South, racial bullying has gone on for centuries (Zinn, 1995), and in South Africa the history of apartheid traces back to the 16th century (Ohsako, 1999).

Loach and Bloor (1995) have cautioned that because racism is subsumed under the heading of bullying, it could be seen as a relatively simple problem. This reasoning ignores its often brutal reality and, in addition, could result in the complexity of the problem being overlooked or even hidden. They warn that bullying is a convenient way for institutions, such as schools, to acknowledge the *fact* of racism in the schools without having to face the *meaning* of it. The result in that case would likely be dealing with the symptoms, such as aggression, rather than the underlying problem of racism.

RACIAL BULLYING IN THE SCHOOLS

Racial bullying in schools often occurs out of sight of teachers. Even when teachers are on playground duty, they are often unaware of it or deliberately ignore it. One approach here would be to alert the staff to the potential problem, improve their surveillance patterns, and specify their obligations. Some of the staff may themselves be racists or be in sympathy with racism (Gillborn, 1992). Regardless of these personal beliefs, the school administrators are obligated to ensure that they do not undermine the school's policy concerning racial bullying. Every effort should be made to create a school ethos that refuses to tolerate the oppression of one person by another. The goal, a difficult one to attain, should be to have the school personnel and parents work together to counter the adverse effects of racial and other kinds of harassment.

In an excellent article, Sullivan (2000) described aspects underlying racist bullying that teachers striving to develop effective ways of dealing with it must take into consideration, whether on a day-to-day basis or over the long term. He defined racist bullying as

> an abuse of power that involves either physical or psychological bullying (including name calling and exclusion) or both to demean or harm a person from another ethnic group. Racist bullying can occur on a one-to-one basis, which can be termed individual racist bullying; can be carried out by a group of people, which is collective racist bullying; or can occur because of societal structures, which is institutional bullying. (Sullivan, 2000, p. 81)

Sullivan (2000) has proposed that a school needs to adopt a two-tiered approach to be effective in its strategies against racist bullying. In the first instance, this means having a clearly articulated and inclusive school philosophy and values statement that is the foundation on which any program or response is built. In the second instance, it means attempting to understand the aspects in the areas of racism and bullying, particularly how they overlap and how they differ. The process of developing a school philosophy should be open and be seen to be open. Members of the school community, that is, teachers, administrators, support staff such as playground supervisors and cleaning staff, the pupils, parents, and members of the community, need to be involved in the development of a philosophy and of policies and programs that grow out of the philosophy.

Sullivan (2000) believes that the most fundamental remedy against bullying of any kind is the creation of a safe environment. In the case of racist bullying, this involves an added dimension that can be termed *cultural safety*; this means that in the school setting, ethnic origins and cultural needs and perspectives are acknowledged, respected, and accommodated (Sullivan, 2000, p. 86). Victimized children are more likely to have low self-esteem, have poor health, have frequent absences from school, be loners, have high levels of depression, and consider and sometimes commit suicide (Rigby, 1996). A similar viewpoint has been proposed by Maslow (1970) in his needs hierarchy theory of personal adjustment. He contended that children must grow up in an environment in which five sets of needs are met if they are to be healthy, well-adjusted adults. These are physiological needs, safety from physical and psychological threat, the basic social needs of being loved and accepted by others, esteem needs (success), and self-actualization needs (reaching one's potential). If children do not feel safe physically, psychologically, or culturally, their ability and learning potential are likely to be seriously jeopardized.

Institutional racist bullying occurs when culturally different students respond to activities in the majority culture classrooms in ways that are inconsistent with school norms but are consistent with their own cultural norms and values (Corson, 1992). As a result, teachers make inaccurate assessments of these students' ability, particularly when the distance is great between the teacher's culture and that of the child. Jones (1987) described an excellent example of institutional racist bullying in a New Zealand case study of an Auckland girls' secondary school in which there were two classes of fifth-form girls, one largely European (n = 5), the other Polynesian (n = 5). The former girls were able to use the teacher as a vehicle for obtaining knowledge, to question and challenge what the teacher said. In contrast, the latter girls did not challenge the teacher because in their culture a teacher is a person who not only should not be challenged but also should not be asked questions, since to do so would be seen as disrespectful as well as indicating that the questioner had not been listening. Jones saw this as "symbolic" bullying because the Polynesian students fail their exams and are destined for low-paying jobs that will not tax their natural ability.

THE IMPORTANCE OF CONTEXT

Human rights versus cultural relativism underlines the importance of the culture and values of the groups to which the bullies and victims belong. In the evaluation by Moore, Adair, Lysaght, and Kruiswijk (1997) of the Eliminating Violence program, one of New Zealand's three major initiatives on bullying, they identified a potential source of conflict in the physical disciplining of children that has implications for bullying between European and Polynesian New Zealanders. Although physical punishment is condoned in some Pacific societies, it is considered unacceptable in New Zealand society in general:

> In our Samoan way you should smack the child out of love not out of anger. There are good values in our culture, but with my

> personal upbringing, a problem is that my parents would have smacked me more out of being angry, rather than smacking me for doing the thing that is not right. (Moore et al., 1997, p. 123)

An unusual case of racism occurred in 1995 at a Seattle high school where Caucasian students were a minority group. The student said that insults and threats started on her first day of school. The problem escalated rapidly. She faced merciless harassment both inside and outside the class, including insults from fellow students that focused mainly on her race: "White slut," "stupid White girl," "White bitch," "Go back to Bellevue (wealthy, primarily White school district)," and "This is *our* school." There were constant threats of violence and humiliating and lewd propositions. The harassment kept her from participating in high school activities, such as trying out for sports teams. She reached a point where she would skip a class rather than face her tormentors. One day she feared for her safety enough to run to the principal's office, only to be told that the principal would not see her. When she went to a security guard, he told her to ignore the problem, that she was better than the bullies, and anyway would soon graduate. Her mother said, "There was no place she was safe." She and her parents tried to make the school personnel address the problem, but without success (Denn, 2001).

Shortly after graduation from high school, the student filed an unusual reverse-discrimination lawsuit against the Seattle Public Schools claiming that African American students at the school had targeted her because she was Caucasian, leaving lasting scars and bitterness on her education and her life. The lawsuit claimed that the district and her principal had allowed a hostile environment to continue, one in which she was subject to race and gender discrimination, thus violating state and federal laws. The student has finally been vindicated. In 2001, she reached a settlement agreement with the school district.

The problem of racial bullying has been a cause for alarm in some English schools (Kelly & Cohn, 1988). The following account is an interesting example of an effective approach initiated by Leroy Taylor, the head of a Manchester, England school, who became concerned when he overheard children in his school mimicking older children's racist words and phrases. Because racism was a problem in the area, he moved quickly to show that racist talk would not be tolerated in his school. He contacted neighboring schools, and together they formed an antiracism liaison group to discuss what could be done to stop the racist behavior. The techniques they decided on were not new, but they did target different facets of the racist problem.

The first of these procedures was *circle time*. The children sat in a circle and talked about how they felt about racist behavior, their experiences with it, and their concerns about it. Taylor said,

> It was very effective, they handled some very sensitive issues about race, name-calling, and relevant things they had heard about in the community. It proved to be a very effective way of learning about different ethnic cultures and the issues involved in racism. (Leach, 2001, p. 21)

Next, they began a *mentoring program* in which older children from Year 10 would first present a topic related to racism to younger children (Year 5). They then sat in a group and discussed any questions the younger ones raised or any comments they made. Meanwhile, they used assemblies of larger groups of children to talk about racism. The assemblies were planned by older students. Throughout the program they had monitors who reported any racist comments or behavior. In the event of an incident, Mr. Taylor talked to both sets of parents because he felt that it was important for the victim's parents and the victim to know that there was support for them. Also, it was important for the perpetrator not to escape censure. Two and a half years later, there had not been a single significant racist incident.

Racism in any form is an issue that no school should ignore (Kelly & Cohn, 1988), but as racial bullying, it is particularly insidious. It can range from offensive and insulting name calling to assault with a deadly weapon, as in the case of Ahmed Ullah. In 1986 this 13-year-old boy was murdered on the playground of Burnage High School (Manchester, England) by Darren Coulborn, a White student and known bully and racist (Burnage Report, 1989). Name calling continues to be one of the most painful and pervasive forms of racial bullying. The critical difference between racist name calling and other forms of name calling is that the latter are individualized taunts relating specifically to the victim (e.g., "beanpole" or "butthead"), whereas racist names refer not only to the victim but also to the victim's family and whole race (e.g., "Jew Boy" or "Golliwog").

RACIST NAME CALLING

In the most extensive project on bullying to date, the Sheffield Bullying Project in Sheffield, England (Sharp & Smith, 1994; Smith & Sharp, 1994), there was a substantial body of evidence that racist name calling was a major problem. A survey by Whitney and Smith (1993) found that of 6,000 English school children, 14.8% in junior/middle schools and 9.4% in secondary schools complained of "being called nasty names" about their color or race. In a predominantly White school, racist name calling distressed Asian children and was often cited as the reason for their dislike of White children. Moore et al. (1997) reported the same problem in New Zealand schools. According to Sullivan (2000), racist name calling is the tip of the iceberg and an indicator of other forms of racism that are much more difficult to identify as specifically racist.

In some schools, little is done to counter racism because school personnel are reluctant to admit that there is a problem: "There is no problem at all about racism in this school" (principal of an elementary school in which racial bullying on the school bus was a major problem); "The parents and children are overreacting" (response of a principal about complaints of well-documented racial bullying; Akhtar & Stronach, 1986, p. 23). When complaints of racial harassment are brushed aside, the school personnel are, in fact, tacitly condoning racist behavior.

WHEN DOES RACISM BEGIN?

Racism begins in the preschool years (Klein, 1994; Kureishi, 1986). Sometimes it is acquired through the process of incidental learning, that is, by observation of others' behavior (Bandura, 1977), but more often it is transmitted intentionally from parents to their children. The following exchange occurred between two 5-year-old boys at the Stanford University Nursery School:

> *Tom:* After Christmas I'm going to a better nursery school.
> *Bobby:* Why is it better?
> *Tom:* Because there won't be no Black kids there.

The following quote is a heartening example of a teenager, Bridget B., who saw her parents' prejudice in its true light:

> Yesterday was my Junior Prom, which I did not attend. Ever since I was in the ninth grade, I've been thinking about the Junior Prom. What if I don't get asked. . . . The thing is that I did have someone I could have asked, but my parents wouldn't let me because he's Black. My parents say I don't need that kind of date. He's just a friend, but I talk to him every night. He's the only Black kid in school, and he hangs around all White people, so he's just like me except for his color. I get so frustrated. I wish I could explain to my parents that despite what they believe, I believe

> something different. And I couldn't tell him that my parents are prejudiced. He would have felt like crap. Because it isn't his fault. So I just told him I didn't feel like going. (Salinger, 1995, p. 16)

In discussing the intergenerational transmission of racial prejudice, Davey (1983) said that the crux of the problem of racism is an implicit consensus in our society about the status of different ethnic groups. Children learn from this consensual perspective how to evaluate different groups.

Some ethnic groups are seen as easier targets than others for racial bullying. Afro-Caribbeans, for example, are notably able to stand up for themselves and are also well represented in sports and athletics. Consequently, students with racial bullying tendencies treat them with reluctant respect. In contrast, Asians are seen as easy targets. And because they are strongly motivated to be well educated, many see them as a financial threat, a negative attitude that is likely to be communicated to their children. In a study of English secondary school children, Riley (1988) reported that 7 out of 10 children nominated by peers as bullies were found to have racist attitudes. At recess, the groups of ethnic minorities and other students in this school were polarized. In the Netherlands, an interview study of 800 schoolboys ages 12 to 18 from four different ethnic groups (Junger, 1990) found that 20% of the boys were physically harassed from time to time and 6% quite often. The same pattern occurred in the prevalence of verbal abuse. Of particular interest was the finding that there were no differences in victimization by bullying across the four ethnic groups: Turkish, Moroccan, Surinamese, and Dutch. Apparently those harassing these boys viewed any ethnic minority as a justifiable and satisfying target.

Community attitudes exert a pervasive influence that may further cement the parental teachings. Pipher's (1994) description of the small Midwest community where she grew up was permeated with racism:

> Our town took great pride in having no Black or Native American citizens. Restaurant signs that read, "We have the right to refuse service to anyone," were used to exclude non-Whites. Adults told racist jokes and held racist beliefs about ethnic groups they had never met. My father warned me never to dance or talk to Negroes when I went to college or people would think I was low-class. Terms like "jewing people down" and "Indian giver" were part of the language. (p. 241)

For many ethnic minority children, racial bullying is the gauntlet that they have to run in the classroom, playground, and neighborhood every day of their lives. Living in racially hostile neighborhoods often erodes their sense of self-worth long before they reach adulthood; their community devalues them and clearly regards them as an inferior class. Each incident of racism functions cumulatively to further reduce their sense of self-worth.

The police force generally exerts a tremendous influence on how a community views racial bullying and how incidents of racism can further diminish self-esteem in ethnic minority children and adults. In New York, racial bullying by the police is frequently a problem especially for young Blacks and Latinos. Although many of the harassing police are White, significant numbers of Black and Latino police are among those engaging in this abusive behavior. Bob Herbert, a *New York Times* reporter, stated (1997, p. A17):

> If you go into a predominantly Black or Latino neighborhood all you have to do is talk to young people at random. They will tell you how they are stopped, frisked, searched, threatened with arrest if they don't produce identification, cursed at, slapped around, spread-eagled on the ground, thrown against walls, run off of street corners, threatened with weapons. Inevitably some are falsely arrested. Some are brutalized.
>
> A sobering example of this unjustified harassment was reported by Angelissa Hernandez, age 17, who was talking to three friends when the police drove up with their lights flashing. She said, "'What's the problem?' They made all of us turn around and put our hands against the wall. The cop searching me put his hand on my behind very firmly and he squeezed it. I was very upset. I moved forward and I looked at him. He said, 'I thought I felt a weapon there.'" After searching Angelissa and her friends, for no apparent reason and with no explanation or apology, the police left.

WHAT CAN PARENTS DO?

When children are targets of racial bullying, their parents should follow the general procedures for bullying described in chapter 3. However, when the children are subjected to racial name calling, they should ignore the problems of those engaging in this antisocial behavior and make no attempt to change their attitudes or to reason with them. This is a waste of time. Apart from encouraging target children to say in a very firm voice, "Stop that, I don't like it when you call me names" and then to continue with their activity or walk away, parents should focus on helping the children in other ways.

Attack the problem *directly* by listening sympathetically and offering reassurance about their right to feel angry (at the same time being clear about not retaliating with physical attacks because this immediately puts them in the wrong); briefly discuss the ignorance underlying racial name calling; then mention incidents from your own past, how you felt, and how you handled them. Occasionally, when the children are present, one parent should talk about a current incident in which he or she was the target, and then discuss with the other parent what happened, how it felt, and so on. Make a distinction between this specific experience, in which *one* person made racist remarks, and the danger of stereotyping, which is believing that because a White person called you names, then *all* White people are suspect. Acknowledge that it often looks as if a very large number of people fall into the negative category, but emphasize that this does not justify regarding all people in a negative way.

Much can be done *indirectly* to help children who are potential targets for racial bullying. When the children are at an early age, possibly age 3 or 4, begin to include fiction and nonfiction books that deal with prejudice among the stories that you routinely read to the children. Insert these with no particular emphasis, sometimes discussing them, other times not. Often the children will make spontaneous comments that lead to a discussion. At no time imply that the children can expect the same negative experiences as those described in some of the books. (The Annotated Bibliography at the end of this text lists fiction and nonfiction specifically related to understanding and dealing with prejudice.) Work on the children's appearance so that neither their clothes nor hair styles are so far out of line with the norm for their grade level that they are likely to elicit verbal attacks. Spend time teaching them the social skills that they need to handle with ease commonly occurring interactions with other children and adults. Playing simple board games, for example, teaches taking turns, following rules, having only one turn at a time, playing in order, and losing (or winning) with reasonable grace. Teach the children to be assertive. Have them practice how to respond politely but firmly to unjustified criticism—for example, what to say when unavoidably late or when unable to complete an assigned task. Too often in this kind of situation, children become mute while simmering with anger at the unfairness of an accusation. Encourage the development of skills, especially one athletic skill, and talents. When children are stars in some area, prowess is likely to take precedence over racial and rreligious differences. All of the foregoing will result in increasing independence and feelings of being in control, along with heightened self-esteem.

Sexual Harassment

Sexual harassment is defined as unwanted and unwelcome sexual behavior that interferes with another person's life. In his book, *Unwanted Sex: The Culture of Intimidation and the Failure of Law,* Stephen Schulhofer (1998) described two types of sexual harassment. One occurs when a person with authority over others, such as a student, parent, teacher, or employee, uses that position to offer favors in exchange for sex and threatens the victim with punishment for failing to comply. The other kind of harassment occurs when peers create a hostile environment within a setting such as a school, school bus, or office. In these situations one or more people make inappropriate sexual comments, gestures, or accusations of homosexuality and put severe pressure on an individual for sexual favors.

In the United States sexual harassment is rampant even in elementary and secondary schools (Colino, 1993; Stein, 1993). Unequivocal evidence of its extent comes from a 1993 survey sponsored by the American Association of University Women (AAUW) that documented the incidence of sexual harassment in 8th- through 11th-grade students (N = 1,632) in 79 public schools across the continental United States (AAUW Educational Foundation, 1993).

The study was conducted in an exemplary fashion. Classes were randomly selected, with no teacher participation in the data collection. The questionnaires were anonymous, with the questions referring to school-related experiences during school hours. The respondents were asked how often, if ever, they had experienced 14 types of sexual harassment, half of which involved physical contact and half no physical contact (see Figure 5.1). Also included were questions of when and where sexual harassment was first experienced; if they themselves engaged in it; why they did so; whom they told about it, if anyone; and what impact the sexual harassment had had on them educationally, behaviorally, and emotionally.

The results were staggering: Eighty-one percent of the respondents reported some experience of sexual harassment in school, most of which occurred in the hallways and classrooms, and of this group, 1 in 3 girls and 1 in 5 boys had experienced it frequently. Peers were responsible for 4 out of 5 incidents, but adult school personnel sexually harassed 1 in 4 girls and 1 in 10 boys. Students usually did not report any incidents to adults, especially not to teachers, and boys were less likely than girls to tell anyone. On the issue of being called a lesbian or gay, girls felt that they would be very upset, and boys rated it as the most disturbing form of sexual harassment. Suffering, in such forms as not wanting to go to school, being embarrassed and upset, and feel-

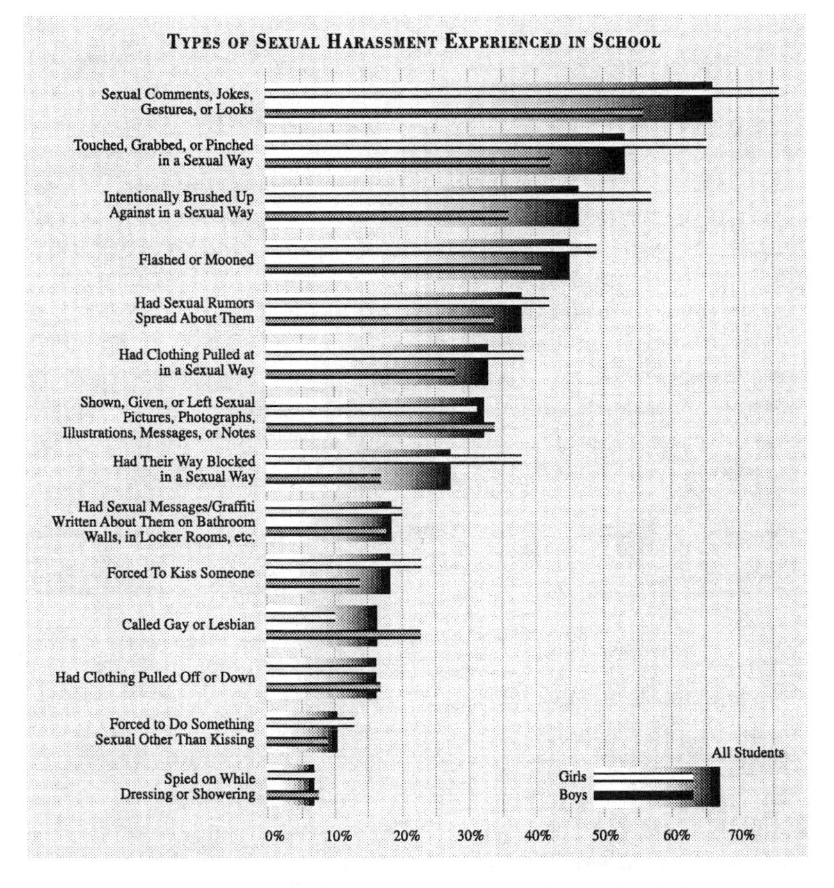

Figure 5.1. Types of Sexual Harassment Experienced in School

Reproduced with permission of the AAUW Educational Foundation. (1993). *Hostile Hallways: The AAUW Survey on Sexual Harassment in America's Schools* (p. 9). © American Association of University Women Educational Foundation.

ing a loss of confidence, was experienced less by boys than by girls, particularly White and Black American girls. The latter group were subjected to an alarming amount of sexual harassment involving physical contact. Figure 5.1 shows the percentages by gender for each of the 14 kinds of sexual harassment experienced in school by the respondents (81% of the 1,632 students) who reported being harassed.

In 1992 a national scandal erupted over the behavior of aviators in the U.S. Navy and Marine Corps attending their annual convention of the Tailhook Association. An aide to Admiral Jack Snyder, Lieutenant

Paula Coughlin, had gone to the association party to deliver a message, been swept unwillingly into a mob of drunken aviators, and then been sexually assaulted. Her attempts to report and complain about the experience were first brushed aside by the Admiral and then moved so slowly through the complaint hierarchy that she next took her case to the news media and then the courts. More than 80 women also stated that they were assaulted or molested. Lieutenant Coughlin won her court case, and 12 other lawsuits were pending. Some high-ranking officers were demoted and a number of promotions withheld (Zimmerman, 1995). This incident is included here because it bears a chilling resemblance to the kinds of sexual harassment that a group of 13- and 14-year-old girls from a junior high school in Washington State described to me as commonplace at their school. Table 5.1 contains their comments, along with quotes from Zimmerman's book (pp. 17, 18, 25) on the Tailhook scandal.

Table 5.1. Parallels Between Tailhook and Sexual Harassment in Junior High School

Tailhook	Junior High School
Women were getting "zapped," having squadron stickers slapped on strategic parts of their bodies.	Girls get "graded"; the guys have stickers with letter grades, and they put them on your breasts and butts and other private places.
Suddenly there were hands reaching out at her, a frenzy of groping, touching, and feeling. She felt hands insert themselves inside her blouse, hands up her skirt. She screamed, "Stop." Nobody stopped. "Here were 5 or 6 guys . . . grabbing my crotch from different angles."	"I dived off the highboard and when I came up the guys were all round me. Then they put their hands inside my top and others squeezed my butt and tried to tear my suit off and some were poking their fingers in my crotch. I yelled for help and their hands were all over me." No one helped.
"I told another aviator and he grinned and said, 'I guess you've just been through the gauntlet.' "	"When I told the man at the pool he just laughed, 'You just got caught in the whirlpool, baby.' "
. . . he had hold of her breasts as if he thought they were handles.	". . . he grabbed my boobs and it was like he was steering a motorbike."

Another case of sexual harassment by the Navy involved a lone female sailor aboard a torpedo retriever boat stationed in Puget Sound, Washington. Two sailors under the command of Boatswain's Mate 2nd Class Dean A. Raymond were charged with throwing the female sailor into frigid waters off Vancouver Island in February 1993. One of the pair admitted that he had grabbed her and simulated sexual intercourse while the other confessed to yanking her hair while making demeaning sexual remarks. This appalling and dangerous behavior took place after the crew had attended sexual harassment prevention training, which raised serious questions about the content and quality of the training (*Seattle Post-Intelligencer*, 1993).

Particularly disturbing is the fact that sexual language, touching in a sexual way, and other inappropriate sexual behaviors are reported to be commonplace even in the primary grades. The following instances of sexual harassment of a 7-year-old in an elementary school in an upper-middle-class district in Washington State are representative of how she had been treated (Harrell, 2000, p. B3):

> Two boys grabbed her and threatened her, held her down and told her another boy "was going to have sex with her on Valentine's Day."
>
> Several boys "called the girl names, pinned her up against a wall and poked her breasts with pencils."

Further evidence of young children's familiarity with sexual language comes from teacher reports. A group of primary grade (K-3) teachers at a conference said that all of the following words were used "quite frequently" by children in their classes, particularly Grades 2 and 3: lesbie, gay, gay-gay, boobs, buns, and fucker. Teachers as well as school psychologists stated that these words occurred far more frequently than had been the case 10 or 15 years ago. The children rarely understood the meaning of the words, but they did see them as negative and sexually related. One Grade 2 teacher (J. J. Underwood, personal communication, April 1969) said she overheard two girls in her class discussing lesbians:

> *First Girl:* What's a lesbie?
>
> *Second Girl:* It's when two ladies do things in bed with no clothes on like mommies and daddies do, you know? Only two ladies do it and it's a wicked thing to do. And that's why I called Jenny a lesbie 'cos she's wicked.

The same teacher heard a boy telling another boy that gay-gay meant a boy could never be a man when he grew up. He was not sure what would happen, but he did not think that the man could be a lady either because gay-gays never had babies.

What has caused this precocious, pseudo-knowledgeable awareness of sex? *Social learning theory* offers the explanation that the older children in a K-6 school are usually high-status models: Younger children imitate them, and sexual taunts lend themselves to imitation because they have an appealingly daring quality. *Sex on television and in films* is becoming increasingly more frequent and explicit and is being shown at times that favor child viewing. As Bandura (1986) has shown, children imitate television models almost as much as they do live models. Sexual actions (groping, pulling up girls' skirts, bra-snapping) and words are acquired by the viewers. *Girls and boys are maturing earlier.* An increasing number of girls are beginning to menstruate and show signs of physical maturation before 10 years of age. This earlier maturation results in an earlier interest in sexual matters, which, in turn, leads to more usually uninformed discussion with peers. Sexually related taunts also follow, rather than the more commonplace ones about general appearance such as red hair or freckles. In addition, all the public discussion about AIDS, the need to use condoms, and abortion issues has focused children's attention on sexual activities.

SCHOOL LIABILITY FOR SEXUAL HARASSMENT

Teachers whom I have spoken to generally feel ill equipped to handle sexual taunts and unwanted physical contact. Consequently, when a child gets up the nerve to complain about sexual harassment, the teacher often brushes it aside, usually accompanied by platitudes. This reaction is especially true of male teachers. The failure to act is seen by the perpetrator as condoning his or her actions, and so the behavior continues. Halting the harassment usually occurs only when parents enter the fray with implicit threats of lawsuits and consequent financial loss to the school district. Consider the following example (Stein, 1993).

Beginning in December 1992, a fifth-grade girl, LaShonda Davis, was harassed repeatedly over the course of several months by a boy in her class. The offenses included trying to touch her breasts and genital area, saying "I want to feel your boobs" and "I want to get in bed with you," and rubbing his body against her. At one time he put a door stop in his pants and acted in a sexually suggestive manner. As the harassment continued, LaShonda's previously high grades dropped, and in April 1993, her father (according to court testimony) discovered a suicide note that she had written. Following a series of complaints to the school, all of which were brushed aside, her mother called the sheriff and LaShonda filed a federal lawsuit under Title IX of the 1972 Education Amendments to the Civil Rights Act, which bars sex discrimination in schools and colleges that receive federal funds. School officials had no choice but to take action, and the boy pleaded guilty to sexual battery. The case went to the Supreme Court, and on May 24, 1999, in a landmark 5-4 ruling, Justice Sandra Day O'Connor declared that schools receiving federal funds can be held financially liable for damages when school personnel react with "deliberate indifference" to known acts of student-on-student sexual harassment. She also wrote:

> Schools are liable only where they are deliberately indifferent to sexual harassment of which they have actual knowledge, that is so severe, pervasive and objectively offensive that it can be said to deprive the victims of access to the educational opportunities or benefits provided by the school. (Page, 1999, p. A18)

In an extraordinarily weak dissent, Justice Anthony M. Kennedy wrote:

> The real world of school discipline is a rough-and-tumble place where students practice newly learned vulgarities, erupt with anger, tease and embarrass each other, share offensive notes, flirt, push and shove in the halls, grab and offend. (Page, 1999, p. A18)

Justice Kennedy's reaction to LaShonda's plight reflects a curious similarity to the "boys will be boys" line of thought many men have about even severe bullying. Going a little farther afield, this indulgent point of view also applies to the slap-on-the-wrist type of punishment doled out to drunk drivers whose actions have caused deaths. There is certainly an undercurrent of admiration for all these behaviors, possibly because they are erroneously thought to represent a kind of desirable masculinity. This implicit admiration affects behavior well beyond the school settings for children and adolescents. Two other settings involving adults are described next.

SEXUAL HARASSMENT IN THE OFFICE SETTING

Although sexual harassment has been a problem whenever men and women have shared the same working environment, research on this problem did not begin until the late 1970s (see, e.g., Collins & Blodgett, 1981; Hern & Parkin, 1987). It has been defined by Gutek,

Cohen, and Konrad (1990, p. 560) as "any non-work related behavior having a sexual component, including harassment, flirting, and making sexual jokes." This definition covers a wide range of behaviors, from making subtle comments to women employees in front of other workers to rape. Over 50% of employees report some kind of social/sexual problems in the workplace (Gutek, 1985), and 10% of women resign from the workplace because of these problems (Randall, 1997). Sexual harassment does happen to men in the workplace but far less often than to women (Burke, 1995). One reason for this difference is that men are less likely to lodge a formal complaint, but when surveyed in private, they form a relatively high percentage of those experiencing it (Randall, 1997).

The effects on the victims are clearly negative. Burke (1995) reported that women who experienced sexual harassment in the workplace were dissatisfied with their jobs, had lower overall satisfaction with the firm, were determined to resign, but were pessimistic about obtaining a fair process when reporting this harassment. Consider this case study (Randall, 1997, p. 71):

> Carol was a newly married 22-year-old clerical worker who was delighted to get a job in a planning office. She rapidly became the sexual joke of the four men in the office. Claiming that it was only fun, they touched her legs, bumped into her breasts when passing, and frequently leered at her. At first she laughed rather nervously with them but after some weeks told them to stop it. One of them grabbed her hair and another threatened to beat up her young husband. The sexual behavior stopped but the physical intimidation increased. Carol began to lose her appetite, her periods became erratic and her sexual relationship with her husband ceased. . . . She was "cured" instantly upon getting another job in an all-female office.

Aversive sexual behavior, common in office bullying, includes any non-work-related behavior having a sexual component. Examples here are inappropriate touching, unreciprocated flirting, and crude sexual jokes (Gutek et al., 1990):

> Tom brushes against Marie, his subordinate, and makes suggestive comments. Marie feels that if she ignores him, he will stop. But he does not stop. He waits until they are alone and then he touches her. She tells him to stop, but Tom says, "You didn't stop me before. If you tell anyone, I'll say you encouraged me. Anyway, it's only a bit of fun." (Randall, 1997, p. 119)

SEXUAL HARASSMENT IN MEDICAL SCHOOLS

When Frances Conley was admitted to the Stanford University School of Medicine in 1961, she and the other women students in her class were as well prepared as the men for the rigor of medical training. None of them, however, had anticipated that they would also face the problem of sexual harassment from residents to attending physicians. This ranged from sexual innuendos, to blatant verbal descriptions of sexual activities, to unwanted physical contact. Conley was able to wend her way through the recurring roadblocks that many women experienced to become the first tenured professor of neurosurgery in the United States and was widely recognized for her breakthrough research on brain tumors. This sterling record was not strong enough to offset the medical school's response to the enormous negative national reaction and resultant negative publicity directed at Stanford Medical School that occurred following the publication of her account of what went on at the medical school (Conley, 1998). One of the humiliations heaped on her was the immediate withdrawal of her access to her laboratory privileges, which, in effect, halted ongoing and future research. She subsequently resigned, which resulted in another wave of nationwide criticism of the university. Her book made a real contribution: It made public what many victims had been powerless to withstand, provided strong support for potential victims, and imposed the threat of retaliation against aggressors. It also provided a channel of communication for those women in medical fields to describe their own experiences of sexual harassment in support of Conley's account, as a national rather than an individual problem.

In the early 1990s, surveys of female physicians across the United States revealed that 50% to 80% had experienced sexual harassment or gender discrimination during their time as medical students and residents (Conley, 1998). In the medical field, particularly surgery, it was accepted that women were "fair game." This view applied to any level, from clerical staff up to qualified doctors. Extortion was not uncommon: Satisfying doctors' sexual appetites could mean preferential treatment, a job, or career advancement. Refusal could result in a negative report or even dismissal. Operating nurses were subjected to considerable abuse (breasts fondled, crotches grabbed), which they could not control without breaking a sterile field and potentially endangering the life of an unconscious patient. When sexual harassment complaints were filed, they generally were ignored. If the victims persisted, they were often terminated for nonspecific reasons such as "poor performance on the job."

In 1992 Adriane Fugh-Berman, MD, wrote a blistering condemnation of the Georgetown Medical School based on her experiences there as a student. Minimal changes occurred nationwide as a result of her charges. At most medical schools the solution to the sex harassment problem was to appoint a relatively low-level person in the administration, usually a woman, to be "sexual harassment coordinator." Very few of these appointees had a direct line to the top administrators, and the allegations were usually dismissed. Two notable exceptions (Conley, 1998) are Yale and MIT, where those responsible for reviewing complaints of harassment did have direct access to the university president and complaints were properly handled.

Homosexuality

Homosexuality is a normal variant of human sexuality that is primarily genetically determined (Pollack, 2000). It is not a disease, nor is it a direction that adolescents and young adults *choose* to follow. Instead, it is an aspect of themselves that between 5% and 10% of men of all nationalities and racial and ethnic backgrounds discover in adolescence or early adulthood. Although being gay is clearly extremely difficult for many people, attitudes toward it have changed to some extent. In the 1950s boys felt that being gay was strictly forbidden and even talking about it was viewed as extremely dangerous. This attitude persists today in that the initial reaction of gay adolescents is usually an attempt to hide this knowledge from their families, other adults, and friends. However, many schools now are emphasizing that whether one is gay or straight is simply another variable in the person's personality. In a large, nationwide interview study of boys in general, Pollack (2000) found that many of the boys thought that a person's sexual orientation should not affect how he or she was treated by their peers. Typical of this attitude is the following response by an 18-year-old boy:

> The Matthew Shepard case (murdered because he was gay) offers a lot of lessons. It teaches us that we should all try to be open to one another, that no matter who we are, we should be able to get along. . . . The news that someone had killed him because he was gay made me incredibly angry. . . . The news made me want to change things in our society. (Pollack, 2000, pp. 284, 287)

Further support for gay people comes from the Presbyterian Church (U.S.A.). At the recent Presbyterian General Assembly, the gathering voted decisively to end the prohibition on noncelibate gay clergy, elders, and deacons that had divided the denomination since 1978. To take effect, the Assembly's stance must be ratified within 1 year by a majority of the 173 regional presbyteries. The man chosen to lead this cause is theologian Jack Rogers, who decades ago helped the church to embrace the ordination of women, and 8 years ago came to see that the Presbyterian ban on openly gay clergy was just as wrong as its earlier support of slavery and racial segregation. At the Presbyterian General Assembly, he was overwhelmingly elected to the top position of Moderator, and he will spend most of the next year convincing churches to embrace their gay members (Price, 2001).

Despite these gains, much of the discomfort that many gay people continue to experience is not the result of their homosexuality but rather society's fear of homosexuality, that is, homophobia. In America, homophobia is the cruelest form of what Pollack (2000) has called the *Boy Code prejudice*. It prevents gay people from being completely integrated into the social group. Gay students are more likely to succumb to the harassment of their straight peers and to skip classes, drop out of school, or commit suicide. In fact, gay students account for up to 30% of teenage suicides (Pollack, 2000). A recent report from the Gay, Lesbian, and Straight Education Network (GLSEN, 2000) showed that 58% of gay students who were interviewed did not feel safe at school, over 90% heard homophobic taunts there, and 28% had been physically harassed. Similarly, a recent study by the Massachusetts Department of Education (2000) reported that 24% of gay and lesbian students were either threatened with a weapon or injured with one, compared with 8% of other students, and 19% had stayed home from school in the past month because they feared for their safety, compared with 6% of other students. Consider the following case of a boy erroneously taunted as being gay:

> William J. moved from the northeastern to the southeastern part of the United States when he was in the fourth grade. He was small and less well developed than most of the boys in his new class, and he had less physical ability for sports and games. He appeared timid and withdrawn when he entered school, and his mother came with him the first day to help him become familiar with the new location. On the second day Willy, a very large student in class, began teasing William about the way he talked, making fun of William's accent and calling him a Yankee and a queer, two very unpopular terms in that geographical location. William began to cry, which provoked Willy to become even more aggressive. Willy told the other students that William's tears proved he was right because queers and Yankees cry a lot and are

> sissies. This caused the other students to laugh at William, and others began teasing him about his accent, too. Each day the taunting and teasing increased and several of the boys began to push, trip, and shove William. No students came to William's defense, and he continued to withdraw and began getting sick each day before school. (Horne, Glaser, & Sayger, 1994, p. 1112)

A major problem for gay men and lesbians (and children like William) is that they often do not get adequate support from school personnel. When two high school students in Reno, Nevada, threw a lasso around the neck of a gay fellow student and threatened to drag him from a pickup truck, he sought help from school administrators only to be cautioned by the principal against "acting like a fag." This student has since filed a federal lawsuit against the school district (Kirby, 2001).

The homosexual as the victim in the bully–victim sequence is an undisputed fact. Kirby (2001) has raised the possibility of a reversal of roles, that the homosexual may assume the bully role. He reasoned that society's negative attitudes to homosexuality may prompt gay men and lesbians who are determined to conform to their ideals to become bullies themselves: A gay man from Los Angeles said that when his classmates started to pick up on the fact that he might be gay, he masked his sexual orientation by bullying another boy on the school bus every day. He said, "I really abused him a lot. I knew I was wrestling with my own sexuality. When you are being oppressed, it is easy to become the oppressor" (Kirby, 2001, p. 32). Kevin Jennings, the executive director of GLSEN in New York, concurred. He stated, "Few are seeing the all-too-obvious pattern. Young people are being taunted with antigay epithets and are then lashing out" (Kirby, 2001, p. 32).

COMMENT

In a remarkably short time the social environment has embraced an atmosphere of blatant sexuality that permeates most facets of daily living. From an early age children are exposed to explicit visual presentations in television, magazines, and films that even as recently as 15 years ago would not have been allowed. Much of what is seen far exceeds most children's capabilities for understanding the social elements and consequences. Yet these children acquire a superficial and glib grasp of adult sexuality, with its sheen of sophistication and accompanying demands, that they are ill equipped to handle. Peer pressure to conform becomes a potent force in an already high-anxiety situation. The effect on the child is to heighten a desperate need to talk to someone, yet too often the line of communication with parents is too weak to handle genuine problems and anxieties that are troubling the child. To break through this impasse, it is essential that parents learn how to talk to their children about meaningful and sometimes threatening topics as a first step in offering constructive support and guidance. A particularly fine book has come out on communicating with sons. Titled *Real Boys' Voices* (Pollack, 2000), it should be mandatory reading for all parents. Although it is solely about boys, the principles involved in it would also apply to girls.

Bullying of Adults

Randall (1997), in his excellent text on adult bullying, made the following comment:

> The beginnings of this book lie . . . in the surprising finding that many adult victims are so desperate for help that they were prepared to use a hotline established for children. When . . . Mike Donohue and I set up a community anti-bullying project and included the hotline as part of its services we were greatly surprised to find that a third of all the callers were adults seeking help for themselves because they were being badly bullied. As their stories unfolded we discovered that adult bullying has a shocking reality that is unsuspected by the majority of the population.

Interest in the bullying of adult workers began in Sweden in the 1960s when Heinz Leymann, MD, PhD, began treating the Swedish victims of bullying (he used the term *mobbing*) in the world's first clinic for adults who had been traumatized at work. Leymann defined *mobbing* as psychological terror in working life that involves hostile and unethical communication and is directed in a systematic manner by one or more individuals toward one individual who is pushed into a helpless and defenseless position and held there by means of continuing mobbing activities. These actions occur at least once a week and over a period of at least 6 months duration. Because of the frequency and duration of the hostile behavior, this maltreatment results in considerable mental, psychosomatic, and social misery (Randall, 1997).

Leymann believed that the chances of healing from acute trauma from bullying were reduced if the victim faced continuing threats. He also described the level of posttraumatic stress suffered by mobbing victims as more intense and persistent than that felt by train operators who have witnessed suicides by people leaping onto the railroad tracks in front of them. Leymann's ideas focused attention on what had become a widespread problem, and in the early 1980s, when his scientific publications on mobbing first appeared, they served to delineate and clarify the issues.

In 1994 a Swedish ordinance on measures against victimization at work was enacted, further consolidating Sweden's position as a front runner in the workplace bullying field. Other countries lagged behind: England was 10 years behind Sweden, and the United States was at least 20 years behind in focusing on workplace bullying (Adams, 1992).

The research on victimization has shown that many victims who were miserable throughout their school years generally are much happier in early adulthood because they can choose their place of work and also their friends (Ross, 1996). However, some victims continue to present a victim demeanor and are easy targets for bullies in supervisory positions of power. In fact, workplace bullying has become a serious problem in the United States. Every day it keeps thousands of people away from work; causes tension and, in some cases, illness; and prevents otherwise able adults from realizing their potential (Randall, 1997). According to the American Institute of Stress (Namie & Namie, 2000), job stress of all kinds including bullying-related stress is the leading source of stress for adult Americans. The National Safety Council (Namie & Namie, 2000) estimates that 1 million employees are absent on an average workday because of stress-related problems. Job stress is estimated to cost American industry between $200 and $300 billion annually.

Employers and senior personnel have frequently been slow to recognize the seriousness of this problem (Adams, 1992), possibly because bullying is looked on as a childhood problem. Consequently, interpersonal abuse in the workplace is not dealt with in a supportive manner. In addition, employees (particularly if new on the job) are often reluctant to complain to management; when they do so, their accounts are likely to be brushed aside by their immediate superiors. The crux of the problem may often lie in the submissiveness of the victim that characterized his or her inability to cope effectively with bullying in the victim's school days and continues to be a major problem for him or her in the workplace (Randall, 1997, p. 27).

BULLYING IN THE WORK SETTING

Joe, a 37-year-old man, referred himself through an antibullying hotline because he had become so ashamed of his submissive behavior.

His line manager was a large, physically intimidating, ex-rugby player who had taken a delight in making Joe, a thin, asthmatic, bespectacled man, back down whenever he could. Joe found himself being used to demonstrate rugby tackles and karate kicks and punches. The line manager also took great pleasure in telling Joe, in sexually explicit detail, what he would like to do to Joe's wife. Over a period of time Joe found that he had gradually adopted a strategy of inviting the bully's coarse humor early in the working day because once the bully "got it off his chest" the rest of the day would be reasonably comfortable. Joe was painfully aware that this submissive behavior could become a permanent habit pattern. . . . He wanted desperately to know how to end the misery (Randall, 1997).

Premeditated aggression is a common type of bullying in the work setting. It includes a large assortment of aggressive behaviors such as violent assault, threats of violence, verbal attacks, subtle harassment, as well as blatant racial harassment, gossip, rumor-mongering, and being ignored. Consider this example of racial harassment:

> A group of workers makes jokes about black people in front of Sarita, who at first pretends not to hear, then tells them they are offensive. They retaliate by saying, "That's the trouble with Pakis—no sense of humor," and increase the frequency of the racial comments. One member of the group pushes her roughly when she comments about their racism. She tells the supervisor, who says, "They're only having a joke. Don't be so sensitive." (Randall, 1997, p. 120)

Bullies in the work setting usually engage in indirect bullying. Their behavior is generally common knowledge but is often not reported to superiors. Sometimes they make inaccurate and unfair criticisms of the employees under their jurisdiction as a way of advancing their own goals. Some do not last long in the job because their behavior is so clearly counterproductive, but others are successful despite their bullying because they are clearly intelligent workers capable of making significant contributions to the organization (Murano, 1995). Consider this case study from Randall (1997, pp. 58–59):

> Jean Reynolds held a middle-management post in one of a chain of small supermarkets. Her regional boss, Anne, was a relentless bully, she started "the minute I entered the shop. . . . I overheard her telling one of the assistants that I might look good but that I probably was some blonde with an empty head. . . . The whole of the first week she kept on making derogatory remarks. I felt

> totally amazed . . . we didn't even know each other before I worked with her."
>
> "I confronted her and asked what she meant by it. She just looked embarrassed and said I was making it up. After a series of other completely false complaints about me (contradicted by compliments from other staff about my work), I just caved in."
>
> "Later, she reported me for making one local personal telephone call and gave the impression that I was always doing this. She told the Area Director I was a totally inadequate person who was always coming to her for help and was a liability around the shop. All this, despite the fact that I was doing what I was supposed to do well and had compliments from the other staff for it.
>
> "The next major thing that happened was that I found out that she had been encouraging suppliers to make complaints about me on the grounds that I had been rude or inefficient with them. She listened to my conversations with our buyers and went back to them later to change my decisions with them.
>
> "The last thing to happen was that she tore up a sick-note from my doctor and told the Area Director that I had been malingering. By this time other people had begun to side with her; they were afraid not to. In the end I just caved in."

A particularly insidious type of adult bullying occurs in situations that would be difficult or impossible for the victims to leave. The Armed Forces are an example of such situations, so it is not surprising that bullying has always been a problem (A. O. Ross, personal communication, May 1996). Armed Forces personnel cannot readily resign before their tour of duty ends without having damaging comments such as "unlikely to become an effective soldier" on their record. Complaints to a senior officer usually lead to retaliation from the bullies. Whether physical or psychological, short or long term, the intention is always to inflict pain and humiliation. The long-term effects can be extremely serious:

> The grandson of a Black American GI joined an English regiment when he was 16. He was bullied for 7½ years. Among the many serious racial abuses he was subjected to were being found "guilty" by a kangaroo court of being Black. He was then given a bath of bleach and urine and scrubbed with brushes. While serving in Germany he was frequently referred to as "nigger boy," "Black boy," "wog," or "coon." He left the army in 1991 and in 1993 he was awarded 8,000 English pounds compensation for the bullying he had experienced. (Randall, 1997, p. 12)

BULLYING OF SCHOOL PERSONNEL

Bullying occurs from the top to the bottom of the status range. In England, many school teachers are being made miserable because of bullying by the heads and governors of schools as well as by parents. In 1995, more than 10,000 members of the National Association of Schoolmasters Union of Women Teachers responded to a national survey of claims of bullying (Dean, 1995). Members were asked to describe in detail the form that bullying took.

The first results revealed widespread bullying of teachers by school managers who were clearly overstepping the boundaries of hands-on management. One in five victims said that they had resigned from their teaching positions rather than be subjected to further bullying. The most typical forms of bullying ranged from destructive innuendo and heavy unjustified sarcasm to daily unannounced entry into ongoing classes by school governors, untrue accusations of insubordination, threats of future dismissal, and assaults by parents making unjustified demands about their children's grades.

An official who was conducting the survey said that a male head of school had grabbed a pregnant teacher and dragged her into his office before berating her for becoming pregnant 6 months after being promoted. A female primary school teacher wrote (Dean, 1995, p. 6):

> The acting head of the school is a bully. He used to corner me and other teachers, and put his face very close to ours and grill us. Sometimes he'd shout at us in public. He would cause a public scene over the most stupid, trivial things.

A male secondary teacher who was bullied by a female head of department complained (Dean, 1995, p. 6):

> She overloaded me with unnecessary extra work, made unreasonable demands, discredited me in the eyes of parents, pupils and colleagues, displayed a contemptuous, insulting attitude toward me, and generally made life as difficult for me as possible.

There is no question that harassment has forced many teachers in England to quit. The growing number who have left the profession early through ill health or stress-related illnesses has increased dramatically from 2,449 in 1984–1985 to 5,535 in 1993–1994. The majority of these teachers had excellent records and were highly regarded by their colleagues.

BULLYING AT THE COLLEGE LEVEL

Bullying is also a major problem in colleges in England, with one in seven lecturers being the victim of severe and unjustified harassment. An intensive study of bullying in the university setting showed that between 15% and 22% of full-time lecturers had been victims of bullying at some point in their careers. Eighty percent of lecturers thought that work-related stress in colleges had reached unacceptable levels (Nash, 1995). The types of bullying included sexual and racial discrimination, threats of redundancy, spreading malicious rumors, public humiliation, demotion for no justifiable reason, unfairly heavy teaching schedules, and isolation by not allowing lecturers to attend department meetings. Many senior staff who were bullied retired; other victims reported extreme insomnia, depression, eating disorders, and increased alcohol consumption. Many also began to blame themselves rather than the perpetrators for their predicament. It is interesting that this reaction is also common to a wide range of victims: Children who are bullied often feel that they deserve such treatment, and wives who are abused by their husbands commonly come to believe that the abuse is justified. Research at the university level shows that this distortion of reality extends even to highly educated university personnel. Corroborative evidence that those with management responsibilities were using intimidation and other bullying tactics comes from the Industrial Society, the College Lecturers' Union, and the Campaign for Academic Freedom and Standards, in addition to a cluster of research studies (Nash, 1995).

The causes of this deteriorating situation are somewhat convoluted, but all point to poor management. Government pressures for cost-saving measures have led to mass redundancies even among the highly capable. The result has been the promotion of inexperienced subordinates to management status, or as the Peter Principle states, "the scum rises to the top." It is clear that colleges need to review and revise their management practices, because in the clamor to cut costs by devolving duties and teaching responsibilities to lower paid, inexperienced staff, an army of incompetents is taking over.

It would be interesting to know if some of the adult bullies who have been described here are a late-onset bullying group. For example, are some of the school principals, military personnel, and prison guards who are bullies individuals who in childhood and adolescence secretly envied aggressive bullies? It is possible that they were deterred from exhibiting bullying behavior until they found themselves in positions of power, coupled with low supervision and subordinates who were in no position to complain.

The frequency of the foregoing bullying problems is on the increase. One solution to this problem would be to have adequate personnel harassment policies and complaint procedures in place that are fully backed by support from the highest levels of management, with consistent enforcement and regular monitoring by senior managers who will take action as problems occur. This is essentially a *management* approach to the problem of workplace bullying. The ideal plan would be to combine the management approach with a *preventive* one by having compulsory programs in all public schools. These would focus on teaching acceptance of other races and religions, stopping bullying and teasing, and providing intervention for children with bully or victim tendencies. A particularly vital component of this intervention would be intensive assertive training to counteract the submissive tendencies in potential victims.

LESSONS FROM WORKPLACE BULLYING AND SCHOOL BULLYING

In a commentary to a special issue of the *Journal of Community and Applied Social Psychology*, Smith (1997) advocated a creative approach to extending our understanding of bullying with the question, What can studies of workplace bullying and school bullying learn from each other? He believed that "there are useful lessons—ideas for potential research, and warnings of potential difficulties—to be learnt in both directions" (Smith, 1997, p. 250).

Starting with the fact that the bully in the workplace is often in a line management position to the victim (Randall, 1997), Smith (1997) pointed out that the direct analogy in the school situation would be a teacher's bullying of children. In view of Bandura's (1986) prolific research on the effects on observers of aggressive models, it is surprising that the effects on children of a teacher who is a bully have apparently never been subjected to empirical test. Using Smith's analogy of the teacher as a bully, several basic research questions immediately come to mind: How many teachers are bullies? In classes where the teacher is a bully, are there more bullies than in classes where the teacher is not a bully?

A second analogy in the school situation would be a principal's bullying of teachers. Although this possibility has rarely been investigated in the United States or Canada, it has been the subject of a number of recent surveys in England, where school teachers and university faculty members have been subjected to such abuse by those who are higher in the chain of command that resignations are rampant, leaving many school districts desperately short of qualified people. Clearly, a bully in charge qualifies as a warning of potential difficulties.

In his commentary, Smith (1997) noted that research on the organizational characteristics of schools that facilitate or inhibit bullying is in the earliest stages. One such characteristic that should be investigated is *traffic flow*, a problem given high priority in the workplace in the interests of increased productivity and economic gain but of little concern in the schools. In many new schools, the halls are too narrow, stairways are overcrowded at intervals during the day, and restrooms (one of the preferred places for bullying) are inadequate in number and typically too small for peak period usage. Crowded, noisy conditions provide protective coloring for bullies. One solution would be to stagger the times that different groups eat, go to recess and lunch, and are dismissed, a solution that works in large offices and factories. There is no reason why it could not be implemented in the schools, although the school bus timetables would require some juggling.

In the reverse direction, several procedures used in reducing school bullying could benefit the workplace. In schools, trained personnel (school psychologists, counselors, and student advisers) are usually available for troubled students to consult. These professionals often provide training, such as assertiveness training and other forms of social support, for those students who need it. In contrast, the employees in the workplace must generally take complaints to an immediate superior, who usually is the reason for the complaint and so is unlikely to be either sympathetic or impartial. There should be trained personnel routinely available for consultation with employees with bullying superiors. For students, hotlines similar to ChildLine (MacLeod & Morris, 1996) and complaint boxes provide assured anonymity to students with complaints. Such procedures would meet a real need in the workplace.

6 Teasing: An Overview

Childhood teasing is a universal form of social interaction. The same teasing patterns found in the inner-city children of Philadelphia, for example, have been observed among the Kaluli aborigine children of New Zealand (Kutner, 1981) as well as the children of Ireland (A. A. Gaffney, personal communication, April 1986) and Brazil (L. P. Towne, personal communication, July 1982). Visitors to some non-English-speaking countries report their surprise at hearing children chanting the melody and format of the familiar singsong taunt of their own early school years: "Markie's a pooper, Markie's a pooper."

Most childhood teasing is a destructive verbal attack that is directed at specific features of the child, features that other children see as negative. The intent is to hurt, annoy, upset, and goad the target to tears. The potential for upset is generally the greatest if the topic of the tease is true, negative, and beyond the victim's control. It takes considerable skill to respond quickly and decisively to such a tease. Children who are repeatedly teased by their peers are at risk for a cluster of maladaptive outcomes including depression, anxiety, school avoidance, physical disturbances such as sleep problems, and, in some instances, suicide. Parents often do not know how to handle the problem effectively and neither do many schools. There are procedures for stopping teasing that any interested adult can use. These procedures are designed to equip victims to handle teasing situations themselves. Thus, in addition to ending the misery of being teased, the victims have the immense satisfaction of having pulled off this coup with no adult present. If bystanders are present when the victim figuratively squashes the teaser, his or her status in the peer group will almost certainly rise. Chapter 7 contains descriptions of these procedures.

This chapter starts with the many meanings that are attributed to teasing in informal conversation and then moves on to the problem of definition. The term *teasing* has been used to describe a diversity of behaviors such as taunting, repeated questioning, mimicry, pretended astonishment, poking fun, kidding, harassing, and exaggerated scolding for a trivial offense. It also refers to actions such as baiting another person, flirtation where much in the nature of sexual activity is implied but little is acted on, and advertisements that purposely withhold some information to arouse consumer interest.

Until recently there has been almost no attempt to arrive at a formal, widely accepted definition of teasing. Table 6.1 contains a representative group of recent definitions of it. The *Oxford English Dictionary* (1993) defines *teasing* as a "mildly annoying, harassing, or irritating occurrence done in sport or mischief, typically of a trifling or petty nature." The same range of affect is apparent in synonyms of teasing. Some are more hostile (*badgering, tormenting*), but others are more playful (*bantering, chaffing*). The positive affect implicit in this definition and some of the synonyms has had the effect of engendering a misconception among adults and providing a convenient alibi for adults and children who tease that teasing is "only joking" and, as such, is not to be taken seriously. In fact, as Pawluk (1989) has pointed out in a scholarly treatise on teasing, it differs from joking in that it involves a perpetrator and victim and often occurs at the latter's expense by relating specifically to one of the victim's characteristics:

> As soon as they found out I couldn't see very well, they started taking my things and hiding them. It's been going on for years now. When I start looking they sing "Bottle Bottoms's on the trail again" and slap me with rulers (9-year-old boy called Bottle Bottoms because of the very thick-lens glasses he wears). (Randall, 1997, p. 10)

Joking, by contrast, reflects a more equal dyadic relationship and can relate to people other than the victim and to impersonal topics. Whereas teasing may elicit reactions ranging from extreme upset to amusement, true joking usually results only in amusement. It also lacks the essential serious component of teasing, namely, the potential for developing into something that is painful and destructive. Teasing that is unquestionably cruel should be accorded the status of a behavior problem in its own right. This category of teasing is the focus of this chapter.

However, before we turn to the cruel and destructive qualities of teasing, aspects of teasing in general are discussed, with emphasis on the developmental sequence that it follows from the preschool period through adolescence. Unlike bullying, teasing can be fun, playful, and unequivocally constructive. Teasing between parent and child, for example, can be used to build up strong relationships in the family. Using references that only the family understands can enhance feelings of solidarity and closeness (Eisenberg, 1986). For example,

Table 6.1. Definitions of Teasing

Alberts (1992, p. 155)	"A tease may be profitably viewed as an aggressive verbalization couched in some situational qualifiers indicating playfulness."
Boulton & Hawker (1997, p. 54)	"While it is clear that teasing consists of verbal name calling, taunts, and derision, the intention of the teaser may vary. Thus, some people equate teasing with playful verbal statements of a trifling or petty nature, whereas others stress its destructive, hostile nature."
Eder (1993, p. 17)	"Here teasing will be defined as any playful remark aimed at another person which can include mock challenges, commands, and threats as well as imitating and exaggerating someone's behavior in a playful way. While the content of teasing would often be negative or hostile if taken literally, the playful meaning is determined in part by cues from the teaser indicating that the remark should be taken in a playful manner."
Mooney, Creeser, & Blatchford (1991, p. 103)	"Whereas teasing can be both playful and malicious in intent, bullying can never be considered as playful."
Shapiro, Baumeister, & Kessler (1991, p. 460)	"Teasing is a personal communication, directed by an agent toward a target, that includes three components: aggression, humor, and ambiguity."
Voss (1997, pp. 241–242)	"Like Eder (1991), I define teasing as humorous taunts. For teasing to be successful, the target must respond in a playful manner. . . . If the target responds in a hostile, impatient, or angry fashion, teasing may escalate to ridicule."
Warm (1997, p. 98)	"Teasing is a deliberate act designed by the teaser to cause tension in the victim, such as anxiety, frustration, anger, embarrassment, humiliation, and it is presented in such a way that the victims can escape if they catch on."

> A family traveling by car across the U.S. border unexpectedly had to take their cat with them. The mother cautioned their three young children that "We mustn't talk about the cat." When the Customs Officer at the border asked if they had anything to declare, the 3-year-old girl piped up, "We mustn't talk about the cat." The Customs Officer looked startled, then grinned and moved on. For years thereafter, when anyone in the family wanted no mention of some topic, someone invariably said, "We mustn't talk about the cat" and everyone, including the former 3-year-old, laughed. (M. M. Smith, personal communication, August 15, 1994)

The Ambiguity of Teasing

Teasing is characterized by ambiguities and intangibles that make it a difficult problem for parents and other adults to handle effectively. What distresses one child may not bother another at all, and even the same incident may not consistently elicit distress in the child. As a result of this variability, children's complaints about being teased often are more likely to exasperate adults than to arouse sympathy. Furthermore, it is relatively easy for persuasive teasers to convince adults that they were "only joking," thus placing the victim in the category of one who makes a fuss about nothing. (This defense may have an element of truth in it: Besag [1989] reported that many teasers genuinely appear to see their teasing as far milder and of less consequence than the victim sees it.)

Added to the ambiguity is the fact that it is sometimes difficult for the child who is teased to know whether to take a specific tease seriously. As Blau (1993) has noted, the very essence of a tease is that its meaning is usually open to interpretation, a feature that is not characteristic of most other components of bullying, such as physical aggression, extortion, and social exclusion. Some light has been cast on this dilemma by Pawluk (1989), who identified several characteristics of teasing episodes that should determine whether teasing is taken seriously. It is often not so much what is said or how it is said but rather *who* says it that determines whether a specific tease will be offensive. Sometimes the teaser means the teasing to be taken lightly and conveys this by certain contextualization cues (Gumperz, 1977) such as a singsong intonation, facial expressions of exaggerated sorrow or alarm, or winks and smiles at apparently inappropriate times. Certain characteristics of the content of the tease may also determine its reception. If the tease contains negative comments that the onlookers know are patently false, the recipient is more likely to take it lightly.

The Problem of Definition

In an article that provides the best discussion and definition to date of what teasing is, Keltner, Capps, Kring, Young, and Heerey (2001) stated that although teasing is prevalent in everyday life and is a descriptor that is widely used, it has not often been subjected to empirical study. They attributed the apparent lack of investigative interest in teasing primarily to the fact that it has never been adequately defined and consequently resists measurement and manipulation. They also acknowledged the many procedural problems associated with conducting controlled experiments on teasing. For example, experiments that specify who teases whom, or provide the verbal content of teasing interactions, cannot capture the essence of spontaneous teasing.

Starting with the question, *What is teasing?* they drew upon Goffman's (1957) analysis of strategic interaction and particularly his concept of face (defined as "an image of self delineated in terms of approved social attributes" [Goffman, 1957, p. 215]) to define a tease as "an intentional provocation accompanied by playful off-record markers that together comment on something relevant to the target" (Keltner et al., 2001, p. 234). A provocation may refer to something about the target, the relationship between the teaser and the target, or an object or activity of interest to the target. *Provocations* can be physical and verbal or nonverbal. *Off-record markers* are tactics such as exaggeration and understatement that indicate that the provocation is not to be taken seriously but rather treated as a comment to be taken in jest. One function of the off-record marker is to differentiate teasing from other behaviors that are often used as examples of it. Note that Keltner et al. emphasized that if the provocation is not accompanied by off-record markers, it is *not* teasing.

The foregoing definition of a tease encompasses the diversity of behaviors that have been reported in studies of teasing, clarifies ambiguities in concepts such as aggression and play that are often involved in teasing, differentiates teasing from bullying and other behaviors frequently incorrectly labeled as teasing, and shows how teasing can lead to more prosocial or antisocial outcomes. Keltner et al. (2001) pointed out one limitation of their approach to what teasing is: There is no information about the effect of the target's response on the interaction. This topic is of considerable importance because often the target can put an end to a teasing interaction with the right response, whereas the wrong response will almost certainly prolong the teasing (Ross, 1973, 1996). A good example of the efficacy of the right response to teasing came from an 11-year-old boy who was known at school as "the Professor." He appeared to be an excellent target for teasing. He had red hair that seemed to stand on end, masses of freckles, and unusually big ears. On his first day in a new school, an older boy who was a confirmed teaser started in on him with teases such as "Spotty," "Elephant ears," and "Carrot-top." The teaser had barely started when the target raised his hand and said, "Whoa! I have to get this down." He then whipped out a small notebook and started writing. The teaser looked disconcerted and asked him what he was doing. The target did not answer but instead asked the teaser a series of questions such as, "Was Spotty the only name you could think of?" "Can you think of some other names now?" "Tell me how old you are and your birthday," and "If you think of some other names later be sure to tell me." Then he explained that he was doing a study of teasing. The teaser became quite defensive and asked, "Who says you can write down what I say?" to which the target replied, "Who says I can't?" The teaser never bothered him again.

Of particular interest is Keltner et al.'s (2001) comment regarding the need for research to clarify the boundary between teasing for fun and teasing that goes too far. Such a boundary would certainly be of great help to parents and school personnel, who often are unsure about where to draw the line. However, it is our opinion that the range of boundaries would be extensive and that the visible reactions of the victims would in many cases mask their hurt feelings and acute embarrassment about being teased. Consequently, the apparent boundaries would not be accurate. Even if the children were interviewed, some of the data would likely be inaccurate because many children are reluctant to admit to adults that being teased bothers them.

When Does Teasing Begin?

Teasing begins before the child is capable of attaching a verbal description to his or her teasing behaviors. Like most attempts to assign clusters of behavior, such as teasing, to age categories, the boundaries are blurred and individual differences rampant. Nevertheless, the categories do provide a framework for ordering progressions in developmental sequences.

PRESCHOOL YEARS

Kutner (1981) described the most primitive form of teasing as that seen among toddlers when one child holds a toy out to another and then pulls it back out of reach as the other child's hand makes a grab for it. Two- and 3-year-olds can accurately identify the cues signaling the playful nature of a teasing interaction and can join in it (Eisenberg,

1986; Miller, 1986). In preschool settings teasers often say silly things that are not specifically related to the target. A group of 4-year-olds, for example, suddenly started amidst raucous laughter to call another child vegetable-type names: "Bernie's a beanie, Bernie's a beanie. Now he's a cornie, now he's a cornie." They quickly lost interest when the intended target's only reaction was a puzzled glance before he resumed play. At this age level the playful nature of most teasing serves the important function of providing practice in beginning to acquire a certain tolerance for name calling that is a distinct advantage when the child enters kindergarten.

Opinions differ on the age at which teasing with a deliberate intent to hurt begins. Besag (1989) believed that toddlers are well aware of the feelings of others and the irritation they can arouse with teasing. Kutner (1981) agreed that teasing begins at the toddler stage, but he contended that, although young children may recognize that their gibes can anger their targets, they are still unaware that someone might feel hurt by what they say. Maccoby (1980) argued that teasing designed to be deliberately hurtful cannot occur until children have reached a level of cognitive development that provides them with an understanding of the self and the feelings of others. Reaching this level can be facilitated by teaching children at an early age that their comments can hurt others, and this intentional training can be strengthened through the incidental learning that occurs as a result of witnessing familial and televised verbal aggression. That preschool children are able to identify and implement ways of deliberately upsetting other children is evident in the following conversation that I overheard at the Stanford Nursery School:

Janie: Let's go call Charlie names.
Debbie: What'll we call him?
Janie: Charlie gongarlie, tee-legged Charlie, tee-legged, toe-legged, bow-legged Charlie.
Debbie: Will he cry?
Janie: No. Cowboys don't cry. Maybe he'll get mad and chase us. Maybe if we push him down and tie him up he'll cry a teeny bit.

They are also capable of making value judgments. Sigelman and Begley (1987) have reported that preschool children tend to devalue peers who are physically or behaviorally different; for example, they have negative stereotypes of the obese (Jarvie, Lahey, Graziano, & Framer, 1983). One 4-year-old girl, whose mother described her as "chubby" but was in fact obese, went eagerly to preschool the first day but flatly refused to go after several days. When her mother questioned her, the child said tearfully that the other children called her nasty names like "Fatty, fatty, Patty" and laughed when she could not manage a climbing apparatus (P. Rowe, personal communication, July 14, 1961).

MIDDLE CHILDHOOD

Many 6- and 7-year-olds are capable of more varied forms of teasing: They are able to present the tease as playful or as a deliberate attempt to hurt (Eder, 1991). At this stage children are particularly vulnerable to others' opinions because they are struggling to feel confident in the public school situation. Consequently, they are easily upset by unkind comments. Being one of the group is very important. Conformity is the rule, and those who are noticeably different (e.g., shy; small for age, particularly for a boy; dressed differently) frequently are the targets of unkind comments. If these elicit visible upset, the comments may change to teasing that is both individualized and deliberate. Such teasing is especially likely if the differences are ones that the group regards as babyish (Klein, 1975). One 5-year-old kindergarten boy, Peter, who still sucked his thumb despite his parents' determined efforts to stop him, stopped completely after 3 days of peer disapproval. On the playground and on the school bus the group chanted a reminder:

> Kids who suck their thumbs aren't cool
> Go back, Peter, to preschool.

This was supplemented by one that, according to the teacher, the class thought was more scary:

> Roses are red, violets are blue,
> If you suck your thumb you'll be in the zoo.

These rhymes become part of the teaser's arsenal, as much to show mastery and group spirit as to attack, but a target is still needed regardless of the motive.

As children move toward the end of the middle childhood years, three qualitative changes occur in their teasing. In the first of these, the teasing becomes sharper, more incisive, and cutting, partly because of increasing verbal skill but also because acceptance by the peer group has now become a top priority. Being recognized as one who is skilled in quick, often cruel rejoinders is one way to be well up in the social hierarchy if other attributes, such as appearance or wealth, have not assured the child of such acceptance. Teasing at this level can be a way of showing other children that *they* are not one of the group.

In a discussion of why teasing becomes increasingly nasty, Thompson and Grace (2001) believed that teasing becomes a weapon in the struggle to be cool. Children say that the cool kids are the ones who are able to *put down* other kids effectively. Thompson described a school that he visited in which life in the fifth grade was completely dominated by the culture of the put-down game. The teachers were very upset about this daily game, which consisted of a surprise verbal attack by one student of a classmate. The latter had to reply quickly with repartee that showed that he was not at all hurt by the initial assault. To make this clear, he had to retaliate with something wittier. The student who initiated the exchange then had to show that he could handle the comeback by outdoing the rejoinder. Originality counted. Two collections of put-downs had circulated in the class. If a child used an insult from one of the books and the source was recognized, he was shouted down. What is particularly interesting about this game is that it originated as a street game decades ago and was one that Black American boys had played in the inner city.

Teasing may also be a sign of social acceptance:

> An 11-year-old girl, a newcomer in the school, was the first to wear knee socks with horizontal stripes. Despite an element of nastiness in some of her peers' comments, she clearly perceived remarks about going out for the boys' soccer team and wearing jail garb as indicative of a degree of social acceptance. She told her mother, "It was the best day so far, the other kids, especially the guys, made more cracks about my socks than they've made the whole time I've been here." (J. S. Ross, personal communication, 1964)

At the same time, there is a trend toward a more positive judgment of teasing, a recognition of some teasing as being funny or as an effective way of sending useful messages to the recipient.

The second change that occurs in teasing with increasing age is a gender difference that was not apparent in the early school years. Boys "go for the jugular" (Blau, 1993, p. 67): They challenge each other's masculinity and try to identify another boy's Achilles' heel. When they do, they focus on it while doing their best to embarrass him:

> What! You still haven't got a date for the dance! Maybe you need Viagra. It's never too early to start, so they say. You spend too much time with that gay guy in the band. The guys are talking

> about you. (conversation of a 13-year-old on the phone to a friend, overheard by his mother, September 2001)

By comparison, girls are more subtle. They spread rumors about other girls and use social exclusion rather than confrontation:

> Lately Sylvia's friends at school have been acting strangely toward her. When she goes to sit with them at lunch, everyone stops talking. When she passes people in the hall, she hears them whispering behind their hands. And then just yesterday she overheard that Mindy was having a birthday party, and she hasn't been invited. What Sylvia doesn't know is that Mindy has been spreading gossip about her to their mutual friends ever since Sylvia beat her out for the lead in the school play. (Crick et al., 2001, p. 196)

Some of their teasing may appear to be playful, but the playfulness masks thinly disguised hostility (Eder, 1991; Pipher, 1994).

The third change is characterized by an underlying sexual quality to the teasing. The child who is often seen talking to one of the opposite sex is at risk for being teased about "liking" the other child. Two fifth graders talking in front of a third girl had this exchange:

> *First girl:* I think someone around here likes Andy *a lot!* Like, why does she go to the library so much? She doesn't even like reading.
> *Second girl:* Yeah, and now she goes home the long way—past his house. Why would she do that except to (pause) you know. . . .
> (The third girl managed to look quite indifferent except for a blush.)
> (J. Eliot, personal communication, September 16, 1985)

The effect of this heterosexual teasing is to construct and monitor boundaries between the sexes, keeping them as separate groups having only limited informal contact in public. In a study of 5- to 11-year-old children, Thorne and Luria (1986) commented that the probability of being teased for such contacts is so great that cross-gender friendships that originated in other settings sometimes "go underground" during the school day.

ADOLESCENCE

In early adolescence unfriendly teasing of a general nature starts to disappear partly because young adolescents often are more empathic and so are more reluctant to attack certain attributes of others, and partly because they begin to look at negative attributes in others in terms of controllability (Royal & Roberts, 1987). They usually react more punitively to peers with apparently controllable negative attributes, such as obesity, than to those with uncontrollable conditions like cerebral palsy. A good example of this selective behavior pattern was seen in a middle school where I was doing research. A grossly overweight boy who ate huge lunches was cruelly teased by his classmates: "Hey, Watkins! Give Richie (fat boy) some of your cake. He's getting real skinny. We don't want him to faint in P.E., we'd have to carry him to the nurse" (Ross, 1977–1979).

However, when the boys' class was chosen to put on a marching display and their P.E. teacher asked them how they felt about having another classmate, a boy with cerebral palsy, participate, they voted unanimously to include him even though they knew that his gait would detract from their performance. On their own, they adjusted the speed of certain parts of their routine to accommodate his slower gait.

By the end of eighth grade most adolescents have experienced, witnessed, and in some cases subjected others to a variety of teasing in the form of name calling, needling, abrasive mimicry, and derision. Their reactions to these experiences are the basis for being recognized as one "who can take it" or being labeled as "a wimp." As one 13-year-old girl commented, "If you can't keep your cool about a few names and cracks by the time you're our age, you'll never make it in high school." Those who have mastered these teasing experiences are indeed well equipped to handle the bantering, ribbing, and exchange of pseudo-insults (insults that are really a sign of goodwill or friendship) that characterize much of the social intercourse in adolescence.

However, when teasing does occur, it is more likely to be cruel in a deadly way. With increasing cognitive maturation there is a concomitant increase in verbal skills, particularly in the ability to convey more subtle and punishing barbs. The adolescent is often very adept at pinpointing the most private areas of vulnerability in the victim. An example of this level of teasing appears in the autobiography of Graham Greene (1971), in which he described the vicious teasing he had experienced from a schoolmate. The teasing related to the conflict of loyalty position that Greene was in because he and his older brother attended an English school in which their father was the headmaster:

> There was a boy at my school called Carter who perfected a system of mental torture based on my difficult situation. Carter had

> an adult imagination—he could conceive the conflict of loyalties, loyalties to my age group, loyalty to my father and brother. The searing nicknames were inserted like splinters under the nails. (Greene, 1971, p. 82)

In adolescence, the heterosexual teasing of the middle childhood years intensifies and branches out into three clusters. One of these is teasing that serves to initiate heterosexual interactions. Much of this teasing is characterized by playfulness and ambiguity, a combination that allows the teenager to express liking for a person of the opposite sex without being held accountable for these feelings (Oswald, Krappman, Chowdhuri, & von Salisch, 1988). In a second cluster, the teasing becomes somewhat insulting, often focusing on sexual patterns such as homosexuality. This focus often functions as a way for the teaser to deal with his own sexual fears by attributing them to others, particularly to the least prestigious targets such as the isolates in the group. Many adolescent girls are aware of the cruelty inherent in these sexual taunts and will go so far as to reprimand the teasers (Evans & Eder, 1993). Teasing in the third cluster is sometimes extremely crude, as McCoy (1992) reported:

> A social service professional asked her 13-year-old daughter, a good-looking star soccer player, why she seemed so unhappy. The girl started sobbing, then admitted that for the past six months whenever one boy saw her in the hall, he would lean toward her and say things like, "You big fat whale, you zit-faced slug, you ugly witch." He did this up to ten times a day and used a lot of four-letter words. (p. 199)

Sometimes teasing is a well-orchestrated revenge attack by the victim:

> See, this real snotty girl, Mary Rose, was the best dressed kid and the meanest in the whole school. We called her Miss Perfect. She teased me all the time about this scar on my face and my clothes, which were *really awful*. Then I read this story about a girl who got teased really badly and one day she started teasing the teaser about something that wasn't true at all and the girl who teased her got real mad and cried and stopped teasing her. So I thought I'd try cross-eyes and when Miss Perfect came over and started on my scar I stared at her eyes as hard as I could and I didn't say *anything* or act upset like I usually do. She said, "Why are you staring at me like that?" And I said, "Golly Gee, Mary Rose, I

> didn't know you were cross-eyed," and she got real upset and red in the face and before she could say anything I said, "They don't cross all the time but they are crossed right now, it looks really funny." My friend, Sally, came by and I gave her a wink and said, "Isn't it too bad Mary Rose's eyes get crossed sometimes like now?" And Sally, who is a real liar, said, "Yeah, but they don't cross *all* the time, just a lot." And Mary Rose just walked away, she was almost crying, and she never, ever teased me again. But I stared at her a lot. (M. L. Stone, personal communication regarding a girl aged 11, July 12, 1982)

The Problem of Cruel Teasing

The discussion so far has centered around teasing in general, with the emphasis on the developmental steps from preschool through adolescence. The remainder of the chapter focuses on teasing that consists of destructive verbal attacks (Smith, 1991) that are usually, but not always, repeated over time, the goal being to create increasing misery in the victim. There is no ambiguity here in what is said: The intent is to hurt, annoy, upset, or goad the victim and to bring this fault to the attention of onlookers in an embarrassing and humiliating way. The potential for upset is even greater if the topic of the tease is true, negative, and beyond the victim's control. Such teasing is a test that most victims are likely to fail unless they have been trained in coping effectively with teasing or have been exposed to models who were able to field destructive verbal attacks without too much difficulty. As Willis (1977) has pointed out, it takes some skill to initiate a teasing attack, but it takes far more to respond quickly and decisively.

From the teaser's viewpoint teasing is most successful when the victim's reaction is one of immediate visible upset. Colloquially, this behavior is recognized as having "scored a direct hit." One of the most detrimental reactions the victim can make is to reject the teasing in a weak defensive way, coupled with visible upset. Although walking away, theoretically, should mean that the teasing has failed, in practice it is extremely difficult for the victim to carry it off without appearing to be making an escape. Walking away is usually accompanied by further taunts such as, "What's the matter, Joan, are you too chicken to stay?"

From the reports of children who have experienced a substantial amount of teasing and from interviews with self-acknowledged teasers, hurtful teasing generally follows an orderly sequence. The tempo of the teasing begins slowly and then accelerates. The teaser first probes tentatively with some exploratory insults and negative comments. If the potential victim responds appropriately with visible upset or anger and appears to be avoiding the teaser, the teaser goes ahead with the tried-and-true teases. However, he or she still spends some time trying to identify new "sore spots," which are then added to the repertoire. Thus teasing is, in most cases, almost a leisurely process in which the teaser gradually accumulates a set of effective teases for a specific victim. From the point at which the first probes clearly work, the teaser feels in complete control of the teasing interactions.

INCIDENCE OF TEASING

Although there is a paucity of incidence data, there is no question that teasing in school-age children is widespread in parts of Western Europe, the United Kingdom, the United States, and Canada, as well as Japan, Australia, and New Zealand. The few studies that have been published support the view that the incidence of teasing is a problem in the schools, but there is less firm empirical support than might be expected because teasing usually is included as a *component of bullying* in questionnaires. The child is asked some form of the question, "How many times have you been *bullied* in the past week, month, etc.?" whereas to determine the incidence of teasing as a separate problem the question should distinguish between *teasing only* and *teasing as secondary to other components of bullying.* Some investigators have used questions that permitted this distinction. For example, Yates and Smith (1989) asked 234 pupils in secondary school, "In what way have you been bullied in school?" Seventy-one percent of the respondents stated that they had "been teased only." Similarly, when Boulton and Underwood (1992) asked 296 elementary school children to check specific categories of bullying, they found that 58% of the group checked teasing only, and in an important review article, Smith (1991, p. 245) stated that most respondents who reported being bullied said it took the form of teasing.

WHO IS A TARGET FOR SERIOUS TEASING?

No theory adequately explains why one child and not another becomes the target of teasers. For a long time it was assumed that being *different* in some way was the criterion. Then in 1984 Olweus introduced the *victim theory* discussed in chapter 4, that is, that children are bullied, or in this case teased, because their whole demeanor labels them as easy targets who are unlikely to retaliate. Olweus (1993a) never suggested that this theory explains all teasing; however, popular acceptance of it has tended to obscure its limitations. The fact is that both the difference and victim theories make a contribution.

DIFFERENCES LIKELY TO CREATE PROBLEMS

Differences play an important etiological role in the teasing problems of four groups of children who, when teasing is first initiated, are not characterized by the victim syndrome. The first group are children who are beginning public school, usually kindergarten, and have two characteristics. One is a *significant lack of social experience* because of some reason not related to any inherent inadequacy that repels their peers. As a result, these children are inexperienced in even mildly negative social interactions with children other than those in their own families. The other characteristic is *some visible difference* in dress, speech, or gait that sets them apart from the other children. When the differences elicit negative comments of a general nature, these children usually become angry or visibly upset, or they withdraw. Any one of these reactions is sufficiently rewarding to other children so that they continue along the teasing track. Although a victim personality may develop as a result of the teasing, it is not the cause of it.

The second group of children is made up of those who are extremely shy with strangers and overly cautious in new situations to the point where they may withdraw altogether. Although almost all children are shy sometimes, the children in this group consistently exhibit shyness to an almost debilitating degree. A mother with an extremely shy son attributed his shyness to newness: "If something is new and different his inclination is to be quiet and watch. . . . It's unfamiliarity that is the cause of his behavior. Not just new people, but *newness*" (Galvin, 1992, p. 41).

Jerome Kagan, who has been studying shy children since 1978, at first thought that their extreme shyness was an acquired trait, the result of rejection by family or peers, poor school performance, or some other identifiable reason (Galvin, 1992). He now believes that, although one cluster of these painfully shy children has acquired shyness as Zimbardo (1982) has demonstrated, the remaining children were born with this temperament, a quality that Kagan calls *inhibition*. Kagan has documented impressive empirical support for genetic and physiological bases being partly responsible for inhibition.

Because shyness in our society can be a major handicap, it is fortunate that both acquired shyness and inhibition-related shyness are modifiable. Zimbardo (1982), through his Shyness Clinic at Stanford University, has made a major contribution to those whose shyness appears to be acquired, particularly those in the adolescent through young adult age groups. His texts on overcoming shyness (Zimbardo, 1982, 1990) offer invaluable help for the parents, teachers, and other professionals who seek to modify shyness in those in grade school through young adult age groups. Kagan (Galvin, 1992) has data on changes with age in inhibition-related shyness. Some changes may occur spontaneously, but more likely they are the result of determined parental intervention. On the basis of his findings with a group of extremely shy children studied from infancy, Kagan estimated that for every 10 children who are extremely shy at age 2, only 5 will still be shy by kindergarten or first grade, and only 3 by adolescence (Galvin, 1992). The behaviors characteristic of extreme shyness could be viewed by peers as a negative difference such as standoffishness, thus creating a logical link to peer rejection and teasing.

A third group of children who are teased are those with differences that are extremely unsightly, the salient characteristic being a marked degree in deviation of their negative attributes from the physical appearance norm. The aftermath of serious burns, facial disfigurement from an accident, and unsightly skin conditions that border on the grotesque are the kinds of differences that draw immediate attention. In this group the cases that we have seen were all children who previously had been "normal" in all respects, including popularity with peers.

We first became aware of this group when we asked children with leukemia to tell us what was the worst pain they had experienced (Ross & Ross, 1988). The answers we expected were some treatment-related pain such as spinal taps or bone marrow aspirations. Instead, for many of these children and for those with the aftermath of serious burns, the worst pain was going back to school and being teased about their appearance. Treatment with prednisone and chemotherapy typically results in leukemic children being bald and obese and having a curiously spongy look to their skin along with extreme pallor. Often the children feel as though they look like aliens from another planet, as do some children with the aftermath of severe burns.

The slowly accelerating tempo of the teasing described earlier is not a characteristic with this group. These children are not selected by the teaser but, instead, more or less burst into his or her sphere on their first day back to school. The teasing always focuses on the markedly deviant attribute, such as baldness, regardless of the target's other teaseworthy negative characteristics. The teasing also tends to be highly repetitive, with little or no variation.

It is our opinion that these tempo and content differences are indications that the teaser feels a loss of control, and the all-out teasing attack is a fear reaction to seeing the dramatic change for the worse in a previously normal-appearing child. It was clear in talking to the teasers that the changes in the leukemic children came as a terrible shock. The teasers clearly did not know how to cope. One 8-year-old boy said, "I just started yelling at him (the leukemic child), I said all kinds of terrible things, I couldn't stop." The same sequence of shock at changed appearance leading to fear and attack has been documented in animals (Bergman, 1973).

The fourth group whose teasing problem is etiologically related to a difference are children in the first or second year of school who are different in some conspicuous but minor way and whose teachers set them up as targets for teasing by their classmates. To understand how such a thing can happen, it is important to remember that the teacher has a great deal to do with how children see themselves and how others in the class see them. The power of teachers is tremendous: They can take a boy who is different in some way from his classmates, set him apart from them in a negative way, and in the process possibly do him lasting psychological damage, or they can make him a valued member of the group.

An impressive empirical demonstration of this phenomenon has been provided by Whalen and Henker (1976). They have unequivocal evidence that the world of the classroom can function as a *provocation ecology* that accentuates the differences between average children and those who are different in a way that their classmates can be led to see as negative, or as a *rarefaction ecology* that diminishes such differences. It is the classroom teacher who determines and controls the ecology of the classroom, as the following example clearly shows. Robert, an unusually bright 6-year-old, suffered frequent mortification and shame because he was unable to tie his shoelaces. His teacher clearly had rigid norms about what boys in kindergarten should be able to do:

> She frequently would ask in a world-weary tone that conveyed complete scorn for Robert's lack of agility, "Will someone please come up and tie Robert's shoes for him so we can go outside for recess? He can't seem to do it for himself yet." And there Robert would stiffly sit—no recourse but to face front—toward tables lined with jeering faces, hearing the barely suppressed giggles, the stage whispers behind loosely cupped hands. There he would sit while some better-coordinated classmate, sometimes a boy, sometimes a girl, would bend over him condescendingly and tie his laces into a bow. (Klein, 1975, pp. 127–128)

Given this scenario, the potential teasers in the class would feel with justification that their teacher was tacitly endorsing the teasing of Robert. As Zimbardo (1982) commented: "The power of a teacher to erode a child's self-confidence is overwhelming. And the power of a teacher to turn otherwise nice children into tormentors is frightening" (p. 12).

WHAT ARE THE EFFECTS ON THE VICTIM OF BEING TEASED?

Adults would not be so ready to brush teasing aside as a passing problem that all children go through if they realized that teasing has important immediate and long-term effects on the victims. The immediate effects, which are often felt throughout the elementary and high school years, are for the most part like those of bullying. The victims come to dread school; are reluctant to attend formal and social groups that the teaser attends; begin to see themselves as worthless and inferior beings; avoid other children, including former friends; and suffer from anxiety, acute loneliness, and depression. Fabian and Thompson (1989), for example, have reported a significant relationship between the current level of depression in 13- to 15-year-old girls and their history of being teased. If the teasing continues over a long period and if the girl receives no social support from parents and others, her depression about her inability to cope with what she sees as a hopeless problem can have drastic results. Her thinking may become confused to the point at which only one action occurs to her: *If I destroy myself, then the problem is destroyed.* The case of Nathan Faris is a textbook example of this sequence (Greenbaum, 1989).

Nathan was a bright, slightly overweight boy in seventh grade who had been teased relentlessly by his classmates since the third grade. He hated going to school: The others continually harassed him with names such as "fatso," "chubby," and "walking dictionary." Nathan felt tormented and vowed to take revenge. One day in 1987 he brought a gun to school, killed one boy who tried to take the gun away from him, wounded two others, and then killed himself.

From the newspaper accounts and from postsuicide interviews with classmates, the teasing that Nathan was subjected to seems rather mild. As one girl said, "Nobody really had anything against him, he was just someone to pick on." But it was bad enough from Nathan's viewpoint for him to kill himself. This points to the *subjectivity of the pain of being teased:* Others' opinion of the teasing is completely irrelevant because their judgments have no relation to how the victim feels. Children's appraisals *must* be accepted at face value: If they say it is terrible, then it *is* terrible. This is an extremely important requirement and one that cannot be overemphasized.

The long-term effects, that is, in post high school and adulthood, continue to exert a punishing influence on the victims. People teased about their appearance by peers in childhood more often evaluated their appearance in adulthood negatively than those who had not been teased. As a woman whose nickname in childhood was "elephant legs" said: "I still can't bear to look at myself in a full-length mirror. . . . My legs still look huge to me even though my husband tells me they look fine" (Cash & Janda, 1986, p. 33).

Minor deviations singled out for teasing in childhood may, without intervention, escalate in adulthood. Wiehe (1991, p. 29) reported the case of a woman in her early 30s who was teased and ridiculed so often as a child about a minor speech problem that she is reluctant even now to speak up for herself. What started as an inability to say certain words correctly developed into the belief that people would laugh at the *content* of her conversation:

> My brother would tease me about not saying certain words correctly. Some words I could not pronounce correctly, so he would get me to say them and then laugh at me. (Now) I feel like people will laugh at what I have to say or they will think it's dumb.

WHAT DO PARENTS DO WHEN A CHILD COMPLAINS OF BEING TEASED?

Parents are likely to handle a complaint of cruel teasing in any of the following ineffective ways.

Urge the Child to Pay No Attention

The suggestion to ignore the teasing is often accompanied by the old adage, "Sticks and stones may break my bones but names will never hurt me." This myth is perpetrated by adults who have forgotten how painful being teased can be for a child. This advice is of little or no help to the victims; instead, it convinces them that their parents do not understand how much teasing hurts and, in fact, will be of no help.

Minimize the Problem

The parents attempt to downgrade the seriousness of the teasing by joking about it. A mother told her 9-year-old daughter, "When you're 10 you'll remember being teased and wonder why it bothered you so much." This is patently false. There is unequivocal evidence that many adults never forget the misery of being teased in childhood and, in fact, remember the sequences in great detail. One woman told me that when her 6-year-old daughter complained of being teased,

> It brought it all back, my first day in Grade 1. I wore a very unattractive dress and the other girls made horrible comments. When I had to stand up and describe my favorite story there were

> smothered giggles. The minute I got home I started to cry. I told my mother I didn't want to go to school.

What parents do not understand is the effect that their failure to offer sympathy has on the victim. One 8-year-old boy thought that the worst thing about being teased was that none of the people whom he had assumed would help him did. He said sadly, "It's the most alone I've ever been."

Complain to the Teaser's Parents or to the School

This is seldom a successful tactic because two essential conditions are almost never present: The interaction must be handled with unusual skill, and the adults involved must be genuinely concerned about the problem. Otherwise, this tactic could make matters worse. The child could be labeled as a tattle-tale by the peer group and viewed as a trouble-maker by school personnel, leaving the victim worse off than was the case prior to the "help."

Present It as "Character Building"

Although it is true that almost everyone experiences teasing at some point in childhood, not everyone is subjected to the intensive teasing that drives them to complain to their parents. The idea that handling the teasing themselves will make the children stronger typically convinces the victims that they are wimps, that their parents are disappointed in them, and that their parents either will not or cannot help them.

Do Nothing

Some parents do practically nothing about the problem because they view teasing as a common and transitory childhood event that will work itself out in time. Others do not take any action because they really do not know what would be the best thing to do: They truly believe that anything they do might exacerbate the problem.

On a superficial level, it is easy to feel critical of these ineffective actions. But parents today lack a traditional framework as a support for many child-rearing decisions. Very little that their own parents did is viewed as applicable to today's children. So each generation is, in effect, starting from scratch. Also, consider the barrage of mixed messages about handling almost any problem that parents get from professionals. In the case of teasing, in the advice columns, magazine articles, and talk shows, the volume of contradictory advice offered as fact is extraordinary. If parents were given as much conflicting and inappropriate advice about physical health problems as they get about behavioral problems, many children would never reach adolescence.

WHAT PARENTS SHOULD DO WHEN A CHILD IS CRUELLY TEASED

Start by listening sympathetically and with obvious interest. It is imperative to make an effort to see the problem from the child's point of view. Ask the child to describe the teasing starting from its onset. Usually a child who is upset will have difficulty talking about it in a coherent manner. If the parent listens patiently, without interrupting, and nods in agreement at appropriate times, the child will gradually settle down. It is essential that the child's account and appraisal of the teasing be accepted as fact. Arguing about it or criticizing the child's handling of it will almost certainly inhibit further meaningful communication: The child would be likely to censor further comments about the teasing or withdraw. The fact is that the child is in too precarious a state to cope with *any* disapproval.

The parent must offer unqualified social support in the form of clearly understanding why being teased is so upsetting. It is helpful at this point to draw on true or hypothetical instances of being teased. Perhaps an older sibling had been unable to handle teasing effectively, or the parent's best friend had been cruelly teased and needed a lot of help from his parents and the school. Teasing is a fairly common problem that should never be tolerated. Neither the parents nor the child should accept it as inevitable or wait for it to be over. The parent should assure the child that he or she knows a way to stop the teasing and will teach the child how to do it (see chapter 7).

Throughout this discussion, the focus should be on the teasing rather than on the personality of the child. Without sounding indifferent, try to keep the discussion as impersonal as possible, at the same time making sure that you have answers to the following questions:

1. Who is the teaser and what is his or her status? Is it someone the child knows well? A friend? If so, is it likely that the purpose of the teasing is to exclude the child from a group or sever membership in it?
2. If the identity of the teaser seems unimportant, then ask about the *content* of the teasing. Is it directed to some characteristic of the child that is reversible? Or is it something such as a speech deficit that is largely irreversible?
3. Does the child appear to feel to blame for the teasing and therefore deserves to be teased?
4. Are there problems with the teacher(s)? Does the teacher set the child up for teasing?

This information gives the parents or professionals a base from which to attack the problem. In addition, the parents should consider the child's assets and liabilities as objectively as possible and obtain opinions about the child from reliable sources to identify behaviors and other aspects of the child that should be modified or changed.

It is pointless for the parents to advise the child simply to ignore the teasing. Such advice merely confirms the child's suspicions that they do not understand. It is almost impossible to ignore being teased without appearing to be a coward. Further, being ignored causes the teaser to intensify the verbal attack, the child's reactions become increasingly ineffective, and any remaining self-confidence dribbles away. As Kutner (1981) has noted, when the victim reacts ineffectively, the battle is lost and the child becomes an easier target next time.

Mention should be made of two courses of action frequently advocated to parents as solutions to the teasing problem. One of these, complaining to the school (Scialli, 1991), is not recommended unless it is one of the very rare schools in which there is genuine concern about teasing, combined with skill in handling it without branding the child as a tattle-tale or worse. Unfortunately, most teachers are not sympathetic about the problems of teasing (Olweus, 1993a). The other action involves rewarding the teaser in some way (Spock, 1986), such as having the victim's mother invite the teaser over for a snack and a friendly chat and offering some privileges. This approach should be avoided at all costs. What it teaches the victim is, first, that if someone bothers you, try to buy them off (a course of action difficult to distinguish from paying for protection) and, second, that parents cannot be trusted to deal with their children's problems because they are likely to defect to the enemy.

WHAT THE SCHOOL CAN DO FOR A CHILD WHO IS TEASED

Most schools in the United States show a disappointing lack of interest in bullying, and teasing ranks even lower on their agendas. However, if a teacher is genuinely concerned about the problem of teasing and is willing to help a specific child, there are some steps that can be taken:

1. If the victim has some behaviors or other modifiable attributes that annoy or repel others, or is lacking in skills that enhance his or her presence in the peer group, the teacher could work with the parents and victim to effect changes in the victim.

2. Class discussions about teasing (with no reference to the victim) could evolve from stories, role play, and problem questions about common teasing situations such as, "What should you do if you see a big boy teasing a small boy?"
3. Situations could be set up in the classroom that allow the victim to perform well. Contests or other activities involving chance could be rigged occasionally so that the victim wins or, even better, scores the winning point for his or her team.

WHAT PARENTS CAN DO IF THEIR CHILD IS ACCUSED OF TEASING OTHER CHILDREN

The parents of the alleged teaser should listen to the complaint from the school or the victim's parents and make a note of specific instances and behaviors. Ideally, such complaints should be received in a low-key, objective way with the emphasis on obtaining specific details of the teasing incidents. Rebuttals at this point should be avoided, the only commitment being that the parent will talk to the teaser and get back to the complainant. Next, parents should sit down with their child and discuss the complaints with him or her. If the child denies the teasing, define it for him or her using the reported instances as examples, and discuss why the complainants would make the charges if they are untrue. Drawing on their own assessment of the child and of the complainants, the parents should come to some conclusion about the validity of the complaints. If the child appears to be telling the truth in denying the accusations, then a meeting with all involved persons might shed some light on the problem. If both factions are adamant about their interpretation of events, then the parents of the accused child should, in private, spell out what they mean by teasing and emphasize that the child must not engage in teasing of others and that there would be negative consequences should he or she do so.

If, on the other hand, the child admits to the teasing, then the parents must make it very clear that the teasing must stop immediately. They should define behaviorally what is meant by teasing and the consequences to the child if the teasing continues. Some time should be spent with the teaser discussing the immediate and long-term effects of teasing on the victim. Have the teaser read some fictional accounts of teasing; discuss the importance of having a sympathetic imagination (seeing what a stressful event is like for another child); emphasize the potentially serious effects on the victim of being teased; and discuss some age-appropriate examples of victims who committed suicide. Also point out that if the teaser dislikes the victim, he or she does not have to voluntarily have anything to do with the victim, and dislike does not give the teaser the right to harass the victim.

Independently of the child, the parents should consider the state of the child's life. Is the child under stress? Frustrated by specific ongoing events or by his or her failure to achieve in some respect such as making the team or being chosen for some office? Is there anything about the child's life that can and should be changed? If so, they should consider talking to their child's teacher, since the teacher's observations about their child's behavior in school might cast some light on the problem.

WHAT IS THE OPTIMUM SOLUTION TO THE PROBLEM OF CRUEL TEASING?

In the case of Nathan Faris described earlier, many letters to the newspaper charged his parents with negligence in failing to protect him from his tormentors. What these writers did not grasp was that in most instances real protection is not having a stressor such as being teased eliminated by some kind of parental intervention. Instead, *real protection* is teaching children how to cope effectively *themselves* with many of the stressors of childhood. The fact that there are no physical or instrumental (weapons or other tangible objects) aggressive components in verbal teasing sets the stage for the victims to handle it themselves. What they need is a strategy, a plan of action to use in confronting the teaser. With a strategy they will feel less helpless, and this will reduce their anxiety and distress. With a successful strategy, children who are teased will feel an enormous sense of accomplishment. Other children will see them as ones who can manage: They may not like them any better, but they will treat them with some respect.

Admittedly, teasers enjoy some clear advantages: They can take as long as they want to think of a taunt and then wait for the ideal time to deliver it; they have the protection of strong sanctions against tattling, coupled with the known embarrassment of admitting to parents that one cannot cope with being teased. There is also the element of surprise: Victims are often caught off balance and are usually disconcerted, yet they must respond quickly and decisively if they are to stop the verbal attack and save face in front of bystanders.

Even so, it *is* possible for children to devise successful strategies, particularly if they have reason to *anticipate* that they will be teased. Consider the following instances:

> A teenager whose school locker was adjacent to those of two boys was continually harassed with suggestive comments that were

> clearly intended to upset her. For some time she followed the advice of her parents and other adults and just ignored them, but it had no effect. Finally, she said she got fed up and counterattacked:
>
> "When they started in on me, I turned around, put on a big smile, and said in the most sultry voice I could manage, 'Well, *hello!*' They got this real shocked look on their faces and mumbled about how they had to be somewhere and they left me alone for the rest of the year." (Minton, 1994, p. 30)

An 8-year-old girl who was new to the school and unquestionably fat was teased for several days by a classmate who always addressed her as "fatty," "hippopotamus," and other obesity-related terms. After several days the victim waited until other children were nearby and then, when the teaser started, turned to her with a wide smile and said, "You have the *strangest* way of making friends. Does it work?" The bystanders burst out laughing as the teaser walked away and never bothered the victim again.

Another example in this mode of taking the initiative was a strategy that involved describing in detail how awful the negative attribute was. This made teasing pointless because everything that could be said had been freely acknowledged by the potential victim. The boy who thought up this tactic had an unsightly and serious skin condition that imposed severe limitations on his activities. On his first day in his new school he gave an unemotional account of the problem to the class: He described the painful treatment, showed photographs of his skin at its worst, explained the limitations, and discussed his depression about the grim outlook as well as the financial problem for his family. He was never teased and, in fact, was welcomed by his classmates.

These examples are not at all representative of the children who are established or potential victims of teasing. Very few victims of teasing would have the necessary attributes of bravery, confidence, and risk taking, as well as creativity in planning a novel strategy. They are included here as emphasis for our view that strategies *can* be developed for coping with teasing and that victims *can* carry them out successfully with no negative fallout. To achieve these goals, programs specifically designed to teach the child the skills for managing teasing are needed.

COMMENT

It is clear that in some respects teasing presents more problems for the target child than does bullying. Whereas bullying is invariably seen as antisocial and negative, teasing is not. It takes many forms, as evidenced by its many meanings, and the act of teasing often is characterized by an ambiguity that the target child must interpret correctly because the "right" response is of great importance in the peer group. As children wend their way through the developmental stages from early preschool to late adolescence, there is a concomitant series of changes in the teasing interactions that confront them. At each stage there is a fine line between constructive and destructive teasing, and the target child or adolescent must know which side of the line the teasing is on. Cruel teasing can be an unremitting source of misery with both short- and long-term effects of a negative nature. Some children are able to take such decisive direct action that the teaser searches for another victim. Sometimes social support is forthcoming. But for many children the outlook is dismal. Often they are unable to generate solutions to the teasing, and they come to view themselves as incompetent and to blame. However, even for these children there is reason for optimism. There are teasing programs that can be easily mastered with an adult or older adolescent's help. In chapter 7, four of the available approaches for handling teasing are described, concluding with a detailed description of the highly successful program that I have developed (Ross, 1973; Ross & Ross, 1984).

7 Teasing Programs

Unlike the procedures for stopping ongoing bullying that were described in chapter 3, those for stopping teasing are designed to equip victims to handle teasing situations themselves. Thus, in addition to ending the misery of being teased, the victims have the immense satisfaction of having pulled off this coup with no adult present.

Since the development of the first teasing program (Ross, 1973; Ross & Ross, 1984), three other programs (Kellerman, 1981; Phillips, 1989; Smith, 1986) have appeared in the literature. All four use some or all of the following elements in varying combinations. *Nonreward* involves not reacting overtly to the teaser in any way that would encourage further teasing. *Verbal punishment,* by contrast, has the vitims striking back verbally in a way that actively discourages continued teasing. *Assertive training* focuses on changing the demeanor of the victims so that they cease to be passive recipients who appear to have no rights. *Understanding the teaser's motives* helps victims select the most effective retaliatory verbal responses and also shows them that they are not totally responsible for their status as victims. In this chapter, these programs are described and their various strengths and weaknesses discussed, beginning with Kellerman's nonreward approach.

Kellerman's Program

Kellerman's (1981) program is based on the fact that behavior that is consistently nonrewarded will eventually drop out; that is, extinction will occur. In his text, *Helping the Fearful Child*, Kellerman (1981) stated:

> There is only one way that I know of to get rid of teasing behavior. And that is to ignore it. Most children tease, and most are teased. Teasing is a special kind of power play. The payoff that comes from ridiculing someone else is the loss of control that the victim exhibits in terms of an angry or frustrated response. The object in teasing is to "get to the other guy" or make him "lose his cool" (translation: lose emotional control). By removing the payoff for teasing, we *extinguish* such obnoxious behavior. (pp. 97–98)

As Kellerman (1981) pointed out, a problem with extinction is that it does not occur immediately. Nor does the unwanted behavior follow a steady downward gradient. Instead, when behavior such as teasing has been consistently rewarded, the immediate effect of withholding reward is to intensify the teasing. Only if the victim can maintain a nonrewarding stance will the teasing eventually stop altogether. The crucial question with this program then becomes, *Can the victim hold out until the teasing stops?* which Kellerman cautioned may take weeks.

Should victims attempt to use nonreward but fail, the consequences are punishing: Their misery increases and their already shaky self-esteem is further damaged. Consider our hypothetical case of two 10-year-old girls, Karen and Mary. Karen teases Mary at school every day about her clothes ("Where'd you get the dress, Mary, the Salvation Army or are you just learning to sew?") or her protruding teeth ("Here's some celery for lunch, Mary, I told my Mom we had a new little bunny at school"). Mary gets upset and shows it. Sometimes she cries. She tries unsuccessfully to avoid Karen and her attempts at counterattacking are pathetically weak. Finally, she tells her mother, who assures her that if she just ignores Karen completely the teasing will stop. Because her mother is almost always right, Mary goes happily to school and tries to ignore Karen, only to find that Karen redoubles her efforts and the teasing becomes more severe. Mary is unable to maintain a nonreward demeanor. She lapses into her old pattern of upset and weak rejoinders, and Karen continues to enjoy teasing her.

Kellerman (1981) would attribute this result to a "maybe-the-next-time" attitude on Karen's part. Her first thought when Mary fails to respond with upset to the teasing is, "I'll keep trying. Maybe the next time I'll get her to cry." However, it also points to a failure on the part of Mary's mother to prepare her adequately: Mary needed to be warned about the strong possibility that the teasing would increase, and she should have been given practice in ignoring the teaser. Note that Kellerman (1981) has emphasized the importance of warning the child that the teasing is likely to increase if the teaser is ignored. He has also recommended that the period between the child's first attempts to extinguish the teasing and the point at which it finally stops will be easier to endure if the power struggle can be presented as a game, a Science Experiment. In this game the victim is a scientist who is observing the teaser (an animal) and keeping a record (data collection) of the frequency of teasing.

With sufficient preparation (and a child who is able to meet the demands of the nonreward method), Kellerman's (1981) approach should be successful. Consider the hypothetical case of Stevie, age 10:

Mother: Hi, Stevie. How was school today?

Stevie: That Gary! In P.E. he called me a *pansy* and he got the guys to smell me like I was a flower. And at lunch he said I was a *drip* and to turn off the tap. *Very* funny! *They* all laughed.

Mother: I bet you didn't like that at all. I would have hated it.

Stevie: He makes me feel terrible and kinda stupid. And the guys *always* laugh.

Mother: You know, this reminds me of how I was teased in fifth grade. I was *really* fat and they'd say, "What's shaking? Oh, it's just Porky Peggy. Hi, Fatso." I used to cry. I hated them and I hated going to school.

Stevie: You were teased, Mom?

Mother: Sure. So were Daddy and Roger (older brother). It doesn't mean there's anything wrong with you. Most kids get teased. I know how you can stop it. I know a way that worked for Roger. You want to try it?

Stevie: Sure, Mom. Hey, imagine *Roger* getting teased!

Mother: Well, when Gary teases you, don't look mad, don't look upset, act as if Gary isn't there at all. Look very, very interested in something else that's going on.

Stevie: That sounds hard to do. Like Gary is *right there* calling me a cupcake or something.

Mother: It *is* hard at first. But you can do it. Gary only teases you because he can see that it makes you mad. Being able to make kids like you mad makes Gary feel good. He feels powerful like Superman. What would help you a lot is if you could get *interested* in the teasing like you would in a game.

Stevie: (outraged) Mom, this *isn't* a game.

Mother: It could be sort of a game. How many times does Gary tease you in a week? Five times, ten, twenty?

Stevie: Hundreds of times.

Mother: (laughing) This game is called Lucky Number. (She gets out playing cards, excluding face cards, and two envelopes which she labels "Mother" and "Stevie.") Now pick two playing cards and don't look at them and put them in a sealed envelope with fifty cents. Now here's a teasing card with squares. Starting Monday you put an X in a square every time Gary teases you. Keep the teasing card where other kids can't see it and on Friday we'll count up the Xs and look at our playing cards that were in the envelope and whoever has a playing card closest to that number of Xs on their teasing card wins all the money. If your card(s) is exactly the same as the number of Xs you win *double* the money.

Stevie: Wow! It's like what we do in Science—data collection.

Mother: That's right. Now when Gary teases you and you ignore him, what do you think will happen?

Stevie: He stops teasing me. Right?

Mother: Wrong. He tries harder to make you mad, he gets meaner. He knows you've always been a good one to tease—you get mad. Gary thinks, "Why isn't Stevie upset the way he used to be? I'll have to try harder." And he does. So what do you do?

Stevie: Keep ignoring him?

Mother: Right. You have to say to yourself, "I can outlast you, Gary, keep trying, it won't get you anywhere." And you must not slip up and get upset, not even once. Now, I wonder who will win the game. Let's practice. I'll be Gary and I'll tease you and you show me how you ignore him. (They practice, then reverse the roles. Stevie performs competently.)

Mother: Good work, Stevie. You didn't look upset at the things I said and you didn't even look as if you heard me. Remember this will work as long as you can outlast Gary. He is sure to get meaner the minute he sees that you are trying to put a stop to the teasing. After a few more tries he'll probably go off and find someone else to tease because you know what?

Stevie: What?

Mother: You're stronger than he is. You know what's going on so you aren't going to slip up and get mad when he teases. I wonder who had the lucky card.

Although Kellerman (1981) did not make any specific suggestions about the mother's behavior during role play, I recommend that the following procedure be used. When the child is first acting as the teaser it is essential that the mother (victim) make errors, for example, she should look upset and look as if she is trying to ignore the teaser but cannot quite manage it. In other words, she must act as a coping model (Thelen, Fry, Fehrenbach, & Frautschi, 1979), one who performs poorly at first but gradually improves. The rationale for this procedure is as follows: Being teased has been a very painful experience for the victim. It is not easy for him to acquire these new responses even in the safety of role play with his mother. By having the mother experience some difficulty, the child is unlikely to feel discouraged by his own less-than-perfect performance. However, if the mother acts as a mastery model (Thelen et al., 1979) by immediately exhibiting effortless competence and great self-confidence, the child may be easily discouraged and decide that the task is too difficult for him.

Note that the game serves a dual purpose. It adds a note of interest to the teasing experience with a consequent lessening of the victim's negative response to the teasing. If the victim tends to exaggerate the negative aspects of the teasing situation, that is, to catastrophize (he is teased "hundreds of times"), the game provides an accurate record of the frequency of the teasing.

COMMENT

Kellerman's (1981) program has a narrow focus, with its emphasis on nonreward. As a concept, nonreward has both theoretical and applied support and is unquestionably an effective tactic. The problem lies in the difficulty most teasing victims have in meeting its no-response requirement. It is often difficult for a victim to remain completely silent in a teasing interaction. If the victim walks briskly and purposefully away from the teaser, remaining silent should not pose any problem although it could result in the teaser taunting him or her about being too "chicken" to stay. But if the victim is rooted to the spot by the teasing, it may be very difficult for him or her not to reply. Because there is no provision in this program for teaching the victim effective retaliatory verbal responses, he or she may respond with weak rejoinders or ineffective denials that lessen the impact of showing no upset and cancel out the strategy of ignoring the teaser. It would be easier for the victim to remain silent if in addition to presenting a calm front the victim was also taught some nonverbal behaviors that he or she should exhibit. The teaser's sense of being ignored would be heightened if the victim yawned sometimes and looked around the area. If others are present the victim could occasionally laugh at some ongoing event at a distance from the teaser. These behaviors would convey an important positive message to the teaser and at the same time give the victim something concrete to do. One final point: It takes longer to bring an end to the teasing because the teaser does not grasp that the victim is slipping away from him or her until some time after the victim's nonreward strategy has been introduced. During this interval the victim is subjected to an intensified attack and is equipped with only the one strategy to handle it.

Phillips's Program

Phillips (1989), like Kellerman (1981), used nonreward for helping a victim put an end to painful teasing. In the case described below, Phillips preceded the teasing training with a series of therapy sessions because the child was singularly lacking in assertive skills. Phillips defined assertiveness in operational terms, for example, being able to express one's feelings easily and calmly rather than aggressively or with hostility; being straightforward and forthright in difficult situations rather than embarrassed or defensive; and being an active person rather than a passive one. Note that being assertive does not involve being overbearing, pushy, or aggressive. Rather, it is the ability to act in a confident way, be competent in social situations, and cope effectively in everyday social interactions as well as in conflict situations. Phillips's approach to teaching a child assertive skills and how to combat teasing is described in sufficient detail in her book, *How to Give Your Child a Great Self-Image* (1989), which any competent and caring parent could use to help a school-age child or adolescent to become more assertive in teasing interactions and consequently more competent in handling such attacks.

It is my opinion that most children who are teased could benefit from learning how to be more assertive, which does not mean that they need therapy sessions. Instead, most children who are experiencing ongoing teasing can benefit from some practice in looking and sounding confident and untroubled when teased, maintaining a relaxed stance and eye contact with the teaser, and not backing off when confronted by the teaser.

The case of Rachel, age 10, reported by Phillips (1989), provides a good example of her approach. Rachel's problems started when she entered a new school. Although she was unquestionably intelligent and quite creative, all her fellow students saw was a short, underdeveloped, unimpressive-looking girl who seemed to be a good target for teasing. She was teased wherever she went in her school. Although there were other students who normally would have been friends with her, they were intimidated by those who were harassing her: The teasing had escalated to being vicious. A boy on her school bus, for example, told her, "You're ugly. You're the ugliest girl on the bus." Another boy in her homeroom said, "I bet you don't even wear a bra yet," and a girl whose name she did not know approached her and said, "No boy will ever ask *you* out." When the class had to fill out medical forms, someone said, "I wonder what Rachel is going to put down for 'sex,'" and everybody laughed.

Rachel's parents knew she was miserable, but only gradually was Rachel able to tell them that she was being teased and did not like anything about the new school. They did what most caring parents do—they assured her that the teasers were insecure and that many people they had known as children had grown up to be successful and popular despite earlier teasing. Rachel's parents then went further by admitting that they had been teased and had tried unsuccessfully to stop the teasing by such tactics as crying, lying, running away, fighting back, one-upping, tattling, and changing their behavior to "suit" their tormentors. They then sought professional help from Phillips.

Phillips focused first on training Rachel to become more assertive, the goal being to help her to feel stronger, which, in turn, could be expected to manifest itself in an assured, confident demeanor that would discourage teasing. Through a combination of positive reinforcement and empathic listening, Phillips was able gradually to get Rachel to express her feelings freely. She was not allowed to be merely a passive recipient of treatment but, instead, was assigned homework that required her to think about her feelings and translate her thoughts into action by expressing her feelings to others in her family. None of this was easy for Rachel, but with Phillips's help she persevered with great success. Only when Rachel showed that she could express her feelings to a variety of people within and outside the family did Phillips turn to the teasing problem.

Knowing how uncomfortable Rachel was about the teasing, Phillips proceeded cautiously. She elicited information about a great moment in Rachel's life when, at her previous school, she had been given a standing ovation for her performance in the school play. Phillips then instructed Rachel in how to use this experience as an escape hatch whenever talking or thinking about the teasing made her anxious or upset. Rachel's task was to substitute thoughts about her success in the play whenever any aspect of the teasing or any other aspects of her life bothered her.

Phillips had also learned who was teasing Rachel, what they said, and how she reacted. Using role play, including reversal of roles, she taught Rachel to respond to teasing in an assertive and nondefensive manner by standing up straight, making extended eye contact (looking the teaser straight in the eye and not looking away), not showing any upset, and never arguing, in fact, not responding verbally at all unless what the teaser said was true, in which case Rachel was to agree in an unemotional but nondefensive way ("You're right. I do have hundreds of freckles.") Agreeing is disconcerting to the teaser; it deflates him or her and reduces the impact of the teasing.

To combat the problem of remaining silent, a demand most children find difficult, Phillips taught Rachel to use an emotional shrug, that is, to assume the demeanor that conveys "So what," or "Who cares, I don't." It is a look of confidence and indifference that indicates that the teasing really does not matter at all. Although this method is hard to master, Rachel persevered and soon noticed that she was being teased less and less. She also found that when she was teased she felt "stronger and more in control" (Phillips, 1989, p. 133). Her weekly therapy sessions dwindled to monthly sessions and then stopped altogether. At last report Rachel was no longer being teased. A measure of the value of Phillips's approach was that Rachel attributed the change to her self-confidence and assertiveness rather than to a change of heart on the part of the teasers.

COMMENT

Phillips's (1989) program offers a number of important features for the adult who wants to help a child combat teasing. It is easy to teach. Procedures such as role play along with reversal of roles, homework assignments that put some responsibility on the victim, thought substitution, the emotional shrug, and positive reinforcement are clearly described and skillfully incorporated into the teaching sessions. For children such as Rachel, beginning with assertiveness training means a significant delay in attacking the teasing problem with its attendant misery. Phillips's program, like Kellerman's (1981), requires the victim to remain silent in the teasing interaction (except in Phillips's case when the victim agrees that a tease is indeed true); it is often difficult for a child to do this. I suggest having some nonverbal behaviors that the victim should exhibit in order to fill the verbal gap.

Smith's Program

The third teasing program to be discussed here was developed by Smith (1986) and was included in a guide for parents to use in teaching children and adolescents to be assertive. Titled *Yes, I Can Say No,* it describes his Social Thinking and Reasoning Program referred to as STAR. The emphasis throughout the program is on teaching the child what to *say* in social conflict situations such as coping with peer pressure, rather than on what to *do*. To this end, Smith teaches a set of general verbal strategies and skills for use in coping with a wide variety of conflict situations. Included in this set are the following:

- *Free Information*: Information you provide spontaneously without having to be prompted. It is the basis of good social conversation.
- *Self-Disclosure*: Making personal statements about yourself, expressing opinions about what you think, and describing how you feel. This strategy makes it easier for the other person to talk to you because he or she can become involved by following

up on your personal statements: It can turn a stilted verbal exchange into a two-way conversation.

- *Fogging*: Agreeing with another person's critical comments about you when there is no objective way of proving whether they are correct. It involves responding to his or her *observations* about your behavior, ideas, and so on, but not to his or her *judgment* about them ("Perhaps I am" and "Maybe").
- *Mirroring*: Repeating back what has just been said.
- *Broken Record*: Saying what you want over and over again until the other person realizes he or she is getting nowhere with you. Prefacing a Broken Record comment with a Mirroring statement helps convince the other person that he or she is getting nowhere.
- *Positive Assertion*: Stating that you are right. Asserting your positive qualities.
- *Negative Assertion*: Agreeing with a critic that what he or she says about you is true, or admitting that you have made a mistake. Note that where Fogging is somewhat ambiguous, Negative Assertion is clear-cut.
- *Negative Inquiry*: Exploring the other person's opinion in a nonchallenging and nonthreatening way rather than apparently accepting it (as in Mirroring).
- *Workable Compromise*: Assuming that something can be worked out so that both participants gain something from the interaction.

Smith (1986) stated that the teaching format for his program is based on one principle: Give an idea, then practice on an example. The child must learn the strategies by rote, understand what each one can accomplish, and then practice them in as many different social interactions and conflict situations as possible. Considerable practice is required because children do not easily transfer skills, such as those learned in one situation in this program, to similar situations outside, if there is anxiety associated with the second situation. To provide the practice needed for such transfer of training to occur, Smith included sample dialogues demonstrating their use in a wide variety of social interactions that are likely to be encountered by children and adolescents.

When the specific topic is teasing, Smith (1986) asserted unequivocally that chronic teasing can be extinguished simply and effectively using his method. Children learn how to respond to teasing in an assertive but nondefensive and unemotional way. With the help of selected assertive verbal skills, the child's behavior when teased changes from an automatic and ineffective response ("can so," "it is not," "are not") to a voluntary thinking response.

In support of the efficacy of his program, Smith (1986) described its use with 8-year-old Mary, a shy, self-conscious girl who was teased unmercifully by her brother and her second-grade classmates. When Mary's rate of absenteeism increased with the concomitant fall in her grades, her teacher and a psychologist experienced in the use of the STAR program devised a plan to help her. First, they gave a few students in Mary's class demonstrations on how to cope assertively with teasers. The children were told that using the STAR techniques would lessen a child's upset when teased and at the same time would exhaust the teaser by repeatedly seeking explanatory information about the topic of teasing without any sign of upset. After several demonstrations Mary volunteered to participate in a trial. The rest of the class were told to tease and criticize her. For 20 minutes the psychologist coached Mary on how to respond assertively to her classmates' taunts. Smith stated that by the end of the demonstration Mary could handle their teasing. Further, during the following weeks she used her newly acquired skill repeatedly with no help from others, to cope with being teased.

In evaluating the coaching by the STAR psychologist, it would be helpful to know if he provided Mary with *specific responses* (e.g., "I don't understand. What is it that I do that makes you call me stupid?") or made *general suggestions* about how to reply ("Keep asking her questions about why she doesn't like your dress"). In any case, what this classroom demonstration shows is that during what was probably a 40–45-minute session that included discussion by a psychologist about a single assertive response, Negative Inquiry, demonstration of its use by peer models, and 20 minutes of intensive coaching of the target child, Mary learned to use this procedure and transferred the learning to the playground. It is a far cry from this level of competence with one assertive response to the level of expertise with multiple assertive responses to teasing that is demonstrated in Dialogues 70 (pp. 202–204) and 72 (pp. 207–209) in Smith's (1986) book.

In our following hypothetical dialogue illustrating the application of Smith's (1986) procedures, a 12-year-old girl struggles ineffectively in a defensive and nonassertive way to deal with teasing by her 15-year-old sister. The younger girl is working on a poster when her sister enters the room:

Older sister: What's the great Picasso doing now?

Younger sister: (reluctant to show work but does so after persuasion) It's my Safety Contest poster. I think it might win a prize.

Older sister: Get real! A dumb poster like *that?* Well, if no one else goes in the contest . . . or if only preschoolers do . . .

Younger sister: That's mean! Why do you always make fun of me?

Older sister: I'm saving you from making a fool of yourself and looking even stupider than you are. You're too stupid to know you should just forget the contest.

Younger sister: All you know is how to be mean. I thought it was looking good and now you've ruined it.

Older sister: What's ruined? There's nothing to ruin.

Younger sister: There is so. I've been working on this for more than two hours.

Older sister: Well, you must be *really* stupid to spend that long on a pathetic poster like this.

Younger sister: (crying) It is *not* pathetic.

Older sister: Sure it is. It's making you cry, isn't it?

Younger sister: Mother!

A second dialogue shows the younger girl responding according to Smith's (1986) program, that is, in a nondefensive but assertive way in the face of her sister's gibes:

Older sister: What's the great Picasso doing now?

Younger sister: (reluctant to show work but does so after persuasion) It's my Safety Contest poster. I think it might win a prize. (Self-Disclosure)

Older sister: Get real! A dumb poster like *that?* Well, if no one else goes in the contest . . . or if only preschoolers do . . .

Younger sister: You think it's dumb (Mirroring). What's dumb about this poster? (Negative Inquiry)

Older sister: I just told you. It's dumb like all your pitiful attempts at art. Like when something's *dumb,* it's dumb.

Younger sister: Maybe (Fogging). But I still don't know what's dumb about it (Negative Inquiry and Broken Record). I'd like it if you'd tell me some specific things in it that make it seem dumb to you. (Self-Disclosure)

Older sister: You go on and on like a stuck record. It's like you don't know many words. Like you're as dumb as your poster.

Younger sister: How about if I give you time to think what exactly is dumb about it? (Workable Compromise)

Older sister: I'm getting out of here (leaves in disgust).

In sensitive situations such as being overweight, just learning not to be unduly upset is rewarding for the child being teased. In the following dialogue based on Smith's (1986) method, an obese girl keeps her composure by responding in a nondefensive, assertive, and unemotional way to a teaser:

Teaser: Here is Hippo the Blimp getting fatter every day.
Victim: You're right. I am getting fatter. (Fogging)
Teaser: You're the fattest kid in the whole school. Soon you'll need two desks.
Victim: I probably will. I've never seen anyone fatter than me at school. (Fogging)
Teaser: I hate looking at you.
Victim: Why do you look at me if you hate it? (Negative Inquiry)
Teaser: I just told you, you bucket of lard. Because you're so fat, you're *gross*!
Victim: What else makes you hate looking at me? (Negative Inquiry)
Teaser: Would you stop asking so many questions?
Victim: I don't understand why it bothers you. (Self-Disclosure)
Teaser: I've got better things to do than talk to you (leaves).
Victim: I'm sure you do. (Fogging)

COMMENT

On the basis of his experience in using the STAR program to teach children assertive skills, Smith (1986, p. 202) contended that "chronic teasing can be extinguished simply and effectively" with the foregoing procedures. This statement implies that his assertive training can be readily mastered by the average child. It is an erroneous conclusion. A child would have considerable work to do before approaching the level of competence evident in the Chronic Teasing Dialogues 70 (pp. 202–204) and 72 (pp. 207–209) in *Yes, I Can Say No* (Smith, 1986). Learning the general strategies by rote first and then understanding what each one can accomplish is a major task in itself. Furthermore, a substantial amount of practice would be needed in a wide variety of social situations for a child to become competent in selecting at a moment's notice the appropriate strategy for a specific ongoing conflict situation. To use the strategy effectively constitutes a further challenge. However, once a child has mastered the assertive techniques in Smith's program, there is no question that there would be immediate and long-term benefits.

A surprising omission in the STAR program concerns the *nonverbal* components of assertiveness. No mention is made of teaching children to stand up straight, look the teaser in the eye, and try for a neutral look devoid of upset. Nor is any attention paid to eliminating defensive behaviors such as backing away from the teaser, folding arms across one's chest, or fidgeting from one foot to the other. It is a mistake to assume that the nonverbal components of assertiveness will appear spontaneously as the child experiences some success in coping with teasing by using the verbal procedures in this program.

The Frames and Scripts Approach

Hoover and Olson (2000a, 2000b) have developed a method, called a *frames and scripts model*, to help children deal effectively with being teased and understand the reactions of others being teased. In the model, *frame* refers to the symbolic space around two children involved in an ongoing teasing episode, and *scripts* provide children with the internal language needed for dealing with the episode. Scripts are provided for different age categories beginning with ages 1 to 4 and continuing through ages 12 and up. From the information provided, it is difficult, for example, to see how a very young child could use the method successfully or how an older child could mentally run through the recommended strategy of *stop, think,* and *decide* (whether or not to tease) when faced with the immediacy of a possible teasing opportunity. In the absence of any supporting data, including unsolicited subjective accounts of the method's efficacy, it is difficult to regard the method as anything but a novel approach with possible potential. The method is described in detail in their book (Hoover & Olson, 2000b) and in an article (Hoover & Olson, 2000a).

The Ross Teasing Program

Ross (1973; Ross & Ross, 1984) designed the Ross Teasing Program to teach victims of ongoing teasing strategies to stop the teasing.[1] The underlying rationale of this approach is as follows: Teasers expect their victims to show upset, exhibit avoidance and withdrawal, and be ineffective in retaliation attempts. They are unlikely to continue teasing children who appear to be untroubled by the teasing, who stand their ground in an assertive but not aggressive way, and, above all, who counterattack promptly and effectively. Effecting these changes in children who are teased is the goal of this program.

The program is for individual school-age children and adolescents for whom ongoing teasing is clearly a problem. It can also be used as a preventive intervention with children who are unequivocally at risk for teasing, for example, the facially disfigured child. The program should *not* be used with children for whom teasing is a problem secondary to other kinds of bullying, particularly physical aggression. It should never be used in schools in which guns and knives are commonplace.

---

[1]©1973, D. M. Ross. Reprinted with permission.

Most children complete the program in 3 to 5 hours, spread over several days or a week. No teaching session should exceed 1 hour, and for some younger children, a full hour may be too long. The program falls logically into four parts. It is essential to stay with one part until the tasks in it have all been mastered. Children must be allowed to work through the program at their own pace. Should a child clearly be unable to handle the demands of the program, some other intervention should be considered. Under no circumstances should the child be forced to continue. There should be no direct or implied suggestion either of incompetence or that the program was then being terminated midway.

Any competent adult or older adolescent can teach the program. An assistant, who may be an adult, adolescent, or child, is needed to help with role-play demonstrations. Having the child's parent(s) teaching or assisting is an advantage because the more knowledgeable they are about the program, the more supportive they can be. Any siblings who participate must be congenial with the child, sympathetic about the teasing, and completely trustworthy about *never* discussing the ongoing program with outsiders. There have been instances of siblings telling others about the ongoing program, with the result that the victim was confronted with merciless taunts about going to "teasing school."

Between training sessions, practice in the form of homework usually reduces the time needed to complete the program. For some of the homework tasks, it helps to have someone in the home environment work with the child. Children will become proficient in handling staged teasing incidents during the lessons. But if the program is to benefit them, they must also be able to use their new skills in outside situations, that is, they must be able to generalize. Because generalization usually does not occur spontaneously, it is intentionally worked into this program through homework assignments and other procedures.

In the following description of the program, the person teaching it is referred to as the Teacher, the assistant as the Helper, and the child as the Victim. Note that whenever examples of teasing sequences are used, the teaser should be the same age and gender and in the same grade as the Victim. A brief outline of the program's content appears in Table 7.1.

PART 1

Begin by giving high priority to reassurance and face-saving. Victims, especially boys, often feel defensive and embarrassed about being teased, particularly if the teaser is the same age. Assure the Victim

Table 7.1. Ross Teasing Program

Part 1
Provide reassurance about the normalcy of being teased and consequent upset.
Explain that Victim's own behavior partly determines whether teasing will occur and whether it will continue.
Assure Victim that there are ways to stop ongoing teasing.
Discuss the concept of *payoff*.
Explain procedure for role-play demonstrations.
Teach four nonverbal behaviors that the Victim must not exhibit when teased.

Part 2
Review payoff and nonverbal behaviors that must not be exhibited during teasing. Teach nonverbal behaviors that must be used.
Have Victim act as a critic as well as a participant in role play.
When Victim is competent, he or she must use the appropriate nonverbal behaviors in the actual teasing situation.
Explain that Victim is to collect data in the teasing situation.

Part 3
Victim learns verbal retort strategies, beginning with the mildest (nonreward) and continuing with the more severe (punishing) strategies.
Victim chooses strategies to use in the next actual teasing situation.

Part 4
Criteria for initiating a test run in the actual teasing situation.
Importance of reporting back after the first trial.
Criteria for considering the program a success.

that it is normal to be upset about being teased. It does not mean that he is a wimp or a sissy. Tell him that he will soon learn how to stop the teasing. Misery loves company (Cottrell & Epley, 1977), so the Victim will feel more at ease with a Teacher who has experienced the stress of childhood teasing and talks freely about it. If possible, obtain anecdotes from the Victim's parents, too, about being teased and not knowing how to handle it.

In your account of how you (the Teacher) were teased as a child, work in the following ideas. You did not know how to handle being teased or what to say to the teaser, and you were so upset that sometimes you cried. You tried to avoid the teaser but he always found you. You were too embarrassed to tell your parents or teacher. The teaser teased you for a long time and got other children to tease you, too. Use your account of being teased to introduce two important ideas that the Victim must accept: First, how a child behaves often determines if he will be teased at all, and, second, how he reacts when being teased usually determines if the teasing will continue.

To help the Victim understand why children are teased, discuss the concept of *payoff*, that is, the effect of reward on behavior. Start with some age- and gender-appropriate examples of payoff (reward): a girl baby-sits because she earns money (payoff) doing it; a boy works hard at swimming so that he can make the school team and go to swimming meets (payoff). Ask, "Would they continue to do these things if there were no *payoff?*" Emphasize that payoff may take many forms, for example, satisfaction, pleasure, or feelings of accomplishment, in addition to monetary benefits.

Now discuss the payoff for the teaser in the Teacher's story. Explain that it made the teaser feel good, powerful, and in control to upset someone else, to see them cry, and to have them be afraid. Stress that as long as a child makes teasing pay off by acting upset, crying, hiding from the teaser, and not telling someone who could stop the teasing, the teaser will keep on teasing. Help the Victim to see that by providing payoff, he is largely responsible for keeping the teasing going.

Next, have the Victim watch while you show him how a mean kid named Jeffrey teased a boy you know, and ask the Victim to tell you what the payoff is for Jeffrey. The Teacher and Helper now role play a sequence in which the Helper, acting as Jeffrey, calls the Teacher names. The Teacher looks upset, stands in a hunched-up position not looking at Jeffrey, moves away cautiously, starts to cry, and mumbles, "I am not." The teasing continues. Discuss what the Teacher did that was the payoff for Jeffrey.

The Victim may find this demonstration upsetting because he is seeing *for the first time* how he looks when being teased, an unquestionably powerful learning experience and motivator. Some Victims start to cry. One 10-year-old boy said, "I'm a *real* wimp. I oughta just hang a sign around my neck that says, 'Kick me. I won't do nothing if you do.'" But not every Victim is upset by this demonstration. Some watch the role play with interest and are able to state clearly what the payoff is and how the victim (the Teacher) should have acted.

Ask, "What would happen if the teasing did not have any payoff? What if the boy had not become upset when Jeffrey teased him? That's not much fun for Jeffrey, is it?" Role play this sequence, then tell the Victim that a teaser *may not stop* after just getting no payoff once. He will *probably* try harder to get the Victim upset. Why? Because he does not want to lose someone who has given him a lot of payoff. But assure the Victim that if he keeps on not getting upset, the teasing will stop. Role play a sequence in which Jeffrey tries harder and the Teacher doesn't give him the payoff he wants so, after several attempts, Jeffrey just walks away.

Next, the Victim must learn not to exhibit the following nonverbal behaviors when teased:

1. *Any kind of upset* such as crying or looking embarrassed.
2. *Physical withdrawal* such as moving away or deliberately trying to avoid the teaser.
3. *Making any kind of physical contact* with the teaser because even minor physical contact can escalate into behavior such as pushing or hitting that is likely to result in punishment from school personnel.
4. *Standing so close to the teaser* that it implies threat.

Using role play by the Teacher and Helper, demonstrate behaviors from each of the above categories. Make a simple, easy-to-read list of these nonverbal behaviors and assign for homework the task of thinking which of the incorrect ones the Victim shows when teased. If possible, someone in the Victim's family should work with him so that he can practice not looking upset, and so on. The Victim must master the contents of Part 1 before starting on Part 2.

PART 2

Review payoff and the nonverbal behaviors that the Victim must *not* show, then move on to the nonverbal behaviors that the Victim *should* show when teased. The Victim must do the following:

1. Look interested, laugh sometimes, appear to be untroubled, yawn sometimes, suddenly stare at something going on elsewhere, and then, if appropriate, turn to the teaser and ask him what he just said.
2. Assume an assertive rather than a passive stance. He must stand his ground, feet slightly apart, arms at side or hands in pockets (this suggests confidence that nothing of a physical-attack nature is going to happen).
3. Maintain eye contact with the teaser, a very important move.
4. Move closer to the teaser rather than moving away.

In trying to look interested or bored, some victims may present exaggerated versions of these expressions (De Paulo, 1992). As you use role play to demonstrate each of the above nonverbal behaviors, try to overdo some of them. Laugh too much, for example, or lean forward and stare instead of just maintaining eye contact as you would in normal conversation. When you do this, have the Helper tell you to stop, demonstrate the exaggerated behavior, and then give you a hand mirror so that you can see how you look.

It is not easy to control facial expressions under conditions of stress. The Victim will soon see that the intent to present a particular facial expression cannot always be accomplished successfully (De Paulo, 1992). Nor will it be easy for the Victim to exhibit nonverbal behaviors, such as an assertive stance, to convey an external impression that is at odds with his internal state. For homework the Victim must learn these behaviors and then practice in front of a mirror, first being the teaser making a mean remark and then being himself exhibiting the appropriate behaviors. Demonstrate these sequences for the Victim and have him practice them.

Start having the Victim act as a *critic*. Have the Teacher and Helper use role play to show a teasing interaction in which the Helper exhibits some nonverbal behaviors that he *should not* use and some that he *should*. Have the Victim sit on the sidelines and when the role play ends, ask him to tell the Helper how he should have reacted. This critique procedure allows the Victim to be the "expert" as well as to have some control over the situation, both being experiences that he sorely needs.

Next repeat the role play with the Helper following the Victim's instruction in a not-too-competent way that leaves room for improvement. The Helper, for example, might withdraw a bit or start by looking untroubled but then look upset. With this degree of semicompetence, the Helper becomes a *coping model* who initially does not perform perfectly but clearly tries hard. The rationale for some Helper incompetence is based on the following points. It is not easy for the Victim to make these quite drastic behavioral changes. If the Helper, too, is somewhat incompetent at first and gradually improves, the Victim will feel more at ease when he participates in the role play than he would if the Helper performed with the ease and confidence of a *mastery model*. Coping models are more effective than mastery models in reducing anxiety and uncertainty in the observer (Meichenbaum, 1971). Also, the idea that both the Teacher and Helper make "mistakes" serves to focus the Victim's attention.

The Victim and Teacher now role play a teasing interaction while the Helper sits on the sidelines and provides feedback in the form of specific descriptions of what was done correctly and praise for it, as well as comments on what needs to be done differently. (In these interactions, concentrate on the nonverbal behaviors that the Victim *should* show but also include some that he *should not* show.) The Victim and Teacher reenact the sequence and then they reverse roles. Role play in which the Victim first plays himself and then takes the teaser's role serves as a vehicle for integrating and mastering the teasing experience. It allows the Victim to see teasing from the viewpoint of the teaser, thus giving him a different perspective about being teased.

When the Victim demonstrates competence in the nonverbal behaviors that he *should* show, he must use them outside when he is teased. Encourage him to reward his efforts with positive self-statements, for example, "I'm really eyeballing him, I bet he's wondering what's going on." He must also report back to the Teacher, who should show great interest and approval of any reported success. Sometimes have the Victim show how he acted, so that you can both enjoy his success. Some Victims stated that when they used the nonverbal behaviors the teasers sometimes were "real nasty, meaner, and talked louder" but did not stop teasing. Use any such reports to review the payoff idea, that the teaser might have sensed a change in the Victim and so had redoubled his attacks to ensure that the Victim remained a victim. Emphasize that the teaser's behavior shows that the Victim's tactics are having a real effect and so far, the Victim has not even said one word!

When the Victim has clearly assimilated the nonverbal behavior tasks, tell him that soon he will learn what to *say* when he is teased. Explain that for this step you need his help, because what he says has to *fit* the teasing. Explain *fit* using examples such as clothes fitting or having the right tool for a job. Ask the Victim to start the next time he is teased to remember exactly what the teaser says and to write it down as soon as possible. Give him a small notebook and treat him as an expert, an essential member of the team. Gear the job title to the Victim's age, for example, data collector, ace reporter, advance scout, or scientist.

The whole data collection experience should be as enhancing as possible for the Victim. When he reports actual taunts, show great enthusiasm, for example, "That's a winner!" "We'll get him if he tries that one again," "We'll nail him for that one," or "We can think of something better for you to say back." If the Teacher and Helper show clearly that the Victim's input is valuable, he will begin to see being teased as a source of ammunition to use against the teaser, rather than solely as persecution against himself.

> One 7-year-old boy who was working very industriously at collecting the teaser's taunts absent-mindedly replied, "Hey, that's a great one—we can use that," after a particularly nasty crack. The

> teaser was clearly disconcerted at the Victim's comment and asked what he meant. The Victim, who was becoming increasingly confident, just laughed and for the first time *the teaser walked away*. (Ross, 1977–1979)

Parents sometimes express concern that rehashing the teasing episode will upset the Victim further. In fact, it often defuses the teasing because the Victim places a less painful interpretation on it. An 11-year-old girl said:

> It's real interesting how I feel now about Missy teasing me. Like I really have to listen carefully because I'm in the front line and the people back in the planning room are counting on *me* to bring in the reports. And I have to remember them 'til I can write them down. I just don't have time to get upset at what she says and anyway it sorta doesn't seem so bad anymore. (Ross, 1977–1979)

PART 3

Even if the Victim handles his nonverbal behavior correctly when he is teased, his remaining silent has an element of payoff because the teaser can interpret the silence as upset or fear. What the Victim needs now is the quick, *specific* retort that fits the teaser's scornful comments. Generalities such as "Are not," "Who says?" and "You're crazy" are very weak retorts lacking any element of fit. By now the Teacher will have accumulated a list of specific taunts and topics of attack by the teaser for use in building up a retort repertoire. Retort strategies range in a hierarchy from mildest (nonreward) to strongest (punishing). The nonreward category will be covered first because even the mildest retort can become a major hurdle for a Victim who has never previously made a strong rebuttal. Although it is usually best to begin with the least threatening (to the Victim) and proceed up the hierarchy from there, occasionally a Victim will react negatively to the nonreward strategies and ask for something "more mean like what he says to me." When this occurs, bypass the nonreward strategies and teach the punishing ones.

It is important for the Victim to know what *not* to say. If the teaser's comment about the Victim is true, the Victim must neither deny it nor argue. Instead, the comment should be either ignored or agreed with. When onlookers see that the Victim does not deny what is clearly true, the tease is defused and the Victim's other retorts gain stature.

There are three nonreward strategies: exhausting the topic, making an asset of the topic, and giving the teaser permission to tease. The teaching procedure for all of the retort strategies is as follows: First, the Teacher and Helper enact one of the teasing interactions (with teaser payoff) that the Victim has actually experienced. Then they repeat it using a retort strategy combined with the nonverbal behaviors that should be exhibited. Next, all three discuss the strategy, think of other replies the Victim might have made, and then the Teacher and Victim reenact them. The Helper watches, offers suggestions, and gives a critique of their performance.

Nonreward Retort Strategies

1. *Exhausting the Topic.* This is a good strategy to use when the teaser's taunts are true. The Victim must first acknowledge in a matter-of-fact, unemotional tone that what the teaser says is true. He then shows interest in hearing more about the topic. In the following scenario the teaser taunts the Victim about being fat:

Teaser: Fatty, fatty, two by four.
Can't get through the kitchen door.

Victim: You're right. I am fat. (moves closer, makes eye contact, shows no upset) Could you say some more about fatties like me?

Teaser: You're beyond fat, you're like a hippo.

Victim: Yes, I am very, very large. When did you first get interested in kids like hippos?

Teaser: Who says I'm interested? All I'm saying is you're a big blob of fat.

Victim: You're quite right. I am a big blob. Tell me more.

Teaser: Oh, shut up.

Some teasers lose interest at this point. Others redouble their efforts to get a rise out of the Victim. No matter what the teaser says, the Victim continues to agree, act interested, show no upset, and seek more information.

2. *Making an Asset of the Topic.* This strategy is most useful when the teaser's taunt is indisputably true and the Victim is clearly not to blame for the target characteristic. It has been particularly successful with leukemic children whose baldness and pallor are the aftermath of chemotherapy (Ross & Ross, 1984). The Victim's task is to look undisturbed, reply quickly, acknowledge the truth of the taunt, and point out the positive aspects of the characteristic:

Teaser: Hey, guys, look at Steve! Is that a head or a skating rink?

Victim: Hi, Mitch. You're right. Not one hair. You know what's great about it? (pauses while the teaser looks puzzled) You don't know? It's the only time in my whole life that I could wash my hair in ten seconds.

Teaser: You look like a freak from Mars. I bet it never grows back in.

Victim: I sure do look like outer space but I hope it doesn't grow in for a while. If it just stays this way 'til Halloween I'm going trick or treating as ET (Telly Savalas or some other bald TV or athletic star).

The Teacher knows in advance what this Victim will be teased about and should help him think of replies.

3. *Giving the Teaser Permission to Tease.* At the first taunt the Victim takes control by saying kindly to the teaser that he can say that if it makes him feel good. Being given permission to tease is very irritating, but often the teaser is genuinely puzzled about why it is irritating:

Teaser: Wow, Karen, where did you get that freaky dress? Straight from Dudsville! Did your little sister make it?

Victim: (smiling sweetly) You can say that if you want to, Cheryl. Don't stop.

Teaser: Gee, you're *stupid*, Karen.

Victim: You can say that as much as you want, Cheryl.

Teaser: (annoyed) Stop telling me what I can do! Who do you think you are?

Victim: I'm Karen (this is a very effective retort to "Who do you think you are?"). I just want you to know you can keep talking about my dress.

Teaser: Oh, shut up! (walks away. This is a typical response: The teaser cannot grapple with the situation and the Victim is clearly in control.)

Now that the Victim has had experience with the three nonreward retort strategies, give brief demonstrations of each. Ask him to pick two of these to use in an actual teasing situation, then give him intensive practice with the selected strategies. The Victim is given a choice because being allowed to choose makes him feel in control. He must feel comfortable with the strategies that he uses to counterattack, otherwise he will not sound convincing. In addition, being actively involved in retort selection will make him more likely to use the retorts, and he will also try harder and longer to make them work (Bandura, 1969).

Punishment Retort Strategies

The next eight strategies use verbal punishment. Here the Victim must attack, rebut, and downgrade the teaser's taunts, the goal being to annoy, discomfit, and embarrass the teaser particularly when other children are present. Onlookers are like sheep—they soon side with whomever is winning.

Remind the Victim that the three strategies that he has just learned will annoy the teaser because he is not getting the expected payoff (reward). Explain that now you are going to teach him how to *punish* the teaser. A teaser will soon stop teasing a Victim who not only is not upset by the teasing but also starts getting tough, picking on the teaser, and making him look dumb. Use the same teaching procedure that was used for the nonreward retort strategies.

Note that some of these strategies may sound somewhat inflammatory and are likely to elicit aggression. However, the teaser has *not* been physically aggressive. *This program is designed for children who are being subjected to teasing only,* and in the first period that the program was used there were only three reports of resultant aggression. Two of these involved mild pushing and shoving; the third one resulted in a nose-bleed for the teaser. Since then, the program has been used with no negative reports of any kind concerning its use.

1. *Unable to Remember the Teaser's Name.* No matter what the teaser says, the Victim starts to reply using the wrong name. The message here is that the teaser is of so little importance to the Victim that she cannot remember the teaser's name:

Teaser: Here comes Carrot-Top. Here comes Red Light. You look like a traffic stop-light.

Victim: Uh, Betty. No. Your name isn't Betty. Don't tell me, I want to think of it myself. (Pause. Victim looks apologetic then says) I have the *hardest* time remembering your name. I never have *any* trouble with anyone else. (Victim looks around and quickly names five or six girls.) See, I know *their* names.

Teaser: It's Jessica.

Victim: Oh, sure, *Jennifer.* (The Victim must use a name with the same first letter.) I guess there's just nothing about you that helps me remember your name. (Pauses and looks thoughtfully at the teaser.) Or maybe it's just that *I never think about you.*

During this kind of exchange the Victim *must* respond quickly and smoothly and look puzzled at the appropriate times. The teaser will usually be thrown off balance by the Victim's counterattack: This gives the Victim an immediate if temporary edge and her confidence soars. There should be no trouble about alternate names: The Victim knows who is likely to tease her, so "wrong" names can be decided on in advance and included in the practice runs. Initially, it was anticipated that the teaser would feel insulted or angry. But, in fact, most teasers were reported to be genuinely upset that the Victim could not remember their name.

2. *Turning the Tables on the Teaser.* This strategy can be used only if the topic is general enough that it could apply to the teaser. It consists simply of listening to the teaser's opening statement and then responding with, "It takes one to know one, doesn't it, (teaser's name)?" Often the teaser becomes really angry. Sometimes he is speechless and when this happens, the Victim should leave with a pseudo-kindly comment, "Well, I'll leave you to think about it."

3. *Reversal of Teasing. Any* kind of teasing can be reversed. The Victim must use the attribute that he is being teased about:

Clothes: Pick out one item that the teaser is wearing and say, "Where *did* you get it? Did your *Mom* pick it out? Do *you* like it?" Stare. Point it out to others.

Hair: "Was *your* hair *always* a bit thin? Do you know that some people go bald *before* they're 20?" Stare at hair and shake head (used very successfully by children with leukemia) (Ross & Ross, 1984).

Hat: "I guess you notice *my hat* because *you* look so *funny* in *that* hat." Pause. "You don't think so? Really?"

Teacher's pet: "You think *I'm* the teacher's pet. Well, it takes one to know one. I guess you're feeling a bit jealous. It's hard when someone else takes over your place."

General: No matter what attribute the teaser uses, throw it back at him or her: "I can see why you noticed that I'm (fat, skinny, etc.) because you're getting that way, too." If the teaser denies it, ask a series of questions about it, for example, "How much do you weigh? Did you always weigh that much (or little)?"

Now follow the same procedure given at the completion of the Nonreward Retort Strategies: The Teacher and Helper demonstrate the three Punishment Retort Strategies, the Victim chooses the one that he would like to use when teased, and he is given intensive practice in it. (If he wanted to start out with "meaner" strategies, he should choose two strategies and practice both.)

For the remaining strategies, follow the same procedures described earlier: discussion, demonstration, incorporation of some of the nonverbal behaviors that should or should not be exhibited, less-than-perfect role play by the Helper, reversal of roles, critiques, and ample rehearsal by the Victim.

4. *The Victim Shows He Is the Boss.* One way for the Victim to show that he is in charge is to take the teaser's taunt (e.g., "You're just a cripple, you

got lousy legs") and ask with a puzzled look, "What did you say?" Repeat this with, "Could you say that again?" Often the Victim can get the teaser to say this three times before the teaser catches on. When this gambit is successful, the Victim should praise the teaser in as condescending a manner as possible: "Good work, Jones, you said that three times. Come back at lunchtime and I'll have you say it some more."

Note that as part of the "boss" behavior, the Victim uses the teaser's surname (boy) or proper name (girl: Margaret, not Peggy) in any verbal exchange. Whenever possible, he gives orders and points with a jabbing motion but does not touch the teaser: "Be here tomorrow, Patterson. Same time. I'll talk to you some more about my ankles." He should take every opportunity to play to the spectators. In the above situation, he should say in an aside to the spectators, "I'm having Patterson come tomorrow."

5. Making the Teaser Look Foolish When He Says the Obvious. "She knows I'm in a wheelchair! Wow! What else do you know? (points to familiar objects) What's that, Elizabeth? A tree. Say *tree*." If Elizabeth is so foolish as to say "tree," tell the spectators that you are having her name things. If she does not say "tree," look sympathetic and tell her that "tree" is a pretty hard word for someone like her and suggest an easier word.

6. Making the Teaser Look Ignorant About Medical Conditions. The Victim with any kind of visible medical problem is almost certain to be teased. The teaser says, "You're in a wheelchair, you're never going to walk." The Victim looks surprised and says, "William, are you *able* to read newspapers? or watch TV? I *really* wonder if you can because if you could, you'd know that in medicine there's no such word as *never*." Explain, using joint replacement or heart transplants as examples.

Or the teaser says, "You've got leukemia, you're going to die." The Victim should point a finger at the teaser and say, "Joseph, I have news for you. You're going to die, too. Everyone dies, don't you know that?" At this point the teaser is likely to say that he means the leukemic child is going to die *soon*. The Victim replies, "You're not using the right words. You don't talk about *going to die,* you say *terminal*. Now let's hear you say it again *properly*." If the teaser hesitates, say, "Well, that is a pretty big word for someone like you. Now, I'll help you. Ter - mi - nal. Now you say it." If Joseph says it, praise him in a heavy-handed way, "Good boy," and if he does not say it, say, "Well, even if you can't say it, Joseph, you try to remember it and maybe when you're older you'll be able to say it."

Or the teaser picks on an obese or underweight child, in which case the Victim says enthusiastically, "You're *right!* I'm fat. I weigh . . ." Pause, look closely at the teaser and say, "I bet you don't know how much I weigh." If the teaser hesitates, say, "What's the matter? You scared to try? I'll give you a dime if you get it right." No matter what the other child guesses, laugh uproariously. Repeat his guess, "_____ pounds! Wait 'til I tell my doctor. He'll die laughing." Pause, shake head slowly, then urge the teaser to try again. Offer him three more chances. Tell him to try again the next day. If the spectators press the Victim to tell his weight, he should laugh and say, "I want to give (teaser) some more chances." Try to sound pitying and say "_____ pounds! He thinks I weigh _____ pounds!"

7. *Derogating the Teaser for Repetition of Taunts.* Here the Victim nods occasionally as she listens to the teaser. The first time that the teaser repeats herself (they often do, their repertoire is generally very limited) say, "You know who you remind me of, Ruth Anne, it's a TV commercial, they say the same thing every day. So I want you to sing it this time (to spectators—"I'm having her sing it—she says the same thing about my ankles every day"). Oh, come on, Ruth Anne, sing it." Pause, "Ruth Anne, is it that you don't want to sing or you just can't sing?"

This question is a useful tactic because it puts the teaser in a no-win situation. If she does sing, the Victim should praise her in a condescending manner; if she refuses, the Victim should suggest that she is lacking in ability.

8. *Anticipation of Taunts the Teaser Will Use.* This strategy was suggested by an 11-year-old girl who, like most of the children who worked through the program, became very interested in the Retort Strategies. She thought, correctly, that her strategy would throw the teaser off balance.

The procedure here is for the Victim to accost (go near but not *too* close) the teaser *before* she says anything to the Victim and ask, "What's it to be today, Carol?" and immediately reel off several of the taunts that the teaser often uses. Then take advantage of the teaser's momentary silence to deliver the final blow: Offer to meet with the teaser to help her think up some new taunts.

When these last strategies have been covered, have the Victim choose two and follow the previously described routines for ensuring that the Victim is able to use them effectively in the real-life situation.

PART 4

Assuming that the Victim (a) is skilled in the Retort Strategies that he has chosen, (b) believes that he can use them effectively in counterattacking the teaser, and (c) wants to try them when teased, the next step is a test. In the test situation some of the retort strategies chosen by the Victim would be appropriate, but the content of the interaction is new to him. The Teacher confronts the Victim with a taunt and he must respond. Have a critique of his performance with demonstrations by the Teacher and Helper. Then repeat the same test and see how the Victim performs.

Follow the same procedure with a new test. If the Victim does well, explain that the teaser might not stop and might even become nastier (because he senses that his source of payoff might be slipping away). But this will be a temporary reaction, so the Victim should continue to handle the teasing using the strategies and behaviors that he has learned. Demonstrate this possibility with the Teacher and Helper taking the teaser and Victim roles.

When the tests have been completed satisfactorily, the Victim should now be ready to confront the teaser in the actual teasing situation. Urge him to note as many details of the interaction with the teaser as he can, so that he can report back. It is *essential* to make the Victim feel important when he does report back and to be untroubled by any slip-ups on the Victim's part. Enlist his help in incorporating any changes needed for the next trial. If the Victim wants to temporarily postpone the next trial, let him, but continue working on his verbal and nonverbal behaviors using the test procedure. An unexpected finding occurred at the first-trial point in the training sequence: If the Victim handled the verbal responses well, the teaser's repertoire seemed to narrow and become more stereotyped, possibly due to frustration over the Victim's unusual behavior. The effect was to reduce the number and variety of taunts that the Victim had to handle, thus making his task much easier.

Of the first group of children who were taught this program, most had no further difficulty with the teasers, according to the children themselves, their parents, their teachers, and their pediatricians (when the latter were involved in the case). Three children, two girls and one boy, were apparently too timid to put the program into action even though they had demonstrated impressive competence in the training situation. The fourth child, a boy, had also been successful in the training situation but was unable to apply the skills that he had learned. Under no circumstances should such failures be punished in *any* way including a show of even the mildest disappointment on the part of the Program Teacher. Instead, consider some other form of intervention more suited to the child's temperament.

COMMENT

In a number of ways, the Ross Teasing Program is an apparently simple one: No professional help or training is necessary because the straightforward instructions can be followed by reasonably competent adults or adolescents who are motivated to help teasing victims. No special equipment is required, and a room large enough for three people is all that is needed. So it is interesting to consider *why* the program has been effective in helping many children to eliminate the teasing problem.

The context is strongly supportive with the Teacher and Helper acknowledging that the problem is a serious one warranting their undivided attention and help. The Victim achieves repeated successes until he no longer feels upset in the teasing situation. The training procedures defuse the Victim's attitude to being teased by having him observe and participate in role-play incidents, some of which are similar to his real-life experiences. As Bandura (1969) has pointed out, fears can be mastered in this way. In addition, the Victim takes an active rather than passive part by providing essential information crucial to the training. In doing this he begins to look at the teasing situation in a more detached and, therefore, unemotional way. The extensive training generates a feeling of being in control of the teasing interaction, and this inner change effects a change in his demeanor. The Victim no longer is an obvious target for teasing.

In addition to the benefits directly accruing from participation in the program, parents have frequently reported other positive changes in their children, changes that they found hard to describe. One man, for example, said that his 8-year-old son "was tougher about things now," and a mother described her 10-year-old daughter as "much more mature." I believe that these changes may occur as a result of coping effectively with the teasing. The victim's confidence and self-esteem are bolstered: The result is what Rutter (1987) called a psychological stiffening or steeling (*not* to be confused with rigidity) that helps the former victim confront new experiences of a stressful nature with greater composure than had previously been the case. It is this *increase in composure* in the face of stress that underlies the positive changes that the parents report.

Conclusion

Cruel and destructive teasing may start as a daily hassle, but all too often it quickly assumes the status of a major life event (Lazarus, 1966), a stressor that the victim is ill-prepared to cope with. What is needed is direct action in the form of a quick, sharp rebuttal, but the victim seldom manages anything more than a feeble comeback. This is not surprising because the dynamics of the teasing interaction usually put the victim at a great disadvantage. The teaser can choose the topic, which is often indisputably true and consequently difficult to refute; the ideal time for the verbal attack; and the place to deliver the barb. In the early stages of teasing, the victim is often taken by surprise and may be unable to conceal the hurt and discomfiture engendered by the teasing. At this point social support from bystanders would give the victim a tremendous boost, but such support is rarely forthcoming. More often the bystanders side with the teaser when the victim is clearly unable to handle the situation. It is not surprising that victims in this situation often end up blaming themselves for their inadequacies. At this point, it is of critical importance to provide social support.

No child should have to endure destructive teasing. It is inexcusable to have a child's life marred for weeks or months by the misery of cruel teasing and, in addition, have the possibility of negative effects well into adulthood. Any interested, reasonably competent adult with a capacity for empathy could teach the Ross Teasing Program and, in the process, equip the child to cope effectively not only with the immediate painful problem of being teased but also with the inevitable verbal sparring of early adulthood.

8 Counseling

In this chapter three approaches to therapy and counseling with school children are described. The first of these, developed by Hazler (1996a), discusses in detail the therapeutic approach used over a period of time with three different cases of bullies and victims in conflict. Particularly important is the fact that before therapy directed at the reason for referral can begin, for the greatest chance of success the tension and anger between the bully and victim must be modified to a level that allows the therapist to begin active intervention with the combatants. Hazler's book, *Breaking the Cycle of Violence* (1996a), is one that every adult who is concerned about children who bully or are bullied should read. In addition to describing the therapeutic approach used with specific bullies and victims, it contains case studies of bullies and victims, actions that the school and community should take to create safe schools, advice to teachers who must deal with bullying, and actions that parents should take with the problems of bullies, victims, and bystanders.

The second approach to counseling focuses on children and adolescents who have a variety of school-related problems including bullying and victimization. The method used here is called solution-focused counseling. It is described in detail by Murphy (1997) in his text, *Solution-Focused Counseling in Middle and High Schools*. It is a unique method of problem solving that focuses on promoting changes in school problems in a very short time. There are excellent case studies that illustrate Murphy's approach along with clear descriptions of how to talk to the child with problems and how to make effective use of his or her resources. Two very practical chapters describe when and how to end counseling and what to do when things do not go as planned. Parents and teachers will find this method invaluable in dealing with the home and school problems that occur on a daily basis. This is another book that every parent should read.

The third approach described in this chapter is peer counseling. The assumption underlying it is that sometimes a child with problems will discuss them more freely with another child than with an adult. As one might expect, the peer counseling approach has met with mixed reactions. One group is convinced that it is useful if the peer counselor is given sufficient training and trained supervisors are available for evaluation of the handling of clients and for consultation about cases. The opponents are strongly against this practice. In this section both viewpoints are presented along with the training procedures for peer counselors.

Hazler's Approach

In *Breaking the Cycle of Violence,* Hazler (1996a) described a three-step therapeutic technique that he developed called Promoting Issues in Common (PIC). It is an excellent model for productive intervention with adolescents and adults having problems with relationships. It is particularly applicable to bullies and victims in conflict who previously have had a neutral or positive relationship that they would like to reestablish. However, parts of it are also appropriate for victims with no previous relationship with their bullies. It is most effective when it is one part of an established intervention for dealing with the problems of bullying and victimization. When this last criterion is met, the PIC model should prove to be a constructive approach for handling a variety of bully/victim problems.

GAINING CONTROL OF THE CONFLICT SITUATION

In this first step, the goal is to create the condition that will facilitate effective counseling at a later point in the course of therapy. Two conditions must be met before counseling can begin. From the first meeting with the counselor, the situation must be unequivocally safer than the bully/victim conflict setting for both participants. It cannot begin, for example, if the bully is covertly intimidating the victim or overtly fighting or bullying others. Lowering sources of tension to at least a moderate level takes precedence over other therapeutic goals. As soon as possible the school authorities who are responsible for official actions should be named so that it is clear to the participants that the counselor has the support of a strong backup team.

During this first step, all judgments concerning who is in the wrong are withheld to convey to the clients that the therapist intends to hear all sides of the problem. By delaying a final judgment, the therapist increases the probability of developing a positive working relationship with those involved, an essential feature in subsequent steps. To illustrate the application of the PIC model, three of Hazler's (1996a) cases (Ahmad, Yolanda, and Allen) are described as they progress through therapy.

Case 1: Ahmad

Ahmad was a junior in high school. Although he was frequently teased and bullied throughout his school years, he had become adept at avoiding his tormentors. Then disaster struck. Early in his junior year he was so severely beaten by two gang members that his injuries were life threatening. Although his assailants were expelled from school and faced charges in juvenile court, Ahmad had no reason to feel safe because of the probability that their fellow gang members might retaliate against him.

Ahmad wanted to quit school so that he could find a job, and he also wanted to seek revenge on his attackers. However, his mother recognized the importance of finishing school as a means of getting out of their neighborhood and into some kind of productive and reasonably well-paying work. Under those circumstances, revenge was clearly impossible. Home schooling was a poor alternative because Ahmad would be deprived of peer interactions and would, for all practical purposes, be in hiding. In the meantime, Ahmad was at home recuperating from the injuries he had sustained in the beating. He could see no future and was terrified.

It is clear from Ahmad's case that only parts of the PIC would be appropriate for him. He was greatly in need of a professional to talk to about the attack, but the goal of a more positive relationship with his assailants was neither feasible nor desirable. He was a random victim of a vicious attack by assailants whom he did not know and was unable even to talk about the attack. Intensive professional help was indicated for him as well as some help for his mother.

Case 2: Yolanda

When Yolanda was in fourth grade she began maturing rapidly. She was acutely uncomfortable with the noticeable physical changes and did her best to hide them. When there was visible evidence that she had begun menstruating, she could no longer hide the fact that she had matured far ahead of her classmates. Her reaction was to strike out verbally at them. The resultant feeling of power served to discourage friendly questions about what the changes meant. The effect was to cause a lot of talk, uneasy jokes, some teasing, and anonymous notes that accused her of having sex with older boys.

Yolanda flaunted her new maturity so aggressively that even her best friends, who wanted to help her, struck back. The more Yolanda retaliated, by intimidating some of her classmates and psychologically abusing others, the more the negative responses from former friends increased. The school year that had started on a positive note for her deteriorated rapidly.

There was no evidence that Yolanda's fourth-grade classmates wanted to be mean to her. In fact, many of them had been her good friends. Rather, it was her inability to handle the unexpected and visible evidence of the onset of physical maturity that created the problem. To cover her embarrassment and as a misguided attempt to show how powerful she was, she began to strike out verbally at other students who had been her friends. Her classmates responded in kind. Even those who would have supported her avoided her as much as possible. Her best friends were confused because their offers of help and support were rebuffed. Their relative immaturity added to their bafflement because it created feelings of uncertainty and anxiety.

The situation rapidly worsened when Yolanda began intimidating younger classmates. A teacher witnessing Yolanda psychologically abusing a younger girl named Alice intervened verbally, to no avail, and then physically. Her commendable goal was to stop the abuse but refrain from making a snap judgment until she could obtain more information about the incident. Because a better relationship was clearly desired by the majority of those involved in this case, the PIC was unquestionably the optimum intervention for Yolanda.

Case 3: Allen

Allen was in eighth grade. He was the kind of student that most teachers quickly come to dislike. He had a poor attention span, and the little work he did was not done well. His interactions with his teachers were almost invariably negative ones. Relations with peers were also negative: He regarded other students as weaklings and described them as "damn wimpy" kids who felt superior to him. They paid for their feelings of superiority when teachers were not around: Allen used extortion, physical force, intimidation, and other bully tactics to keep them in line. These behaviors made the school day tolerable for him.

Allen had no real friends at school. His real friends were a small gang of older boys, all school dropouts. With them, he felt strong and effective, feelings that were in sharp contrast to the inadequacy he felt in class. By eighth grade, he could not wait to get out on the streets where his high status was unquestioned.

Although Allen's behavior often caused the school personnel trouble, they had done everything possible over a period of time to show that they believed he could change and become an asset in school activities. In the interest of treating him fairly and not labeling him with a bad name, they delayed making final judgments about him when he misbehaved. Their attitude was the antithesis of an all too common adult reaction to a substantial record of bad behavior, that is, to assume the worst and act accordingly.

Fortunately for Allen, the reaction of the school personnel to active conflict in the school was to take control of a conflict situation in an orderly, unemotional way; assess it objectively; and convey appropriate concern without undue anxiety. This approach is effective in preventing further escalation of a conflict. Consider the following incident:

> The school principal, Mr. Denson, saw a younger boy, Seth, accidentally brush up against Allen. . . . He could see Allen take this as a challenge. . . . Mr. Denson decided to move before actions and emotions escalated. He said, "Hi. How you doing?" Allen was temporarily deflected from getting to Seth . . . the tension was lowered. . . . As they walked together down the hall Mr. Denson could see that Allen still had his eye on Seth . . . the principal decided to escalate the importance of the situation with Allen. . . . "I saw Seth accidentally bump you. It made you mad, huh?" "Damn right," Allen said. "Looked like an accident to me," Mr. Denson said. "This is not one to get yourself in trouble over, Allen." Allen backed off. He did not want to be in trouble with the principal . . . and Mr. Denson knew it. (Hazler, 1996a, pp. 77–78)

In a subsequent conflict situation when Allen bullied Seth, no final judgments were made until things calmed down. The effect of this tactic was to increase the probability of developing a positive working relationship between school personnel and the two boys. During the delay the boys were informed that both would be allowed to give their accounts of the conflict. At this point in a conflict sequence, Hazler (1996a) emphasized that both participants must understand enough of the basic process to ensure their ability to answer three questions: Do they recognize why the situation is deemed a problem by some, if not all, participants? Do they know why those seeking to gain control of the conflict situation are behaving in this way? Do they understand what will happen next and why it will happen? The benefit of a delay is to allow both boys to become significantly calmer than they were during and immediately after the conflict.

EVALUATING THE PEOPLE AND THEIR PROBLEMS

In this second step of the PIC model the process of evaluating bully/victim conflicts typically begins with individual interviews, first with the bully, then with the victim. Seeing the bully first should facilitate the building of a positive relationship between the bully and the therapist. It also protects the victim. One goal is to learn as much as possible about each of the clients and the needs common to their relationship. Another goal of this evaluation process is to determine the appropriateness and feasibility of joint counseling. Individual counseling will come first because the protagonists are likely to need individual counseling sessions to provide help with their own problems. However, help with the relationship problem is best handled with joint counseling. A major shift in the interviewing process occurs in this period when the therapist tries to help the student who is being interviewed to see the other person's point of view. The task of considering the other's feelings and situation is a difficult one for most clients. At this point any other individuals familiar with the situation should also be interviewed. Evaluating everyone's views of the problem is essential if the next step, the direct intervention process, is to begin with the maximum probability of success.

Case 1: Ahmad

Although Ahmad had recuperated from the physical injuries of the beating, the psychological effects of the most recent attack and his previous experiences as a victim had not disappeared. He wanted to leave school and get a job or home school until he graduated. His two assailants faced charges and were unlikely to directly cause Ahmad more trouble. However, he quite realistically feared that others from the same gang would seek revenge. Ahmad's mother took him to a counselor against his will. He did not know that the counselor had talked to two other boys who were still in the school and who had bullied Ahmad from time to time. The counselor saw these two first to reduce the probability of them blaming Ahmad. This tactic gave the counselor a chance to talk to Ahmad about the possibility of improving his relationship with these boys instead of continually looking for ways to escape peer relationships such as these. Ahmad's talk with the counselor did leave him with a more positive feeling about his future.

Case 2: Yolanda

Some of the problems that confront school counselors are relatively straightforward ones. Yolanda's was a good example of this. Her counselor began by making it clear to Yolanda that she was there for several reasons, including not getting along with some girls, being mean to others like Alice, and poor grades. Yolanda struck back by blaming Alice. She told the counselor that "that damn Alice just doesn't get it. She ought to know by now that her and her friends better quit talking behind my back or I'll take care of them." She was reluctant to continue counseling and felt that everyone blamed her unfairly: "No one cares about my side anyhow."

The counselor used a very direct, matter-of-fact approach with Yolanda. After a brief discussion about how things were going with her, Ms. Kline, the counselor, stated what she had heard about Yolanda's problems with her classmates, her aggression toward Alice, and her falling grades. She expressed great interest in turning these problems around and said that she hoped Yolanda would work with her to do so.

Note that Ms. Kline made it clear that she was being straight with Yolanda and at this point was not blaming her. When Yolanda asked angrily if Alice had squealed, Ms. Kline assured her that she had not talked with Alice yet and was depending on Yolanda to give her more information about the problems. The counselor was focusing on building an honest working relationship with Yolanda and she was succeeding: Yolanda began to trust Ms. Kline.

Case 3: Allen

Allen's counselor, Mr. Jones, took a different approach from that used so effectively by Ms. Kline. He wanted to give Allen a chance to initiate the direction of the counseling. Instead, he should have directly confronted him with the issue that was the point of the session: to get Allen talking about the situation with Seth. His failure to be direct convinced Allen that Mr. Jones was just another example of school personnel who could not be trusted.

Building a level of trust at this point is of critical importance. The counselor should be matter-of-fact about why the client has been referred for counseling and should briefly summarize the information he has about the problem, in this case, the bullying incident. Next, both clients' understanding of the conflict should be obtained in separate interviews. Gaining an understanding of the incident from the client's view is traditionally known as seeking empathy for the individual. Empathy is an attempt to identify with another person's situation and feelings. The individual interviews emphasize the first phase of empathy: gaining an understanding of what happened in the conflict situation. By obtaining a clear picture of the development of the conflict from the diverse viewpoints of both participants, the counselor has a better idea of the parts of the situation that will warrant therapeutic attention. This discussion must not deteriorate to an interrogation level: The emphasis must remain on the student's view of the situation.

In the second phase of empathy the counselor's task is to get beyond the objective facts of the bullying incident and explore the feelings, thoughts, and attitudes that underlie the behaviors of the boys. In this case, he found that Allen was very concerned about being in control of the people and events around him. Allen's account was that Seth had annoyed him greatly in the past and that the recent annoyance of Seth brushing up against him was the last straw. Further discussion of the event leads Mr. Jones to comment that it seems very important to him to feel in control. Allen confirms this emphatically, "Damn right it is. Letting people know you are in control is what it's all about." As the session progresses, Mr. Jones finds that Allen is very afraid of losing control of the people around him. Allen worries that he is unable to control people's ideas, he has no control over his chaotic home situation, and he does poorly in school. To counteract these anxieties, he has convinced himself that school and home are of no importance to him and further self-reassurance is provided by the power he had over students like Seth. He had been pleased, for example, to find that Seth had been far more worried about the impending talk with the principal and teacher.

Unlike Allen, Seth was a victim. He was terribly afraid of what Allen could do to him, and he was well aware that he lacked social support both at school and at home. In the latter situation it gradually became apparent that his mother made all his decisions and allowed him no responsibility in handling problems. As a result, he felt alone, isolated, not too competent, and willing at all costs to avoid being hurt. These feelings are characteristic of many victims in the school setting (Smith, 1991). More than anything else, Seth needed to know that help was available in his school.

In marked contrast to the approach that Mr. Jones used with Allen, he was very direct when he saw Seth. He told him that he knew that there had been problems between Seth and Allen and that he would like to help them solve the problems. He made it clear that he needed to hear Seth's side of the story. With considerable tact and skill, he established that the problem relationship between the two boys had a long history. Seth explained that it had started when Allen came up to him, punched him for no reason, and started yelling at him. Throughout the session Mr. Jones also worked hard to gain Seth's trust and confidence in the idea that the goal of the counseling sessions was to help him.

The information about Allen and Seth demonstrates the value of exploring the feelings of those involved in bully/victim problems. This approach often provides information that will lead to a very different assessment of those involved than would be the case if counseling focused solely on the factual description of the conflict situation. It is important to note that the purpose of the PIC method is not to bring the bully and victim together for a stormy and pointless confrontation. Instead, when each has shown that he has grasped the other's point of view, the goal of the PIC method is to bring the combatants together for joint counseling sessions.

The next and more difficult task for the counselor was to help each boy to become aware of the other's point of view. The shift from discussing their own feelings about their situation to how others feel is not an easy one to make. Indeed, Hazler (1996a, p. 98) emphasized that the timing of this topic is best introduced early in a counseling session. The counselor must be reasonably confident that both the bully and victim have enough recognition of the other's world to cope with the challenges associated with this step.

Near the end of Mr. Jones's first counseling session with Allen, he had talked briefly about the need for Allen to understand something about Seth if the two were going to have a better relationship. This idea had been very coolly received. However, in the next individual sessions with each boy, he had persisted with this topic by having each boy look for issues that they might have in common. In separate sessions they decided that each had feelings of powerlessness and loneliness: Seth with his fear of Allen and lack of real friends, and Allen believing that he could not impact how he was treated at home or at school, where other children disliked him. Hazler (1996a) emphasized that bringing bullies and victims together can succeed only if they clearly have problems in common. If they do not or cannot recognize these similarities, it is probably better to continue with individual therapy.

DIRECT INTERVENTIONS

The third step, direct intervention in the bully/victim problem, cannot begin until control of the situation has been established and a thorough evaluation of the problem has been conducted. The PIC model is more concerned with the optimum process for providing direct intervention than with specific therapeutic tactics. Decisions of direct interventions are made on the basis of how much each individual is in need of personal, social, and psychological therapy. It is important to delay working in pairs or larger groups until the therapist is confident that the individual is independently prepared to do so.

Case 1: Ahmad

Consider the plight of Ahmad. He had seen the counselor twice, and they had developed a positive relationship. They had discussed some of the pain and fear associated with Ahmad's life-threatening beating. Although Ahmad had talked about other boys who had bullied him, he often had become very emotional when discussing events associated with being bullied, particularly when the discussion turned to the most recent severe beating. He clearly felt comfortable with the therapist, but he continued to experience major anxiety attacks including cold sweats, generalized fears, and hyperventilation. These attacks had also occurred at school and home without any identifiable initiating factors.

Ahmad's reactions to being bullied far exceeded those of the other two cases. It was clear that at the time of counseling, he was unable to change his victimization status. He needed a two-pronged therapeutic intervention: first, intensive individual therapy designed to help him to achieve some control over his anxieties and begin to develop confidence in himself; second, training in assertive skills, social skills, and some sports activity that he appeared to have the potential to master with a reasonable degree of proficiency.

Realistically, neither of these interventions was likely to provide maximum benefit unless Ahmad also had a new social environment: a new neighborhood and school somewhat distant from his current home. Unless these changes could be accomplished along with a substantial amount of professional help and some social skill training, it is difficult to see how he would ever become a reasonably confident young adult.

Case 2: Yolanda

Yolanda could clearly benefit from individual therapy although her problems were less severe than those of Ahmad and Allen. Bullying had not been an established pattern of her behavior prior to the fourth grade. She had always done well in school, both academically and socially, and she had a positive home environment. Also, her inappropriate reactions to the physical maturation changes that were at the root of her problems would diminish in effect as her classmates also matured. Consequently, individual therapy with Yolanda should be relatively brief. In fact, unless unexpected problems arose, a shift to joint therapy might be more productive by allowing a focus on promoting positive peer relationships with other girls such as Alice whom she had antagonized. Yolanda and Alice appeared to be ideal candidates for joint therapy. Their past relationship was a positive one, they had previously had many peer friends in common, and they both wanted to be liked by others.

Yolanda had developed confidence in her counselor. Ms. Kline had not attributed any blame to Yolanda or her classmates at any point in the counseling sessions. Instead, she had concentrated on building an honest and positive working relationship with Yolanda. Her approach was productive. Yolanda's new-found confidence in

Ms. Kline enabled her to confide some of the problems that had occurred with her sudden maturation and the reactions of peers to it. Ms. Kline decided to begin joint therapy with Yolanda and Alice.

Prior to joint meetings the protagonists must have their personal concerns clearly identified, understand how the joint meeting will help them, and know which issues they have in common. The primary therapy goal of each joint meeting is establishing a working, but not necessarily friendly, relationship between both parties. The PIC technique emphasizes an ongoing model for improvement that relies less and less on the therapist for improving the relationship and more and more on the clients to do so.

The two girls communicated very effectively in joint sessions about the problems that they had had and each other's point of view. Things went so well that Yolanda wanted to be best friends with Alice, who happily agreed. Ms. Kline tactfully suggested some more limited short-term goals: It came as no surprise to her that this sudden closeness did not last. She also helped the two girls realize that more progress was needed before best-friends status became a reality. After several more joint meetings, Ms. Kline told the girls that the joint meetings would soon end. They were very upset.

The Termination Procedure

Deciding on the number of joint meetings in the PIC model is the responsibility of the therapist and depends on the progress made. The procedure is described here because Yolanda was the only one of the three students to complete the third step. In the second-to-last meeting the therapist should ask the students to think over what they have accomplished, including how their feelings for each other have changed. In the final meeting there is a discussion of these accomplishments with some emphasis on what the two students have done on their own to improve their relationship. It should also be emphasized that it is reasonable for them to feel sad or a little anxious about ending the therapy. At the same time, stress the fact that they can come to talk with the therapist should other problems occur.

Ms. Kline followed these procedures, and the sessions concluded satisfactorily. Both students maintained the progress that they had made, and no further problems arose.

Case 3: Allen

Allen had used bullying successfully for a fairly long period of time. His parents and other adults either ignored or punished this behavior but failed to reward him when he did make positive changes. As a result, there was no incentive for Allen to eliminate his bullying behaviors. Punishment acted as a positive model for him: He saw the power of his punisher and felt that he, too, could be powerful by bullying other children. He concluded that the best way to get along with others and make them do what he wanted was to be in the power spot.

Individual therapy for Allen was difficult because he had a cluster of well-established defenses and beliefs. However, Mr. Jones was both persistent and patient. He could see that Allen was gradually thinking more and more about issues that in his first session he had just brushed aside. A major shift had occurred: Previously, staunch denials were based on the firm conviction that others were to blame for any problem, whereas now there were some tentative inklings that he *might* have been partly to blame for some of his difficulties. This change constituted a major step forward.

At this point in the intervention process no predictions could be made as to how much individual therapy Allen would need. He has already shown signs of thinking about issues previously suppressed. Mr. Jones's goal is to get Allen into joint sessions with Seth, but serious problems remain. Classroom- and peer-related problems are long-standing, he has no real motivation to improve his relationship with Seth, and he has strong defenses against people who do not reward his bullying behaviors. Allen is likely to be reluctant to admit to commonalties or be interested in considering positive options for improving his relationship with Seth. He is certain to remember that meetings about his bullying behavior were invariably followed by negative events. Furthermore, his attempts to control his relationships rest on shutting people out if their actions are incompatible with his bullying behavior. Seth is not confident about his ability to be effective in a joint meeting with the enemy, Allen. His mother has always intervened to handle problems for him. He would need a lot of reassurance from the counselor about his ability to be effective in a joint meeting with Allen; in fact, the prospect terrifies him. Both boys would probably need many more individual therapy sessions before joint sessions can be considered (if ever). Realistically, there is little reason for optimism about the boys' ability to work together.

Solution-Focused Counseling

Solution-focused counseling (Murphy, 1997) is a practical, empirically based method for promoting changes in elementary, middle, and high school students' problems and doing so in a relatively short time. It is ideally suited to the large caseloads and time constraints that confront school counselors. The focus in this approach is on small changes and reasonable goals. It shows school counselors how to make the best use of every counseling session. In his 1997 text, *Solution-Focused Counseling in Middle and High Schools*, Murphy first described each intervention strategy, then presented case studies demonstrating their use for a variety of school problems. Most case studies include excerpts from actual counseling sessions. School teachers, social workers, and concerned parents could benefit greatly from many of the ideas and strategies involved in this form of counseling.

For the school counselor, working with the middle or high school student is often difficult, particularly when the referral is for misbehavior. The student's attitude toward seeing the counselor may be part of the problem. He or she may stubbornly refuse to admit that there *is* a behavior problem. He or she may challenge the counselor's ideas to a degree not possible in most classrooms and in this way gain control of the counseling sessions. As one student explained, "I set up road blocks to the counseling," one result being that a power struggle may erupt, diverting attention from the original problem. Resistance such as this is clearly detrimental to helping students resolve problems. It could replace the reason for referral and become the primary focus of the counseling sessions (Murphy, 1997), a colossal waste of both student and counselor time. Adding to the counselor's difficulties is the view of some students that there is stigma associated with being referred to the school counselor. Consider these comments by high school students: "When I got counseled the other girls on our basketball team gave me funny looks and they talked different to me like there was something strange or suspicious or something about me. It made me feel really weird" (girl, age 13). "I never let anyone know I had to go to the counselor because last year when Pete (friend) had to go and the guys found out and all, they wondered what was *really wrong*—it sure wasn't his grades" (boy, age 14). "Well, I heard that once you go to counseling the next thing is a *shrink!* I stopped seeing a lot of Joline after she went. I mean you don't really know, do you?" (girl, age 14). Some attitudes toward counseling have a certain validity: "It was kinda weird, you know? Like she (the counselor) asked really embarrassing questions and then it's probably on your school record for ever and ever. I wished I hadn't gone" (girl, age 13) (D. M. Ross, personal communication, April 3, 1998).

Another factor making for difficulties in the counseling session may be the counselor's beliefs regarding the problem. If, for example, the counselor accepts the stated reason for the referral as *fact*, this belief will largely determine the initial approach to the student. The counselor would likely feel no need to begin the first session with a preamble designed to put the student at ease before assessing his or her view of the problem but would, as one counselor said, "Get right down to business." This unquestioned acceptance of others' views of what is wrong with the student will focus the first session on ways to stop the misbehavior, to the exclusion of other possible interpretations of the situation including those of the student.

Consider the following hypothetical case applying Murphy's (1997) approach. Jessica, a 14-year-old ninth-grade student from Florida, was new to the Boston area. Although her grades were excellent, she was frequently sent out of class for disruptive behavior. According to Jessica the girls in her homeroom had taken an instant dislike to her, and after 2 months of school she still did not have a single friend. The girls teased her relentlessly about her clothes and makeup, both of which were unquestionably unusual; spread rumors that she was a light-skinned Black whose father was a Communist; ignored her attempts to socialize; and told girls in other classes to ignore her. After a series of initial attempts to make friends, Jessica ignored them all.

Because of her disruptive behavior and inappropriate dress, Jessica was called to a meeting with the school principal, a school psychologist, and her homeroom teacher. She was sternly rebuked and also told that she must conform immediately to the dress code. She refused point-blank even in the face of a warning that she could be suspended from school. She was then referred to a school counselor who, like the three professionals, showed no interest in any facet of Jessica's personal experience of school. Instead, as the following excerpt shows, the counselor was of the "get right down to business" school of thought starting with blunt, uncompromising accusations about the reasons for referral:

Counselor: I see that your classroom behavior is very disruptive, Jessica, and your clothes do not meet our dress code. Is this how you behaved in your school in Florida?

Jessica: No.

Counselor: Then why are you acting this way here? *Our* girls are *very* well-behaved. (Jessica laughs derisively.) Why are you doing this, Jessica?

Jessica: I don't know.

Counselor: You're getting a bad reputation and you've only been here two months. What does behaving like this do for you?

Jessica: It's just something to do.

Counselor: I just don't understand you. If you continue to behave this way you'll get an out-of-school suspension.

Jessica: Who cares?

Counselor: Don't you want to finish high school?

Jessica: (For the first time she pauses to think.) Not when high school is like this.

Note that the counselor does not pursue the fact that Jessica does not like the school. Instead, as the session continues she persists with the same approach despite its ineffectiveness, and Jessica replies with indifferent and sometimes insolent negatives. Finally, the counselor focuses on the problem of Jessica's inappropriate style of dress.

Counselor: You could be attractive if you would try to dress better. (Jessica does not answer.)
Counselor: What do you want from counseling, Jessica?
Jessica: I want to get out of this school ASAP.
Counselor: (who clearly feels defeated by Jessica's attitude) I'll see you next week, Jessica. Try to improve your behavior in class and do something about your clothes. OK?
Jessica: OK! OK! OK! (She leaves, slamming the door.)

After several more counseling sessions that might more accurately be described as sparring bouts, Jessica's classroom behavior continued to deteriorate. The counselor became increasingly frustrated by her lack of progress coupled with the pressure of time constraints and teacher impatience for visible improvement in Jessica's classroom behavior. However, instead of approaching the problem from a different angle, the counselor continued with the same combination of asking Jessica why she behaved the way she did, alternating with pleading with her to change (aptly described by Jessica to her parents as "stuck-record counseling").

When a concerned adult tries to resolve a problem by trying harder and harder with no change of tactics, while the adolescent becomes increasingly disinterested at hearing more of the same, Durrant (1995) called this counseling sequence an example of falling into the "responsibility trap." In a situation such as this, other approaches are clearly indicated. For example, psychologists in the Mental Research Institute (Watzlawick, Weakland, & Fisch, 1974) would recommend interrupting the problem pattern by making all those involved do something completely different, and Lambert (1992) has identified the following cluster of empirically derived common factors that contribute to successful outcomes in counseling. Some of these procedures should have been an integral part of the first session with Jessica regardless of the counselor's theoretical orientation. The first and most powerful are *client factors*, such as the skills, experiences, unique strengths, and ability to enlist the support of others that the student brings to counseling. The second most powerful are *relationship factors* such as empathy, acceptance, and warmth. Less powerful but still very important are the *expectancy factors* that convey hope for improvement and change. Last are the *theoretical orientation* and *intervention techniques* used by the counselor.

Jessica's parents had become very concerned about the school situation and consulted a psychologist who recommended sending her to a colleague who practiced *brief therapy*. Before this approach could be implemented, Jessica's father was unexpectedly transferred, and she left the school.

BRIEF THERAPY

Brief therapy is generally well suited to school counseling referrals that are concerned with specific current problems that can reasonably be expected to require relatively brief intervention. Many professionals view Milton Erickson, a psychiatrist, as the founder of brief therapy. While he did not endorse any particular theory of psychopathology, in his approach a minimum of time was spent on the client's problem. Instead, Erickson focused on the solution. He conveyed this to his clients by shifting their attention from their past problems to a better future. He emphasized using what the clients brought to therapy and was always alert to small changes in the direction of the client's goal. For an interesting example of his approach, see the case study of the student who refused to read (Murphy, 1997, p. 33).

Murphy (1997) has acknowledged the major impact that Erickson's work has had on his own development of solution-focused counseling. He has also acknowledged the value of the pioneering ideas and interventions of colleagues from two other brief therapy groups: de Shazer (1984) and his colleagues at the Family Therapy Center in Milwaukee, Wisconsin, and Weakland and his colleagues at the Mental Research Institute in Palo Alto, California.

Solution-focused counseling (Murphy, 1997) with its practical, empirically based brief therapy approach would have been admirably suited to the problems Jessica had had. Characteristics that make it particularly effective for counseling adolescents in general include the following. It recognizes that most students need help in resolving a specific ongoing problem. They are not primarily interested in gaining insight (although this likely will occur as an offshoot), modifying their personalities, or discussing their early childhood. Instead, the focus is on the future, not the past. Instead of challenging the student's position, the solution-focused counselor collaborates with the student's beliefs. Collaboration is typically far more effective than coercion in promoting change. Coercion increases resistance and often results in a power struggle to the detriment of effecting change in the referral problem. The counselor adapts his or her procedure to the student rather than expecting the student to adopt the format prescribed by the counselor. For students of other races or religions, the counselor uses a culture-sensitive approach. From the first session the counselor's relationship with the student is a cooperative rather than an authoritative one. The student's own assessment of his or her relationship with the counselor will have a major effect on outcome (Orlinsky, Grawe, & Parks, 1994). To this end, the counselor accepts and uses the ideas that the student brings to counseling because this is the most effective way to facilitate acceptance of interventions. The counselor focuses primarily on what is working in the student's life, not on what is wrong. Two basic guidelines of solution-focused counseling are (a) If it works, do more of it, and (b) If it does not work, do something different. The counselor also matches the student's language, a helpful technique in any counseling situation but particularly so with students. In the following examples (Murphy, 1997), note how the first counselor imposes a different set of descriptors on the student's account of the problem, the result being that the student shuts down or tunes out. By contrast, the second counselor accepts and matches the student's language and is able to establish a cooperative rather than combative relationship with him.

(First) Counselor: Why do you think Mr. Riehle (eighth-grade science teacher) referred you to me?

Eighth-Grade Student: He's a jerk, that's why. He *gets on me* all the time. He has it out for me. . . . Nobody likes him. He *gets on a lot of people.* He can't teach, so he yells at us instead. He ought to refer himself for counseling. I'm tired of him *getting on me all the time.*

Counselor: C'mon now. That's pretty harsh, isn't it?

Student: What do you mean?

Counselor: Well, don't you really mean that he is firm and wants to run the class in an organized way?

Student: What?

Counselor: It sounds to me like the two of you have a communication problem or a personality conflict.

Student: If you say so (shrugs shoulders, pulls hat over forehead, scoots down in the chair, and is on the way to being labeled a "resistant" client).

(Second) Counselor: Why do you think Mr. Riehle (eighth-grade science teacher) referred you to me?

Eighth-Grade Student: He's a jerk, that's why. He *gets on me* all the time. He has it out for me. . . . Nobody likes him. He *gets on a lot of people.* He can't teach, so he yells at us instead. He ought to refer himself for counseling. I'm tired of him *getting on me all the time.*

Counselor: How does he *get on you?*

Student: He's always asking me questions that he knows I won't be able to answer. He sends me out of class to the principal's office for little stuff. There are some people in there that mess around a lot more than me and never get sent out.

Counselor: What else does he do that *gets on you?*

Student: He says bad stuff about me in front of the whole class. Instead of talking to me in the hallway, he does it in front of everybody else. I hate that.

Counselor: Have you found any things that you can do in class that make him *get on you less* or be *less of a jerk?* (Murphy, 1997, pp. 55–56)

In Murphy's (1997) approach the assumption is that most adolescents already have the requisite resources to modify the referral problem, and that with effective counseling the student can be encouraged to apply his or her own resources to the problem. The counselor's suggestions are more likely to be implemented if they are consistent with the student's *position* concerning the problem. The concept of position consists of two aspects: the student's view of the problem and its best solution, and his or her commitment to change the problem (in Murphy's terms, this latter aspect is called *customership*). Commitment to change ranges from unwillingness to acknowledge that a problem exists (students that fit this description are called *visitors*), through being willing to concede that there is a problem but showing reluctance to make an effort to resolve it (called *complainants*), and finally, agreeing that there is a problem and being eager to be actively involved in resolving it (called *customers*). Murphy (1997) cautioned that treating *visitors* like *customers* is likely to seriously impede progress in counseling. Respecting and cooperating with these positions facilitates subsequent specific interventions.

The First Counseling Session

In solution-focused counseling, interviewing is the first step in intervention. In the all-important first meeting, both participants are assessing each other: The counselor is assessing the student and his or her problem, and the student is assessing what he or she thinks of the counselor. During the session the student (not the counselor) should describe his or her problem in his or her own words. With help from the counselor, the student can define the problem in specific behavioral terms, the circumstances related to the onset and stability of it, and any effective and ineffective attempts that the student and others have made to resolve it. The student should also state how important the problem is to him or her and describe the form of resolution of it that he or she would most like. Next the counselor must find out what characterized the times when the problem was not occurring at all, or when it was not as bad as usual (these times are called *exceptions*). Using exceptions helps the counselor and student identify aspects of the problem that are already moving toward a solution.

Goals

In helping the student to describe the goals he or she would like to reach in counseling, it is essential that the goals are the student's rather than the counselor's and that they are formulated in the student's own terms. Two types of questions can help the counselor in this task. *Scaling questions* lead the student to view progress through counseling as a series of small steps rather than as a tremendous breakthrough. For example, "On a scale of 1 to 10, with 1 being the way things are right now and 10 being where you want to be, how will things be different when you move from 1 to 3?" *Miracle questions* (de Shazer, 1988) help the student to clarify his or her goals in concrete terms and focus on future solutions: "If this whole problem (reason for referral) suddenly disappeared, what would you be doing tomorrow at school that would be different from what you usually do?" Note the use here of *presuppositional language*, that is, language that includes words and phrases that presuppose change and solution. It conveys positive expectations of change and also mobilizes the student's resources. If truancy is a problem, for example, the counselor might ask, "How *will* things be different at school *when* you start attending regularly?" or in the case of poor grades, "What *will* be different about how your parents act toward you *when* your grades improve?"

The following hypothetical account illustrates the first session that Jessica might have had with a counselor using the solution-focused approach:

Counselor: Jessica, you've just moved here from Florida! Wow! This must be quite a change! My Dad was in the Army and we moved around to be near him so I went to a lot of schools. How do you like this school?

Jessica: I hate it! It's horrible! A lot of girls in my class pick on me and the rest ignore me.

Counselor: I hated some of my schools, too. In one school the kids made fun of the way I looked and the way I talked. (Notice that the counselor collaborates with Jessica's view of school rather than challenging it.) I don't know you very well yet, Jessica, but I do not see why the other girls would pick on you.

Jessica: It's my clothes, my Florida accent, and me.

Counselor: Your *Florida* accent! That's crazy! Say something in Florida talk.

Jessica: (giggles helplessly)

Counselor: If you could change one thing about this school, what would you change? (miracle question technique)

Jessica: (after a thoughtful pause) I'd have two or three really nice girl friends. I haven't any friends at all in this school. (Note: The miracle question identifies one goal for the counselor—to get her into the peer group.)

Counselor: That sounds horrible! You must feel really lonely! Have you tried to make friends with some of the girls in your homeroom?

Jessica: (bitterly) I sat down at a lunch table where there were some girls in my class and they just got up and moved to another table. In biology we were each supposed to pick a partner. I asked two girls and they both said that they already had one. No one picks me. No one ever speaks to me. It's like I'm not there.

Counselor: When doesn't this kind of thing happen? (exception) There must be some times when it doesn't happen or when it isn't as bad as this sounds (exception).

Jessica: Even when they're forced to be right near me like in auditorium meetings or P.E. it's just the same. It's like I don't exist.

Note how the counselor introduces information designed to change the way Jessica views the problem. This is called *reframing,* and it is based on two assumptions. One is that there are several plausible interpretations for any problem, and the other is that the student's interpretation of a school problem may not be the most useful one in resolving it. In reframing, the counselor uses the tentative *ambassador approach*: He or she addresses the student from the perspective of an ambassador in a foreign country requiring the citizens' help in clarifying the nature of the problem, their position and resources. Examples of this low-key approach are comments such as "I'm wondering if this would be a possible way to handle the problem . . . " or "Could it be that one of the reasons the other girls aren't friends with you is that . . .?"

Counselor: I don't know if this would interest you (ambassador approach), but this makes me think of a course on animal behavior I had in high school. With animals, if there's an established group and a newcomer who is different in some noticeable way tries to enter the group, the rest drive him away. But if his difference disappears, they soon accept him. I think this idea could help us. Jessica, are you good at any sports or acting or something that students do in a group?

Jessica: I'm really good at baseball, especially at batting. In my last school I hit the most home runs. And I'm good at acting. I had the lead in the school play.

Counselor: Well, I'm not sure if this idea is even a base hit (uses her language), stop me if you don't think this is a good idea. What would you think of going shopping this weekend and dressing like the other girls here and then signing up for the baseball team trials next week? The team would get you into another group of students who have similar interests. What do you think?

Jessica: I could give it a try—anyway it would be fun to play baseball again. (Note that she has shifted from the *visitor* category and is closer to being a *customer*.)

Counselor: That's great! If it doesn't work we'll just try something different. Also, at lunch time, what would you think of sitting at some table where there are none of the girls from your homeroom and starting up an animated conversation? If you're good at acting you should be able to manage this. Think of some topics ahead of time and look as if you're having a good time.

Jessica: (dubiously) I guess I could manage that. I'll try it.

Counselor: I know you can. I'll see you next week.

Jessica: You bet. (She leaves quietly.)

Note that the counselor conveys to Jessica that they will work together on the problem and that the counselor is very interested in her goals and appraisal of the counselor's suggestions. In discussing the value of working on what the student thinks is important, Wexler (1991, p. 94) commented: "When adolescents feel forced into something, they resist. On the other hand, when they feel that they are choosing to do something for their own self-interest, their motivation can be intense."

A school counselor provided the following unusual example of the power of intense motivation: A senior with a long-term record in high school of "successful" bullying requested counseling to help him stop his bullying behavior. For ethical reasons the counselor would say only that the student had a powerful motive driving him to this unusual stance: A girl he was extremely attracted to had refused to date him unless he stopped bullying once and for all. The counselor added that to the surprise of the staff and some of his fellow students, the boy did stop bullying.

In situations of this sort, solution-focused counseling would be highly appropriate. Before the first session, it would be prudent of the counselor to be aware of the forces that are against stopping the bullying. Bullies are often respected and even admired by a sizable number of students, and they frequently have a group of loyal followers (Olweus, 1993a; Smith, 1991). They often have a very positive attitude to bullying, bolstered by surprised denial of "real" wrongdoing. Consider their answers in interviews as to why they bully: "To have fun, to really have fun"; "If you don't feel like you can do anything else and you can beat up everyone in the school, at least you can do something well"; "Bullying is where it's at, man, you're in the power spot" (Priest, 1987). Adding to the hurdles that the counselor must overcome is the fact that bullies may be apprehensive about losing face if they suddenly stop bullying.

Keeping in mind the general principles underlying the solution-focused approach and its descriptive framework assisting the counselor in adhering to the principles, the sessions with the student who wants to stop bullying should include the following kinds of content. One goal in the first counseling session would be to determine if the student appears to be genuinely committed to stop being a bully. Obtaining a definition of the bullying problem in specific behavioral terms might involve the following questions. When does the bullying occur? Who is around during the times when bullying occurs? Ask the student to describe a recent example of when bullying someone got him or her into trouble. What is the student doing or has already done in an effort to stop bullying?

It would be unrealistic to expect the student to come to a complete stop on bullying. Small steps rather than an immediate breakthrough would be more effective in achieving the long-term goal of elimination. Stopping bullying on two specified days a week would be a good beginning, followed by a gradual increase in the nonbullying days. In line with the principle of no coercion, this idea should be suggested in a tentative way, possibly when goals are being discussed ("What would you think of this idea as a start . . . ?"). Time should also be spent on discussing ways the bully could handle questions from cohorts about his or her refusal sometimes to engage in bullying. For example, the counselor might ask questions that indicate that it would be reasonable for the boy to have some ambivalence about stopping bullying completely, such as: "What are the disadvantages for *you* of stopping bullying completely?" and "Wouldn't it be hard to stop completely when you've been a bully for quite a long time?"

Then the counselor might say, "I've never experienced a problem like this, it's *quite* unusual. We need to really think this over carefully. What would you think of this idea for a start? No bullying at all on two specified days a week?"

Another set of questions should be aimed at clarifying the student's resources, the assumption being that some of his resources likely would facilitate the desired behavior changes: "What do you like to do outside school?" "What does the person who helps you the most do or say that really helps you?" and "Is there anything else besides bullying that you would like to change about what is happening in your life now?"

In subsequent sessions the counselor must determine the social and temporal circumstances surrounding periods when the bullying does *not* occur, consider ways that the student's resources (skills, social support, etc.) might be useful in interrupting the bullying pattern, help him make the decision to increase the number of nonbullying days, and find ways to help him see bullying in a less favorable light. In an example of the last task, one high school junior, a confirmed bully who was exceptionally strong and well coordinated, was "picked" to become an assistant in an after-school self-defense class for men; the combination of the resultant status and time commitments resulted in a decrease in the frequency of his bullying as well as a loss of interest in continuing it.

When the counselor and student are confident that the latter's problem behaviors have been greatly improved or eliminated, the counseling sessions usually end. How to do this without leaving the student with a feeling of being abandoned is a task the counselor must accomplish successfully. Sometimes students become emotionally attached to the counselor and would like to continue meeting even though they are moving steadily toward a resolution of the referral problem. This attachment is in no way a "crush"; rather, it reflects a warm relationship that has grown during the sessions as a result of the psychologically comfortable interactions between the counselor and student. One way to handle ending the sessions would be to tell the student that the door is always open should he or she want to drop in occasionally to chat. Murphy (1997) has suggested other constructive ways of handling this. One of these involves offering the student membership in the Consultant Club, which is composed of former students who have demonstrated expertise in solving their own school problems and who would be willing to give advice to other students with the same type of problems.

Peer Counseling

One of the problems that confront school personnel concerns adolescents who experience a bullying problem and are then more likely to tell their peers or someone at home rather than a teacher (Whitney & Smith, 1993). Because school personnel generally want to know when students are bullied, peer counseling has appeared to be a solution to this gap in communication. Major assumptions underlie acceptance of this approach: Adolescents will find peers more approachable than adults, and with training, peers can be trusted with confidential information, will make good decisions, and will offer appropriate advice.

Peer counseling focuses on students helping other students with nonacademic problems (Carr, 1988; Cowie, 1999). The peer counselors are usually secondary school students carefully selected from the student body. They are given training in listening and other communication skills, such as talking to victims and bullies in a nonjudgmental way, as well as opportunities to practice these skills under the supervision of a professional counselor. The issue of confidentiality is emphasized, and if a problem is too difficult for the peer counselor to handle alone, help from professional counselors is always available (Sharp, Sellars, & Cowie, 1994).

As one would expect, the quality of the training and supervision of peer counselors varies. Carr (1988) has shown that it is possible to develop an exemplary training procedure and follow-up assessment. Her City-Wide Peer Program included 30 hours of basic communication skills, 30 hours of training in special issues, and 45 hours of supervised, in-school work experience, all of which were provided by an experienced counselor. Carr used video recordings of the peer counselors, self-reports, and teacher and parent reports to evaluate the efficacy of the program. From every perspective, Carr viewed the service as clearly an unqualified success. The students demonstrated their ability to help their peers manage complex problems as well as everyday difficulties. They primarily encouraged self-exploration and decision making on the part of the troubled peers. Carr commented that the peer counselors were caring young adults who gave advice and other practical assistance when it was appropriate to do so.

Content of peer counseling programs also varies. Gougeon (1989) recommended that the initial training should combine training in essential listening and helping skills as well as supervised opportunities to practice these skills. In an excellent training course for secondary students, Robinson, Morrow, Kigin, and Lindeman (1991) emphasized personal growth, acceptance of diversity, self-assessment, and basic counseling skills. Their program includes trust-building exercises as well as role play to facilitate skills practice.

Support for the assumption that students are more comfortable in discussing their problems with other students than with adults comes from a study by Owens, Slee, and Shute (2001). They asked Australian teenage girls what could be done about bullying in their schools. In general, the girls showed a lack of confidence in adult help. They thought that teachers should stay out of it: "Teachers make it worse." "I don't think that teachers and counselors are very well educated about how to handle the problem." They also disparaged parental help on the grounds that parents often tried to deny that any problems existed. Instead, they urged the girls to "ignore it and get on with your schoolwork."

An informal survey I conducted found similar negative attitudes in a group of randomly selected American teenage students. In addition to a lack of confidence in the school counselor, students sometimes also expressed doubts about the confidentiality of the information given in the counseling sessions:

> The one (counselor) I went to used to give me *the look*, you know, and she said, "You can tell me *everything*, it is *completely* confidential," and I thought, yeah, I bet it is. (boy, age 14)
>
> I went to counseling last year and almost right after I finished some teachers like Miss (homeroom teacher) started acting mushy and real sympathetic to me like I was a *real nut case*. (girl, age 13)

Positive Reactions to Peer Counseling

Generally, the reports on peer counseling have been favorable. One counselor said,

> We knew we were handing the children a lot of power and that this was risky. . . . But this initiative is about children working with their peers and a year on, we feel very impressed with how seriously they have taken their work and how professional they have been about it. (Neustatter, 1994, p. 6).

A 15-year-old girl counselor said,

> I've been counseling for a year now and sometimes it's really been hard. I've had kids who say they want to run away and a couple have talked about suicide—that's how bad it feels when the bullying goes on and on. . . . Then there are wonderful moments like when a boy who had been bullying for quite a long

> time said to me: "I'm not proud of what I've done. Bullying isn't nice." (Neustatter, 1994, p. 6)

Negative Reactions to Peer Counseling

Brown (1994), a former teacher, believes that the responsibilities assumed by peer counselors are dangerous for all concerned. Referring to an account in the *Times Educational Supplement* (Neustatter, 1994) of a peer counselor working with bullies, would-be suicides, and other problems, Brown (1994, p. 2) wrote:

> Surely this is a professional job, with the need for years of maturity and training. As with any such process—or, indeed, no process—there will be cases where the counseling seems to work, and the bully stops. But the problem might have resolved itself anyway.
>
> Without control the bully would, in any case, go on to operating while awaiting the cure. Who would be responsible if real damage were done to another pupil at this stage? How would the adolescent counselor deal with her feelings if a victim of one of her caseload committed suicide? How would she handle a case of a would-be suicide who decided to go ahead anyway after counseling? Where would the responsibility lie, personally and in law, for such an event, especially if it were suggested that a line of counseling had been wrongly chosen for the case or a proper treatment not given for a real disorder?
>
> Pupils need protecting from too much responsibility. The responsibility belongs with the head or staff. If they need help, or feel unable to cope with a pupil's problem, they need to seek out the relevant expertise, not push the matter on to a pupil.

I am in complete agreement with Brown (1994). Peer counselors are given responsibilities far beyond their capabilities and should not be permitted to assume the functions of adult professionals.

Peer Supporters

More recently, other efforts to use peers have appeared in the counseling literature. An alternative form of peer support is *befriending*, an approach that consists of training peer supporters, who are often self-nominated, to give direct, relevant support to peers who are troubled. This form of peer support differs from *peer counseling*, which is more closely related to a professional counseling model. Whereas peer supporters typically receive need-based, goal-directed, and experiential training and often are supervised on a regular basis, peer counselors are generally carefully selected by a professional and, as already discussed earlier in this chapter, are equipped with a set of counseling skills and supervised in ways that are modeled on professional counseling practice.

In a 9-school interview study in England (Cowie, 1998) and in a larger survey 2 years later in 51 secondary schools with well-established peer support systems, Naylor and Cowie (1999) found that peer support systems were used by the victims of bullying and generally seen as helpful by a high proportion of the users. The peer supporters clearly enjoyed the chance to work on a real problem in their school community and clearly valued the skills they had learned in the course of training for tackling problems.

Having a peer support system in a school was not without problems. Cowie and Olafsson (1999) reported that some adults in the school setting were reluctant to share power with young people and some school environments were actively obstructive to the work of peer supporters. Further, there was evidence in the form of "hoax calls and referrals," "adverse comments," and other negative reactions to the service offered by the peer support systems. These negative reactions clearly played a part in the reluctance of boys to participate as peer supporters and their higher dropout rate.

One of the most consistent findings in the 1999 Naylor and Cowie survey was that in the space of 2 years the peer support systems had undergone a change. In the Cowie (1998) study the systems clearly had a peer counseling-based approach. Two years later they had become more flexible. Overall, there was a shift away from formal, peer counseling-based models to a more informal, befriending approach. Naylor and Cowie (1999) found that the majority of students interviewed had a good knowledge of the peer support system whether they had been bullied or not. The peer supporters were convinced of the value of their services and clearly had an enhanced sense of self-confidence. On the negative side, some of the peer supporters felt that there was a serious lack of adult supervision or the opportunity for debriefing. Boys were still underrepresented in the group of peer supporters, possibly because they are less empathic, particularly to other boys who are in trouble (Olweus & Endresen, 1998), but are more responsive to girls.

Any school with a bullying problem or other problems that school-age children experience would benefit from reading the article by Cowie, Naylor, Talamelli, Chauhan, and Smith (in press) and should consider setting up a befriending peer support system in their school. Note that it would be essential to have staff enthusiasm and willingness to commit time to such a project.

9 School Programs

School bullying gradually became a topic of widespread concern in the last two decades of the 20th century as evidence accumulated about the often severe effects of bullying on children. Many programs were designed to combat school bullying, but very few were subjected to empirical evaluation. Among the exceptions was Olweus's excellent program developed in Norway in the 1980s in which schools were encouraged to adopt antibullying measures at the whole school, class, and individual levels. Evaluation of the program after 2 years showed a decline of 50% in reported bullying and a decline in other antisocial behaviors, along with an increase in student satisfaction with school life. How did he accomplish this result? With the Whole School Campaign coupled with impressive parent support.

Olweus's Whole School Campaign

The basic premise of the Whole School Campaign against bullying is that bullying is an intentional act and, consequently, one that can be controlled provided that there is a strong commitment to work together on the part of school personnel, parents, and children (Olweus, 1993a). To stop bullying, intervention is needed that can accomplish two changes. First, all attacks on others must be stopped and firm comprehensive action taken to ensure the safety of victims, and the social behavior of the bullies and victims must be changed. Second, bullies must redirect their energy in more positive directions, and victims must be helped in gaining confidence and becoming more assertive so that they do not attract bullying.

Before a Whole School Campaign is initiated, it is essential to have a code of conduct operating smoothly in the school. A *code of conduct* is a whole school disciplinary policy with a clearly stated set of rules for behavior in and around the school, effectively communicated to all students, and enforced without exception. For violations of the code, nonphysical sanctions such as deprivation of privileges should be used (Olweus, 1993a).

INTRODUCTION OF THE CODE OF CONDUCT

First, a copy of the code must be mailed to all parents, whose responsibility is to read it, go over it with their children, and return it signed to the school. Next, there must be a whole school assembly in which the principal goes over the code of conduct and says that from now on the school will be a *telling school*. Immediately after the assembly, all homeroom teachers should go over the code with their classes and answer questions. It will be every homeroom teacher's responsibility to review the code in class once every 2 weeks throughout the year. It would be naive to assume that, without any further mention of the content of the code, the children would continue throughout the year to be aware of it. Consider the following comments by a 16-year-old girl talking to ChildLine (MacLeod & Morris, 1996, p. 88) who was asked if she thought the code helped prevent bullying:

> It (the code of conduct) does in some ways, but it goes out of your head. The first years when they come in, they'll know it and they'll stick to it. But as you get older you forget about the code of conduct, you don't even know it's there half the time. You get told it once a year about, it's on all the doors but you don't really look at it.

In contrast is the comment from a group of Year 6 pupils for whom antibullying has been a regular classroom theme: "Bullying . . . yeah, we've been doing bullying for two years . . . it's our job to stop it happening . . . it's really important" (MacLeod & Morris, 1996, p. 88).

School personnel usually can expect considerable resistance to the whole concept of the telling school possibly because children and adults fail to distinguish between legitimate telling (for bullying and antisocial behaviors in general) and tattling (reporting behaviors that cause no injuries to self or others and no damage to others' property, the purpose being to get someone in trouble). To overcome the ingrained belief that a teller is a "sneak," the school can use the following rationale in presenting the idea to students.

Children have rights, one of which is the right to feel safe in school in an atmosphere conducive to learning. Bullying is a violation of children's rights: Children who are bullied or who witness bullying incidents generally do not feel safe. Consequently, they neither benefit from school as they should nor do they enjoy it. Any child who is bullied by another child or adult, or who sees another child being bullied, is urged to report the incident to designated school personnel. There is a designated teacher to report to along with a comprehensive reporting routine that records all the details of bullying incidents. Children who report such incidents are promised anonymity, a promise that must be ironclad.

Some children (Elliott, 1991) see bullying as endemic, like the common cold, an inevitable part of growing up. This attitude acts as a deterrent to bystanders' willingness to report bullying. Reluctance to intercede or help a victim in any way may be due to dislike of the victim. Research by Perry and his associates (Perry et al., 1988; Perry, Williard, & Perry, 1990) has shown that as a group, victims are disliked. Consequently, children have less concern for a victim who is assaulted than they do for peers in general. Another factor is apathy or unwillingness to get involved. In a study by Boulton and Underwood (1992), 20% of the respondents said they would not help a victim of bullying because it was none of their business. One third of the respondents said that they could see why bullying happens, a reaction that seems to imply condoning of bullying.

In addition to bystanders' unwillingness to report bullying incidents, many victims are also reluctant to do so. One possibility for this is that they often do not equate indirect aggression, such as social exclusion and spreading rumors about the victim, with bullying (O'Connell, Pepler, & Craig, 1999). Even when they do include such behaviors, they may fear further retaliation if they tell, anticipate ridicule from peers, or have no confidence in their home or school support systems (Cowie & Olafsson, 1999). Evidence in support of the latter possibility comes from Craig and Pepler (1995), who found that even peers who professed interest in helping victims and had been trained for an antibullying support system settled disputes and made decisions in favor of the bullies. Naylor, Cowie, and del Rey (2001, p. 119) commented that

> this finding highlights the continuing difficulty in targeting bullied children who are reluctant to ask for help. . . . There is an urgent need to identify these children and to find ways of enabling them to seek out the help that they need.

As long as the victims, bystanders, and others who hear about the bullying protect bullies by keeping silent, bullying will flourish because secrecy is necessary for bullying to thrive. The children in a telling school must do their part in reporting bullying incidents, and school personnel must also do their part by punishing bullies. Such punishment should be clearly spelled out so that there is no doubt in the children's minds about the consequences for the bully. There must be no exceptions.

UNEQUIVOCAL ENFORCEMENT

To bring about any long-term change in behavior, the system of reward and punishment must be consistently enforced, without exception. Enforced rules can make the difference between law and order for all and the reign of terror that exists in many schools (Besag, 1989; Prothrow-Stith, 1991). If rules vary from one teacher or one setting to another, the students can, with some justification, challenge them: Variations provide an alibi for rule infringements. Consistent enforcement of the code of conduct requires active vigilant supervision and is one of the most effective and economical preventive strategies (Besag, 1989). An important supervisory contribution can be made by the nonteaching personnel (custodians, school secretaries, lunch ladies, safety crossing guards, and parent volunteers), many of whom know some of the children well. Here, too, the procedure would be to report punishable incidents to the designated teacher.

When the school has settled into the code of conduct routine, a whole school approach can be mounted to tackle the problem of bullying. A group of specific intervention procedures that could then be incorporated into Olweus's school-based plan are described in chapter 10. It is imperative that the whole school plan be operative and functioning smoothly before the first of the specific interventions is included. Similarly, these interventions should be introduced one at a time and only when the previous one is working well.

SCHOOL LEARNING CLIMATE

To qualify as a good school, it is essential for a school to foster a positive learning climate. The climate of a school is an intangible that nevertheless exerts a considerable influence, whether good or bad, on the well-being of the students. In schools with high levels of bullying, the effects of such behaviors permeate the entire school experience. In an atmosphere of fear, students do not feel safe and are often dissatisfied with school life. For many students, particularly those who are victims, fear can interfere with their academic achievements and enthusiasm for learning (Olweus & Limber, 1999). Such an environment can be damaging in other ways even for those not directly involved: Those who witness bullying may see that other children and sometimes the teachers are supportive of bullying behavior. As a result, a certain number of students are likely to slowly come to see bullying as an acceptable behavior. To modify their approval, schools should take firm action (Olweus & Limber, 1999). In its absence, over a period of time the bullying episodes will have a negative effect on the social climate, and new episodes of bullying will be fostered. A similar effect occurs in the opposite direction as a result of a positive social climate; such a climate elicits positive behaviors from the children.

In 1989, Stephenson and Smith did a survey of the amount of bullying among 1,078 children in the final year of 26 primary schools. For each class, each of the 49 teachers completed two questionnaires for each child in the class. The first focused on characteristics of the child, particularly in relation to any tendency to bully or be bullied, and the severity and form of the bullying. The second concerned the organizational structure of the school, the teacher's experience of bullying and attitude toward it, and the teacher's view of the efficacy of various procedures for dealing with bullying. The questionnaire data showed clearly that bullying occurred more frequently in some schools than in others. In 3 schools there was no bullying at all, whereas in 1 school over 50% of the students were involved in bullying.

The next step involved a more detailed investigation of the 6 schools with the highest and the 6 with the lowest incidence of bullying. In all but 1 of the low-bullying schools the teachers expressed considered and purposeful views on bullying that emphasized the importance of prevention, whereas this was less apparent in the high-bullying schools. Further, only in the low-bullying schools was there consensus on a policy on bullying. The following statements are representative of the teachers' attitudes to bullying (Stephenson & Smith, 1989, p. 50):

> Low-Bullying Schools: We do not accept bullying. We observe very carefully, particularly children admitted from other schools and stress that we are all friends and live happily together. A stern warning is given to any child who shows any sign of aggressive behaviour. The child is reminded what behaviour is expected and is helped to achieve this.
>
> High-Bullying Schools: It is not possible to generalize—we use a variety of approaches. We attempt to reason with the bully. Take away privileges. Show affection to both the bully and the victim. A good telling-off. A do-as-you-would-be-done-unto approach.

The responses by teachers or other adults to children's complaints about being bullied fall into three general groups: (a) a refusal to accept the seriousness of the problem for the child; (b) a suggestion that the child must sort it out without outside help; and (c) a follow-up with decisive action on behalf of the child (MacLeod & Morris, 1996), a relatively rare occurrence. Some teachers combine acknowledgment that bullying occurs in their schools with no responsibility for eliminating it. A parent visiting his son's school, which clearly was not a safe school, said: "Just walking through the school you can feel the undercurrent of violence, to continue to send my son to the school is unthinkable." A teacher at the same school commented: "This is a boy's school. You have to accept bullying. If a child can't take it they should be in another school" (Lane, 1989, p. 95).

Stephens (2000, p. 9) described a safe school in the following terms:

> A safe school is in place when students can learn and teachers can teach in a welcoming environment, free of intimidation and fear. It is a setting where the educational climate fosters a spirit of acceptance and care for every child; where behavior expectations are clearly communicated, consistently enforced and fairly applied. Unlimited options and potential exist for safe school planning. It requires only the ability to get started.

THE CORE PROGRAM AGAINST BULLYING AND ANTISOCIAL BEHAVIOR

For most of the past two decades Olweus has concentrated on developing intervention procedures against bullying or peer harassment for the school setting. The key element in this project has been his Core Program Against Bullying and Antisocial Behavior (Olweus, 1999a, Part IV; Olweus & Limber, 1999). The empirical basis for his approach is a limited set of principles derived primarily from research on the development and modification of antisocial behavior, particularly aggression. These principles have been used to develop specific measures to be used at the individual, class, and school levels. The primary goal of the program is the restructuring of the social environment. This change is effected through changes in *reward* structures and *opportunity* structures for bullying behavior, the result being fewer rewards when bullying does occur and fewer opportunities to bully others. The fact that this approach to intervention is both systems- and individual-oriented is generally regarded as a strength of the program and one of the factors that helps explain its efficacy.

The first intervention project demonstrated clearly positive results (Olweus, 1991, 1993a) with regard to bully/victim problems and the social climate of the classroom. Preliminary results of the intervention part of the new Bergen Project (14 intervention schools and 16 comparison schools; Olweus, 1999a; Olweus & Limber, 1999) also showed positive results. These gains increased more when further evaluations were made in the second project year, with the greatest increases occurring the more closely the teachers followed the program.

The program has recently undergone a grueling evaluation by a committee of American expert assessors and has been selected as 1 out of 10 "model" or blueprint programs. It will be used in a national violence prevention initiative supported by the United States Department of Justice. At the present time the Core Program is being implemented in a large number of schools across the country. The main components of this program are the *Revised Olweus Bully/Victim Questionnaire* (Olweus, 1996); the textbook, *Bullying at School: What We Know and What We Can Do* (Olweus, 1993a); Olweus's *Core Program Against Bullying and Antisocial Behavior: Part IV* (1999a); and the video, *Bullying* (South Carolina Educational Television, 1996).

The criteria for selection were established by the committee at a very high standard. The first of these was a strong research design that included random assignment, low rates of participant attrition, and adequate measurement procedures. Next, evidence of significant deterrence effects was required, an obvious minimal criterion for claiming program effectiveness. The third criterion called for multiple site replication, an important element in establishing program effectiveness in varying settings. This is particularly relevant for selecting blueprint programs for national use because it is no longer possible for a single program designer to maintain personal control over the implementation of the program. Finally, there should be sustained effects beyond the conclusion of the program.

Preliminary analyses of the intervention show reductions of about one third in the levels of bully/victim problems, whereas in the comparison schools that were doing antibullying work of their own design, there was little or no change in "being bullied" and an increase of 35% or more in "bullying other students." At the present time the program is being implemented in a considerable number of schools in various parts of the United States. This will be a stringent test of the efficacy of Olweus's (1999a) Core Program because bullying is a much greater problem in the United States than in Scandinavia. In 1985 Olweus estimated that 15% of the students in Norwegian schools were actively involved in bullying, approximately 7% as bullies and 8% as victims. Note the contrast between Olweus's data and those of a recent study of a representative sample of 15,686 students in Grades 6 through 10 in public and private schools throughout the United States (Nansel et al., 2001). A total of 29.9% of this sample reported moderate or frequent involvement in bullying (13.0% as a bully, 10.62% as a victim, and 6.3% as both bully and victim). The outcome of this stringent test is of crucial importance for the problem of the effective management of school bullying. If the results, as expected, are positive, it will be a giant step forward in combating school bullying. Olweus's (1985) estimate of school bullying in Norway, coupled with the subsequent success of his Whole School Campaign, had a catalytic effect on concern about school bullying in some countries, but especially in England.

Action Against School Bullying: England

Action against school bullying in England was spearheaded by Peter K. Smith and Sonia Sharp. They began by examining the relative success of procedures that had been used in attempts to reduce school bullying. Much of their information came from their own series of research projects in 23 schools over a 30-month period. In terms of the number of children participating this was, to date, the largest monitored intervention project targeting bullying in the United Kingdom. Their findings were reported in a text titled *School Bullying: Insights and Perspectives* that was edited by Peter K. Smith and Sonia Sharp (1994). They also edited a companion handbook titled *Tackling Bullying in Your School* (1994) that described in detail a group of practical procedures for combating school bullying that had been tested and proven to be effective in school settings.

HOME OFFICE POLICE RESEARCH GROUP PROJECT

In 1992 an unexpected and very welcome group of program developers, the Home Office Police Research Group, was formed in England to carry out research projects in the social and management sciences relevant to the work of the police. As part of a broader Home Office initiative aimed at reducing domestic violence and neighborhood conflict such as violence in the street and racist aggression, the Group developed a program to tackle bullying in two secondary and two primary schools in Liverpool and London and summarized it in *Preventing School Bullying* (Home Office Police Research Group, 1996). A questionnaire survey of the students in these four schools had established that there was a high level of violent and antisocial behavior in the schools and surrounding areas, that Bengali and Black students appeared to be disproportionately victimized, and that students usually lacked the confidence to report bullying incidents.

The goal of the project was to produce a program to combat bullying and a strategy for its implementation through a process of staff/student consultation and collaboration. As such, it is not simply concerned with the creation of new rules and the control of individual behavior. Instead, the focus is on *organizational* change, an approach that has had more impact on bullying than other kinds of intervention

(Olweus, 1991; Rutter, Maughan, Mortimore, & Ouston, 1979; Smith, 1991). This type of intervention operates at a number of levels and involves all members of the school: administrators, teachers, students, and ancillary staff. It can have lasting beneficial effects for both bullies and victims. The three-level structure (individual, class, and school) of the highly successful intervention program developed by Olweus (1991) is a good example of an organizational program.

The development of the program was designed to minimize demands on the staff and cause as little disruption as possible to the school. In the fall term, three meetings were held in separate staff and student groups, and thereafter the groups were mixed. It was felt that the staff agenda might differ from that of the students and that the latter might speak more freely with no staff present. During these three sessions experienced professionals worked with the students to elicit their suggestions about organizational change, and subsequently with the staff and students to develop procedures relevant to each school. The key elements in the development process were to facilitate communication among all members of the school community and harness their collective resources in combating bullying. Although the precise components of the strategies varied from school to school because each one had a different culture, confronted different problems, and consequently chose different solutions, in all four schools consultations preceded the acceptance of a solution.

Initial Staff Consultation

The goal of this initial staff consultation was to generate as much relevant information as possible, as quickly as possible. It was important to establish that while the leader might make suggestions, the school personnel were the experts in the victimization problem at their school, so final decisions were their responsibility. The information needed in this meeting concerned what works and what does not work, what rules or practices are clear or unclear, what the school's policy is and what it might be, what support and backup are needed in dealing with bullying in the school, and an indication of the sanctions, resources, and practices that are needed for the staff to operate effectively at the school, class, and individual student levels.

At this time, the teachers were also given an example of a bullying incident and were asked to state in writing how they would handle specific aspects of it, what they would do if the incident recurred, and what sanctions and restrictions they would impose. Other questions covered topics such as how bullying could most easily be observed and how safety could be improved on the students' journey to and from school.

Initial Student Consultation (Secondary School)

The students were given the same bullying incident and similar questions appropriate to their student status. Other questions concerned where they would be in the most danger if they were being bullied, when it was most dangerous, what kind of help they would need, and how classmates and teachers could best help them. Another set of questions related to how the student would respond if bullying another student, for example, what promises by the victim would halt the bullying, what sort of sanctions or threats would stop it, and whom to talk to if concerned about being a bully.

Secondary School Students' Ideas

The students' ideas, which were excellent, focused on the prevention of bullying and racism and, to a lesser extent, sexism. On bullying, for example, they thought school suspension was useless, the punishment should be visible and in school, and the bully should apologize in front of the whole school. On racism and sexism, no name calling should ever be tolerated, and antiracism should permeate the curriculum; in sports, girls should have equal status, and if a girl could qualify for a boys' team she should be on it. In addition, students wanted more responsibility and more opportunities to work with the staff; they did not know what the school policies (rules) were, and this lack of knowledge also applied to some of the staff. Of particular interest were their views concerning future staff/student consultations. Confidentiality was most important: Participants did not want anything that they said to get back to the bullies. As a starting point for future meetings, the staff could be given a list of the questions that the students wanted to ask.

Final Decisions From the Staff/Student Meetings

Consensus on the various points raised by the staff/student consultations resulted in a number of decisions including the following. It was felt that it would be better to confront a bully in front of the class rather than the whole school, but the whole school should know who the persistent bullies were. There should be a program of lunchtime activities that would help reduce bullying. To meet the need for teachers to follow through on complaints of bullying, a Bully Box should be constructed so that students being bullied could leave a petition to discuss the problem with the teacher of their choice. Suspension for bullying would work only if the student had to complete a bullying-focused workbook during the suspension. Student/staff antiracist and antisexist working parties should be convened and should meet regularly to discuss how things were working and how they could be improved.

Important Features of the Preventive Program

In the two primary schools workshops of four to six children were held, using a video, to explore why bullying occurs and how it could be prevented. The video was thought to be an excellent medium for generating a discussion of bullying. The staff and students produced a video on the school behavioral policy to show to students new to the school. A program of peer education was also begun in which older students worked with younger ones to identify what bullying is and to develop school rules to stop it. In the two secondary schools the staff developed an eight-session program for all students that focused on self-esteem, prejudice, stereotyping, assertiveness, and conflict resolution. In addition, the staff/student working party decisions resulted in a survey of the school site to identify areas in which students were most at risk for bullying and a meeting with the local police to clarify the roles and responsibilities of the police and school. These and other bullying-related issues effectively established bullying as a part of the curriculum.

At the end of the first 2 years of implementing the preventive program, follow-up questionnaires were used to monitor its impact on the four schools. The percentage of students who said that they had been bullied once or more in the preceding 3 months fell in both the London (62% to 47%) and Liverpool (72% to 48%) primary schools and in the Liverpool secondary school (34% to 21%). In each of these three schools all types of bullying decreased. Some factors that played an important part in reducing bullying were an increased confidence on the part of students to report bullying, an increased readiness of the teaching and ancillary staffs to intervene in ongoing bullying, and the development of a shared perception in adults and children of behaviors that could be tolerated and those that were unacceptable.

In the London secondary school, however, bullying did not decrease over the 2-year period. A number of counteracting forces were identified, a major one being the strong racial tensions in the locality that spilled over into the school environment in the form of strong demands for allegiance to one's own racial group. A number of former students who hung around the school gates undermined staff and students' feelings that the school was a safe place.

It is clear that for a school situation such as that of the London secondary school, even a carefully developed program like the one described here cannot overcome the powerful opposition of deeply embedded racial prejudices. One approach might be to attempt to involve the students' families in the activities and goals of the school, in combination with a system of rewards and punishments related to the cultural backgrounds of the students. For the Japanese, for example, the threat of losing face would be a strong deterrent to antisocial behavior.

Action Against School Bullying: United States

An important pilot study (Twemlow, Fonagy, Sacco, Gies, et al., 2001) of a social systems/psychodynamic antiviolence intervention program was designed to compare the impact of this program on the learning climate in an elementary school with that of a control school over a 4-year period. The two U.S. schools were matched for demographic characteristics, and both had high levels of disciplinary problems, including serious fighting, high suspension rates and disciplinary referrals, gang recruitment activity, a high number of dropouts, drug and alcohol use in nearby middle and high schools, low overall academic achievement, a high level of teacher dissatisfaction, a low level of parent involvement, adversarial relationships between school personnel and the parents of problem children, and school tolerance of power struggles without an active plan to identify and manage them (Twemlow, 2000).

The change procedures were developed after dialogue with *all* the adult school personnel and the parents. Twemlow (2000, p. 747) stated that the method used "was based on understanding and addressing the etiology of the problem, rather than on forceful attempts to superimpose a corrective experience such as truancy programs based on improved detection and increased penalties." The control school was allowed regular psychiatric consultation. The experimental school interventions focused on dealing with the complex dialectical relationships among three groups of students: the victims of serious bullying, their bullies, and the bystanders. The essence of the unusual approach of this program is that victims, victimizers, and bystanders are targeted simultaneously without attributing an abnormal condition that prevents normal functioning to any child. The more able children helped the more disturbed ones in the participating classes, thus avoiding the possibility of stigmatization, a most humane procedure.

The experimental group's antiviolence program had four components. Component 1 was zero tolerance for behavioral disturbances such as bullying, victimization, and standing by doing nothing during violent acts. It worked by increasing cognitive skills and awareness of roles and by changing language usage. Component 2 consisted of a discipline plan for modeling appropriate behavior. In it, children were taught to view any behavioral disturbance as an interaction of all three roles (bullies, victims, and bystanders) so discipline focused on this aspect rather than attributing pathology to the bully. Component 3 was a physical education plan designed to teach self-regulation skills in physical education classes. These included martial arts, role playing, and story reading; the emphasis was on anger management and encouragement in adopting one or more of the three roles during conflict. Component 4 was a mentoring program for children and adults to help children avoid one of the three roles. The focus here was on playground, lunchtime, and school corridor conflicts.

RESULTS

The experimental school reported dramatic reductions in discipline referrals coupled with significant increases in scores on standardized academic achievement measures (*Metropolitan Achievement Tests,* 1993). Suspension rates for the experimental school were significantly lower in each of the first 3 years, whereas those for the control school remained unchanged. Subjective reports from teachers showed a variety of improvements in the children: Passive, withdrawn children became more verbal and outspoken; the children became more relational and more reflective; they became less reactive, having developed response options that did not include bullying, coercion, or anxious–depressed retreat. In the 4th and final year the stability of the effects of the intervention was evident in the continued progress in the experimental school despite the fact that there was little support from the research team (Twemlow, Sacco, & Twemlow, 2001).

Prior to the intervention, the staffs at both the experimental and control schools were plagued with high levels of disciplinary problems and fighting that was serious enough to require police intervention. In the postexperimental results, the control school showed no changes from their pretest scores. By comparison, the experimental school showed significant improvement in a reduction in out-of-school suspensions and other serious infractions, as well as the important behavioral changes in the students described earlier. Of particular importance was their continued progress even in the final year of the intervention, when support by the research team was minimal. It was conclusively established that the learning environment improved as a result of the intervention procedure.

Although the results of this low-cost pilot study of antiviolence intervention were impressive, Twemlow, Fonagy, Sacco, Gies, et al.

(2001) expressed concern about two aspects. One was the fact that the allocation of experimental and control groups had not been random. This basic limitation has been addressed in an ongoing controlled study of the program in nine elementary schools in Topeka, Kansas. The other was their uncertainty as to whether all the multiple components in the program were essential. This concern does not appear to justify any changes in the program or further trials varying the components in each one.

Action Against School Bullying: New Zealand

As part of their Law-Related Education Program, the New Zealand Police developed the Kia Kaha (Maori for "be strong") Anti-Bullying Kit in 1992. This resource kit is designed for teachers of children 9 to 15 years of age. The kit includes a booklet describing the steps for school personnel to follow in setting up an antibullying campaign, beginning with the readiness of the school staff to use the program. Two staff meetings provide an overview of Kia Kaha: Procedures for involving the parents are discussed, postprogram evaluations are described, and a clear explanation of the rationale of the program is provided along with the aims and objectives, how it can fit into the school curriculum, and how to introduce students to it.

The core of the program is a 14-minute professionally produced video made up of five bullying scenarios. Following the first scenario, effective antibullying strategies are discussed. Between each of the scenarios, bullying-related questions are asked. The accompanying booklet also includes exercises that are relevant to the video, a series of antibullying strategies that children can use, a five-step plan to defuse a bullying situation, and cards for encouraging children to brainstorm about bullying scenarios and to suggest solutions.

In 1996 three international focus groups evaluated the Kia Kaha Kit. Along with a number of positive comments, several recommendations for possible improvements were made. Of interest here are some of the negative criticisms from these groups, beginning with the message from the program that "the only way to meet power is with power." Also, the bullies in the video were not made to take any responsibility for their actions and were portrayed as cowards who were not intelligent. Too much pressure was put on the victims to adopt an assertive stance. It was felt that the actors involved were "one-dimensional," meaning that people are more complex than those shown in the video. Some of the comments suggested that the video would be most appropriate for children up to 10 years of age.

These problems could largely be overcome by astute teacher discussion. Particularly commendable is the participation of the police in focusing on what is essentially a preventive approach to a problem that, if unchecked, may escalate rapidly at the young adult level.

Action Against School Bullying: Italy

Concern about the quality of the school climate led to a carefully conducted 3-year project in a small-town middle school near Florence, Italy (Menesini & Smorti, 1997). The focus in the first year was on training the teachers in how to handle the problem of psychosocial risk factors, such as high aggression or hot temper, in the school children. At the same time, data were collected on bully/victim problems, using anonymous questionnaires (Genta, Menesini, Fonzi, Costabile, & Smith, 1996; Olweus, 1993a; Whitney & Smith, 1993). In the second year, the teachers were provided with a counseling service to help them cope with school problems and difficult children. Also set up were a series of teachers' and parents' meetings on school bullying. Active intervention occurred in the third year: At the whole school level, all those involved (children, teachers, parents, and other school members) collaborated on developing a school policy against bullying, as well as a plan to build up a positive school climate. At the class level, teachers were trained in two kinds of interventions: role-playing activities to raise awareness of the issue and quality circles (see chapter 10) for problem-solving bullying issues.

There was evidence that a relatively short-term intervention such as this one can improve the social interactions of children as well as decrease bullying behavior. There was a significant decrease in reports of bullying and a related increase in prosocial behavior. A particularly interesting finding was that peers treated bullies with more understanding and tolerance than adults did: Both teachers and parents were ready to deal with victims' problems, but bullies received very little attention.

Action Against School Bullying: England

Despite cultural differences that tended to dilute concern about bullying, there was a shift in the 1990s to action against bullying not only by the schools but also by foundations such as the Gulbenkian Foundation; organizations such as ChildLine, which sponsored a Bullying Line (LaFontaine, 1991; MacLeod & Morris, 1996) so that children could telephone qualified adults about being bullied; the Home Office Police Research Group, which developed an antibullying program

(Pitts & Smith, 1995); and the Department of Education and Employment (1998), which made it a legal requirement for schools in England to have an antibullying program in action by September 1999.

How effective were these efforts in reducing bullying in the schools in England? Smith and Shu (2000) conducted a survey to obtain data on this question. They sent a questionnaire concerning antibullying activities in the school to a random sample of 440 schools. Replies were received from only 140 schools, a lower return indicative of the general attitude of indifference to the bullying problem. From this group, 100 schools were then sent a letter explaining the purpose of the proposed study and offering the results of a free survey of bullying in their schools as an incentive for their participation. Of the 30 schools indicating positive interest, 19 were able to complete the questionnaires within the time limits of the survey. Altogether a total of 2,308 pupils (1,238 boys and 1,070 girls) ages 10 to 14 years took part. Although the initial random sample represented a cross-section of urban/rural areas across different parts of England, Smith and Shu cautioned that the final sample of 19 schools could not be considered representative of English schools in general because of the self-selection aspects of the procedures.

The questionnaire that each child was given was an adapted 24-question version of the widely used Olweus questionnaire (Olweus, 1993a). All questions about being bullied and bullying others had a time marker so that the frequencies and experiences could be related to a specific time period. All questions had a multiple-choice format. A teacher at the school who was not the class teacher administered the questionnaires and emphasized the anonymity and confidentiality of the responses.

Although the overall level of bully/victim problems remains a cause for concern, the findings from this survey show a noticeably lower level than that reported previously by Ahmad and Smith (1994) and Whitney and Smith (1993) using a similarly adapted Olweus questionnaire. Smith and Shu (2000) concluded that there is some evidence for a decrease in rates of reported bullying and victimization in English schools, which could be the result of the antibullying activity in England during the period 1990–1997.

Although the duration of bullying experienced by the victim was relatively short, with two thirds of the respondents reporting less than 1 month, 22% were bullied for a year or more. Clearly, neither the victims nor their schools were able to deal effectively with the bullying problem. The most common strategy that victims used to combat bullying was to ignore it. This reaction may be useful for nasty teasing but seems very ineffective for physical attacks and other harsher types of bullying. Age was a factor here: Older children more often were used to ignoring, whereas younger children reported more crying and running away.

The predominant attitude on the bullies' part was that the victim deserved it. Some "justified" their bullying on the grounds that the victims were weak, had no friends, or were generally rejected by the peer group. However, on the plus side, victims reported that telling someone usually helped and rarely made it worse. Teachers could be a powerful source of help, if told, but there was a slight (but significant) risk of things becoming worse when teachers, compared with family or peers, were told. It is clear that if teacher intervention is attempted, it must be done with skill.

The most sobering findings of all were the increasing apathy on the part of bystanders, the rise in self-justification with increasing age on the part of bullies, and the "culture of silence" that often surrounds bullying, giving it a protective coat. Thirty percent of the victims had not told anyone of their being bullied.

Schools are faced with many challenges as they work to develop and put into effect antibullying policies and strategies. However, Smith and Shu (2000, p. 207) concluded from their survey that "good schools can reduce the extent of school bullying."

When the excellent comprehensive school-based intervention program, the Sheffield Project developed by Smith and Sharp (1994), was used under their careful supervision, only a 15% to 20% reduction in school bullying was achieved. This level of reduction is certainly evidence of progress in combating bullying, but it falls far short of the 50% reduction that Olweus (1993a) reported for Scandinavian schools. The question then is, Why is it that English schools are unable to match or even come close to Olweus's results?

Reasons for the Discrepancy Between the Scandinavian and English Results

CULTURAL DIFFERENCES

Cultural differences between Scandinavian and English adults provide one explanation. Olweus (1997) contended that reducing school bullying is primarily a question of changing the attitudes as well as the behavior and routines in school life. The attitudes of Scandinavian parents are unquestionably supportive of decisive action against school bullying. In 1982 when the report came out that three 10- to 14-year-old Norwegian boys had committed suicide as a result of severe, long-term bullying, parents and school personnel were outraged. Norwegians rose en masse and demanded and got immediate government action in the form of a school-based intervention program to combat bullying (Olweus, 1993a).

However, in England, reports of bullying-related suicides have never elicited a comparable reaction. When suicides do occur, there are expressions of distress and sometimes a flurry of concerned letters to the local newspapers, but no decisive action is taken or even contemplated by the government. The fact is that in many ways England accepts school bullying. Consider the bullying that occurs in many English boys' boarding schools. School personnel are well aware of it. Prefects (senior boys) have "fags" (junior boys) who are required to perform a variety of tedious and often demanding tasks for them. If the fag displeases the prefect, he may be caned by him, often quite severely. For generations, upper-class British boys have been sent off to boarding schools at the age of 8 or 9, with the unreassuring advice to "keep a stiff upper lip" and to "take it like a man." Because many of the fathers have been through the same experiences, they are quite aware of how miserable their sons are likely to be. Typically, they are convinced that the experience will "make a man" out of their sons, a tall order for a child of 8.

With this parental background, it is logical that English parents are much less decisive than their Scandinavian counterparts when their children are being bullied. In a study by Elliott (1986) of 4,000 children, the parents were asked how they coped when their children were bullied. Only 4% tried to intervene to stop the bullying. Fifty-seven percent of the children who had told their parents about it experienced either no change in the bullying problem or a negative result (MacLeod & Morris, 1996). Although many parents expressed some concern about the bullying, the majority had reasons for not getting involved at all: "It's an age-old problem—always happened, always will," "Let the kids sort it out," and "Just hit back." There was parental indifference to what the children were experiencing:

> A gang of girls are bullying me at school. They pick on me, pull my hair and push me around. They tell the teacher I've been doing naughty things. My mum told the teacher and the girls were told off; but they've started again. My dad says I have to fight my own battles. (Kerry is 10 years old.) (MacLeod & Morris, 1996, p. 43)

A simplistic approach to the problem of bullying has been proposed by Knight (1997), an English columnist. He advocated less rather than more adult intervention on the grounds that it can stifle learning and that children need unrestricted and unsupervised peer interaction to prepare themselves for later relationships in which they must cope with conflict on their own. He apparently equates teaching children antibullying strategies with increased dependence on external help, thus undermining their ability to resolve conflicts themselves.

Knight's (1997) superficial take on the whole problem reflects a number of misconceptions (if not downright contradictions of valid research findings): He agreed that some children repeatedly persecute other children, sometimes violently, but stated that these victims can suffer serious short-term side effects. No mention is made of the unequivocal evidence that the side effects are usually anything but short-term. He imposed an adult view on indirect bullying behaviors (name calling, spreading rumors, being ignored) as being negligible, but from a child's viewpoint, such behaviors by others can be far more demoralizing than physical attack. When ratings are obtained of the seriousness of a particular behavior, children's ratings seldom match those of adults. Even more surprising is his totally erroneous statement that "we may be able to give pointers, but social skills can't be taught or enforced" (Knight, 1997, p. 18). In view of the evidence that even mentally retarded children can be taught social skills (Ross, 1970; S. A. Ross, 1969), this argument is ludicrous.

It is unfortunate that Knight's (1997) approach provides support for parents and others who believe that "boys will be boys" and that children must "stand on their own two feet," "fight their own battles," and so on. These sentiments completely disregard the fact that the odds are so stacked against the victim that immediate retaliation is almost always completely unrealistic. For those in agreement with Knight, his column will strengthen their convictions and thus deprive the victims of bullying of the support they sorely need.

DYSFUNCTIONAL PARENTING

Dysfunctional patterns of child rearing will undermine and counteract any school-based intervention programs for coping effectively with bullying. A child who goes home every day to a dysfunctional household is unlikely to experience any behavior changes in response to the school program.

In Scandinavia, most children come from reasonably stable homes in which the parents are supportive of the intervention program and have access to counseling, small discussion groups, and regular teacher conferences. Genuine concern about bullying has been an ongoing reaction for more than two decades. It has attracted the interest of the scientific community and has achieved widespread media coverage. The focus on the bullying problem has not been obscured by other problems such as school shootings and student drug usage, as is the case in the United States (Pollack, 2000).

In England, school bullying has its origins in dysfunctional parenting as well as in factors in the school environment (Hazler, 1996a). When parents are aggressive models who exhibit violent behaviors, use harsh and inconsistent discipline, show indifference to the child's needs, are absentee parents, or, in the case of mothers, are cold and rejecting, the child is often an active and confirmed bully (Prothrow-Stith, 1991). A child who experiences dysfunctional parenting is unlikely to benefit from the regular school program (in addition to being a constant irritant in the classroom) or from even a top-quality school-based intervention program such as Olweus's (1993a) bullying program (James, 1994).

A classic example of the poor school and behavioral prognosis associated with dysfunctional parenting is the case of Robert Thompson, age 10, who was the leader in the 1993 brutal murder of 2-year-old James Bulger in Liverpool, England (Morrison, 1994). When Robert was 6, his father left to live with another woman. The situation deteriorated even more after he left. His mother, in anger and despair at being abandoned, began most nights drinking heavily in the local pub. Robert had four older brothers who used physical aggression freely: Each one regularly beat up the next younger one, and the mother either was unable to stop it or was too drunk to try. Robert was sent to school at 8:30 a.m. every school day and told to be home by 6:00 p.m. if he expected dinner. He was usually allowed out after dinner. He had a poor truancy record, having been absent 37 of the previous 60 school days. His mother was a bundle of inconsistency in child rearing, but with compulsory school she was forced to try to get Robert to school. She coped ineffectively by hiding his shoes, locking him in his room, and taking him to the local police for a lecture. Some of his brothers and his mother attempted suicide. There were many reports by the neighbors of neglect and violence against Robert. Children in his class at school claimed that he "used to ask us do we want to be in their gang, we're going to kill someone" (Morrison, 1994, p. 49). On their way to kill James Bulger, Robert said to his friend Jon, "Let's get this kid lost. . . . Let's get him lost outside so when he goes into the road he'll get knocked over" (Morrison, 1994, p. 55). The police who interviewed Robert described him as "cold, manipulative, adult . . . streetwise, aggressive, defiant, cunning . . . he treated his interviews with the police as 'a battle of wits'" (Morrison, 1994, p. 55).

Scandinavian school personnel and parents were solidly behind efforts to halt bullying and wholeheartedly supported intervention programs. By contrast, neither English school personnel nor parents took as firm a stand. The Scandinavian parents were the ones who demanded and got government support for intervention. When their children told them that they had been bullied, the parents were always ready to take decisive action.

Similarly, in Scandinavian schools most principals and teachers take a firm stand against bullying. Complaints of being bullied and reports that others have been bullied are acted upon immediately with rebukes and nonphysical forms of punishment. School principals in England often react so ineptly to complaints of bullying that they make the situation worse:

> A parent called the Bullying Line about her daughter, Julie, who was being subjected to what she described as "daily verbal torture" by two girls who used to be friendly with her. The parent had reported the matter to the headteacher who had put Julie in front of the school during assembly and asked the bullies to stand up. Since then the bullying had intensified. Julie was becoming hysterical about going to school and had refused to allow her parents to talk to the school. The mother was desperately worried about her and said Julie was becoming rude and uncommunicative. (MacLeod & Morris, 1996, p. 50)

Sometimes the principal will steadfastly deny that there is a bullying problem because he or she is solely concerned about the image of the school. Even long-term or repeated complaints may have no effect, and the parents may resort to sending their child to another school:

> A 13-year-old boy caller told us of a year of misery at a school where his and also his parents' attempts to get the problem tackled had had no effect. His parents had finally decided to move the boy to another school which had worked out very well because, the boy reported, the headteacher was very clear that bullying was out of order and everyone knew this. (MacLeod & Morris, 1996, p. 13)

Often the teachers also deny that there is a problem. They contend that the victim provoked the bully or was oversensitive. English school teachers are not as well prepared as their Scandinavian counterparts to cope with bullying. The problem of bullying has been largely ignored in English teacher-training courses (Smith, 2001). This omission is surprising in view of the substantial body of empirical evidence that school bullying is a major problem that causes serious harm to many victims (Hawker & Boulton, 2000). According to a questionnaire study with 270 teacher-training students in England,

Nicolaides, Toda, and Smith (2002) reported that the majority of the English respondents viewed school bullying as an important problem but often lacked accurate knowledge about it. In addition, they were often not confident about their ability to deal with bullying at school, with bullies, or with the parents of bullies. Note the uncertainty that this teacher expressed:

> It's just so hard to know what to do . . . I mean it (bullying) seems so hard to pin down and other times I just know that there is bullying going on but I don't know how to approach it . . . it's different from other kinds of discipline matters I feel much less confident somehow. (Sharp & Smith, 1993, p. 128)

They showed more confidence about dealing with the victims of bullying and their parents. Not surprisingly, they were strongly in favor of courses about combating bullying. Nicolaides et al. (2002) supported this view and, in addition, recommended including courses in other areas in which trainees clearly lack confidence. In a comment at the British Psychological Society Conference in 2001, Smith said:

> It's now a legal requirement that schools have an antibullying policy, and parents are very aware of the issues. We have seen legal cases against schools where issues have not been dealt with properly. We are arguing that this should be reflected in the training teachers get, which at the moment is haphazard. It seems to be dependent on one-off courses or tutors who have a particular interest. We think it should be a core part of teacher training.

THE CODE OF SILENCE

There are marked differences between Scandinavian and English school children in willingness to tell adults that they or another student have been bullied and to name the bully. In the Scandinavian school intervention program (Olweus, 1993a), there were three important classroom rules:

1. We will not bully other students.
2. We will try to help students who are bullied.
3. We will make it a point to include all students who are easily left out.

Although it does not explicitly say so, one function of Rule 2 is to encourage children to tell their teacher or parent when a fellow student is bullied. To counteract any tendency on the part of the child to think that he or she is guilty of tattling, the teacher explains that a child who reports bullying is simply following Rule 2 by trying to help a student who has been bullied.

In contrast to the foregoing sanctioning of telling tales, the code of silence in England is ironclad. To report a peer for bullying is almost always regarded as appalling behavior in English schools. Once at a Sports Day at a boarding school, I commented to a student how well another student performed on the high jump. The student replied contemptuously, "Oh, that's Dawson. He's good at it because he will never get into any of the team events. So he practices the high jump all the time. He's really rotten." When asked what was rotten about Dawson, the student said, "He told when another boy beat him up." A student nearby added, "He would. He's a real grasser (one who tells tales). No team would ever have him."

Evidence that the code of silence is still operating in English schools comes from two studies. In a survey of 2,308 pupils ages 10–14 years and from 19 schools (Whitney & Smith, 1993), 50% of the self-reported victims had not told anyone that they had been bullied; in a more recent study (Smith & Shu, 2000) 30% had told no one. On the basis of victim reports, telling someone that they had been bullied usually helped. Teachers proved to be a powerful source of help when told, although there was a small risk of things becoming worse when teachers were told. Overall, though, the outcome was usually seen as positive.

The real beneficiaries, at least in the short term, are the bullies who have the protection of the code of silence. Half of this group said that no teacher or parent had ever talked to them about their bullying. Most of the victims who told no one were boys or older children, a tendency that increases with age. Smith (2000) believed that it reflects the more serious nature of victimization for the older age group. Presumably, embarrassment at not being able to cope acts as a deterrent to seeking help.

COMMENT

It is clear that wide-ranging differences between the Scandinavian and English way of life provide a reasonable basis for explaining why school-based intervention procedures for reducing school bullying are far more successful in Scandinavia than they are in England. The combination of cultural differences in attitudes toward bullying, willingness to report infractions, support by school personnel and parents, and family climate offers a valid explanation for the disappointingly low reduction in school bullying in England. In fact, when one considers the obstacles in the way of reducing school bullying in England, achieving a 15% to 20% reduction begins to seem like a minor miracle.

THE PROBLEM OF HARD CORE BULLIES

The consensus among school personnel and other professionals is that there is a hard core of bullies who are highly resistant to the forms of intervention currently in use. Two recent studies provide some support for this statement. One, by Sutton et al. (1999), concerns the popular stereotype of the oafish bully as a not-too-bright, somewhat clumsy individual whose success is largely a function of physical strength, combined with the ability to identify victim potential in others and an inability to understand the mental states, beliefs, and emotions of others, particularly of their victims. Sutton et al. argued that the view of bullies as lacking in social perspective-taking skills has no empirical basis. Accordingly, they started with the question, What empirical proof is there for this assessment of the bully? To investigate the validity of the belief that children who bully are lacking in social perspective-taking skills, Sutton et al. used a set of 11 stories designed to assess the theory of mind ability (Taylor, 1996) of 7- to 10-year-old children (N = 193) involved in bullying. Theory of mind refers to the ability of children or adults to attribute mental states to themselves and others to explain and predict behavior (Premack & Woodruff, 1978; Taylor, 1996). The set of stories used by Sutton et al. was designed to answer the question, How well do bullies understand the mental states, beliefs, and emotions of others?

Their findings do not lend credence to the view of the bully as stupid and oafish. Instead, they provide support for a subgroup among aggressive bullies, a group who are cold, manipulative, highly skilled experts in social situations. They organize top-level groups of loyal followers with real skill and foresight and generally use subtle, indirect methods in their interactions with others. They scored significantly higher on the theory of mind stories than did anxious bullies, victims, and peers who stepped in to help victims of bullying.

Sutton et al. (1999) raised the question of where these highly skilled children end up in adulthood and speculated on the possibility of a negative effect of social cognitive skills in adult bullying:

> Victims of bullying in the workplace often refer to managers who cunningly manipulate their workers, for example, creating "furtive alliances" and using "entrapment," and who also man-

> age to hide their behavior from their superiors, passing it off as an "autocratic style." (p. 445)

Subgroups of bullies with these social cognitive skills could be identified early in the school system and taught positive uses of this set of skills. With this training, these skills would then become a definite asset, particularly on the work front.

Data from a second study (McBurnett et al., 2000) provide further support for the existence of a hard core of bullies who are impervious to the current educational and counseling interventions. In this 4-year study, McBurnett et al. found that extreme antisocial behaviors, including bullying, were strongly associated with lower than expected levels of salivary cortisol in 7- to 12-year-old boys ($N = 38$). Although the number of boys involved was small, level of salivary cortisol also correlated very strongly with the cluster of behaviors described as child-onset conduct disorder.

Cortisol typically is released in response to fear, such as fear of punishment for misbehavior. Its low level in bullies and other antisocial boys suggests that these boys do not fear negative consequences for misbehavior. In fact, bullies often brag that they can take whatever disciplinary actions school personnel use against them. Consequently, the usual deterrents to misbehavior are ineffective. Because their misbehavior may be biologically based, current treatment regimens may be of little use. K. McBurnett (personal communication, January 10, 2000) speculated that it might be necessary to discard traditional approaches to treatment of these children and instead focus on helping them to find a niche in society where their aggressiveness and lack of a sense of danger would be an asset.

What is unique about Sutton et al.'s (1999) and McBurnett et al.'s (2000) studies is the concern that is voiced about helping the bully to use his or her particular talents effectively rather than focusing on interventions designed to force the child into a mold at odds with his or her own potentially strong assets. This positive approach also has implications for a number of other childhood behavior problems.

Bystanders: A Potential Positive Force

Until the 1990s, only a modicum of investigative interest was shown in the social roles that bystanders might play. In the early 1990s, a Finnish research group (Salmivalli, Lagerspetz, Björkqvist, Österman, & Kaukiainen, 1996) conducted a series of studies focusing on the different social roles that children assume in the process of victimization. The starting point was an interview study to determine what one group, bystanders, actually do during an ongoing bullying episode (Salmivalli, 2001). It was immediately clear that bullying is not just a bully/victim interaction. Instead, "passive bullies" or "henchmen" (Olweus, 1978) influence the ongoing bullying, usually with encouragement.

An important advance relevant to the effect that bystanders might have on a bullying episode has been made by Salmivalli (1992, 1999, 2001). She distinguished between two kinds of victimization. In one, the victim is the target of systematic antisocial aggression that is characterized by a power imbalance and may involve one or more bullies. In the other, the victim is just one part of a process that has developed over a period of time within the context of a whole group. Involved in this process are several group mechanisms such as social contagion and diffusion of responsibility (Olweus, 1978, 1991). From the latter viewpoint, Salmivalli (2001, p. 398) contended that "being a victim can be viewed as a social role in the group." It follows that victimization should be studied not only as the outcome of a pattern of antisocial behavior but also as a social phenomenon that must take into account the group context in which it occurs (Fraczek, 1996).

Through a series of studies, the Participant Role Questionnaire (PRQ) was developed to measure the participant roles in bullying. It is a peer-evaluation instrument in which every child assesses each classmate's typical behavior in bullying situations as well as his or her own. The 22 statements in the PRQ form five participant role scales: bully scale, assistant scale, reinforcer scale, defender scale, and outsider scale. Victims are identified by a separate peer nomination procedure. Table 9.1 provides short descriptions of the participant roles as well as some examples of items on each scale. Scale reliabilities are good: Cronbach's alphas range from .80 to .94. The criteria for assigning a certain role to a child are (a) the child scores higher on that particular scale than on the other scales, all of which were standardized by school class, and (b) the child scores above the class mean on that standardized scale. The criterion for a child being identified as a victim of others' harassment is that 30% or more of classmates of either sex nominate him or her as a victim. One possible problem with the procedure of standardizing scores by class is that a child could be categorized as having no role owing to an extreme score from another child in the class.

The social roles that students take with respect to bullying have been conceptualized by Salmivalli et al. (1996) as participant roles in the bullying process. These are the roles of bully, assistant to the bully, reinforcer of the bully, defender of the victim, outsider, and victim.

Table 9.1. Descriptions of Participant Roles and Examples of Items on Each Scale

Participant role	Description	Examples of items
Bully	Active, initiative-taking, "ring-leader" bullying behaviors	Starts bullying. Makes others join in the bullying.
Assistant	Following the bully, assisting him or her	Joins in the bullying. Assists the bully.
Reinforcer	Providing bully with feedback that encourages him or her	Comes around to watch the situation. Laughs.
Defender	Taking sides with the victim	Says to the victim, "Never mind." Tries to make the others stop bullying.
Outsider	Withdrawing, not reacting to bullying	Is not usually present (in bullying situations). Does not even know about the bullying.
Victim	Target of systematic harassment (identified with a separate peer-nomination procedure)	

Source: Reproduced with permission of the author and publisher from Salmivalli, C. (2001). Group view on victimization: Empirical findings and their implications. In J. Juvonen & S. Graham (Eds.), *Peer Harassment in School: The Plight of the Vulnerable and Victimized* (pp. 398–419). © Guilford Press.

The concept of participant role includes a potential for change, so that these six roles should not be viewed as relatively permanent personality characteristics.

Salmivalli (2001, p. 411) acknowledged that the social role approach may involve some problems:

> Social roles . . . sometimes become self-fulfilling prophecies. . . . When a person has taken . . . a certain role, he or she may find it difficult to get rid of it. The group punishes behaviors that are contrary

> to that role and rewards behaviors that are in accord with it . . . it may be difficult for an individual to switch to a very different role.

It follows that changing the bully's appraisal of ambiguous events faces obstacles, such as a loss of face when his or her customary immediate attack on the victim is not forthcoming, as well as the disapproval of his or her assistants and reinforcers. However, changing the bully's behavior could be facilitated by also focusing on some of the children in the participant roles: If the assistants, reinforcers, and outsiders could be persuaded to take a stand against school bullying (as part of a whole school program), this loss of supporters and audience could undermine the bully's customary antisocial response pattern. Or if the bystanders could be actively discouraged from watching bullying incidents, the bully would be deprived of an important source of reinforcement, in his or her estimation, an admiring audience.

Some investigators have focused on how bystanders would react if they saw ongoing bullying. Boulton and Underwood (1992), for example, asked middle school children how often they tried to stop ongoing bullying: 41% said sometimes, 16% said almost never, 31% did not know, and only 12% said they almost always did do something. To the question "What do you do when you see a child of your age being bullied?" 49% tried to help the child in some way, 29% said they did nothing but thought that they ought to try and help, and a dispiriting 22% said they would not help because it was none of their business. One third of the children in the study said that they could see why bullying happened, a response that seems to suggest acceptance or an implicit condoning of the bullying.

In line with the last view are the findings from a study by Whitney and Smith (1993) in which 18% of the children in junior/middle and secondary schools said that if their friends were bullying someone, they would join in. One respondent offered the following rationale for this behavior (Whitney & Smith, 1993, p. 18):

> I think it's like because if somebody's bullying them—you don't want to be friends with them (the victims) . . . because everyone will tease you for being friends with them . . . so everyone'll join in the bullying.

Some children feel guilt at not intervening if the victim is a friend: "I don't like it that Gill is bullied but I can't do anything about it or they will turn on me, too" (Elliott, 1993, p. 9). Others worry that they might be the next target and seek advice. One 7-year-old boy said,

> They call him Big Mac, he's only seven like me but he's as big as my brother who's nine. I wish I knew how to fix it so he doesn't know I even am at this school. If you was a boy like me, what would you do? (D. M. Ross, personal communication, October 1991)

In an interview study of sixth-grade children in Finland (Salmivalli, 2001), one aspect involved what bystanders do when a bully is harassing a victim. One boy said:

> Quite a few gather there on the spot . . . if all the boys are there, for instance, they laugh and someone might say, "Hit him properly!" . . . Pekka (the victim) has no one to stand up for him, but if Tapio (the bully) is too superior, then we intervene. (p. 401)

Hazler (1996b) noted that nonintervention takes a psychological toll on bystanders in the form of diminished self-respect, but it can be replenished through help from concerned adults that focuses on regaining the confidence that goes with feeling in control. Generally, this help is most effective when it occurs with groups rather than individual bystanders. As Hazler (1996b, p. 15) noted: "Group teaching, counseling, and training activities help students to recognize the commonality of feelings, concerns, and even the empowerment that comes from a unity of purpose and recognition of available support for individual actions."

Underlying all attempts to help bystanders become active in bullying situations is the need to understand and recognize that their feelings of inadequacy and guilt over their failure to become involved are not unique but are generally experienced to some extent by many of the bystanders. When talking over these feelings in the context of the group, participants begin to see the potential power of the group in intervening in peer-on-peer abuse. Once this stage is reached, the group will then be able to come up with many ideas on how to cope when faced with a bullying incident. One principle involves attacking what the abuser has done to a victim rather than the abuser himself, that is, focus on the action rather than derogating the personality of the abuser. Discussion of various possible ways of intervening should include a run-through of the steps and their possible consequences as well as an evaluation of each proposed intervention. Chances for successful intervention are obviously greatest when substantial numbers of bystanders are present and also have a well-thought-out plan for united action. If this requirement is lacking, merely increasing the number of bystanders does not increase the likelihood that they will intervene. In fact, research on adult bystander behavior (Latane & Darley, 1970; Latane & Nida, 1981) has shown that as the number of bystanders at an incident increases, the probability of constructive action on their part decreases. A "good" example of this phenomenon occurred in the case of James Bulger (Morrison, 1994): At least 40 adults saw the 2-year-old boy crying and clearly miserable as he was being dragged along by the two 10-year-old boys who were taking him to a place where they could kill him. Not one adult intervened. This pattern of behavior, common among bystanders, is aptly called *diffusion of responsibility*.

In a thoughtful discussion of the potential role of bystanders, Hazler (1996b) contended that although child bystanders are generally passive spectators to ongoing bullying, they could be a major force in coping with the bullying problem. He attributed this tendency to stay on the sidelines of ongoing bullying to the bystanders' uncertainty as to what action they should take, their fear of becoming a target themselves, or their concern that they might do the wrong thing and so intensify the bullying.

Although avoiding direct confrontation with the bully or bullies is certainly a prudent thing to do, one of the several negative results is that it creates a feeling of powerlessness in the onlooker. To help bystanders gain control in a bullying incident, Hazler (1996b) developed a set of guidelines that should be mandatory reading for school personnel and others who would like to ensure that bystanders play an active and effective role in combating bullying.

The group should also spend time considering ways of giving a victim support outside of the bullying incident. These might include talking to the victim in a casual way, including him or her in some activities, and making other overtures in a subtle rather than obvious way. Some thought should also be given to the group's feelings about the abuser, particularly when there is confusion caused by mixed feelings about abusers who have some positive qualities. The group could possibly think of ways to capitalize on these qualities by diverting the abuser into situations in which these qualities would be praiseworthy.

According to Olweus (1978), in most school situations, four group mechanisms are operating that can result in bullying and other antisocial behaviors. These are social contagion, weakening of inhibitions against aggressive tendencies, diffusion of responsibility, and gradual cognitive changes in the child's perception of the victim. In his new *Core Program Against Bullying and Antisocial Behavior: Part IV* (Olweus, 1999a), there is further description of the reactions of students to cruel bullying. It is clear that there are distinct patterns of behavior that dif-

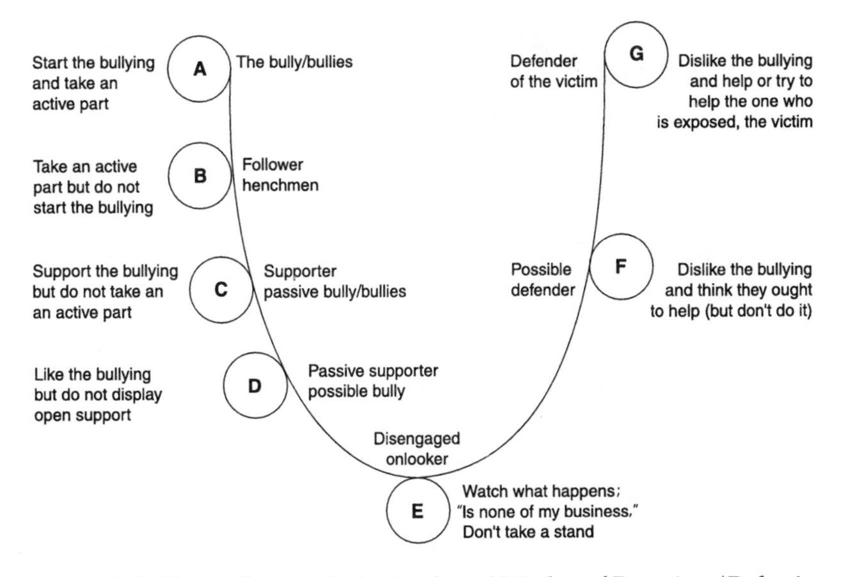

Figure 9.1. The Bullying Circle: Students' Modes of Reaction/Roles in an Acute Bullying Situation

Reproduced with permission of the author and publisher from Olweus, D. (2001). Peer harassment: A critical analysis and some important issues. In J. Juvonen & S. Graham (Eds.), *Peer Harassment in School: The Plight of the Vulnerable and Victimized* (pp. 3–20). © Guilford Press.

ferent students display. These responses represent the student's attitude to the problem of bullying, for example, positive, neutral–indifferent, and negative, and the way the student will respond in an actual bullying situation. These roles are illustrated and briefly described in Figure 9.1 above. The Bullying Circle is based partly on Olweus's earlier research and partly on the work of Salmivalli and her colleagues on participant roles (Salmivalli, 2001; Salmivalli et al., 1996). It combines attitude and action/no action.

Olweus (2001) preferred self-reports rather than peer ratings for assessment, but he questioned whether even self-reports will provide the quality of information that researchers are seeking. Apart from the empirical data that the Bullying Circle (Olweus, 2001) may provide, Olweus considered it to be a useful pedagogical device for discussions with parents and school personnel about the problem of school bullying. It depicts graphically the importance of more students moving to the right side of the Bullying Circle.

Potential Impact of Early Preschool Programs

THE EARLY VIOLENCE PREVENTION PROGRAM

Of relevance here is an outstanding program that is admirably suited to the goals of the approach to bullying advocated here. The Early Violence Prevention Program is intended for preschool and early school children in the age range of 2 to 7 years. It was developed by Ronald Slaby and his associates (Slaby, Roedell, Arezzo, & Hendrix, 1995). It provides teachers and other adults who work with children in this age group with the requisite knowledge and practical strategies for helping to reduce aggressive behavior, preventing violence, and building skills in constructive conflict resolution. Furthermore, it teaches children to be more assertive, empathic, and willing to share and cooperate with others. It combats tendencies to bullying, becoming a victim, and being a racist. Most children who are exposed to this program will be equipped with the social and emotional skills that facilitate entry into the peer group and becoming a good friend. They will be better able to resist peer pressure to engage in antisocial and other harmful activities, and their ability to protect themselves from abuse will be increased.

In addition to the excellent content of the program, it is also easy to use. The materials needed are readily available to most teachers. Everything that an adult needs to know or do is spelled out clearly; for example, the rationale underlying the use of positive and negative reinforcement is presented in such a way that it is completely clear why a particular step is introduced. The 13 chapters in the program set out the objectives so that the material can be used effectively despite the wide age range of 2 to 7 years. One advantage of this age range is that it bridges the transition from preschool to the primary grades. I strongly recommend that preschools and public schools use this excellent program.

THE PERRY PRESCHOOL PROGRAM

In some cases it is clearly apparent in the early preschool years that the quality of a child's home situation is such that antisocial behavior and other problems are a virtual certainty. It is imperative that these children be enrolled in a preschool program and that home visits by a trained adult be provided to ensure that the home reinforces the goals of the preschool program. The period of such intervention should be 2 or more years. A good example of this type of program is the Perry Preschool Program (Barnett, 1993; Berrueta-Clement, Schweinhart, Barnett, Epstein, & Weikart, 1984), a high-quality, active learning program. The recommended classes are small, with one qualified teacher to every six or seven children. The trained adult should make weekly or bimonthly visits to the home and provide social support in the form of discussing family and other problems, as well as support of an informational nature related to child development. Both the Perry Preschool Program and another program, the Yale Child Welfare Project (Seitz, Rosenbaum, & Apfel, 1985), are admirably suited for preschoolers who are clearly in need of a good start.

USING STORIES AND DRAMA TO INCREASE AWARENESS OF BULLYING AND TEASING

One of the most popular activities that can be used at the preschool and primary school levels to combat bullying is the use of stories and drama. Teachers have access to many books that can be used to enhance awareness of the cruelty inherent in forms of bullying (such as social exclusion, extortion, racism, and sex harassment) and to encourage open discussion of these topics.[1]

There are very few books for children about bullies changing their ways spontaneously. There are many about victims turning on the bully or ending the bullying with some strategy, such as a trick. When you read a bully story, work in ideas such as how painful bullying was for the victim, how the bully was punished for what he or she did, and how the bully's behavior made some children scared and a lot of children and adults dislike him or her. In other words, the bully's behavior was costly for him or her.

Start by reading the book or watching the video yourself and thinking about what and where something could be added. A story is a great way to get a lot of bully-related messages across to the children. The content can easily be changed slightly so that ideas about bullying can be emphasized. Drama is a powerful way to raise the level of awareness of students to the misery of being bullied. Watch TV programs for films about children being kind to other children and animals and about school events. Short films about children from other countries would be helpful in discussions about cultural differences.

[1]See the Annotated Bibliography for books and videotapes that should be helpful in increasing children's awareness of the misery of being bullied and teased.

DAY CARE

In the National Institute of Child Health and Human Development (NICHD) study of Early Child Care and Youth Development (Crary, 2001), the longest and largest study of the effects of day care on young children in the United States, a large group of children were followed from birth, and their child-care environments were studied in the context of their family environments. The findings on early infancy were dispiriting. Most children began nonparental care very early in infancy for extensive hours and with multiple caregivers. Although they appeared to receive somewhat more sensitive caregiving than older children did, only one quarter of the infants received adequate stimulation of their burgeoning cognitive and language development.

Child-care experiences are of crucial importance to optimal child development. The quality of the caregiving should be nurturing, dependable, and supportive of language development and learning. About half of the children received care that could accurately be described as moderately to highly positive along these important dimensions. For the remaining half, the quality ranged from minimally positive to mediocre or barely adequate.

Caregivers are able to provide positive caregiving when they are better educated, hold child-centered beliefs about what children are like and what they can be reasonably expected to do at different preschool ages, and have responsibility for a reasonable number of children. The White House and Bush Administration have announced initiatives for modifying the nation's Head Start programs (Naito, 2002) that will shift the focus from learning through social interaction to cognitive learning with emphasis on literacy, language, and numerical skills. This change apparently disregards the findings from the earlier NICHD study (Crary, 2001) in which researchers found that children who spent more than 30 hours a week in day care were almost three times as likely to exhibit aggression, disobedience, and defiance as those who were in day care for less than 10 hours a week. To reduce emphasis on social interaction skills is a serious and unnecessary error. Research by Ross (1970), for example, established unequivocally that learning of number concepts in small-group board games in which the emphasis in the form of direct teaching is on the social skills necessary for playing group games (taking turns, following rules, losing with reasonable grace, and so on), with number concepts introduced only as part of the game (i.e., showing a child how many moves should be made for two moves or what one turn means, but with *no* drill or emphasis on the number aspects of the game), resulted in far higher arithmetic scores on the postexperiment test than the scores of the control group whose teacher had been told exactly what arithmetic knowledge the control group would be tested on and encouraged to use any methods the teacher chose for teaching the arithmetic concepts. In addition, the social behavior skills of the game group were at a far higher level than those of the control group.

The current Head Start programs are experiencing a nationwide teacher shortage that is not surprising in view of the teachers' average salary of $16,000 a year. Although the Bush plan will increase funding from $6.5 billion in 2002 to $6.7 billion in 2003, this amount is inadequate in view of the recruitment needs and the added mandatory retraining requirement. The stated objective is to field-test the Bush plan in 2002–2003 and fully implement it the following fall.

The intent of the plan is clearly a positive direction for the Head Start program, that is, to improve the learning experiences of young children. However, there is little chance for success in view of the inadequate funding and serious teacher shortages already in existence.

I visited 17 preschools on the West Coast several years ago and was appalled at the conditions. They were all grossly understaffed, and some of the staff did not speak English. Children who cried bitterly were seldom comforted or asked what was the problem; instead, they either were scolded for acting like babies or were ignored. The level of noise in most of the preschools was so high that I had to raise my voice to talk to anyone. Often the bathrooms and kitchens were dirty. Chaos prevailed, with the bigger children rampaging around, pushing smaller ones off the swings and taking toys that the smaller children had brought from home. Very few constraints were imposed. Productive use of the children's time was minimal. On an overall assessment scale of 1 to 10, I, as well as a friend who accompanied me, would not have given any of the preschools more than a 3. It was depressing to think that many of the children spent all day, 5 days a week, in those settings. It underlined the absolute necessity of making a number of drop-in visits at various times of the day to any preschool prior to enrolling a child and entrusting his or her welfare to others, and of arranging with the staff that subsequent drop-in visits would be permitted after the child's enrollment.

An Innovative Commentary on the Problem of Bullying Applicable to the Middle School Years and Up

In a commentary on school bullying, a Seattle lawyer, Li (2001), focused on the question of why there has been a recent marked increase in school shootings by victims of bullying. Going beyond the obvious, such as easy access to guns or the graphic violence in movies and video games, he proposed that the core of the problem lies in

> a competitive, materialistic, and increasingly amoral suburban culture that produces, in schools, a cynical, multi-layered caste system. It is a cruel, predatory society in which young people in the upper castes have free license to harass, put down and humiliate, physically and verbally, those beneath them. . . . Bullying (in the affluent suburbs) . . . begins most often with athletes who are physically big and strong, spreads through the ranks of groupies who seek their approval, then filters down through the lower strata. . . . The multiple castes in suburban schools consign a relatively small number to the very bottom, rejected or picked on by almost everyone else. One thing stands out in the past five years: the shooters are almost always children at the bottom of the caste system. (Li, 2001, p. B4)

The following comments (Strasser, 2000), posted anonymously on the Internet, from two former high school students are in agreement with this analysis of a school's social structure:

> I went to three (high schools), and in none of (them) did I for a moment feel safe. High school was terrifying, and it was the casual cruelty of the popular kids that made it hell. (p. 35)
>
> How many kids ostracized, humiliated, and assaulted in American high schools, like the survivors of Columbine High, are left scarred for life? How many commit suicide every year? So long as some kids go out of their way to make high school hell for others, there are going to be kids who crack, and not all of the kids who crack are going to quietly off (kill) themselves. (p. 33)

Those within a high caste cannot fall back on a claim of ignorance concerning the punitive effect their behavior has on their victims. In a recent conversation I had with a 14-year-old girl in the top caste in her school, the girl said that she was uncomfortable about the punishment meted out by others in her caste to those at the bottom, cruelly called the Leftovers. When asked why she thought the other girls persecuted this group, she replied that they thought it was fun. She had tried remonstrating with them, to no avail. Sadly, however, the appeal of group membership clearly overcame her own scruples, and she remains a member of the top caste.

In discussions of school bullying, one aspect of the problem focuses on the necessity of teacher training that really equips most teachers and school administrators for coping effectively with bullying (Nicolaides et al., 2002). In any new programs, it would seem to be essential that schools include training in recognizing the existence of the castes as described by Li (2001). This would involve an intense focus by school personnel on students' behavior, particularly in hallways, playing fields, lunch rooms, and other similar sites around the school. Within class periods, opportunities would also occur for identifying who are assigned to the lowest castes and who appear to be the ringleaders. Isolates in any setting, those chosen last and reluctantly for team activities, and lone children who seem to have the hostile attention of a group of children would be identifiable, as would those whose responses in class are received with negative reactions that are often quite subtly disparaging.

The hidden culture of indirect aggression in school-age girls (Simmons, 2002), particularly those at the upper middle and high school levels, is difficult to detect because it is less concrete and visible than most bullying. Since the middle 1990s, concern about this insidious problem has escalated. Public as well as private schools are inviting the authors of recent texts on indirect aggression to give seminars and lead roundtable discussions about it. Generally, school girls are viewed as the only victims. However, there is another group of individuals who are both miserable about it and unable to intervene effectively. These are the mothers of the victims of indirect aggression. Note the misery and frustration in this mother's comments:

> Having a child who is bullied means seeing your child become an outcast, frozen out and completely isolated. But most of what you read is about bullies and victims who are boys. Bullying is to be found amongst girls, but it is not so obvious from the outside. It is not usually a matter of damaged clothes or damaged arms and legs. . . . How can I as a mother accuse the girls bullying my 14-year-old daughter for having stopped phoning, for not saying hello, for speaking badly of her behind her back, for changing places in the classroom, for always commenting on and making fun of what she says, etc. Nothing they do (or don't do) is against the rules. . . . In desperation I have tried to talk to the mothers of two of my daughter's previous friends. It wasn't particularly helpful; some parents just can't accept that their children are criticized by outsiders. . . . I wouldn't wish the grief and helplessness I feel on any parents, but I wish you and your children could actually feel just for a short time what my daughter and our family have had to live with for the last six months or so. Then perhaps you would understand. (Olweus, 2001, pp. 8–9)

10 Specific Interventions

Support for children who are having social problems is available in the form of telephone hotlines. Children who use these hotlines can, if they wish, discuss their problems with trained interviewers without identifying themselves. There are also small support groups that meet weekly for children with problems, such as how to make friends.

Some schools are telling schools. Children are encouraged to report bullying and other problems, and it is emphasized that this is not tattling. Another program that focuses on bullying and other antisocial behaviors is the Student Watch Program. Designated students patrol the school and report any instances of bullying and other antisocial behaviors to school personnel. An important feature of the Student Watch Program is that the student simply reports the behavior; the school personnel confirm it and carry on from there. There is no problem of retaliation by students who are reported. When video monitoring is available in a school, it is impossible for the student or his or her parents to discount reports of what happened.

The Quality Circle activity enables small groups of students to work out solutions to problems such as bullying on the school bus and to present their solutions to the school administration. Training in conflict resolution is available for able students who patrol the school buildings and grounds and help children who are disagreeing to resolve their problems. Two controversial approaches to getting on with one's peers involve no blame or punishment for bullying methods. One is the Method of Shared Concern; the other is the No Blame approach to bullying. The bullies are not censured for their behavior. Instead, the adult in charge conveys confidence that the bullies will know how to handle the problem so that the victim has no more trouble with being bullied.

One of the most effective ways to combat bullying and teasing is the use of stories and drama, followed by discussion. Many of the topics in this chapter can be enhanced by the use of fictional accounts of bullying and teasing and the occasional use of videos. These materials facilitate and encourage open discussion of topics such as the cruelty inherent in social exclusion and reports by the children of bullying that they have experienced or witnessed. Also helpful are newspaper and television accounts of bullying that are relevant to the intervention procedure being discussed by the teacher. Teachers, as well as students, should be alert for such items.

The whole school approach (discussed in chapter 9) in the campaign against bullying must be functioning smoothly long before most of the specific interventions are selected for incorporation into the school program. When a teacher feels that the class is ready for the next intervention, this step must be taken only when the current intervention has been successfully incorporated.

Telephone Hotlines

GIRLS AND BOYS TOWN NATIONAL HOTLINE

The Girls and Boys Town National Hotline is the only national hotline in the United States and Canada that children and parents can call at any time with any problem (telephone: 1-800-448-3000). It is also the only one that has earned the accreditation of both the American Association of Suicidology and the Council on Accreditation of Services for Families and Children. Since its inception in 1989, the hotline has received millions of calls, currently at an annual rate of about 500,000. The myriad problems include being bullied or depressed and thinking seriously about suicide, taking drugs, alcoholism, fighting with parents, parents frustrated by an out-of-control child, and parents in a medical crisis situation. About two thirds of the callers are female, and just over half of the callers are 19 years of age or younger.

The hotline is open 24 hours a day, every day. Its services are free of charge to every parent and child in the United States and Canada. Callers talk to highly trained professional counselors, and language is no barrier: Spanish-speaking counselors and access to translation services for more than 100 other languages are available at all times. A TTY line (1-800-448-1833) allows counselors to communicate with the hearing impaired.

For additional help, the hotline staff can refer callers to people and services in their own communities and do this in a matter of seconds. When appropriate, counselors actively follow up to see that callers have made contact with the local agency. Sometimes they remain on the line with the caller until help has arrived:

> Brandon, age 14, said he had run away from home to visit the grave of a high school friend who had died in a car accident. He

> said he keeps a knife under his pillow and had been hospitalized for depression recently. Brandon agreed not to hurt himself and to let the Hotline counselor call his psychiatrist. Brandon stayed on the phone with the counselor until the police arrived to take him to his psychiatrist's office. (Boys Town Call Report, n.d.)

CHILDLINE

ChildLine is the toll-free national helpline that was set up in England for children who need any kind of help. The children need not provide any identification and are promised complete confidentiality. Trained professional counselors are available 24 hours a day, every day, to listen to the children's problems and help them in any way possible.

In offering help, the counselors have three goals: (a) to give the children the relief and comfort of telling a nonjudgmental adult what has been happening to them and how they feel about the problem; (b) to help them plan how to handle the problem and, if they have tried to tackle it on their own, to praise them for their efforts and courage; and (c) to begin the process of undoing the harm done to their confidence and development (MacLeod & Morris, 1996). If the children want the counselor to talk to their parents or school personnel, the counselor will do so but offers no guarantees that either parents or school will take any action. This rider sounds a cautionary note that is particularly realistic in view of the children's accounts of their bullying and teasing problems. Although some schools supported the children and the bullying or teasing was stopped, other schools were not at all helpful. Consider the following examples, all from MacLeod and Morris (1996):

> Often the school puts the onus on the child. Sophie, age 11, called about being bullied by Julie, another girl in her class. It had started after some of the boys in their class had called Julie a slag. Sophie said, "She doesn't do it at school; she waits 'til we're on the school bus, then she hits me." Sophie had recently received a black eye from one of these attacks. When she told her teacher, the teacher told her to try to sort it out herself. (pp. 44–45)
>
> Sometimes the school takes action and the bullying stops briefly. When it resumes, the school does nothing more. Kerry, age 10, called ChildLine because a gang of girls was bullying her at school:
>
> "They pick on me, pull my hair, and push me around. They tell the teacher I've been doing naughty things. My Mum told the

> teacher and the girls were told off; but they've started again." No further action was taken by the school. (p. 43)

In some particularly dispiriting cases, the teachers join in with the bullies. James, age 15, reported such a case:

> I was made a fool of in the class today, called a *spastic* and a *mongol* and the teacher laughed. I felt so humiliated. I am very angry with the teachers for letting these boys get away with it. (p. 41)

Toll-free national helplines are also available in Scotland, Ireland, Norway, Belgium, the Netherlands, Canada, and Australia (Smith, Morita, et al., 1999).

CONFIDENTIAL HELPLINE: PRISON

Another group that clearly could benefit from a hotline are 16- to 20-year-old males in prisons and young offenders' institutions. At Cardiff Prison in Wales, prison officials were well aware that the treatment meted out to some of the inmates by other prisoners had to be stopped. As a first step, they conducted a survey that showed that bullying was rampant. One third of the prisoners reported being bullied in the previous month; two thirds said that they did nothing when they saw bullying going on. Some inmates were so desperate for protection that the prison doctor routinely had to stitch up three or four prisoners a week who had mutilated themselves in an attempt to get out of their cells and into the prison hospital. Prison officials were genuinely concerned about the problem because it meant that these inmates were being kept away from mainstream prison life and were unable to benefit as they should from the facilities that were available to them.

Changes and additions were made in the induction program. It was impressed on each young offender that reporting bullying was not "grassing" (prison slang for telling tales) but, instead, was about self-preservation and the safety of others. In addition, each prisoner was allocated a prison officer whom he could approach in confidence with problems. As one would expect, some prisoners were reluctant to follow this procedure. For this group, there was a confidential helpline and a mail box that could be used to give staff details of bullying and the names of the perpetrators. Although the prison staff were skeptical at first, they were surprised at the number of letters they received and, following action taken about the information, the resultant improvement in prison climate (Prestage, 1994).

Support Groups

Children with specific problems whose needs are not being met by existing organizations would benefit from participating in support groups (Katz, 1993). These groups provide a safe, supportive environment for children with behavioral or other problems to talk about them. Support groups satisfy a wide range of needs, such as the need for gaining peer acceptance, dealing with divorce, a recent death in the family, or physical disablement. Before joining a support group, many children feel that they are alone in their misery. Interacting with other children with similar problems markedly lessens their feelings of isolation. One 9-year-old with terminal leukemia lovingly described her support group as "my very own little family." The group consists of a leader, preferably with counseling training, who also has expertise in small-group work. The maximum number of participants is 12 for adolescents, 10 at the middle school level, and 6 in the primary grades. In most cases, each group should be a same-gender one. Before the first session and again at the end of the course, obtain a measure of self-esteem for each participant, using the self-esteem measure that is used in the child's school. In this way the results can be compared with previous evaluations.

At the beginning of the first session, and in all other sessions, welcome the group and call the role. In this session have each child stand and say his or her name, grade, and teacher's name. The length of a session should be determined by the children's behavior. It is essential to stop at the first sign of restlessness or disinterest. After the first two sessions, in which the group leader chooses the topic to be discussed, ask the children what they would like to talk about. Write the suggestions on the chalkboard and have the children vote for the topic that they would like to have discussed. Teaching procedures for some topics such as assertiveness training are suggested here but the topic should not be regarded as mandatory. If the group leader sees aspects of the children's social behavior that warrant discussion, they should be added to the list of topics. When possible, read a short story about the topic, and sometimes relevant videos might be available.

The material in the following sections applies to both boys' and girls' groups—there should be no mixed groups—but it is described as though for a boys' group.

GENERAL PROCEDURES FOR THE GROUP MEETINGS

Discuss the purpose of the group and why the group format is preferable to a one-on-one format. Emphasize that each child may tell his family about the procedures used in the group but may not give out *any* information about any of the other children. Explain confidentiality using as examples information that doctors have about their patients and banks have about their account holders. Classmates or other peers should not be told about the purpose of the group or who its members are: The children in the group will have a whole new problem with their peers if they are labeled as having "to go to bully class." Discuss ways to turn aside questions from peers, and have various members of the group practice what to say. Point out that this ability to turn aside unwanted questions on *any* topic is a useful skill, that just because someone asks a question does not mean that a child has to give the information. There are other responses he can make. For a nosy neighbor, for example, who is asking the child something about his family, the child could say, "I'll tell Mom you are interested and maybe she could talk to you."

The main teaching method used is maximizing the opportunities for modeling and role-play practice in the group setting. Use role play with the teacher acting as the one who cannot turn aside a question and who does it the wrong way. Note that the teacher must first be asked the question and then show the response. Ask one child in the group to ask the question. Have the group critique the teacher's performance. The group must not be influenced by the fact that it is the teacher who is handling the question badly; for example, they must criticize firmly and show no embarrassment about a harsh criticism. Follow this role-play procedure every time a new behavior is introduced.

When asked to participate with the teacher in demonstrating an interaction, the child may fumble the task and appear embarrassed. In a matter-of-fact way, help the child through it. In a short time, the children will be willing to participate and will become more self-assured. Some children may lack social skills. Work these in indirectly through the examples given and the interactions set up. Use real-life experiences whenever possible. Encourage friendships in the group. Always give one or two simple procedures to be practiced at home for homework. Whenever a legitimate opportunity occurs, boost the children's self-esteem.

ASSERTIVENESS TRAINING FOR CHILDREN WHO ARE VICTIMIZED

The topic of assertiveness training will be introduced with discussion along with demonstrations of standing up for one's rights. Although the primary problem for this support group is difficulty dealing with bullies, assertiveness is taught first because an assertive manner will often deter a bully from bothering a child. Assertive behavior is a set of verbal and nonverbal behaviors that provides a child with an air of confidence in social interactions. Responding assertively means that a child will stand up for his rights; respond to adults with a brief explanation of what actually happened when they criticize him for some apparent misbehavior that was not his fault; respond to another child by stating clearly, but not aggressively, what his feelings are about the incident; maintain eye contact; and exhibit relaxed but firm body language. Responding assertively does *not* mean being aggressive, bossy, or verbally loud. Being assertive gives the victim a feeling of security and a sense of control, power, and optimism, particularly when entering new situations. The resultant demeanor lessens the impact of contact with new children and has a deterrent effect on bullies.

Example of a Session on Standing Up for One's Rights

Ask the children to think of a time when someone else took something of theirs and refused to give it back. Ask for a show of hands to indicate that the children have thought of examples and pick one child to describe his example. Help the child who is describing an example by making appropriate comments and questions if the child is having difficulty.

Explain what is meant by standing up for your rights. Use role play with the teacher as the victim and the child as the bully: The child demands that the teacher give him some object and the teacher gives it to him. Then show the teacher successfully insisting on his rights. Tell the group that it will not always work the first time because the bully is used to getting his own way, "pushing other kids around and having it work." Now repeat the procedure using another child's account. Then give demonstrations of the assertive behavior to use when you are standing up for your rights: Start by stating clearly what the problem is: "This is my chair. Please get off it now." Maintain eye contact, use relaxed but firm body language, and speak clearly. Ask for another child's example and use role play to demonstrate, first, assertive behavior and then weak, nonassertive behavior. After each demonstration, encourage the other children to say what was good and not good about how the situation was handled. Frequently take the "not good" role and encourage blunt criticism of how you mishandled it. Continue to give practice using the following situations:

1. How to make requests to another child to borrow homework, bicycle, jump rope. What the other child should say in refusal or in agreement. Discuss ownership here: If it is yours, you may

or may not wish to lend it. In either case, respond courteously.

2. How to give compliments, for example, "I like your dress," "Your painting is really good," or "You're a really good swimmer," and how to acknowledge them with thanks.
3. How to describe your feelings about some event to another child. In describing their feelings, encourage the children to give reasons for the feelings. For example, when a good friend moves far away unexpectedly: "I feel really sad because Jimmy has moved." Or "I'm really mad because someone has picked up my lunch."

Now ask the children for examples of nice and unpleasant things that have happened to them. Emphasize linking the child's feeling statement with the action of the person who is responsible: "I feel mad at you for saying I was no good at playing catch" and "I really liked what you said about my painting."

Emphasize being direct when you want something from someone else: "I forgot my spelling book. Could you lend me yours?" or "I feel like flying kites. Can I have a turn with yours?" If the other child refuses, do not get mad. It is his right to refuse. Give practice in refusing demands from another child. Start with common objects, such as a pencil or book, then move along to the child's lunch and money.

Nonverbal Communication

How the child looks is the first thing that others see, then they hear him talk. Body language tells others a lot about the person. Demonstrate coming into a room, first in a tentative, uncertain kind of way and then with a confident manner (making good eye contact with those in the room, standing firmly on both feet, and having hands at sides or in pockets but not wrapped protectively around chest). Assign as a homework task practicing these behaviors in a way that shows confidence. If possible, do this in front of a mirror. Where a verbal accompaniment is reasonable, have the child say it clearly.

How to Make Friends and How to Keep Them

If a child is absent, ask if anyone knows if that child was in school that day. Tell the group that you are going to talk about making friends with other children. Ask them, What is a friend? What kinds of things does a child do who is a friend? Try to elicit some of the following answers:

- A friend helps you if you have a problem.
- A friend knows how to keep a secret.

- A friend shares favorite things and takes turns playing with them.
- A friend may not agree with you about something but does not get mad and is willing and able to talk it over with you.
- A friend may fight with you but that is not the end of the friendship.

Discuss the concept of *best friend*. Some children have several friends and one best friend. Now ask each of the children to tell one good thing about a friend that they have.

Ask: Do you know what is really special about having a friend?

Answer: You don't *pick* brothers, sisters, parents, teachers, or who will be in your class or neighbors who live near you. But, you pick a friend.

Ask: Is everyone you know (all the kids on the street, all those in your class at school) a friend?

Answer: No. You know them, you know their names, but they aren't friends, at least not yet.

Next, ask the group to think of some children they know that they do *not* want for friends. Why? Ask the children to think of one child that they do not want for a friend and tell you why. Likely answers here are being mean to other children, being mean to animals, always wanting to be in charge, never sharing with others, being a poor loser, being willing to cheat to win a game, making fun of other children's clothes, and pushing other kids around.

Ask: Suppose you see your best friend having fun with another child without calling you to come over and play, too. How do you feel? Mad? Left out? Jealous? Discuss this type of situation with the group, emphasizing that because you are friends, it doesn't mean that you own your friend or that your friend shouldn't have other friends.

Ask: Now, suppose that you and your friend are having fun and another child you know wants to join you. How do you feel about this? Do you want to keep your friend for yourself (discuss the bad points of being too possessive), or do you think it would be fun to include this other child?

Ask the group what they would tell someone who asked, "What is a friend?" Give them a minute or two to think it over, then have them give their answers. Discuss their answers. Now tell them to listen carefully and think what they would do if they had just moved into a new house and did not know anyone on the street or nearby. What should they do when they see that the boy or girl who lives next door is probably about the same age that they are and they would like to get to know this child?

Let the group discuss this problem with only enough input and praise from you to keep the discussion going. Then review the ideas that the group has given. If no one has suggested it already, suggest that one way to start would be to smile, say "Hello," and tell the other child your name. Tell the children not to be pushy (explain this idea). Also, tell them not to try to buy a friend (e.g., by offering inducements). If the other child does not start talking, say "Good-bye (name), I have to go in now." Go in and do not hang around.

CHILDREN WHO ARE BULLIED

A support group would be ideal for the victims of bullying and teasing (Arora, 1991; Besag, 1989). In addition to providing emotional support for the victims, one goal of the support group is to introduce behavior changes that would provide them with protection against bullying and teasing. The group format is ideal for practice in role play, along with reversal of roles as a way of showing the victim how it feels to be a bully or teaser. It is also excellent for assertiveness training as a means of changing the cringing demeanor typical of many victims. For approaches to the teasing problem, see chapter 7 in this text and also Phillips (1989), who offers excellent advice on assertiveness training for individuals that could also be applied to groups.

Most children do not realize that one often has to work at having friends. Until children are about 8 or 9, they think that people who have a lot of friends are just lucky or that children with lots of friends have so many toys or other resources (like a swimming pool) that other children want to be their friends. Have the children tell how they made friends when they moved to a new neighborhood.

Video Monitoring: Catching Ongoing Bullying

Video cameras and other surveillance procedures are being used increasingly in the school setting, especially in secondary schools, as a security measure. Having a record of actual instances of bullying has proved to be highly effective. The school has grounds for accusing the student of bullying and can rebut denial or attempts to minimize the bullying interaction as "just a bit of fun" by confronting the bully with a replay of the recording. Further, if parents question the bullying accusation, as they often do, they can be shown the recording. The tape can also be used to force the bully to examine the antisocial behavior by requiring that the tape be watched and the consequences for the victim be considered. The taped record of bullying events can also help in increasing awareness among pupils, teachers, and parents that bullying *is* a problem in the school. In classroom discussions of the problem, showing a video of an actual bullying incident by a student whom others in the school know provides an excellent starting point. It also puts the bully in an unfavorable light and at the same time removes the secrecy element that bullying thrives on. In addition to picking up instances of bullying, some schools are installing video cameras as security measures against violence and other misdemeanors. In a Toronto suburb, where intimidation and extortion at school had reached epidemic proportions, the school board authorized the installation of closed-circuit TV cameras in isolated sections of the high schools (Fennell, 1993).

At Lyndon Comprehensive School in Solihull, England, cameras that were installed for theft prevention proved invaluable in the school's campaign against bullying (O'Malley, 1993). The cameras, which record 24 hours a day, were installed as a crime prevention measure after a series of thefts had occurred while the school was open for evening activities. Two cameras were positioned to cover the main entrance to the school, the playground and rear entrance, and the changing room corridor.

It soon became apparent to the camera maintenance staff that problems other than theft, such as bullying, could be detected and, more important, documented for later use. The head of the video maintenance staff said:

> You'd get pushing and shoving, maybe with three or four kids on to one youngster . . . or in the playground you'd spot a lump of kids gathering and you would want to know what was going on. . . . They sometimes stand there waiting outside the back door for someone they want to get. (O'Malley, 1993, p. 15)

The procedure was to have the staff member monitoring the four-way split screen in the video office zoom in at the first signs of trouble to see exactly what was going on and then to notify the teacher on duty.

There is a new video technology called Poseidon (Pierce, 2001) that can make school swimming pools safer not only by preventing accidental drowning but also by guarding against near-drowning that results from bullying. If a swimmer is in trouble or remains motionless for too long, the system uses a beeper and monitor to alert lifeguards in less than 15 seconds. The system consists of several interactive components: underwater optical cameras sealed within the pool walls and overhead cameras that look down into the pool and are connected to an on-site computer that analyzes all images instantaneously. These images are displayed on screens that are posted in the lifeguard stations next to the pool. Lifeguards are given lightweight alarm pagers to wear while on duty. When the computer identifies a struggling, slowly sinking, or immobile victim, it triggers an alarm pager at the appropriate lifeguard station. The lifeguard can see exactly where the victim is located and make the rescue.

Problem-Solving Approaches

THE QUALITY CIRCLE

The concept of the Quality Circle (QC) originated in Japanese industry in the 1950s and now is used by major companies worldwide. A QC consists of a group of 5 to 12 people who are interested in solving a problem that they believe has reduced work productivity. To achieve this goal, the QC uses the following five-step problem-solving process. The problem is (a) identified and (b) analyzed. Solutions are (c) developed and (d) presented to the management for (e) their consideration. Throughout this process, a trained QC leader works with the group to foster group cohesion and to acquaint them with the requisite skills and strategies for problem solving, brainstorming, interviewing, and other data collection procedures (Cowie & Sharp, 1992).

Although the QC procedure originated in industry, it is clearly applicable to a variety of social groups. In educational settings it has proved to be effective with staff development problems (Fox, Pratt, & Roberts, 1991) and has been adapted for successful use with school children who were concerned about bullying in their school (Mellor Smith, 1992). Significant results in relation to bullying were also obtained by Cowie and Sharp (1992). In addition, the teachers in their study were impressed with the quality of the children's work and the gains they had made. The children were very enthusiastic about the whole experience. They said it had made them more aware of the bullying problem, more likely to intervene in ongoing bullying, and more careful about their own behavior to others. Indirect benefits are also likely to result from the QC approach. The participants should become more aware of the complexity of the bullying problem and the fact that there are no easy answers to it. The QC procedure shows children how constructively they can work together when all members of the group have equal status. This latter aspect may very well be the first time that some of them have experienced this feeling of equality regardless of age, sex, or skill level.

One approach is to have the group leader suggest a specific topic for the QC to work on, for example, how to combat bullying in the school. Cowie and Sharp (1992) have pointed out that by asking a QC to consider solutions to the problem of bullying, a collective responsibility is developed that could serve to empower and mobilize a highly effective deterrent to bullying: peer pressure. The following sequence of steps shows how a group of concerned students could use a QC to tackle the problem of bullying in their school:

1. A group leader who is experienced in the QC procedure and believes it could be used effectively to combat bullying in the school forms a group of five to seven elementary grade children who are genuinely interested in the problem of bullying in their school. The group leader's task is to foster group cohesion and teach the participants some decision-making skills as well as problem-solving techniques.
2. A brainstorming session is held to decide on the aspect of the bullying problem to be studied. The order in which the group members present their ideas is determined by drawing lots. In the QC method, no member of the group is in charge and no one is ignored. Ideas are thrown out freely, considered, and discarded or accepted. By group consensus, bullying on the playground is selected: It lends itself to observation, interviews, and other data collection methods to determine how important the problem is.
3. A why–why analysis (see Figure 10.1) is used to identify some of the causes of why people bully. Some of the answers will be supplied by the data collection process: "They don't know what they're doing to people."
4. Now the group uses a how–how analysis to develop a possible solution to whatever problem was selected by the group for study. Figure 10.2 shows possible solutions to the question of how to stop bullying on the school bus.
5. School personnel discuss the problem and the proposed solutions in a private session, followed by an evaluation of it in a joint meeting with the QC group. If their solution to playground bullying is accepted, the principal publicly acknowledges the group's contribution.

Another approach is to ask the QC to think of ways in which the school could be a happier or better place. Cowie and Sharp (1992) reported a school in which a QC suggested that pupils who were consistently nice to others should be given some recognition. The QC suggested that in the main hall one wall could be designated the "building a better school" wall where children who were generally

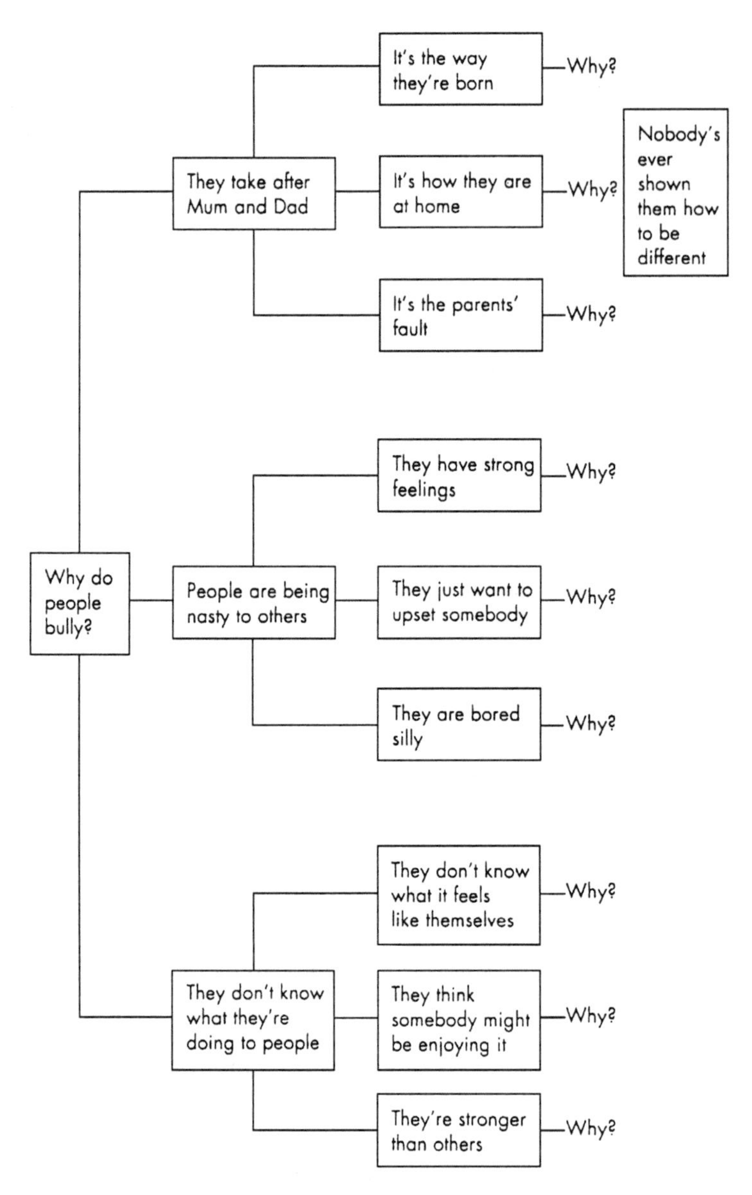

Figure 10.1. An Example of a Why–Why Diagram: A 10-Year-Old's Responses to Why Do People Bully?

Reproduced with permission of the authors and publisher from Cowie, H., & Sharp, S. (1994). Tackling bullying through the curriculum. In P. K. Smith & S. Sharp (Eds.), *School Bullying: Insights and Perspectives* (p. 92). © Routledge.

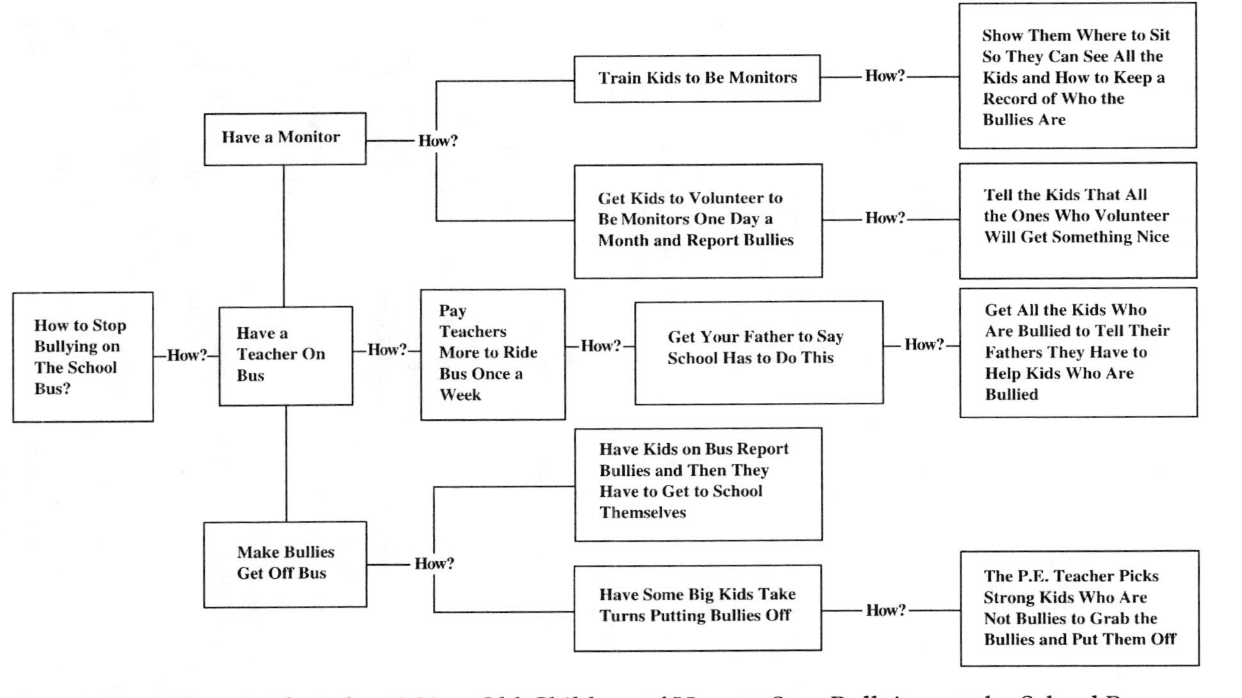

Figure 10.2. A How-How Analysis by 10-Year-Old Children of How to Stop Bullying on the School Bus

Reproduced with permission of the author and the publisher from Ross, D. M. (1996). *Childhood Bullying and Teasing: What School Personnel, Other Professionals, and Parents Can Do* (p. 142). © American Counseling Association.

very pleasant to others could have their names recorded. Both the group leader and school personnel approved the idea, and the wall became an integral part of the behavior management system in the school. Cowie and Sharp (1992, p. 37) commented that "pupils in the school were left in no doubt that the QCs were taken seriously and that their well-worked-out ideas were valued by the whole school."

CONFLICT RESOLUTION

Conflict is an inevitable and potentially valuable part of the human experience. The response to a conflict situation generally is the variable that determines whether the outcome is to be a constructive or destructive one. Because most children have a narrow view of conflict as a win–lose situation best handled by verbal or physical aggression (Deutsch, 1993), much of the conflict occurring in the competitive school environment is of a destructive nature. In most conflicts among children, other alternatives do exist: The antagonists could both win or they could both lose. The purpose of conflict resolution training programs is to help children see conflict situations as having the potential to be win–win. With this outcome as a possibility, children are more amenable to considering constructive, cooperative, and problem-solving approaches in which disagreements are seen as joint problems to be resolved in mutually beneficial ways.

Former U.S. Attorney General Janet Reno recently told educators at a North Carolina meeting that if they want to stop school violence, they should start in preschool and kindergarten teaching children how to resolve conflicts in peaceful and constructive ways (Eden, 2001). How early can this training begin? Until recently, research on this issue has been observational and lacking in methodological rigor, with a focus on naturally occurring conflicts between young children. Training has not been an interest, possibly because developmental psychologists such as Selman (1980) and Nicholls (1984) have contended that kindergarten children do not have the cognitive capacity to focus on finding a solution satisfactory to both protagonists. Social psychologists, on the other hand, have contended that with training, kindergarten children can learn to resolve their conflicts constructively, but, again, empirical evidence has been lacking. However, there is evidence that with training first graders learned as well as sixth graders to engage in integrative negotiations to maximize joint outcomes and find solutions that satisfied both parties (Johnson, Johnson, Dudley, & Acikgoz, 1994).

Of relevance here is Flavell's (1979) theory of the development of metacognition, that is, knowing about one's own thinking as well as that of others. Flavell and his associates identified three levels of metacognitive skills (Flavell, Fry, Wright, & Jarvis, 1968). At Level A, the child is aware that there is a motive underlying an opponent's stand but is not aware that the opponent may know the child's motive. At Level B, the child knows that his or her opponent is capable of attributing the same thoughts to the child. At Level C, the child can now step outside the dyadic interaction and know that both opponents can simultaneously consider their own as well as the motives of the other. Flavell (1979) has stated that it would be difficult to achieve a durable resolution of conflict without being at least at Level B.

Österman, Lagerspetz, Landau, Fraczek, and Pastorelli (1997) performed a cross-cultural study of spontaneous, nonviolent conflict resolution in three groups of children ages 8, 11, and 15 in Finland, Israel, Italy, and Poland (girls n = 1,025; boys n = 1,069). The participants' behavior in conflict situations was measured with peer estimation techniques. Although cultural variation was found, girls, more than boys, tended to make use of dyadic constructive conflict resolution and third-party interventions across nationalities and age groups. Developmental trends were also found: The highest frequency in interpersonal conflict resolution occurred at age 11, when adolescents reach the Level C metacognitive stage of mutual perspective taking (Flavell, 1979).

Österman et al. (1997) have suggested that one reason why conflict resolution does not increase continuously by age may be that the development of metacognition not only affects conflict resolution skills but also facilitates the prevention of conflicts before they become overt. Further, they suggested that a possible explanation for the finding that girls are better at conflict resolution than boys may be that they generally are smaller than boys and not as strong. It follows that when in a conflict situation girls estimate both the effect and danger of different conflict strategies and choose tactics such as constructive conflict resolution or indirect aggression that do not depend on physical strength. Björkqvist et al. (1994) referred to this strategy as the *principle of the effect–danger ratio.*

Three styles of nonaggressive conflict resolution were selected: constructive resolution, withdrawal, and intervening as a third party in a conflict between others. Peer estimation techniques were used in which every child estimated the conflict resolution behavior of each of the other children in the class, including the child doing the rating. Constructive conflict resolution was measured with three items: "solves problems by trying to talk," "finds peaceful solutions," and "manages to calm down the situation." Withdrawal had two items: "goes away" and "gives in." Third-party intervention was measured with one item, "helps others who get teased." Although the summed variables consisted of only six items, they had acceptable internal consistency.

In addition to selecting one of the above items to describe a specific child's conflict resolution behavior, the child doing the rating was also instructed to estimate how often that behavior occurred and mark the estimate on a 5-point scale ranging from 0 (*never*) to 4 (*very often*). These estimates were for the same sex only because within-sex conflicts are more common than between-sex conflicts in the school environment (Lagerspetz & Björkqvist, 1994).

The results were consistent with previous research evidence that girls are better at conflict resolution than boys (see, e.g., Ohbuchi & Yamamoto, 1990). In estimates of frequency, girls used constructive conflict resolution techniques and third-party intervention more often than boys. Both sexes used conflict resolution most at the age of 11, possibly because peer-group conflicts are most frequent in this period and aggressive behavior has a peak at that age (Björkqvist, Lagerspetz, & Kaukiainen, 1992). The peer estimates also showed ethnic differences: Finnish and Israeli children used more constructive resolution behaviors than either the Italian or Polish children. The Polish group used less of all types of conflict resolution than the other ethnic groups.

In a recent study that was a model of methodological rigor, Stevahn and his associates (Stevahn, Johnson, Johnson, Oberle, & Wahl, 2000) evaluated the efficacy of conflict resolution training on kindergarten children in a midwestern elementary school in the United States. The participants were 80 kindergarten children who were randomly assigned to either an experimental or control group in morning or afternoon time blocks. Children in the experimental condition were given 9 hours of conflict resolution training integrated into a curriculum unit on friendship taught daily for 4 consecutive weeks. Those in the control condition were taught the identical friendship unit for the same period of time but without the conflict resolution training. The kindergarten teachers rotated equally across conditions.

Children in the conflict resolution group first learned what a conflict was and was not. Next, they learned the following six-step negotiating procedure for resolving conflicts constructively (Johnson & Johnson, 1995):

1. Recognizing that a conflict exists and expressing a desire to resolve it constructively ("Stop. We have a conflict. Let's work it out.").
2. Stating what you want and giving your underlying reasons ("I want . . . because . . . ").

3. Expressing how you feel ("I feel mad or sad").
4. Communicating your understanding of what the other person wants and why ("You want . . . because . . . ").
5. Inventing three or more optional solutions that maximize mutual gain ("Some ideas are . . . ").
6. Reaching an agreement by selecting and shaking hands on one of the options ("We agree on . . . ").

In being taught these steps, the children engaged in a wide range of pictorial, role-play, sequencing, and other activities designed to help them learn and practice the integrative negotiation procedure.

The results showed significant differences between the experimental and control group children in knowledge and retention of the conflict resolution procedure, ability to apply the procedure in conflict situations, and conceptual understanding of friendship. These results provided unequivocal evidence that the frequent inability of children of kindergarten age to resolve conflicts constructively is not due to their developmental limitations but rather to a lack of appropriate training.

Although early conflict resolution training is often recommended (Eden, 2001; Prothrow-Stith, 1991), special training programs rarely cross the void between research activities and their inclusion in the existing school curriculum. If these programs are seen as an "add on" separate from the required curriculum and as a drain on competing time priorities, they are unlikely to garner sufficient support. However, the probability of making conflict resolution training an essential part of the regular school program increases if the program has a positive effect on student achievement. In Stevahn et al.'s (2000) study, the program was integrated into an ongoing unit on friendship, with positive behavioral results. Previous studies in high school settings (see, e.g., Stevahn, Johnson, Johnson, Green, & Laginski, 1997) found that the curriculum-integrated approach to teaching conflict resolution increased achievement in English literature.

The real problem is that the criterion for success of a particular training program focuses on the immediate posttest results when, in fact, the long-term changes in behavior are a far superior indicator that the program has validity. Over the long haul, a school with an effective conflict resolution program across all grade levels should see a drop in conflict behaviors. Unfortunately, the difficulty of applying stringent experimental controls to statistics from a shifting population over a long period of time would make it highly unlikely that "research" of this kind would ever receive federal funding. Such rigid adherence to the strict protocol for what constitutes acceptable research has cut off avenues of potentially successful investigation.

CONFLICT MANAGEMENT

Conflict management can best be described as a refereed communication process, with the child who is trained in management being the referee. The referees are not concerned with deciding which of the disputants is right or wrong, nor do they reprimand, pass judgments, make demands, or force their services on others. They are peacemakers rather than policemen, with none of the authority usually accorded to teachers and other school personnel. Their goal is to provide an opportunity for direct communication between the disputants, making them responsible for finding their own solutions to their disagreements through negotiation and mediation.

HOW ARE STUDENTS SELECTED FOR CONFLICT MANAGER POSITIONS?

Some conflict management teachers decide which students to select as conflict managers on the basis of their own assessment, along with peer nominations, the rationale being that 20 opinions are better than one. In these instances, however, the teacher makes the final decision. Iwasaki (1992) reported that teachers working with upper elementary school children chose students of average ability on the grounds that these children seldom qualify for any rewards and so need some kind of special activity to maintain interest in school. When conflict managers are elected by their fellow students, Prothrow-Stith (1991) found that according to some teachers, it is the popular children and the bullies who are chosen. The choice of bullies is questionable. Most children in a school know who the bullies are and might be intimidated if a bully is mediating a dispute. Any sense of intimidation negates the whole idea of the conflict resolution as a constructive, cooperative, mutually beneficial problem-solving experience.

Candidates for the conflict management role are given anywhere from 15 to 30 hours of training. Course content includes learning how to use conflict resolution skills to help settle disputes between other children, practice in active listening to disputants' complaints, constructive communication, learning the steps of the mediation process, managing the situation and controlling the disputants in a nonaggressive way, and helping them to work out peaceful solutions. Although some of the training consists of lecture-type sessions, usually a substantial part of the course provides the students with well-planned opportunities to practice the conflict resolution skills in a supportive atmosphere (Haigh, 1994). Role-play demonstrations of conflict situations by "trained actors" are produced so that the students have an opportunity to demonstrate their level of skill in conflict management. During the sessions, the students are observed and given critiques in the classroom. When they are judged to be competent, they are sent out on trial and required to report back in detail to the teacher. Follow-up training is then given as needed.

THE CONFLICT RESOLUTION PROCEDURE

Conflict resolution has a set of rules that disputants must agree to abide by while the conflict is being resolved. These include no interrupting while a disputant is telling the conflict manager what happened, promising to tell the whole truth, no name calling or insults, working to solve the problem, and avoiding any physical aggression.

1. The problem or disagreement is identified, and both sides describe what has happened and what each wants. The conflict manager restates it, and both sides agree that the restatement is accurate.
2. Both sides explain how they feel about the issue and suggest solutions that they would like. There is an element of brainstorming here with no limit on the number of solutions offered. Sometimes the solution is very practical, particularly in bullying cases ("Just stay away from me").
3. One conflict manager writes down all the suggested solutions no matter how unrealistic, and then the pair of managers help both sides to reconsider each idea and choose the one that is closest to best for both, as a mutually beneficial choice is not always possible. Note that the managers do not tell either side what to do.
4. The conflict managers help the sides to work out a balanced settlement that each agrees on and accepts as fair. If appropriate, both sides agree when, where, and how the solution will be carried out. Sometimes this agreement is written up in the form of a contract and signed by both. The whole incident is entered in the school record book and is treated as confidential.
5. The conflict managers then are responsible for following up the incident to see that both sides abide by the decision.

EVALUATION OF CONFLICT RESOLUTION PROGRAMS

Teachers and school personnel report benefits that they attribute to ongoing conflict resolution programs. Conflict and aggression decrease. Teachers see more caring behavior among students (Iwasaki, 1992), and they are impressed by the speed with which conflict managers work through the mediation process. Other professionals and investigators say that children who learn to assert themselves without attacking others not only are less likely to become bullies but are also less likely to become victims of bullies (Prothrow-Stith, 1991). The potential for long-term benefits is considerable: "To encounter it (conflict) naturally, to work out a solution amicably, and to learn to see the situation from the perspective of another, could be one of the most valuable experiences we can offer our young people" (Besag, 1989, p. 106).

No Blame or Punishment

The two methods described in this section are unique in that they advocate a participative, nonpunitive approach to the problem of bullying. Instead of blaming or punishing bullies, the adult in charge conveys complete confidence that the bullies themselves will be able to resolve the problem so that the victim is no longer a target. This approach was developed in 1989 by Anatol Pikas, a Swedish psychologist. A similar, but not identical, procedure was developed in 1992 by two English psychologists, Barbara Maines and George Robinson. Although these two approaches differ in some respects, they share a common target (a group of bullies who are harassing a single victim) and a common goal (finding a solution to the problem of bullying without resorting to punitive methods). Each of these innovative procedures is briefly described along with their differences, reports of their efficacy, and criticisms that have been leveled at them.

METHOD OF SHARED CONCERN

Pikas (1989) developed this counseling procedure for bullying by children age 9 or older. For younger children, Pikas advocated a direct approach: Telling the child firmly to stop bullying at once and seeing that he or she does so.

With the Method of Shared Concern, the goal is to find a solution to ongoing bullying that will result in peaceful coexistence between the bullies and their victim. In pursuit of this goal, no attempt is made to determine blame or to punish any of the participants. An underlying assumption is that in a bullying incident the group of bullies are likely to think and act as one. To change this pattern of cognitive response, it is important to get the group thinking as individuals and being willing to take some responsibility for their own actions. A feeling of shared concern can then be established about the plight of the victim and what can be done about the bullying problem.

The intervention procedure consists of three stages, with approximately 1 week between each one.

Stage 1: "Individual chats" with each pupil involved, for about 5 to 10 minutes per child. The "ringleader" of the bullies is seen first, then the rest of the bullies in the group, and lastly, the child who is being bullied. The talks with the perpetrators are aimed at arousing any feelings of shame and unease that individual members have in regard to the plight of the victim. That some of the perpetrators do have such feelings is evident in the following account (D. M. Ross, personal communication, April 2001) by a 14-year-old girl who is a member of the Top Hats, the most powerful and highest status clique in a junior high school in Washington State:

> They say really mean things to Berta, like "What's Berta the best at in the whole damn school? She's the fattest, dumbest, and smelliest," and then they hold their noses. I tell them not to be so mean, but they just laugh and Nonie says, "We're just having *fun!*" I wish I could stop them. Berta's absent a lot and I know it must be that she can't face a whole day at school. Nobody could. I wish I could help her.

Stage 2: Follow-up interviews of about 3 to 5 minutes with each child.

Stage 3: A group meeting of all the children involved lasting about half an hour.

Pikas (1989) claimed great success for his method on the basis of a small number of case studies. He stated that his "Shared Concern Method has only failed once in hundreds of documented cases throughout Scandinavia. . . . It is now used in 90 percent of Swedish schools" (Dore, 1993, p. 9). Smith and Sharp (1994) used Pikas's method in some schools in their Sheffield Bullying Project and described their experience with it as positive: "It appears that it can be a powerful short-term tool for combating bullying but long-term change could require additional intervention in cases of very persistent bullying" (p. 200). Dore (1993) reported complete success with the method in six outbreaks of bullying. In an unpublished BA dissertation from the University of Sheffield, Lucas (1993) reported that the combination of the Pikas method with removal to another class of one or two of the hard-core bullies seemed to lead to a long-term positive change. She commented (Smith & Sharp, 1994, p. 202):

> Pikas was right in his attempt to break the "group psychology." What the method achieves is an alleviation of the situation for a

> while and a way to identify those pupils who are most disruptive so they can be dealt with by other measures. Once the group has been broken and the leaders removed or their behavior changed, it will not re-form.

Olweus (1988) challenged Pikas's claim that children who bully other children feel guilty on the grounds that there is clinical evidence that bullies do not feel guilty about their behavior or empathy for their victims' feelings (Besag, 1989). He believed that the failure to involve the bully's parents is a serious flaw because they could work with the bully's teachers in strengthening the reportedly changed attitudes of the bully. His most severe criticism is that the procedure is not ethical: It is built on manipulation and latent threats that are presented as bully–teacher cooperation. Olweus contended that it would be more ethical for the teacher to state unequivocally that unless the bullying stops there will be severe consequences.

NO BLAME APPROACH

In 1988, Maines and Robinson developed a counseling-type procedure that rests on the assumption that bullying is an interaction that demonstrates dominance and status at the expense of others (see Maines & Robinson, 1992). A change to more positive values on the part of the bullies is essential if the bullies are to abandon their antisocial behavior and coexist peacefully with the victim(s). The critical elements in effecting this change in the bullies are no blame or punishment of the perpetrators and no policing of the environment. No lasting change in the bullies' behavior will occur if either of the foregoing is operative. The No Blame procedure can be summarized as follows:

1. Sit down with the victim (Peter) and listen carefully to his story. Take notes and use prompts as necessary. Be sure to get the facts about the bullying incident so that when you talk to the bullies you can consider the discrepancies in the two accounts.
2. Pay particular attention to Peter's account of the effects of the bullying on him. Note these down in detail, and encourage him to provide details, either in writing or by drawing pictures.
3. Set up a meeting of those involved in the bullying. The optimum number is six or eight students. If there are only one or two perpetrators, try to include some bystanders who saw the bullying and did not intervene.

4. Explain to the group that Peter has a problem. Tell his story clearly and in enough detail so that the group understands why Peter is upset.
5. Do not blame anyone. Merely state firmly that the members of the group are responsible and can do something about the problem. If some of the group were witnesses, suggest that they must have some ideas about what can be done even though they were not directly involved.
6. Arrange to meet with each member of the group in about a week to find out how things are going. Convey a certainty that action will be taken by the group to help Peter.
7. Throughout this procedure, try to convey that those involved are basically good people, if somewhat misguided in this instance, and that they will be kind to Peter.

Support for the efficacy of the No Blame Approach comes from a report (Maines & Robinson, 1992) of 100% success with this method with primary school children and 97% success with secondary school students. In a particularly interesting chapter on victimization among teenage girls, Owens et al. (2001) endorsed Maines and Robinson's No Blame Approach for teenage girls because of the importance of peer-group relationships for this group in respect to indirect aggression. They contended that the group-oriented and interpersonal nature of the No Blame Approach could be highly effective in resolving teenage girls' conflicts. The approach harmonizes with the verbal skills that girls generally exhibit in the counseling setting; it is consistent with the finding that girls in our society are encouraged to express their feelings whereas boys are not encouraged to do so; and it has the potential to accommodate the nature of girls' friendships and group interactions.

Both the Method of Shared Concern and the No Blame Approach assume that the bullies must acquire more positive values if they are to abandon their antisocial activities and coexist peacefully with their peers. Both also assume that the critical elements in effecting this change are no blame or punishment of the perpetrators and no policing of the environment. If either of these elements is missing, no lasting positive change will occur in the bully's behavior.

The two procedures differ to some extent: Pikas (1989) talks to the bullies first as a means of protecting the victim from possible reprisals for telling the adult about the bullies; Maines and Robinson (1992) speak for the victim and believe that this will have a powerful effect on the subsequent behavior of the bullies. Pikas then talks to each of the bullies, individually, in contrast to Maines and Robinson, who contend that the group process is likely to enhance the impact of the victim's story. Pikas's only comment about the victim's plight is that he heard that the bully had been mean to the victim. He then asks the bully what he or she knows about it. Maines and Robinson recount the victim's story to the bully in considerable detail.

What criticisms have been made of these two methods? Most children, including bullies and victims, find it difficult at the best of times to talk candidly to their teachers about school events. When the topic is bullying, it would be essential to find some way to elicit a candid account and convince the child that confidentiality would be assured. Financial costs include remuneration for initial training of teachers and for subsequent sessions, plus replacement or payment for damaged possessions and extortion of lunch money and bus fares by the bullies. Failure to keep the parents informed about the intervention procedures could have repercussions for the principals, which, in turn, could undermine continuation of the procedures. Lastly, both procedures are inconsistent with the established empirical and clinical knowledge about bullying (Olweus, 1988), which makes the apparent absence of follow-up data to determine the efficacy of the intervention over the long haul a glaring omission.

Bully Courts

In schools with bully courts, children who have been accused of bullying are required to appear before a panel of peers who listen to statements by the victim, accused bully, and witnesses, questioning them as necessary. If the bully is found guilty, the panel decides on the punishment, which, when appropriate, may involve reparation and restitution. An adult, usually a teacher, is present to monitor the hearing, including the punishment, but otherwise interferes as little as possible.

Bully courts vary in organization from the more formal to less formal and in the extent to which their procedures and personnel resemble standard courts of law. Regardless of structural variations, however, the purpose is always the same: to confront the bully or bullies with the victim's account of the alleged misbehavior, have peers judge the seriousness of the allegations, and then decide on appropriate punishment. Two bully courts representing a range in formality are briefly described.

A FORMAL BULLY COURT

The best documented study of a formal bully court (Mahdavi & Smith, 2002) was conducted in a large secondary English school (Year

7 to Year 12). During the school term, from September to December 1999, three bully courts were operating successfully in the school, and 25 cases were tried. The purpose of the study was to describe the operation of the bully court and to determine how it was viewed at that time by pupils and school personnel.

This school has a number of antibullying strategies in place. An "Anti-Bullying Code" is displayed around the school. The school operates a *positive discipline system* in which pupils are rewarded for positive behavior and rewards are cumulative, leading to privileges, whereas bad behavior is penalized. There is a bully register that contains records of every bullying incident along with how such incidents were dealt with by the bully court.

Bullies are summoned to the court for their appropriate year group. The court determines whether the alleged incident did in fact occur, whether the incident should be classed as bullying, and what punishment (if any) should be given. Note that false accusations of bullying and behavior that wastes the court's time may also be punished by the court. After appearing in the bully courts some bullies are called to the *bully court council*, which consists of pupil representatives from Year 7 to Year 12, to answer for their behavior. The council impresses upon them that the school will not accept their behavior and explains why. This meeting is described by Mahdavi and Smith (2002) as "formal, but not confrontational."

The court generally meets once a week and may deal with two or three cases in one sitting. The bully court representatives who are elected at the beginning of the academic year act as a jury and discuss the information that they are given about the bullying incident, ask questions of all those involved, and decide whether the accused is guilty and what punishment should be given. A member of the teaching staff is present but contributes only as needed. The court takes place in a normal classroom but the desks are arranged so that they resemble a court and the procedures are formalized.

At the beginning of the session the staff member in charge discusses any points that the bully court representatives should know. The victim of the bullying is then brought in and the victim's letter describing the bullying incident is read. Usually, the victim then leaves and the representatives decide whether to call witnesses. If so, the witnesses are brought in one at a time and questioned. The accused leaves, a verdict is reached, and all those involved are informed of the decision.

Punishments range from a stern warning to the accused in the bully court to lunch-time and after-school detention. A letter may be sent to the bully's parents requesting that they come to the school.

Sanctions range from picking up litter around the school to a ban on using the school bus. The court can also recommend that the Head Teacher suspend the bully for a period of time.

While punishment is important, there are other aspects of the court procedure that are likely to be painful for the bully. A notice is read out in the school assembly about the date of the next bully court along with the names of pupils who are summoned. What happens during the court hearing is not a pleasant experience for the accused. Also, the bully court register provides records of previous appearances in court and previous offenders are punished more severely than first-time offenders.

The research team was given considerable information about the cases heard during the 3-month period of the study and was allowed to observe the court in action. All 70 of the pupils who appeared in the court during the 3 months as victims (n = 35), the accused (n = 28), witnesses (n = 4), or counselors (n = 3) were interviewed. Each pupil was given the option of withdrawing but none did.

Out of 70 responses, the majority (58 pupils) thought that both the verdict and punishment decided on by the court were fair. The majority of victims of bullying (30/35) found the actions of the court helpful and said that they would encourage a friend to use the bully court. Most of those who had been accused of bullying (20/28) said that their experience in court would deter them from bullying again. Generally, the bully court was seen in a very positive way.

Both staff and pupils strongly supported the bully court, but the low rate of return of questionnaires by pupils in Years 7 and 12, bully court representatives, and staff was disappointing. Mahdavi and Smith (2002) attributed the level of approval to a number of factors. The court had existed in the school for more than 7 years. The bully register provided an accurate report of the number of previous offenses. The court representatives enjoyed the responsibility they were given and so did many of the Year 12 mentors. Mahdavi and Smith (2002) cautioned that the perceived value of the court may vary with age. They hypothesized that the results suggest that the bully court system can be a useful procedure in combating bullying under the following circumstances:

- a well-established and well-publicized system
- adequate staff supervision of the court process and training for those pupils involved
- a well-integrated record system of bullying incidents
- a combination of the court system with a peer mentoring/counselling system that helps/encourages Year 7 pupils to use the bully court. (Mahdavi & Smith, 2002, p. 339)

THE LEAST FORMAL COURT: THE CLASSROOM COURT

These courts meet several times a week in some elementary schools. Students are invited to voice their concerns about any school-related problems rather than focusing exclusively on bullying-related ones. They and the others in the class suggest solutions to the problem, then vote on a decision. The problems are relatively minor ones, with major problems being handled by other school personnel.

The rationale underlying classroom courts is called Positive Discipline (Nelsen, 1985). Advocates of the Positive Discipline approach say that when it is used correctly it helps children get along better with each other and learn to express, analyze, and solve problems on their own. Yoshikawa-Cogley (1995) reported the following sequences that she observed in a fourth-grade class:

> On this day Adrien claims Andy "pumped up" his shoe (today's high-tech sneakers have air pumps to create a snugger fit). Everyone comments, from Andy who says he didn't do it to students who observe inconsistencies in Adrien's or Andy's statements. The discussion continues for 15 minutes, and it appears Andy is responsible.
>
> Hunt (teacher) asks the class: "What is the appropriate consequence?"
>
> Someone suggests Andy should miss two recesses. Another suggests he shouldn't play four-square for the rest of the week. A third says he should miss computer time. As classmates talk, tears begin flowing from Andy's eyes. The teacher decides Andy should miss two recesses and write a letter of apology. Andy wipes the tears from his eyes and kicks his legs in apparent frustration.

Sometimes the problems cut across grade levels or involve same-age children from other classes. When this is the case, the class teacher sends a note requesting the child's presence. In this situation, children from other classrooms are all alone and, in a sense, face a hostile audience. They should be allowed to have someone come with them, possibly a witness or at least a friend. In addition, if they are called with no prior warning, they have no time to marshal the facts and prepare their own defense.

COMMENT

Teachers are ambivalent about the idea of bully courts (Pitfield, 1992; Smith & Sharp, 1994). Apart from a justified concern about the time needed to put bully courts to a fair trial, their other fears are to some extent groundless. They worry, for example, that the punishments for bullying may be too severe (but one or more teachers are always present); that the children on the jury are given too much power; that bullies would not conform to the punishment decided on by the court (in a well-run school, such disobedience would not be an option); and that parents might be alarmed at the whole idea (a general meeting with parents spelling out the need to curb ongoing bullying in the school and the approach that the court will use should eliminate most if not all parental resistance).

Smith and Sharp (1994) believe that "the jury is still out" on the idea of bully courts because there are no well-documented studies of schools in which properly set up bully courts have been used for a reasonable length of time. However, they feel that there could be several positive effects if the necessary time is taken to set up the court properly. These include shared responsibility by the students on the jury, peer persuasion, and the deterrent power of the court and its sanctions. They also point to several possible dangers, such as a possible lack of impartiality in forming the jury and giving verdicts, possible trauma for shy children who must testify, fostering of too punitive an attitude to bullies, and the shifting of bullying to outside the school's jurisdiction. Overall, however, they believe that the idea of a pupil court, or council, to deal with bullying is an interesting one.

Teen Courts

"Teen court" is a generic term for youth courts, peer courts, peer jury courts, and student courts. There have been teen courts in New York State since 1968, and in the past decade the number has increased markedly from 78 in 42 states to over 450 (Godwin, 1998). Such rapid growth suggests that the teen court format is fulfilling an important need. These courts require funding, but because of high levels of volunteers and community support and involvement, they can be relatively inexpensive to operate. A juvenile offender's participation in a teen court is strictly voluntary, and parental consent and participation are mandatory. It may be chosen as an alternative to the criminal justice system's regular court or a disciplinary office. The courts usually have teenagers serving as jurors and may also have them acting as prosecuting attorney, defense attorney, judge, bailiff, or other officers of the court. Referrals may come from a variety of sources in the community, including law enforcement, schools, and juvenile probation offices. The juvenile offender and his or her guardian meet with the teen court staff to review the program requirements and sign the consent forms and other paperwork necessary for participation in the program. Once the offender has been accepted into the program, the case is docketed and a trial date is set.

In most teen courts, young offenders are referred for sentencing rather than for a decision of guilt or innocence (Nessel, 2000). In some courts a set of sentencing options is established with specific guidelines for jurors to follow when determining a constructive sentence. Others give jurors considerable flexibility in determining sentences, which commonly include community service (1–200 hours), jury duty (at least once), restitution, and apologies. Additional sentencing options may include counseling, educational workshops, essay writing, school attendance, and peer discussion groups. Teen courts usually require juveniles to admit to guilt before participating and to agree to accept the charges against them. However, a few courts will determine the guilt or innocence of a defendant who pleads "not guilty" (Godwin, 1998). Anecdotal reports indicate that compliance with the teen court sentence is fairly high. Once the defendant has completed the sentencing program, most teen courts report that they dismiss or expunge the charges. If the offender does not comply, the referring agency is notified so that appropriate consequences can occur. The types of offenses that teen court programs report accepting most often include theft (91.2%), alcohol/drug use (85.3%), vandalism (84.6%), and disorderly conduct (83.1%; Godwin, 1998).

In 1994 a survey of teen courts by the American Probation and Parole Association (Godwin, 1996) identified four trial models. The most common teen court model is the Adult Judge Model in which an adult judge, often a lawyer, rules on courtroom procedure and clarifies legal terminology. Youth volunteers serve as defense and prosecuting attorneys as well as jurors. The Youth Judge Model is similar to the Adult Judge Model except that a juvenile serves as judge, usually after a length of service as a youth court attorney. The Tribunal Model has no peer jury. Instead, the prosecuting and defense attorneys present their cases to a juvenile judge or judges who determine the sentence (Nessel, 2000). The Peer Jury Model uses a panel of teen jurors who question the offender directly. There is no defense or prosecuting attorney, and the judge is usually an adult volunteer.

EDUCATIONAL ROLE OF TEEN COURTS

These courts focus on educating participants not only about specific court procedures, sentencing options, and trial techniques but also about the general structure of our juvenile and justice systems, the meaning of justice, the role of rehabilitation, and the relationship between rights and responsibilities. Teenagers who are equipped with such knowledge are better able to understand the American justice system and to feel that they are participants in it rather than potential victims of it (Nessel, 2000).

TRAINING

The educational role of teen courts is considerably enriched by the orientation procedures and training offered to young volunteers. Some teen courts have an extensive training program for student volunteers who wish to participate as officers of the court or as foremen of the jury. A good example of such a program is the one offered by the Anchorage Youth Court in Alaska, a Tribunal Model youth court in which a panel of three teenage judges decides on the guilt or innocence of the plaintiff and determines the sentence. The trainees must first complete an 8-week (16-hour) training course covering evidence, case preparation, advocacy, procedure, and teen court jurisdiction, then pass a bar examination and complete 4 hours of sentencing training before becoming officers of the court. In addition, they must attend monthly meetings that include 30-minute continuing legal education classes (Nessel, 2000).

CONFIDENTIALITY

Teen court cases are usually strictly confidential. In Washington State, for example, the guidelines are clear and unequivocal:

> Washington State Law dictates that all Juvenile Court Diversion cases are strictly confidential. Outside of the Teen Court Hearing, nothing connected with a specific case may be discussed or even acknowledged by a Teen Court member. If anyone, including a friend or relative, asks a Teen Court member about a hearing or someone involved in a hearing, the member must say that he/she may not talk about Teen Court cases. If the Respondent in a Teen Court case approaches a Teen Court member outside of the Teen Court Hearing and wants to talk about their case (or any other), the member must tell them that he/she cannot talk with them about Teen Court cases. The Respondent should be referred to the supporting YMCA staff member of the Juvenile Court Diversion Unit (*Teen Court Manual*, 2000).

HOW EFFECTIVE ARE TEEN COURTS?

Although individual court programs consistently report positive results, little is known about their effectiveness on a national level. In

1998 the Office of Juvenile Justice and Delinquency Prevention (OJJDP) awarded a grant to the Urban Institute to conduct a national evaluation of teen courts. To document the characteristics of these courts, Urban Institute researchers mailed questionnaires to every known teen court program in the United States and then summarized the results (OJJDP Fact Sheet, 1999). The next phase, to measure the intended outcomes at four teen courts, is expected to be available in 2001.[1]

Although not yet formally documented, there are many benefits associated with teen court programs. They offer communities a prevention and early intervention program that can hold juvenile offenders accountable, educate teenagers in the community on the legal system and the judicial process, help build competencies in young people, help protect the community, and educate youths on the impact their actions have on their victims and the community. Perhaps most important of all is the impact that the experience of participating in the teen court program and actual court sessions may have in causing teenagers to rethink their views on delinquent behavior. Consider the following statement by a 15-year-old girl who, before participating as a volunteer in a North Carolina teen court, had engaged in shoplifting:

> A few years ago I started hanging out with some guys that always got into trouble with the police. I know what they were doing was wrong, but I didn't know exactly what would happen to me if we were caught. It didn't take long for me to . . . fit in well. When we would go into a store, I always knew my part and no one else ever messed up either. We never got caught. . . .
>
> There was one last time when we went into a store five times . . . and the last two times there was a police officer there. It didn't bother us . . . we thought the police were too stupid to catch us . . . an ignorant way of thinking because a week after that my friends were caught at another store. I, fortunately, was not with them, but it got me to thinking. What if I had been with them? If I had been caught, what would have happened? Even though it got me thinking, I didn't quit doing those types of things. I still wasn't sure what could happen if I was caught.
>
> Once teen court started in Asheville, I got into it. I learned what could have happened if I was caught, and that was when I decided not to do anything illegal again. If it hadn't been for teen court, I would never have learned about the consequences of

[1]For further information, contact Jeffrey A. Butts, PhD, Senior Research Associate, The Urban Institute, Program on Law and Behavior, 2100 M Street, NW, Washington, DC 20037 (telephone: 202-261-5514).

> doing wrong things and I would probably still be doing them. (Godwin, 1996, p. 21)

COMMENT

One criticism that is frequently raised against many of the specific interventions in current usage is the lack of empirical data supporting their efficacy. Olweus (1993a, p. 128), for example, commented:

> The recent English literature on bully/victim problems in school abounds with suggestions about measures against these problems. Almost none of the proposed measures have been scientifically evaluated, however, and consequently it is difficult to know what their effects, if any, are likely to be.

There is no question that empirical support is virtually nonexistent for some of the specific interventions in this chapter. But blanket insistence on such a requirement should be tempered by Dubos's point (Siegel, 1986, p. 20) that there is always the danger that rigid adherence to the necessity for empirical data could result in promising ideas being discarded. Empirical tests of the direct, that is, immediate, effects of a specific intervention usually involve measuring changes in the form of increases in amount of information that the respondents have acquired specific to the intervention. While of some academic interest, the data shed no light on the potential indirect but nevertheless real benefits, such as positive behavioral changes, that may be exhibited by the participants long after the end of the training program. Although such benefits would be extremely difficult to measure empirically, it is my position that in well-constructed intervention programs the potential for their existence is unequivocal. For example, the inclusion of specific interventions in a whole school campaign allows a number of students to be actively involved in combating bullying, and in the process to acquire skills such as conflict resolution, problem solving (Quality Circles), and an understanding of trial and other court procedures that would likely be of long-term value. Seeing antisocial behavior punished with the bullies visibly working off their sentences should have a powerful modeling effect on those with bullying tendencies and provide substantial reassurance and hope to the victims of bullying. Perhaps most important of all is the fact that the student body would see the difference between mandatory telling and being a tattletale, and in the process the bullies would be stripped of their greatest source of protection—the code of silence.

11 Violence

Violence is a form of terrorism. It creates intense fear with physical and/or verbal attacks that destroy the individual's confidence in his or her personal world (Zimbardo, 2001). Unpredictable acts of violence are the terrorist's signature. The target's resultant acute fear is a realistic emotional response because the anxiety that acts of random violence create markedly amplifies their impact. Although the concept of violence overlaps with bullying (see Figure 3.1), there are two important differences: Violence need not be repeated, nor must it be characterized by an imbalance of power (Ananiadou & Smith, in press). Some researchers (see, e.g., Olweus, 1999c, p. 12) have limited violence to physical acts, whereas others (Debarbieux & Blaya, 2001), including children, have defined violence more broadly. A 13-year-old girl at a conference on youth violence said: "There is another kind of violence, and that is violence by talking. It can leave you hurting more than a cut with a knife. It can leave you bruised inside" (Horn, 2000, p. 2).

The following account of the "peer violence by talking" that a man had endured throughout most of his secondary school years is a graphic example of being bruised inside:

> When I went into secondary school I found it difficult to adjust to the new situation. By second year I was being subjected to name calling with a mental or obscene connotation—"Weirdo," "Queer," "Mental." I found it disturbing and distressing. I began to internalise and personalise these things. Over a period of time, my mind stopped working, just as if somebody had taken the power out of it. My energy went—physically, mentally, every way. Eventually, I became locked into a role. I was perceived as freakish, peculiar, queer. I began to play their game, to give them what they expected. My self-confidence and self-esteem were so badly affected that I began to doubt myself. I was so distressed, traumatised and hurt that I was rendered literally speechless about what was happening to me. I felt wounded . . . I felt like someone was beating down on my heart with a hammer. (Byrne, 1994, p. 46)

The focus throughout this book has been primarily on bullying. If bullying goes unchecked, the probable next step is violence. A cautionary note has been sounded by the International Association of Chiefs of Police (1999) that "staff, students, and parents/guardians need to understand that bullying is a pervasive problem that leads to violence. Bullying should neither be thought of as a 'kids will be kids' occurrence nor accepted as a way of life." In most efforts to categorize behaviors, overlap occurs in the boundaries between categories, and this is the case with bullying and violence (see Figure 3.1). However, each is a distinct category (Olweus, 1999c): There can be bullying without violence (as is the case with intimidation) and violence without bullying (a playground fight between near-equal combatants).

Violence: A Public Health Epidemic

In the United States the level of violence in the school population in the poverty pockets of the inner cities as well as the more affluent suburbs has been accurately described by Prothrow-Stith (1991) as a "public health epidemic," with the incidence of violence being exceeded only by that in some developing countries. Donna Shalala, former Secretary of Health and Human Services (2001), has added an ominous warning: "In our country today, the greatest threat to the lives of children and adolescents is not disease or starvation or abandonment, but the terrible reality of violence." Further evidence that violence is on the rise in the school-age population comes from a study titled *Youth Violence: A Report of the Surgeon General* (U.S. Department of Health and Human Services, 2001), which concluded that near-record numbers of juveniles are committing a range of violent acts. Apart from this discouraging statistic, the report strikes a strong positive note with its contention that youth crime and violence rates could be substantially reduced simply by reallocating the money that is currently being spent on ineffective policies and programs, such as gun buyback programs, boot camps, and adult detention centers, to those that have proved to be effective. Effective youth violence programs include life-skills training, behavior monitoring and enforcement, social problem-solving and thinking skills, peer-group involvement, parent training, and home visitation.

The need to reallocate funding to effective violence programs brings up the schism between prevention and treatment. Funding for prevention programs in general falls far behind allocations for treatment of existing conditions. Funding sources expect concrete results based on pretreatment and posttreatment comparisons. Prevention programs, by comparison, produce reasoned expectations for changes over the long term but lack the reassurance provided by immediate postprogram data. Spending money on prevention makes sense. If adolescent boys at risk, such as those from terrible home environments in the inner cities, were provided with therapeutic interventions before they had moved on to committing major crimes, intervention at that point would have the potential for effecting a change that could be of lifelong benefit. Very little is spent on young people in high-risk categories. Yet even moderate detention costs are extraordinarily high, not to speak of those that are outrageously expensive.

LIFE IN THE INNER CITIES

Statistics provide one index of the gravity of the problem of violence, but they are often poor approximations of the effects of violence on individuals. Consider the plight of this mother who lives in the poverty pocket of a low-income neighborhood in New York City:

> Tanya Parker is 20 years old. She lives with her infant daughter on East 100th Street in East Harlem. In her neighborhood there is no place to hide. At night, an army of young "soldiers" controls the streets. They shoot powerful semi-automatic weapons at the sky and at each other. For these young men, guns talk. Guns equalize the weak and strong, the rich and the poor. Peace-loving people stay at home but they may not be safe. . . . They can never be certain that they and their children are safe. (Prothrow-Stith, 1991, p. 185)

Mothers living in this type of neighborhood teach their children to lie on the floor while watching television and to sleep beneath the window sills to avoid random bullets that might come through the windows (Prothrow-Stith, 1991). Mothers who have good reason to feel panic and fear every day are so stressed out that it must be difficult for them to be good parents. Children living in these conditions may experience negative reactions ranging from temporary upset to the symptoms of posttraumatic stress disorder (Osofsky, 1995).

The long-term effects of such exposure to violence need to be investigated (Osofsky, 1995). In these neighborhoods even young children have witnessed shooting and stabbing. When third and fifth graders were asked to draw pictures of "what happens" in their neighborhoods, they drew very detailed pictures of shootings, drug deals, stabbings, fighting, and funerals and stated that they were scared of the violence and of something happening to them (Osofsky, 1995). That life in the inner cities is not easy for teenagers either is evident in these excerpts from an essay by a 17-year-old girl who lived in a low-income neighborhood in New York:

> I find trying to survive in this world very hard, but when there's violence on the streets, it makes survival even harder . . . I think about kids getting killed at young ages. . . . I think about all these different gangs that are . . . trying to take over different turfs, which don't even belong to any of them. Each day when I come home from school I stay in the house . . . until it's time to go to school again . . . I wish that the day would come when people could walk the streets, without fear of being shot, stabbed, robbed, or just plain molested. (Prothrow-Stith, 1991, p. 80)

VIOLENCE—THE SEARCH FOR POSSIBLE CAUSES

In the search for the causes of this epidemic of violence many potential contributors to it, such as the poor home situation that exists in many inner cities, child maltreatment, dysfunctional parenting, association with delinquent peers, and membership in antisocial gangs, have been studied at age levels ranging from 5 years through adulthood (Farrington, 1989; Hawkins et al., 2000). One period of life that has aroused relatively little research interest is the 33-month period encompassing gestation, birth, and infancy. This period has been largely overlooked because it has been assumed to be irrelevant not only to a specific crime but also to later behavior in general. It is commonly believed that the infant, and particularly the fetus, lacks the ability to think and the capacity to store enduring experiences.

Of relevance here is an investigation linking the etiology of antisocial behavior to the gestation period and the first 2 years of life. In *Ghosts From the Nursery: Tracing the Roots of Violence*, Karr-Morse and Wiley (1997) started with the question, *Why are children violent?* Using evidence from case histories, crime statistics, and recent research in neurobiology, they presented a convincing argument for the role of pregnancy, infancy, and parental behavior in the genesis of violence: They showed why this 33-month period is so crucial in brain development. From late in the gestation period and after birth, the infant begins to develop a set of expectations about himself or herself and others and the world around him or her. Recent research depicts the 2 years of infancy as the real crucible of human relationships, a period in which the foundations for trust, lifelong learning and thinking, and conscience are laid down, or when a predisposition to violent behavior is causally linked to abuse and neglect. Whether the fetal brain is traumatized by alcohol, drugs, or violence against the mother, or whether the infant suffers from outright physical abuse, other trauma, or prolonged neglect, the effects of all these negative experiences are *cumulative* at each subsequent stage of development.

There is unequivocal evidence that the developing brain must have a steady stream of certain positive experiences to establish the circuits for thinking, feeling, and relating, and some infants are seriously deprived of these experiences. Long before the beginning of language and memory, the brain and body store traces of positive and negative experiences, and these become the basis for subsequent behavior. Karr-Morse and Wiley (1997) noted that the disruptive behavior that is first reported in the primary grades was, in retrospect, often noticed in the 2-year-old child; by age 4, aggression, tantrums, and coercive interactions with others are a consistent pattern of behavior (Walker, 1996). By the time the disruptive behavior arouses concern in public school, it is well entrenched.

Karr-Morse and Wiley (1997) emphasized that no single biological or social factor by itself predisposes a child to violent behavior. Rather, it is the interaction of multiple factors, such as the fetal alcohol syndrome combined with physical abuse of the child and exposure to toxins, which may set the stage for the child's later violent behavior. The key to understanding the genesis of violence is the number of negative intrauterine and early experiences operative in the 33-month period in relation to the number of protective factors available and operative in the child's environment.

Further evidence linking the etiology of some antisocial behavior to the 33-month period encompassing gestation, birth, and infancy comes from a study by Arseneault, Tremblay, Boulerice, and Saucier (2002) on the interaction between specific obstetrical complications (preeclampsia, umbilical cord prolapse, and induced labor) and early family adversity in predicting violent behavior during childhood and adolescence. The assumption underlying this link is that neurophysiological deficits leading to behavioral problems are brought about by fetal brain damage that could have been caused by obstetrical complications. Further, previous research (Piquero & Tibbets, 1999) has demonstrated that infants who experience specific obstetrical complications coupled with early adverse environments are at increased risk for violent behavior during childhood and adolescence. Arseneault et al. (2002) have noted that two developmental pathways could account for this outcome. First, the interaction between obstetrical complications and psychosocial risk factors could have a delayed effect that could create a vulnerability that increases the probability that later, in adolescence, the developmental tasks that are often a challenge at that time, even under the best of circumstances, will be met with a sudden onset of violent behaviors that may or may not disappear in adulthood (Greenwood, 1995). In the second pathway, the obstetrical complications and psychosocial risk factors could have an immediate impact on children's ability to control their physical aggression. In this case, violence and other disruptive behavior in adolescence would be the adolescent expression of the chronic physical aggression that was apparent in early childhood.

In considering how obstetrical complications could influence each developmental pathway, Arseneault et al. (2002) have stated that support for the first developmental pathway (in which antisocial behavior becomes a problem in mid-adolescence) is based on evidence that obstetrical complications contribute to the etiology of schizophrenia (M. Cannon & Jones, 1996; T. D. Cannon, Mednick, & Parnas, 1989). Because schizophrenia is characterized by a late age of onset and an abrupt appearance, obstetrical complications could have an impact on violent behavior that would become evident in mid-adolescence. Support for the second pathway (in which the signs of antisocial behavior appear early in the preschool years) comes from research that links obstetrical complications with cognitive functioning and with neuropsychological deficits, such as impaired verbal and executive functioning, that are involved in persistent antisocial behavior that is present early in life. It follows that obstetrical complications could have an impact on violent behavior that would become evident in the preschool years.

When deciding on the optimum time to begin prevention strategies, the difference between these two pathways is of crucial importance. It is possible that intervention late in middle childhood or very early in adolescence could interrupt the first pathway to violent delinquency, whereas for optimum results the second pathway would require very early intervention in the preschool years, probably no later than at 3 years of age.

The participants in Arseneault et al.'s (2002) study were 849 boys from low socioeconomic areas of Montreal, Quebec, Canada, who were part of an ongoing longitudinal study (Tremblay, Pihl, Vitaro, & Dobkin, 1994) that had started during their kindergarten years. To create a culturally homogeneous group, all those in the sample were White boys whose native language was French and whose parents were born in Canada. In kindergarten, the class teachers from 53 schools rated all the boys on adverse psychosocial conditions, such as early maternal rejection or a disadvantaged familial environment, and physical aggression. Complete data files for behaviors from kindergarten to adolescence were available on all 849 boys, including self-reports of delinquent behavior that were obtained when the boys were 17 years old.

Obstetrical complication data from all of the participants were used to create three scales—Atypical Presentation Situation, Distress Situation, and Deadly Risk Situation—using a nonlinear principal-components analysis followed by rotation. These data were used to determine, first, whether the interaction between specific obstetrical complications and early family adversity could predict childhood physical aggression and, second, whether this interaction accounts for the continuity of violent behavior from childhood to adolescence. High scores on the Deadly Risk Situation of obstetrical complications (preeclampsia, umbilical cord prolapse, and induced labor) increased the risk of being violent at both age 6 and 17 only among boys who grew up in high adverse familial environments. In addition, this interaction partly accounted for the continuity between violence in childhood and adolescence. Arseneault et al. (2002) stated that, to their knowledge, "this is the first study to demonstrate that a specific combination of obstetrical complications was involved in chronic physical violence from childhood onward" (p. 504).

IMPLICATIONS FOR EARLY INTERVENTION

The results of Arseneault et al.'s (2002) study suggest that intensive support for young pregnant women in poor socioeconomic areas could have a significant positive impact on both their parenting abilities and the psychosocial development of their children. In contrast to the findings of Raine, Brennan, and Mednick (1994) that the interaction between birth complications was specific with early maternal rejection, Arseneault et al.'s findings showed that a broad measure of family adversity interacted with obstetrical complications to predict later violent behavior. The interaction effect found with family adversity could be specific to low socioeconomic status populations.

An encouraging development in intervention programs targeting disruptive young children, especially boys, is the inclusion of some form of parental training and support. An example of this approach is the excellent study by Tremblay, Pagani-Kurtz, Mâsse, Vitaro, and Pihl (1995). Tremblay et al. tested the effect on school adjustment of a 2-year bimodal preventive intervention program on a large sample (N = 366) of kindergarten boys from inner-city low socioeconomic neighborhood schools who were randomly assigned to a preventive condition and a control condition. The program consisted of a school-based social skills training component that included home-based parent training. Other predictive studies by Tremblay and his associates

(Tremblay et al., 1992; Tremblay, Pihl, Vitaro, & Dobkin, 1994) have demonstrated the urgency of the need for early intervention with disruptive preschool and primary school boys.

Risk Factors for Youth Violence

SEATTLE SOCIAL DEVELOPMENT PROJECT

In a study of developmental risk factors for youth violence, Herrenkohl, Maguin, Hill, Hawkins, and Abbott (2000) set out first to replicate earlier research findings on risk factors for youth violence, and then to examine the effects on violent behavior of constructs that have been shown to increase risk for other problem behaviors, all within the developmental frame of a longitudinal study. Data were obtained from the Seattle Social Development Project, a prospective study involving a group of youths who had been followed since 1985. At ages 10, 14, and 16 years, measurements were made of the presence of potential risk factors for violence at age 18. At each of the three age levels, bivariate relationships involving risk factor constructs and violence were examined to assess changes, if any, in the prediction of violence at age 18 years. The risk factor constructs covered five areas: the individual boy, his family, school, peers, and community. The overall level of risk at ages 10, 14, and 16 years became the basis for determining if participants at age 18 were correctly classified as to whether or not they had committed a violent act.

In attacking the problem of violence, two strategies have emerged. One of these involves preventive interventions that target known risk factors for violence, coupled with procedures designed to strengthen the individual's resistance to known negative influences (Brewer, Hawkins, Catalano, & Neckerman, 1995). The other provides remedial interventions after youths have been arrested and judged to be delinquent. In this group violent patterns of behavior are generally well established (Reiss & Roth, 1993).

The first step in designing empirically based prevention strategies is knowing what factors put the individual at increased risk for violence. Of relevance here are the five categories of risk factors that Herrenkohl et al. (2000) had used previously (see Table 11.1):

1. *Individual.* A large group of potential risk factors for violence have been studied (Hawkins et al., 1998). Of particular importance are biological and psychological characteristics that are present in early childhood. These may increase a child's vulnerability to social and environmental influences during the

Table 11.1. Risk Factors for Violence Organized by Domain

Individual	Family	School	Peer	Community
Male gender	Parental violence	Low academic performance	Sibling delinquency	Economic deprivation
Hyperactivity (teacher rating)	Parental criminality	Low school commitment	Peer delinquency	**Community disorganization**
Hyperactivity (parent rating)	Poor family management	**Low educational aspirations**	Gang membership	**Low neighborhood attachment**
	Family conflict	**School transitions**		
Risk taking	**Parental attitudes favorable to violence**	Antisocial behavior (teacher rating)		**Availability of drugs**
Drug selling	**Residential mobility**			**Neighborhood adults involved in crime**
Early initiation of violence				**Enforcement of laws against violence**
Child's pro-violence attitudes				

Note: Boldface indicates predictors included in the study with no previous empirical validation.

Reproduced with permission of the authors and publisher from Herrenkohl, T. I., Maguin, E., Hill, K. G., Hawkins, J. D., & Abbott, R. D. (2000). Developmental risk factors for youth violence. *Journal of Adolescent Health, 26,* 176–186.

course of development but, in many cases, they could be modified or even eliminated with early intervention. Gender is considered to be a risk factor for violence simply because boys more than girls are encouraged to engage in physical aggression (Loeber & Stouthamer-Loeber, 1998). Hyperactivity, risk taking, and early evidence of violent behavior are also individual risk factors for serious violence (Mannuzza, Klein, Konig, & Giampino, 1989).

2. *Family.* A cluster of family characteristics places children at increased risk for violence. In families in which violence, conflict, and criminality are condoned and modeled consistently by older siblings and parents, and antisocial norms and values are endorsed, children are clearly at increased risk (Farrington, 1991). Further, the failure to set clear rules and to enforce them consistently, coupled with inconsistent and severe discipline, also increases the risk of violence (Hawkins et al., 1998).
3. *School.* Children who have little interest in school and from a young age perform poorly on academic tasks are on a trajectory of early school failure and dropout, association with delinquent peers, membership in antisocial gangs, and violence (Farrington, 1989; Maguin & Loeber, 1996).
4. *Peers.* Involvement with antisocial or delinquent peers is one of the strongest predictors of serious violence in adolescence (Hawkins et al., 1998; Lipsey & Derzon, 1998). Active gang involvement is also a known predictor.
5. *Community.* Exposure to poverty at both the neighborhood and family levels increases the risk for violence especially if the child is a member of a gang. Having access to drugs can lead to becoming a dealer, with a consequent increase in the risk of violence.

RESULTS

At age 10 years: Of the 15 constructs measured, 10 of them predicted violence at age 18. Odds ratios (ORs) were computed with risk factor constructs and the age 18 violence measure, using a pairwise missing data treatment. The largest OR (2.66) was associated with antisocial behavior rated by teachers.

At age 14 years: Twenty of the 25 measured risk factors were significant. There was a tripling of the odds for later violence in the ORs for five constructs (risk taking, drug selling, early initiation of violence, gang membership, and presence of the neighborhood adults involved in crime). Nine other constructs had ORs > 2.0. These were parental ratings of hyperactivity, the child's proviolence attitudes, parental criminality, poor family management, low academic performance, teacher ratings of antisocial behavior, peer delinquency, community disorganization, and availability of drugs.

At age 16 years: Nineteen of 21 measured constructs were significant. Exposure to two risk factors at age 16 years (drug selling and gang membership) quadrupled the odds for violence at age 18. Tripling the odds were risk taking, peer delinquency, community disorganization, availability of drugs, and presence of neighborhood adults involved in crime. Seven of the remaining 12 constructs had ORs > 2.0.

These results show that risk factors for violence at 18 years can be identified as early as age 10 years. The strength of associations between risk factors and violence at age 18 years generally increased at ages 14 and 16. Risk factors with strong effects were distributed across all five categories.

Several of the results have important implications for preventive intervention programs. Antisocial behaviors as rated by teachers, male gender, and teacher/parent ratings of hyperactivity were all strong predictors of later violence. It is interesting that hyperactivity continued to be a strong predictor at ages 14 and 16. Clearly, diagnosing and treating symptoms of hyperactivity when they are first apparent should be given high priority. The fact that low academic performance consistently predicted violence at age 18 suggests that intervention should also focus on academic achievement.

Herrenkohl et al. (2000) concluded that their ability to identify youths who will go on to commit violent offenses is limited, although relatively few individuals who were predicted to be violent failed to engage in violence at age 18 years. However, 13% to 18% of those predicted to be nonviolent did engage in later violence. These failures in prediction suggest that there may be reason to focus preventive efforts on groups or populations that are exposed to multiple risks rather than limiting prevention efforts only to those meeting a given risk profile. The rationale for this suggestion is that those who may be excluded from intervention programs based on individual risk assessments, but do engage in violence later, would likely be included in intervention programs.

Prevention: A Formidable Task

The importance of prevention in attacking the problem of increasing violence is gaining some support. In 1994 the American Psychological Association sponsored The Commission on Youth and Violence, who concluded that the roots of violence are almost always in the home. An elementary school teacher said:

> The violent kids are the ones who come from homes with anger. They're angry about what goes on in their home. . . . They're angry to start with. They're angry when they walk in the schoolhouse door. (Horn, 2000)

Violence is not a natural state, but is learned by young children observing their parents, siblings, and peers. The Commission emphasized that a child can have birth complications or genetic tendencies but does not act in certain ways unless that is how he or she has learned to behave (Spollen, 1994). If violence begins at home, then so must prevention.

THE ROLE OF SCHOOL PROGRAMS

The fact that violence is on the rise in the school population has been well documented (U.S. Department of Health and Human Services, 2001). Less than a decade ago the National Education Goals Panel (Johnston, O'Malley, & Bachman, 1993) stated that their goal was to have every school in the United States free of violence and conducive to learning by the end of the century. We have fallen far short of this goal and, if anything, deterioration in the situation has accelerated. When violence is a common occurrence in a school, even those who are never bullied but who sometimes are bystanders or are aware of it through word-of-mouth feel a sense of threat. The effect is diminished enjoyment of school and lowered academic performance.

The Covert Power Dynamics Program

There are programs available now that are specifically designed to combat school violence. A good example is the Covert Power Dynamics Program that has been developed by Twemlow, Fonagy, and Sacco (2001). The basic assumption of their psychodynamically influenced model is that in all schools experiencing violence, a covert power dynamic (PD) is pervasive. This dynamic is a conscious or unconscious coercive pattern in which an individual or group controls the thoughts and actions of others. Although at times the PD effect may operate as a subtle and unconsciously motivating force, more often its effect takes the concrete form of high levels of disciplinary referrals and poor academic achievement.

In this PD model, the bully may be a child, teacher, or other staff person, and the victim may be a child or any other school member who feels dominated or abused by this repeated and humiliating coercion. This bullying usually pairs a stronger, more dominant person with a weaker, more submissive one in a situation in which major physical injury rarely occurs. Instead, the major discomfort involved is emotional humiliation.

Although bystanders have been shown to play a variety of supportive and/or disapproving roles in bully/victim interactions (Hazler, 1996b; Olweus, 2001; Rigby, 1996; Salmivalli et al., 1996) such as being an assistant to the bully or taking sides with the victim, the PD model has identified subcategories of the bystander role. Children who are too frightened to resist the bully who is recruiting followers are *victim bystanders*, whereas school personnel who deny the fact that there are problems such as bullying in the school serve as *avoidant bystanders*. A more positive role is that of the *ambivalent bystanders*, who are not committed to the demands of the PD and have the potential to help others resist the pathological roles although they may choose not to do so.

In commenting on the bully/bystander interactions, Fonagy noted that "the whole drama is supported by the bystander. The theater can't take place if there's no audience" (Labi, 2001, p. 47). In a major study of 10,000 children in an East Coast city, Twemlow, Fonagy, and Sacco (2001) found that between 10% and 20% of third through ninth graders experienced a vicarious thrill through watching ongoing bullying. In the PD model some of these *bully bystanders* may subsequently become "puppet masters" who set up their victims to commit crimes for which they themselves do not want to be blamed but may enjoy watching. A distressing example of this dynamic occurred in Pearl, Mississippi, when a 16-year-old boy who killed two students was "coached" by six other boys who were subsequently charged with conspiring to commit murder. A similar dynamic occurred at a school dance in Edinboro, Pennsylvania, when a 14-year-old boy shot and killed a teacher and injured several others after the dance. The "puppet master" bystander came to watch the outcome of his play (Twemlow, Fonagy, & Sacco, 2001).

In obtaining information from students to establish whether a PD exists in the school, the clinical assessment of each child at the preschool/elementary school levels should include questions about the degree to which the child has been victimized and by whom in the school setting. For example:

- Do you like seeing a fight or are you so frightened that you can't do anything?
- Which kids or groups of kids bully others?
- What could you do when another student is always left out?

In middle and high school there may be a hierarchy of social groups (jocks, punks, etc.) or cliques that facilitate the emergence of PDs. Any group can encourage coercive PDs, so ask:

- Is there one dominant group or clique in your school?
- Are there racial/ethnic groups who control the school?
- Do teachers appear intimidated at your school?
- Have you ever reported a student being bullied? What happened?

These and similar questions can be used by a consultant as catalysts for discussion with teachers and students in a school that has too much fighting and bullying as well as serious discipline problems. In applying the Twemlow, Fonagy, & Sacco (2001) model, top priority should be given to "rebalancing" PDs, the most difficult task in effecting change. The potential for change is already present in the fact that the bully, victim, and bystander roles are interchangeable, with children taking on different roles at different times. Twemlow, Fonagy, & Sacco (2001) contended that if all children acquire the verbal and nonverbal skills needed to handle PDs, they can help each other to abandon the pathological roles for more socially desirable relationships.

What evidence is there for this somewhat radical approach? One example of its effectiveness (Twemlow, Fonagy, Sacco, Gies, et al., 2001) comes from a 4-year controlled study with experimental and control matched elementary schools. The antiviolence intervention program consisted of four components:

1. Zero tolerance for behavioral disturbances such as bullying and victimization as well as passive observance of violent acts.
2. Helping school personnel develop a discipline plan for modeling appropriate behavior.
3. A physical education plan that focuses on self-regulation skills including anger management, role play, and martial arts and, later, organized physical sports.
4. The use of peer mentors and adult volunteers to intervene at critical points and times such as getting on the school bus, recess, lunchtime, and free play, and accidental and deliberate school corridor incidents and conflicts.

Disciplinary and academic achievement data were collected at predetermined temporal points from both schools. The results in the experimental school showed significant reductions in discipline referrals as well as increases in scores on standardized academic achievement measures. The teachers reported that many previously passive and withdrawn victimized children became more verbal and outspoken as the program progressed. Bullying and coercion also decreased. The control school showed no such changes.

Two other recent publications by this team of researchers merit special attention. One is an excellent training program for creating a peaceful school learning environment at the elementary school level (Twemlow, Sacco, & Twemlow, 2001). The other is a description of psychoanalytic models of the roots of violence (Twemlow, 2000). Of particular interest are his comments on the tragedy of Littleton.

Victim Slide Show

Professionals who are concerned about the rising tide of violence should be alert to opportunities to use everyday events to teach children how easily severe injuries can occur. The following slide show presentation is an excellent example.

Timo Nuutinen (1999), an experienced member of an emergency team in a Finnish hospital, was shocked and dismayed by the number of young victims who were admitted as a result of violent bullying by other adolescents, and also by the ease at which severe injuries could be inflicted. Seemingly harmless bullying such as tripping a victim on the school playground, a snowball aimed at a peer, or a single blow to the nose often caused concussion or even irreversible brain damage, permanent damage to the eyes, or broken noses.

Nuutinen (1999) assembled a slide show that included color photographs and X-rays of actual cases of injured young victims of bullying. The slides were quite shocking evidence of the damage that could be done. He presented this slide show to school children and adolescents along with a lively account of how the injuries occurred. Word spread about the slide show: It was so popular that during the 1980s it was presented at most of the schools in Finland. The combination of the pictures and Nuutinen's vivid descriptions seemed to shock audiences and ensure their absorbed attention.

Björkqvist and Österman (1999) attributed two important results to the slide show. It provided a graphic demonstration of the real consequences and danger of violence for audiences who were used to seeing violence glorified in films. In addition, pupils who saw the slides could not fail to feel empathy for the victims. The overall effect was a combination of information about the results of unnecessary and pointless violence with empathy training. To measure the attitudes of 12- to 16-year-old pupils to the behaviors described in the slide show, Björkqvist and Österman (1999) used a 5-item scale (α = .92). Although they had not expected any long-term effects, there were, in fact, significant long-term effects on the presumed danger of violent acts as well as significant short-term effects on moral condemnation of bullying.

The Problem of Violence on Television

Violence is a major feature of contemporary television, film, and video games. In children's television programs there is more violence than on prime-time programming for adults. It has been estimated than an American child sees 200,000 acts of violence on television alone by the age of 18 (Robinson, Wilde, Navracruz, Haydel, & Varady, 2001). Media violence is a major barrier to having schools in the United States free of violence. Numerous studies have clearly demonstrated the link between television violence and juvenile crimes. Violent video games have also been linked to juvenile violence. Some juveniles who have been interrogated about violent crimes have spent hundreds of hours playing violent video games (*Seattle Post-Intelligencer*, 1999). As Slaby (1994, p. B1) has so aptly pointed out, "High levels of unrealistic television violence are presented to those most vulnerable to its distorting effects—children."

HARMFUL EFFECTS OF TV VIOLENCE ON VIEWERS

The findings to date provide substantial and well-documented evidence that television violence can produce harmful effects on viewers. Slaby (1994) categorized these effects and identified the characteristics of each category. One is the *aggressor effect*. Although some viewers are more susceptible than others to the depiction of violence, it appears from the research that no viewer is immune. From longitudinal studies, some of which have followed viewers for more than two decades, there is evidence that watching large amounts of television violence in childhood is one of the best predictors for males' violent criminal behavior in adulthood. Seeing violence on television may make it seem appropriate for the child to victimize peers when they will not do what he or she wants. One danger then is that the child can use violence as a problem-solving tool. A *victim effect* has also been documented. Viewers who identify with the victim are more likely to exhibit fear, mistrust, and self-protective behavior, such as carrying a gun. They also have an irrational fear of violence from total strangers. Viewers who become characterized by the *bystander effect* are likely to be more callous than most to the victims of violence and unmoved at the consequences to the victim because they have been desensitized into accepting it. The *increased appetite effect* occurs when viewers, particularly those who have seen violence portrayed in ways that glamorize it, begin to seek out depictions of more intense violence such as what is often available in movie videos. Many of these contain levels of violence that even television will not broadcast, yet the video format permits unlimited replays.

Although the weight of evidence regarding the negative consequences of television violence is irrefutable, the blanket resistance to change on the part of the television industry has led to even more studies in an attempt to convince the industry that change is imperative. In 1996, for example, a $1.5 million survey by TV interests (Slaby, 1994), the largest of its kind to date, involved researchers at four universities who studied 2,500 hours of public television, cable, and network broadcast. They found that 57% of the programs surveyed contained violence, and 33% of them showed nine or more violent acts. In addition, 47% of all the violent interactions showed no harm to the victims, and 58% showed no evidence of pain. Consider the following example of the effects of seeing violent interactions that show no visible evidence of pain in the victims:

> The young gunshot victim in the Boston emergency room astonished his doctors. He said he was surprised that his wound actually hurt. "I thought, boy, he's really stupid," recalled Dr. Deborah Prothrow-Stith, Associate Dean at Harvard University's School of Public Health and author of a recent book on violence. "But it dawned on me that what he sees on television is that when the superhero gets shot in the arm, he uses that arm to hold onto a truck going 85 miles an hour around a corner. He overcomes the driver and shoots a couple of hundred people while he's at it." (Clark, 1993, p. 6)

The results from the survey support critics who contend that televised violence fosters misunderstanding in children by blurring the distinction between reality and fantasy. It is not uncommon, for example, to see an actor "killed" in one episode of a series only to reappear alive in the next one.

Executives of the television industry have rebutted the scientific findings on television violence by denying them or attacking them with totally unsupported counterclaims. They contend that violence is a nonissue, a mere reflection of our society, a way of draining off aggressive energy. They also contend that programs are only giving the viewers what the ratings show they want and that proposals to limit violence are censorship (Slaby, 1994).

As the situation stands now parental control appears to be the only way in which exposure to media violence can be eliminated.

This approach makes enormous demands: Prescreening of programs, videos, and video games is a time-consuming task; establishing and enforcing rules is a must; stamina is required to withstand the negative comparisons with peers' households and freedom and to resist all pleas; and some attention should be paid to substituting appealing activities that cut into the time formerly available for television viewing.

REDUCTION OF TV VIEWING TIME

Despite the evidence of the effects of media violence, very few attempts have been made to reduce this effect (Eron, 1986). An exception is the study by Robinson et al. (2001) that was designed to answer the question, Are these effects modifiable? They ran an experiment in two schools with third- and fourth-grade children and their parents. The schools were randomly assigned to either the experimental or the control group. In September preintervention data were collected on all of the children: The children rated their peers' aggressive behavior and reported their own perceptions of the world as a mean and scary place. At this time parents were interviewed by telephone and rated their children's aggressive and delinquent behaviors on the Child Behavior Checklist (Achenbach, 1991). The control group children had no other interventions, whereas the experimental group were given an 18-lesson, 6-month classroom program designed to reduce their television, videotape, and video game use. The intervention included self-monitoring and reporting of television, videotape, and video game use to motivate the children to reduce the time they spent on these activities. Next, there was a TV Turnoff (Winn, 1987) during which the children were challenged to watch no television or videotapes and to play no video games for 10 days. After this, the children were encouraged to limit these activities to 7 hours per week. Parent newsletters were sent to parents to motivate them to help their children stay within their time budgets. Following the intervention period, in April, the postintervention data were again collected from all of the children and their parents. When compared with the controls, the children in the intervention group showed significant decreases in the primary outcome measures of aggression ($p = .03$) and observed verbal aggression ($p = .01$). The other measures favored the intervention group but were not statistically significant.

Marked decreases in media exposure are beneficial in a variety of other ways. The increase in available free time opens the way for social interactions with peers, pursuit of other interests such as hobbies, and heightened independence in determining what interest paths to follow. A reduction in media use has also been shown to affect adiposity, physical activity, and dietary intake in overweight children (Robinson, 1999) in third and fourth grades. Among other findings, children in the intervention group had significant decreases in adiposity. Because fat children are frequently targets of teasing and bullying, a concerted effort to reduce their media use could have the additional benefit of eliminating one reason for their victim status.

PHILLIPS'S APPROACH

A promising solution and a new direction for approaching the problem of children seeing violence on television has been proposed by Martin Phillips, an English teacher and media advisor at Devon School in England. Unlike Robinson et al.'s (2001) approach, which focused entirely on media use alone, with no attempt to teach critical viewing skills or knowledge and attitudes of an antiadvertising nature, Phillips's (Coughlan, 1995) rationale is that watching TV and videos is likely to continue to be a substantial part of children's daily experiences. Almost all parents watch television, and many households have more than one TV set. Trying to either keep children from watching or severely limit their exposure is usually doomed to failure. Phillips (Coughlan, 1995) argued that, in reality, children need to acquire the critical skills needed to understand what they are watching. The purpose of his study is to teach children to be discriminating viewers who know the difference between fictional violence that is presented for entertainment and the dangerous consequences of real-life violence.

A pilot study is currently being conducted in 10 primary schools to evaluate the first phase of the Devon project. It involves giving the schools a video and printed materials that provide examples and exercises designed to help them understand television. Phillips hopes that the participants will begin to look at television in a more objective way and will be able to distinguish among news programs, documentaries, and action movies. He also hopes that this approach, through education rather than through ineffective bans, will prove to be productive.

In addition to the methodological care that has gone into the Devon study, it is commendable that Phillips acknowledges the role that others have played. The project was set in motion in part by programs in the Netherlands by Dutch schools and by the work of television and media researchers at the University of Leiden.

The problem of violence is frequently attributed to three factors: the ready availability of guns in most of the United States making it easy for boys under 18 years of age to obtain a gun, television programs and other media that endlessly reinforce the message that violence is the normal outcome of human conflict, and the national ideology that portrays violence as a legitimate way to resolve disputes (Prothrow-Stith, 1991). It is important to remember that, in addition to these factors, some forms of violence are condoned. Included here are hazing and violent forms of initiation for joining high school and university athletic teams and other clubs, as well as often overlooked, and therefore implicitly condoned, aggression in sports, such as deliberate attempts to injure players on an opposing team.

HAZING

Hazing is another example of the tacit approval given by a wide range in the population to behaviors that are clearly violent, yet condoned not only by peers but also by many authority figures such as coaches of athletic teams. It is defined as conduct that causes or threatens to cause serious physical injury or psychological damage to another person as a condition for joining a team, organization, or other group. This conduct has become illegal in 40 states in the United States. Although the specifics vary among these states, one element remains constant: When the hazing activities endanger the physical or mental health of anyone, whether a participant in the hazing or a nonparticipating bystander, they become a criminal offense. Even when the hazers cite the victim's consent as a defense, the courts have rejected that argument.

When did hazing start? It dates back to at least the fourth-century Carthage, when students were described as behaving like devils, taunting and bullying first-year students (Sheed, 1993). What are the ritual social functions that have caused hazing to endure for centuries? Charles Moskos, coeditor of *The Postmodern Military* (Moskos, Williams, & Segal, 2000, p. 56), wrote:

> The latent function of hazing is that it differentiates and separates one from, and at the same time makes one feel superior to, whatever mainstream you're defining yourself against. . . . I think it's significant that there was little if any hazing in the armed forces in World War II. It seems like a post-Vietnam-era phenomenon, as the military got separated from the mainstream of society. Insecurity drives hazing. And there are sort of homosexual undertones to much of this male hazing; therefore, you have this sort of irony of going through a kind of homoerotic experience to prove you're not homosexual.

THE ALFRED UNIVERSITY STUDY

This study by Hoover and Pollard (2000)[1] of initiation rites in American high schools focused on hazing, defined as "any humiliating or dangerous activity expected of you to join a group, regardless of your willingness to participate" (p. 4). Hazing fell into three categories: humiliation (socially offensive, isolating, or uncooperative behavior), substance abuse (abuse of tobacco, alcohol, or illegal drugs), and dangerous hazing (hurtful, aggressive, destructive, or disruptive behaviors).

A random national sample of 20,000 high school juniors and seniors was sent a two-page survey questionnaire. Of this number, 1,541 completed and returned usable surveys, a rate of 8.28%. According to Hoover and Pollard (2000), high school students have a consistently low rate of response on mail surveys. The survey covered background, including membership in any type of group, definition of and experience with hazing, and initiation activities that were required for joining a high school group or team. Open-ended questions were asked on such items as prevention of hazing strategies, reasons for participating in hazing, experiences as a consequence of it, feelings afterward, and activities expected of initiates.

Major Findings

Students did not distinguish between "fun" and hazing. In terms of the definition of hazing used by Hoover and Pollard (2000), almost half (48%) of the respondents participated in activities that were clearly defined as hazing, and 29% reported doing things that are potentially illegal in order to join a group, yet only 14% said that they were hazed. Most of the students did not regard even the most dangerous initiation activities as hazing.

Hazing starts at a surprisingly early age. Almost 5% put their first experience of it in middle school, and 42% reported that their first hazing occurred in high school sports. Dangerous hazing is as prevalent in high school students (22%) as it is among college athletes (21%). Within this category, substance abuse is prevalent in high school and more than doubles (51%) in college (Hoover & Pollard, 2000). In line with other forms of bullying, the code of silence deters students from reporting instances of hazing. In this study, 40% of the respondents said that they would not report hazing.

What forms does hazing take? Some initiates have been required to bear extreme cold or burial in sand; others were ordered to exercise

[1]Additional information on the work at Alfred University and a final report on this study, titled *Lethal Violence in Schools*, can be obtained from Edward Gaughan, PhD, Professor of Psychology, Alfred University, Alfred, NY 14802, USA.

until they lost consciousness. Some were kidnapped, beaten, and tied up or abandoned. An example of the last was the initiation imposed several years ago by the men's soccer team at the University of Washington in Seattle. Campus police found three initiates one night who had been bound together and taped to a luggage cart so that they were unable to move. The soccer team was put on probation and all members were required to perform 240 hours of community service.

In view of the increasingly vicious forms of hazing and its increasing frequency, the question then is, Why are these behaviors continuing relatively unchecked? Some school officials persist in denying that a hazing tradition exists in their schools even when confronted with supportable evidence to the contrary. Some high school coaches believe that hazing serves to bond players and increase achievement, so they overlook it. However, Brian Rahill, who runs a Web site (www.stophazing.org), strongly disagrees that hazing encourages cohesion. He stated, "Hazing doesn't bring people together. It only breeds animosity and separates people" (Jacobs, 2000, p. 10).

In discussing the thorny issue of why hazing continues to persist, Nuwer (1999, pp. 114–115) drew on Arnold's (1995) work and made the following comment:

> Hazers, as Arnold has shown, are nothing more or less than addicts in an addictive system. For hazing to continue to survive within the education system, as it has for thousands of years, requires dependence and tolerance—the two common characteristics of addiction identified by deviant behavior researchers—on the parts not only of hazers and the hazed but also of those who supervise them. So long as educators persist in believing that brutish hazing serves a useful purpose that civilized behavior cannot achieve more effectively, the red stain of hazing will continue to besmirch academe's ivory towers. Once educators and young people who are seeking an education can see hazing for the addiction it really is, they will seek proper treatment to end a barbarous custom that has been more than two thousand years in the making.

Still, this implicit condoning of hazing by external influences provides only a partial explanation for the willingness of most hazing victims to accept such treatment. The real motivator is the extraordinarily strong desire and need to fit in to the peer group and be accepted by it.

The effects of the atmosphere of violence that is a part of the child's environment would, at one time, have been counteracted to a large extent by the family as a haven meeting basic needs of acceptance and belonging. In a series of conferences on youth violence, Horn (2000) noted that the importance of a sense of belonging was reiterated throughout the discussions. Its source: the family. Increasingly, however, family bonds have weakened as children see less and less of their parents. Many adolescents spend only a small fraction of their time with their parents and even less with other adults. And when they do see their parents they often find that they cannot really talk to them about things that the adolescent sees as important (Pollack, 2000).[2] Without the family as an anchor, it is logical that the child would seek other means of support. If the choice is a good one, then the void would be filled in a socially and psychologically desirable way, at least to some extent. If this is not the case, the stage is set for major problems. A frightening example that occurred in Vermont is described later in this chapter.

Gangs

A general definition of gangs offered by the California Council on Criminal Justice—that a gang is a group of people who interact at a high rate among themselves to the exclusion of other groups (Barden, 1989)—could be applied to other groups such as private clubs. However, in addition to always having a group name, a gang claims a neighborhood or other territory as its own, and on a regular basis engages in criminal or other antisocial behavior. Gangs are rarely open to everyone: The incumbents usually make new members undergo painful, lengthy, and often criminal initiation rites. Members must spend their time with other gang members and avoid outsiders at all times. They are not free to make new friends independently of the gang (Barden, 1989).

VIOLENT JUVENILE GANGS

In most parts of the United States, particularly in inner cities such as those in Los Angeles and Chicago, violent juvenile gangs are on the increase. A national survey of school crime (Bastian & Taylor, 1991) showed that 15% of the students felt that their schools had gangs, and others concluded that youth gang violence as well as the frequently random killing that goes with it is emerging in almost every U.S. community, regardless of size (Hazler, 1996a).

[2]An outstanding contribution to the understanding of teenage boys and their needs is Pollack's book, *Real Boys' Voices* (2000).

The question of why children and adolescents join gangs relates partially to a background of exposure to violence and decreasing sensitization to it. Many gang members were bullies in school (before dropping out) and were victimized at home and in their neighborhoods. Lacking any sense of belonging within the family and often needing protection within the neighborhood make joining a gang a logical and rational move for the poor, inner-city child. Being accepted by a gang meets a real need: It gives a boy, and sometimes a girl, a sense of belonging. It eliminates the terrible loneliness of "being no one" that a child who has lived in poverty often has. Gang membership gives a feeling of recognition. The more unfavorable the attention that television and other media give gang activity, the more special the gang members feel (Prothrow-Stith, 1991). A Los Angeles school teacher who works at a gang-besieged junior high school in Watts described the attraction of gangs for the children at her school:

> It's a very insecure way of life that they come from and children at this age need a lot of security. They need rules and guidelines. Many of them come with very, very poor academic skills from elementary school. They can't read . . . they're just prime for something positive. The gangs have a structure that they gravitate towards because there are rules, there are colors, there are guidelines. And this is what all kids need. Gang activity manifests itself on a day-to-day basis. For example, I'll come in, in the morning, and my classroom will have been vandalized. And the gang graffiti will be all over the posters and the walls. And the kids see it as a positive way to make a statement. I've been here. I was here. . . . I was part of something. (Brokaw, 1989)

In the gang, each member is valued by the group and in their estimation is someone worth dying for. Sneaky, a 19-year-old gang member and convicted felon from Los Angeles, explained his commitment to the gang, "This is our own little family . . . I love these guys with all my heart" (Prothrow-Stith, 1991, p. 106).

The gangs, usually male, that are formed in early adolescence are generally very organized. They have initiation rituals that provide a way for the adolescent to prove himself by undergoing some sort of trial; they require specific forms of dress, insignia, rules, and hand symbols; and they frequently engage in violence (Klein, 1995). When young adolescent men form a gang, the group exerts a powerful influence that is capable of eliciting vile acts from adolescents who in themselves appear to be rather ordinary (Fagin, 1990). In schools in which there are gangs, the reported number of weapons in the school doubles, and gang members are more heavily involved in violence than students who are not in gangs. A national survey in the United States showed that the reported number of gangs increased from 19% in Grade 6 to about 40% from Grade 9 and up (Bastian & Taylor, 1991).

GIRL GANGS

An increasingly serious problem throughout Western Europe and the United States is the girl gang (Randall, 1997). The rise of girl gangs in the United States has reached such epic proportions that gangs have their own magazine, *Team Angles*. The following case study (Chaudhuri, 1994, p. 6) shows the pleasure that these girls experience from intimidating others:

> For no reason at all the girl sitting opposite the victim on the Bakerloo underground line in London suddenly leaned forward with a hideous expression on her face and said, "Fuck off, bitch." The victim, a reporter, was about to make some suitable reply when she noticed that this girl had three companions, all aged around 16 and dressed in thigh-length black socks, miniskirts and over-sized baseball jackets. Two of them were heavily built and moved rapidly to sit on either side of the reporter. After further threats, one of the girls made to snatch away the reporter's Walkman but was thwarted when the train pulled into the next station. The reporter, not unsurprisingly, said that she was terrified by the experience.

Campbell (1995), who has studied aggression in girl gang members in the United Kingdom and the United States, believes that their cruel aggression is aimed at gaining respect and acceptance among their peer group and particularly their male peers. In one instance, South London police appealed for witnesses to a brutal attack on a 14-year-old girl by three girls ages 11 to 14. She was stripped and beaten and, it is claimed, offered to a gang of boys for rape (Chaudhuri, 1994).

RICH KIDS' GANGS

In the past decade a new type of gang organization has moved into Manhattan. The members of these gangs are some of Manhattan's most privileged teenagers who have joined forces with their ghetto counterparts. Each gang is usually made up of the richest rich teenagers and the poorest poor ones: White, African American, Asian

American, and Latinos all working together. They travel about in rented chauffeured cars selling pot to customers who happen to be classmates at the top private schools in Manhattan. They steal from stores and from other teenagers' homes whose wealthy parents are out of town. They estimate their take in the tens of thousands of dollars. A reporter who rode around with one group for one evening said that these teenagers were not playing at gangster activities, they were gangsters (Sales, 1996). Except that they are free to make new friends on their own, these groups clearly qualify as gangs. They have names such as Blunts, Forties Sex, and Who's King Now as well as their own territories. Their parents have no idea what their children are doing. One member told the reporter that his parents thought that he was a deliveryman. However, that changed when a warrant went out for his arrest for stealing jewelry from another member's apartment. When members were asked where they saw themselves in the next few years, one rich boy said that he would get a legal job and just have another way of laundering the money. He added that he scored 1,520 on his SATs and planned to go to Columbia University.

YUPPY GANGS

In 1994, Prime Minister John Major of England declared war on the "yob culture," his targets being gangs of young men who were associated with disturbances at football matches (Muncie, 1999). However, other adult gangs can arise in all kinds of subgroups, as the following case study of a "yuppy" gang shows:

> Simon, Frank, Joel, Mel and Simone were well-off professional people working in investment services. Their money bought them expensive cars, clothes, food, and holidays, but soon their tastes were jaded and they sought fun elsewhere. Simon and Mel had been physically tough bullies at public school and had enjoyed intimidating weaker boys. Simone was also a bully. . . . Joel and Frank were basically passive watchers of aggression with an undisclosed admiration for powerful bullies.
>
> After a few designer drinks too many after work Mel had suddenly announced that he wanted to give someone, anyone, "a good kicking." He soon found a 15-year-old boy pushing his bike with its punctured tyre. Mel walked into the boy's path, accused the youngster of not watching where he was going, and violently assaulted him. Simone then egged Simon to do something similar, followed by Joel and then Frank. Two days later Simone assaulted a young girl walking her dog, and fairly soon this yuppy

> gang had found its new and thrilling diversion. (Randall, 1997, pp. 40–41)

Home Office statistics show that crimes of violence amongst women are rising. Between 1982 and 1992, there was a 73% increase in the number of women found guilty of violent crimes (Mirrlees-Black, Budd, Partridge, & Mayhew, 1998).

COMMENT

Teenage gangs are not a problem limited only to the United States, Canada, and the United Kingdom; rather, they are an international problem. Particularly dispiriting are the gangs in Russia. Free education in Russia ends after Class 9 when the children are 14 or 15 years old. At that point, some children run away from home or from children's homes. Homeless children have long been a problem in the Soviet Union: By the mid-1990s there were over 200,000 homeless children. Not all are orphans: In 1988, 80% had one or both parents alive. Of those who are still at school or have just left school after Class 9, too many come home one day only to find that their parents have sold their apartment and left, with no forwarding address and only a note saying, "Go to the neighbors." Because the state homes for abandoned children are already overcrowded, there is, in fact, nowhere for a child treated in this way to go. However, if according to police statistics the children are already juvenile delinquents, they are welcomed in the well-organized gangs in Moscow. Gang membership probably represents the only viable solution to the teenager's dilemma ("Free to Roam the Streets in Gangs," 1993).

Approaches to Gang Elimination

Most efforts to deal with the gang problem are based on a treatment approach, which involves working with already established gangs, as opposed to a prevention approach. Horne et al. (1994) cautioned that schools using Olweus's (1993a) program, or other programs designed to reduce bullying, should make a distinction between working with an individual bully and working with a bully gang. They pointed out that it is possible to use the power of the group (e.g., the class and the teachers) when attempting to change the individual bully's behavior. However, a punitive approach with a well-established group of bullies can work against the goal of changing their behavior because it may create an increased sense of solidarity in what is already a cohesive group. Also to be considered is the fact that when a gang jointly engages in bullying another student, some group mechanisms are likely to be operative (Olweus, 1978). These include social contagion, the weakening of control or inhibitions against aggressive tendencies, diffusion of responsibility, and gradual cognitive changes in the perception of bullying and of the victim. Horne et al. recommended a "divide and conquer" approach in dealing with the bully gang. Olweus (1993a) found that when gang members were approached individually, they were more responsive to talking about their bullying and somewhat more receptive to changing their behavior; when treated as a group, they were strongly resistant to any such change.

THE PREVENTION APPROACH

One of the few programs in the prevention category was initiated by the Phoenix, Arizona, Police Department (McEvoy, 1990). Called the Gang Resistance Education and Training (G.R.E.A.T.) Program, its purpose is to provide children in the lower grades with the skills necessary to resist becoming gang members. It targets seventh-grade students, but some schools have offered it to sixth and eighth graders. Also available are a third- and fourth-grade component and a summer program component. The choice of these age groups was based on observers' beliefs that many school children are predisposed to gang membership at those levels and much active gang recruitment occurs at the later elementary school levels and in middle school (McEvoy, 1990). The program is taught by trained uniformed police officers over 9 consecutive weeks in the school year. It covers such topics as

- How to resolve conflicts
- Meeting basic needs without joining a gang
- How cultural differences affect the school and neighborhood
- How drugs affect the individual, the school, and neighborhood
- Crimes, victims, and their impact on the school and neighborhood
- Setting short- and long-term goals
- Responsibilities of students in the school and the neighborhood (Winfree, Esbensen, & Osgood, 1995).

The police officer-instructors have detailed lesson plans that serve as instructional guides. Classroom teachers are given a copy of the curriculum and must remain in the classroom during the lessons. Students who complete the program receive a certificate in the 10th week.

The program originated in the Police Department in Phoenix, Arizona, and in 1991 it was tested as a pilot project in seven school districts in the Phoenix area. By September 1994, a total of 954 police officers in 43 states had completed training. A comprehensive multisite evaluation of the program is currently under way (Winfree et al., 1995).

Law-Related Education

The optimum approach in efforts to eliminate violence and other forms of delinquency is prevention. One such approach that since 1978 has gained widespread and enthusiastic acceptance throughout the United States is a program called Law-Related Education (LRE) for elementary through high school students (Lawrence, 1998). Since 1984, LRE programs have been conducted in 670 school districts in the United States; 52,000 teachers and resource persons have been trained, reaching an estimated 2.4 million students (Office of Juvenile Justice and Delinquency Prevention, 1999).

LRE aims to teach students about the law, the legal system, how the courts work, and why citizens who break the law must be held accountable for their illegal activities. It is designed to help students understand that rights and responsibilities are a part of everyday life. It emphasizes good citizenship and encourages them to become more accountable for their actions. Effective LRE programs engage students in lively debates about school locker searches, freedom of the press in student publications, computer crimes, and environmental laws. By teaching students about the law through active and relevant engagement, it is hoped that they will gain a deeper understanding that will then promote positive attitudes toward the law and prosocial behavior. This is a program that should be a part of every school's curriculum.

Guns

In the last 3 years, there have been more than 12 school shootings, with over 120 students and teachers injured or killed (Nyhan, 1999). Note that Handgun Control, Inc., the most established gun control lobbyists on Capitol Hill, joined forces on October 1, 2001, with the 230 chapters of a Million Moms, the first nationwide grassroots gun control movement. The new combined group will be known as the Brady Campaign to Prevent Handgun Violence. The first item on the group's agenda is closing the loophole that allows minors and others to buy guns at gun shows easily and illegally. The merger of these two powerful groups is cause for real optimism about gun control (Dahl, 2001).

Most of the shootings had three factors in common. One is bullying. Case studies have shown that most of the school shooters had been bullied, ostracized, and generally treated like third-class members of society:

> Every day being teased and picked on, pushed up against lockers—just the general feeling of fear in the school. And you either respond to a fear by having fear, or you take action and have hate. (Brooks Brown, a student at Columbine High who knew both Eric Harris and Dylan Klebold) (Strasser, 2000, p. 26)

Their violent reaction to being bullied is consistent with the conclusion of James Gilligan, a Harvard psychiatrist who has spent years interviewing convicted murderers in Massachusetts. He said, "Nothing stimulates violence as powerfully as the experience of being shamed and humiliated" (Gilligan, 1996, p. 102). A second factor is the ready availability of guns in the United States coupled with the mildest of restrictions on gun ownership and usage:

> The killers (in school shootings) were able to easily acquire high-powered guns, and in many cases, their parents helped the children get them, either directly or through negligence. Guns with rapid-fire capability . . . that can spray a burst of bullets in a matter of seconds, were used in the incidents with the most victims. ("High Power Guns," 1998, p. A3)

The United States has almost 1 gun for every man, woman, and child—260 million people and 240 million guns of all types—a number that is increasing by 5 to 7 million a year, with 3 new guns rolling off the production line every minute (Handgun Control, Inc., 1996). The Second Amendment of the Constitution specifies the individual's right to bear arms. What has happened in the United States is not what the drafters of the Constitution intended, but it has been the basis for the National Rifle Association's (NRA's) position supporting an unlimited right to bear arms. The NRA very conveniently overlooks the fact that the Second Amendment was referring to the militia's right to bear arms, not the general public's right to do so (Rakove, 2002). Although public opinion polls show that 77% of Americans say that the age for owning handguns should be raised from 18 to 21, and that 85% favor trigger locks on new handguns to discourage accidental or impulsive firing, the powerful and well-financed NRA, along with other progun groups, has succeeded in blocking all but the mildest gun law reforms.

Consider the problem of the ready availability of guns in this country. There are 60 million handguns in America (Cook & Ludwig, 2000). Many adults, especially parents, are justifiably bitter about how easy it is to buy a gun. The resistance to gun laws that would impose restrictions on the manufacture and availability of guns is set in cement. Two extremely powerful groups oppose such laws. One is the NRA, a very rich, progun association, and the other is the gun industry. Every year 2.5 million new handguns are sold in the United States. The fact is that the gun industry is a business, and the people who make and sell guns are business people who want to make as much money as possible.

Other countries are not hampered by this misinterpretation of the Second Amendment, and the statistics reflect their different policies. Consider this report from a lobbying group in Washington, DC: "In 1996, handguns were used to murder two people in New Zealand, 15 in Japan, 30 in Great Britain, 106 in Canada, 213 in Germany and 9,390 in the United States" (Handgun Control, Inc., 1996). Note that only a tiny fraction of the guns manufactured in Japan stay in that country. Japan has very strict gun control laws. The majority of the guns manufactured there are shipped to the United States (Handgun Control, Inc., 1996).

In addition, when faced with a gun problem, many countries have in place a framework for taking immediate and decisive action. In Dunbane, Scotland, after a disgruntled Scoutmaster killed 16 nursery school children and their teacher, Great Britain had a law in effect in 2 weeks that banned handguns and required owners to turn them into the police. Following a shooting in Australia when a man using a semiautomatic rifle murdered 35 people, the gun laws were severely tightened. Under existing regulations, these changes could not happen at the federal level in the United States. However, at the state level, changes are possible. Massachusetts, for example, has the nation's best record on regulating firearms. Over the past 4 years, the state has had the lowest violent crime rate per capita in the country, with gun laws requiring training, licensing, a 21-year-old age limit, safe storage, child safety devices, and limits on gun dealers operating out of their cars or at garage sales (Nyhan, 1999).

The third common factor in the school shootings is a more pervasive one: The United States has become a culture of violence. The current school generation is steeped in violence from horror movies, TV programs that cater to children's violent fantasies, warlike video games such as Doom and Duke Nukem, and teenage fiction that describes in detail how to torture someone, plan a murder, or build a bomb. Today's teenagers are accustomed to wars and fighting in other countries, including Ireland, Iraq, and Kosovo, and TV coverage spares none of the details. As a result, many of today's teenagers have become desensitized to violence, often without being aware that there are consequences for their own or others' violent actions. They are out of touch with the hard realities. How else to explain, as cited earlier, the surprise, dismay, and resentment of a boy being treated for a gunshot wound that being shot hurt? Exposure to media violence of a fictitious kind is not conducive to understanding consequences: The actor shot and killed in one sequence reappears later in good health.

One danger of the explicit details shown on TV after a school shooting is that it spawns copycat shootings. After the Littleton, Colorado, massacre in April 1999, schools were warned of this possibility, and in the month following the shootings there were over 100 shootings planned, many of which did not come to fruition. The worst one was in Palatka, Florida, where two boys were intercepted and jailed before they could put their plans into effect. The realities of their legal position were so foreign to them that they boasted to their school principal and the police that their plan was even better in terms of mortality potential than the plan at Littleton had been.

In a national survey of junior and senior high school students (N = 2,017) titled *Lethal Violence in Schools*, Gaughan, Cerio, and Myers (2001) reported that 12% of the students said that there was nothing that could be done to stop school shootings. Those surveyed also believed that revenge was the strongest motivation for school shooting: 87% said that shootings were motivated by a desire to "get back at those who have hurt them" (p. 10), and 86% said that "other kids picking on them, making fun of them or bullying them" (p. 10) causes teenagers to turn to lethal violence in the schools.

After an incident of school shooting, schools generally react by hiring more security guards, installing metal detectors, and searching lockers. While such procedures are often necessary, a growing number of experts say that a more effective deterrent to school shootings and other teenage violence may be to focus on stopping bullying, a task that involves not just the bullies but their victims as well. In the case of the Littleton disaster, such a step would involve a complete examination of the philosophy and goals of the school followed by a massive firing of personnel.

THE LESSONS OF LITTLETON

The Littleton tragedy has aspects that are relevant to the problem of gun violence in the United States (Cook & Ludwig, 2000, p. 5):

> One feature of this attack cannot be ignored: Harris and Klebold, like other student killers before them, used guns to accomplish their grim purpose. They also tried, unsuccessfully, to use bombs, *but without guns, the enterprise would have been unthinkable* [italics added].

The consequences of Littleton and other school shootings go well beyond the injuries and loss of life, one result being a new and valid reason for anxiety on the part of students, their parents, and school personnel (Pollack, 2000). In addition to these emotional costs are the related financial costs to repair the damage to the peace of mind that most parents and children in suburban areas have about the safety of the school setting. For example, in Allen, Texas, a suburb of Dallas, officials are spending $1 million to bring in metal detectors, surveillance cameras, and a new security force and are also requiring students to wear identification badges. In the costly pursuit of safety, common sense is often lost in the process, resulting in zero-tolerance rules that may elicit criticism from parents, which filters down to the children as implicit approval to disregard school safety measures that are of real importance for their safety and well-being. Consider these examples:

> A Pittsburgh kindergarten boy was disciplined in 1998 because his Hallowe'en firefighter costume included a plastic axe. In Cobb County, Georgia, a sixth-grade girl was suspended in 2000 because the ten-inch key chain on her Tweety Bird wallet was considered a weapon in violation of the school's zero tolerance policy. (Derbyshire, 2001, p. 46)

When someone does report a potential problem to school personnel, the feedback that person gets from peers is largely negative even when the subsequent searches provide concrete evidence supporting the likelihood that an attack was being planned. Typical of this negative reaction from peers is the case of Kim (Magnarelli, 2001), who told a school counselor that her former boyfriend had been building bigger and bigger bombs and that he and his friends had marked asterisks on a map of their school that she thought might be for bomb locations. When police raided the boy's house, they found unequivocal support for Kim's suspicions. Despite these events, Kim's classmates harassed her and called her derogatory names, and some accused her of being a part of the plot. Her twin sister deserted her and sided with the others. However, Kim stood firmly by her decision to inform school personnel.

Knowing about such potentially catastrophic plans is no guarantee that officials will be notified about them. In a poll of 2,719 students, 38% said that they had heard a fellow student threaten to kill someone, but only 11% reported it. These findings are consistent with those of other studies (Magnarelli, 2001). Another study found that most perpetrators of school shootings had told others, usually peers, of their plans, which suggests that efforts should be directed at the code of silence. One contributor to maintaining this code is fear of retribution. For students who want to remain anonymous, schools should have tip boxes, e-mail addresses, or anonymous tip telephone lines such as those in Illinois, Georgia, Michigan, and North Carolina. In addition, long-term campaigns should be mounted to reduce or eliminate the stigma associated with reporting potential attacks and other antisocial behaviors.

THE COST OF GUN VIOLENCE

In 2000, Philip Cook of Duke University and Jens Ludwig of Georgetown University coauthored *Gun Violence: The Real Costs*. Their text is the first to document the many ways in which gun violence affects the United States. They have tallied all the direct and indirect costs that we pay for gun violence, including medical costs, metal detectors, taxes paid for the protection of public officials, the cost of urban renewal projects in areas devastated by gun violence, the loss of workplace productivity, the costs of putting policemen and surveillance cameras in public schools, the costs of medical treatment for gunshop injuries, earning losses from gun violence, and many more. Their final figure on the annual costs of gun violence in the United States was $100 billion. When costs of this magnitude and reports of how many people were killed with handguns in the United States in one year are publicized, the NRA has rebutted with indifferent cynicism that "this is the price of freedom."

Cook and Ludwig (2000) set out a policy agenda that they believed had strong possibilities for reducing the problem of gun violence. Their first recommendation was to regulate secondary-market sales, the major source of guns used in criminal activity. This goal could be accomplished by making the registration of handguns a law. Although mandatory gun registration was proposed in 1995 (Jacobs & Potter, 1999), the measure was defeated because voters were afraid that gun registration would make it easier for the government to confiscate all guns at some point in the future (Cook & Ludwig, 2000).

Their second recommendation was that police patrols to detect illegal gun carrying could produce benefits that far outweigh the measurable costs. The critical question here is, Do these net gains outweigh the costs that cannot easily be defined, such as the resentment that could occur among individuals who are stopped and searched? While residents of high-crime neighborhoods would likely be the main targets of police patrols, the benefit of such a policy would also accrue primarily to those neighborhoods.

Their agenda's third recommendation was that increasing the severity of sentences might reduce gun violence, and the available evidence is supportive of this proposal. In the fourth recommendation, Cook and Ludwig (2000) firmly supported the public health departments' demand to regulate firearms as consumer products. They also supported alternatives to direct regulation that would achieve the same result. For example, requiring gun owners to buy insurance for their firearms could substitute the premium-setting process for direct regulation in providing an incentive for greater safety features.

Their fifth and final recommendation was that Congress provide financial support for the collection of better scientific data on all types of injury. The goal of this procedure would be to collect detailed information about all facets of an injury. Although such a system might cost several million dollars per annum to develop and administer, Cook and Ludwig (2000) argued that the potential benefits from such a data bank, in the form of improving program design and gun policy, are considerable.

Note that Cook and Ludwig (2000) asserted that their foregoing proposals are widely supported and they should impact on most gun owners being able to keep guns at home either for their own protection or for sport. In conclusion, they stated:

> The current policy regime has left us with a gun problem that imposes substantial costs on everyone in America. Gun violence can be reduced, and many of the interventions designed to separate guns from violence essentially pay for themselves. (Cook & Ludwig, 2000, p. 134)

The Vermont Crisis

Probably no state was as astonished about the sudden rise of violence in the school-age population as Vermont was, a state that until recently had been ranked at or near the top of America's "safest" and "most livable" states. Vermont's largest city, Burlington, had been singled out for national awards such as the City Livability Award from the U.S. Conference of Mayors and was frequently described as a "kid-friendly city" with superior air quality, impressive public safety, one of the lowest crime rates in the nation, ideal pupil–teacher ratios in the schools, and excellent funding levels for the arts and education in general. Many young couples with children moved to Vermont in the 1980s and 1990s because they wanted to raise their children in "the safety and harmony of a tight-knit community" (Powers, 2002, p. 58).

However, in the last 5 years, there has been a radical change in this picture of serenity. In many Vermont public schools armed and uniformed police guards have become a familiar fixture as an epidemic of bomb threats became a fact of adolescent life. In the mid-1990s, urban youth gangs began to trickle into Vermont from neighboring states, to the delight of Vermont teenagers. Dozens of adolescents, bored with school and their working-class families, joined the gangs and in the process learned new "skills" such as extortion and how to deal drugs. Heroin addiction, which as recently as 1997 had been virtually unknown in the state, was a well-established crisis by 2000. By early 2001, the volume of confiscated heroin had increased fourfold in the previous 2-year period. Every town of substantial size had many young addicts, and the local newspapers began reporting deaths from overdose. In 2001, *The Burlington Free Press* reported that "heroin is almost as easy to get in Burlington as a gallon of maple syrup" (Powers, 2002, p. 64). Concomitantly, there was an explosion of serious juvenile crime: In 3 years, the number of jail inmates between the ages of 16 and 21 jumped by 77%, and the overcrowded prisons had to send prisoners to out-of-state jails. The Department of Corrections supervised or housed 1 out of every 10 Vermont males of school age, and their annual budget during the 1990s increased from $27 million to more than $70 million.

Meanwhile, there was a series of acts of lethal violence committed by apparently "ordinary" teenagers from "ordinary" communities who Powers (2002, p. 58) described as having become "detached from civic life and saturated by the mythic violent imagery of popular culture, and consumed by the dictates of some private murderous fantasy." Representative of these acts was the murder in 1997 outside Rutland, Vermont, of the owner of a tattoo shop by two local boys ages 18 and 16. They were armed with a gurkha, an extremely sharp combat knife. The older boy, who committed the murder to make his car payments, had also invited a 14-year-old boy to come along to watch. In another case, Jane Hubbard, a 59-year-old English woman who supervised foster children, was awakened in 1999 by two of her charges, boys who were 15 and 14. They demanded her car keys, and when she refused, the older boy punched her in the face while the younger one held her down. The puncher idly remarked to his accomplice, "I've never seen anything swell that fast. . . . Just like in the movies." They decided not to kill her but to drive her somewhere and leave her in a ditch, where she eventually was picked up by a passing motorist. The boys returned to her house for guns and ammunition, which they planned to sell. When they were picked up by the police, one of the boys said with a laugh, "If you had to listen to that British voice, you'd want to kill her, too," but they told the police they had "chickened out" about this.

In June 2000, Theo Padnos, who had completed a PhD in comparative literature from the University of Massachusetts and wanted to teach but could not find a university teaching job, applied for a part-time job teaching literature to adolescents and adults in a Vermont Department of Corrections facility and taught there for 13 months. Teachers in this facility were protected from their charges with surveillance cameras and walkie-talkies. Classroom doors were always left open to allow fast entry by guards, and jail "snitches" were placed in the classrooms. Padnos rejected all of these protection moves because he wanted to "humanize" his students. Consequently, he not only closed but also locked the classroom door and even allowed the group to have the jail snitches removed during classes. Most of the students were in for mid-level crimes such as robbery, but there also were gang members, adult rapists, and murderers. Most of the younger ones had not as yet broken through to violent crime, but Padnos (Powers, 2002, p. 68) described them as fascinated by violence in general:

> Violent crime was the one topic to which they could devote sustained concentration. When my classes touched on the subject . . . they became a kind of seminar. Everyone was well informed and prepared to teach something.

When Padnos asked them how often they read the police files, the witness statements, and other information the prosecution had turned over to the defense, they would say, "All the time. Over and over. And over." Arranging their future crimes was the long-term extracurricular project that kept them busy, and they got constant guidance and reinforcement from the hardened jailbirds in their midst. It was clear to Padnos that these youths were not thinking about getting jobs or going back to school.

As Padnos thinks back on this experience now, he concedes that the course was a failure because the inmates were beyond the point of this kind of help by the time they were put in prison. But in his teaching sessions a transformation occurred that he had never anticipated. The prisoners gradually came to accept Padnos as one of themselves, possibly because he had jettisoned the classroom safeguards. Whatever the reason, he found himself privy to conversations that he says were the language of apocalypse:

> The goal of the bright ones is to truly mesmerize the middle class with violence. . . . They've been transfixed by disaster themselves—in their families, at the movies, in the company of their mentors in crime. They've come to feel that there's nothing out there for them, and so they know exactly the effect they're looking for: They keep up with the news. They read about their deeds in the papers. They've been ignored all their lives, and they're pleased to see that the public is finally giving them some of the attention they're due. The papers always describe their crimes as "senseless," and "meaningless," and "unmotivated," and these kids themselves always come off as "cold" and "distant" to the reporters. The details of their crimes are always covered with the tightest possible focus, as if meaning might be found there. The result is just what they'd been hoping for: terrifying, mesmerizing violence, and no context. (Powers, 2002, p. 68, from an interview with Theo Padnos)

Eventually the gangs in Vermont were crushed by a variety of paramilitary tactics including surveillance, nightly phone calls to the parents of adolescents who were suspected gang members, reportedly rough physical interrogations, and infiltration by informants. The situation apparently returned to normal for everyone except the children.

WHY WERE THE GANGS SO ATTRACTIVE?

No one pursued the question that should have been explored, in depth, with the same tenacity applied to the problem of getting rid of the gangs: What was it about the gangs that had made them so appealing to Vermont children in the first place? Little attention was given to the answers from the few children who were asked. According to Powers (2002, p. 65),

> they saw the gangs as a replacement for something missing in their lives—namely, a community that satisfied their longings for worth-proving ritual, meaningful action in the service of a cause, and psychological intimacy.

Confirmation by an adult of this explanation came from an investigator with the state public defender's office. He told Powers that the gangs were not all bad, that they took care of each other, and then he said:

> They come up here to Vermont to chill out, or because there's not as many cops. And who's waiting for them. Our kids. Our kids, the MTV generation. To them, these guys look like TV stars! So our kids . . . who feel lost, disenfranchised—they join up! And why not? They don't have enough support services in this state. I mean, look . . . at the communities in this state that wage war on their youth. You've got Vergennes, kicking kids out of the park. You've got Woodstock banning skateboarding. . . . What I'm seeing in recent years is the total and complete alienation of youth . . . it is not coming from them; it's coming from the adults who aren't bothering to reach out to them. And it is terrifying. (Powers, 2002, p. 65)

The Inevitability of Conflict but Not of Violence

In May 1986, 20 scholars from different countries and representing a number of disciplines, including neuroscience, psychology, and biology, gathered in Seville, Spain, to draft the Seville Statement on Violence (1986/1989). Their purpose was to question certain biological findings that have been used to defend the use of violence and warfare. In their opening statement they made the point that their justification for questioning the biological findings was that these findings have created an unnecessary feeling of pessimism in our time. They contended that it is scientifically incorrect to claim that war or any other form of violence is genetically programmed in mankind. Genes only provide a developmental potential; they do not produce individuals who are predisposed to violence. Further, it is scientifically incorrect to assert that war is caused by "instinct" or any such motivation, or that man has a "violent brain" and has inherited a tendency to make war from our animal ancestors.

The fact that warfare occurs frequently among humans signifies that war is a product of human culture, that is, that language, tools, and technology have made war possible. There are cultures that have never engaged in war and others that are frequently at war. Conflict is an inevitable part of social life, but violence is not. Björkqvist (1997, p. 35) stated that "if modern warfare is a consequence of human culture rather than of human nature, perhaps culture is also the best cure against it." As the Seville Statement on Violence (1986/1989) noted, the species that invented warfare should also be capable of inventing peace. What is needed is a change in the general attitude toward violence.

In an introductory comment in their chapter in the Seville Statement on Violence, the editors (Fry & Björkqvist, 1997, p. 25) noted:

> Scripts for how to behave in conflict situations are learned, and they are to a great extent dependent on culture. Anger, which is a natural human emotion, may serve as an invigorating factor, encouraging the choice of aggressive scripts. Whereas conflict constitutes an inevitable part of social life, violence can be avoided, and alternative scripts employed.

Final Comment

It is clear from the large number of researchers whose work has been referred to in this text that the topics of bullying, teasing, and violence have aroused intensive interest, fueled by humanitarian concerns on the part of the public and by political anxiety about the skyrocketing costs of these antisocial problems. Although some geographical areas have been characterized by a particularly high research output, the many other small pockets of research activity justify the descriptor "global" for the combined efforts. The variety in focus is especially impressive, with some bursts of creativity that have opened up new avenues of research. Particularly praiseworthy are those researchers who have pursued long-term interests and have established definite prevention procedures on an empirical base. In doing so, the opportunity for frequent publications has been bypassed in favor of single substantial contributions over the long haul. Others have sought out alternatives that might exist in fields not generally viewed as potentially pertinent. This form of risk taking has produced some intriguing results.

In considering the overall field, three researchers come to mind as particularly noteworthy for what they have done, how they have gone about it, the caliber of their ideas, and the changes that have occurred as a result of their findings. They are Dan Olweus, David G. Perry, and Peter K. Smith. Future researchers owe them a debt of gratitude for helping to build a solid foundation for subsequent work, not to speak of the many children who have benefited, and will continue to benefit, from their impressive work.

References

AAUW Educational Foundation. (1993). *Hostile hallways: The AAUW survey on sexual harassment in America's schools.* Annapolis Junction, MD: Author.

Achenbach, T. M. (1991). *Manual for the Child Behavior Checklist/4-18 and 1991 Profile.* Burlington: University of Vermont, Department of Psychiatry.

Adams, A. (1992). Holding out against work place harassment and bullying. *Personnel Management, 24,* 48–50.

Adlam, E. (1991, April 12). The tormented pupils. *Times Educational Supplement,* pp. 19–21.

Ahmad, Y., & Smith, P. K. (1990). Behavioral measures: Bullying in schools. *Newsletter of Association for Child Psychology and Psychiatry, 12,* 26–27.

Ahmad, Y., & Smith, P. K. (1994). Bullying in schools and the issue of sex differences. In J. Archer (Ed.), *Male violence* (pp. 70–83). New York: Routledge.

Akhtar, S., & Stronach, I. (1986, September 19). They call me Blacky. *Times Educational Supplement,* p. 23.

Alberts, J. K. (1992). An inferential/strategic explanation for the social organization of teases. *Journal of Language and Social Psychology, 11,* 153–177.

Alsaker, F. D., & Valkanover, S. (2001). Early diagnosis and prevention of victimization in kindergarten. In J. Juvonen & S. Graham (Eds.), *Peer harassment in school* (pp. 175–195). New York: Guilford Press.

Ananiadou, K., & Smith, P. K. (2002). Legal requirements and nationally circulated materials against school bullying in European countries. *Criminal Justice,* 2.

Anthony, E. J. (1974). A risk-vulnerability intervention model. In E. J. Anthony & C. Koupernik (Eds.), *The child in his family* (Vol. 3, pp. 99–121). New York: Wiley.

Ariès, P. (1962). *Centuries of childhood: A social history of family life.* New York: Knopf.

Arnold, J. C. (1995). *Alcohol and the chosen few: Organizational reproduction in an addictive system.* Unpublished doctoral dissertation, Indiana University, Bloomington.

Arora, C. M. J., & Thompson, D. A. (1987). Defining bullying for a secondary school. *Education and Child Psychology, 4,* 110–120.

Arora, T. (1991). The use of victim support groups. In P. K. Smith & D. Thompson (Eds.), *Practical approaches to bullying* (pp. 36–47). London: David Fulton.

Arseneault, L., Tremblay, R. E., Boulerice, B., & Saucier, J. -F. (2002). Obstetrical complications and violent delinquency: Testing two developmental pathways. *Child Development, 73,* 496–508.

Askew, S. (1989). Aggressive behaviour in boys: To what extent is it institutionalized? In D. P. Tattum & D. A. Lane (Eds.), *Bullying in schools* (pp. 59–71). Stoke-on-Trent, England: Trentham Books.

Baldwin, M. W. (1992). Relational schemas and the processing of social information. *Psychological Bulletin, 112,* 461–484.

Band, E. B., & Weisz, J. R. (1988). How to feel better when it feels bad: Children's perspectives on coping with everyday stress. *Developmental Psychology, 24,* 247–253.

Bandura, A. (1969). *Principles of behavior modification.* New York: Holt, Rinehart.

Bandura, A. (1977). *Social learning theory.* Englewood Cliffs, NJ: Prentice Hall.

Bandura, A. (1986). *Social foundations of thought and action: A social cognitive theory.* Englewood Cliffs, NJ: Prentice Hall.

Bandura, A., & Walters, R. H. (1959). *Adolescent aggression.* New York: Ronald Press.

Barden, R. (1989). *The facts about gangs.* Los Angeles: Crestwood House.

Barnett, W. S. (1993). Benefit–cost analysis of preschool education: Findings from a 25-year follow-up. *American Journal of Orthopsychiatry, 63,* 500–508.

Bastian, L., & Taylor, B. (1991). *National crime victimization survey report.* Washington, DC: U.S. Bureau of Justice Statistics.

Batsch, G. M., & Knoff, H. M. (1994). Bullies and their victims: Understanding a pervasive problem in the schools. *School Psychology Review, 23,* 165–174.

Beck, A. T. (1986). Hopelessness as a predictor of eventual suicide. *Annals of the New York Academy of Sciences, 487,* 90–96.

Bentley, K. M., & Li, A. K. F. (1995). Bully and victim problems in elementary schools and students' beliefs about aggression. *Canadian Journal of School Psychology, 11,* 153–165.

Bergman, G. (1973). *Why does your dog do that?* New York: Howell Books.

Berrueta-Clement, J. R., Schweinhart, L. J., Barnett, W. S., Epstein, A. S., & Weikart, D. P. (1984). *Changed lives: The effects of the Perry Preschool Program on youths through age 19.* Ypsilanti, MI: High/Scope Press.

Besag, V. E. (1989). *Bullies and victims in schools.* Milton Keynes, England: Open University Press.

Bierman, K. L., & Smoot, D. L. (1991). Linking family characteristics with poor peer relations: The mediating role of conduct problems. *Journal of Abnormal Child Psychology, 19,* 341–356.

Björkqvist, K. (1994). Sex differences in physical, verbal, and indirect aggression: A review of recent research. *Sex Roles, 30,* 177–188.

Björkqvist, K. (1997). The inevitability of conflict but not violence: Theoretical considerations on conflict and aggression. In D. P. Fry & K. Björkqvist

(Eds.), *Cultural variation in conflict resolution: Alternatives to violence* (pp. 25–36). Mahwah, NJ: Erlbaum.

Björkqvist, K. L., Lagerspetz, K. M. J., & Kaukiainen, A. (1992). Do girls manipulate and boys fight? Developmental trends in regard to direct and indirect aggression. *Aggressive Behavior, 18*, 117–127.

Björkqvist, K., & Österman, K. (1999). Finland. In P. K. Smith, Y. Morita, J. Junger-Tas, D. Olweus, R. Catalano, & P. Slee (Eds.), *The nature of school bullying: A cross-national perspective* (pp. 56–67). London: Routledge.

Björkqvist, K., Österman, K., & Kaukiainen, A. (1992). The development of direct and indirect aggressive strategies in males and females. In K. Björkqvist & P. Niemelä (Eds.), *Of mice and women: Aspects of female aggression* (pp. 51–64). San Diego, CA: Academic Press.

Björkqvist, K., Österman, K., & Lagerspetz, K. M. J. (1994). Sex differences in covert aggression. *Aggressive Behavior, 20*, 27–33.

Blanchard, D. C., & Blanchard, R. J. (1988). Ethoexperimental approaches to the biology of emotion. *Annual Review of Psychology, 39*, 131–134.

Blau, M. (1993). Just teasing. *American Health, 12*, 66–68.

Bolger, K. E., & Patterson, C. J. (2001). Developmental pathways from child maltreatment to peer rejection. *Child Development, 72*, 549–568.

Bolger, K. E., Patterson, C. J., & Kupersmidt, J. B. (1998). Peer relationships and self-esteem among children who have been maltreated. *Child Development, 69*, 1171–1197.

Boulton, M. J. (1999). Concurrent and longitudinal relations between children's playground behavior and social preference, victimization, and bullying. *Child Development, 70*, 944–954.

Boulton, M., & Hawker, D. (1997). Verbal bullying: The myth of "sticks and stones." In D. Tattum & G. Herbert (Eds.), *Bullying: Home, school, and community* (pp. 53–63). London: David Fulton.

Boulton, M. J., & Smith, P. K. (1994). Bully/victim problems in middle-school children: Stability, self-perceived competence, peer perceptions and peer acceptance. *British Journal of Developmental Psychology, 12*, 315–329.

Boulton, M. J., Trueman, M., Chau, C., Whitehand, C., & Amatya, K. (1999). Concurrent and longitudinal links between friendship and peer victimization: Implications for befriending interventions. *Journal of Adolescence, 22*, 461–466.

Boulton, M. J., & Underwood, K. (1992). Bully/victim problems among middle school children. *British Journal of Educational Psychology, 62*, 73–87.

Bowlby, J. (1973). *Attachment and loss: Vol. 2. Separation*. New York: Basic Books.

Brewer, D. D., Hawkins, J. D., Catalano, R. F., & Neckerman, H. J. (1995). Preventing serious, violent, and chronic juvenile offending. In J. D. Howell, B. Krisberg, J. D. Hawkins, & J. J. Wilson (Eds.), *A sourcebook: Serious, violent and chronic juvenile offenders* (pp. 61–141). Thousand Oaks, CA: Sage.

Brokaw, T. (1989, August 12). *Gangs, cops, and drugs* [News special]. New York: NBC News.

Brown, B. (2000). Quote in T. Strasser, *Give a boy a gun,* New York: Simon & Shuster, 2000, p. 26.

Brown, I. (1994, October 28). Nothing nice about tackling bullies. Features, *Times Educational Supplement,* p. 2.

Brown, J. M., O'Keefe, J., Sanders, S. H., & Baker, B. (1986). Developmental changes in children's cognition to stressful and painful situations. *Journal of Pediatric Psychology, 11,* 343–357.

Bugental, D. B., & Goodnow, J. J. (1998). Socialization processes. In N. Eisenberg (Vol. Ed.), *Handbook of child psychology: Vol. 3. Social, emotional, and personality development* (pp. 389–462). New York: Wiley.

Burke, R. J. (1995). Incidence and consequences of sexual harassment in a professional services firm. *Employee Counselling Today, 7,* 23–29.

Burnage Report. (1989). *Murder in the playground.* London: Longsight Press.

Buss, A. H., & Durkee, A. (1957). An inventory for assessing different kinds of hostility. *Journal of Consulting Psychology, 21,* 343–349.

Byrne, B. (1994). *Bullying: A community approach.* Dublin, Ireland: Columbia Press.

Campbell, A. C. (1995). Friendships as a factor in male and female delinquency. In H. C. Foot, A. J. Chapman, & J. R. Smith (Eds.), *Friendship and social relations in children.* New Brunswick, NJ: Transaction Publishers.

Cannon, M., & Jones, P. (1996). Schizophrenia. *Journal of Neurology, Neurosurgery, and Psychiatry, 61,* 604–613.

Cannon, T. D., Mednick, S. A., & Parnas, J. (1989). Genetic and perinatal determinants of structural brain deficits in schizophrenia. *Archives of General Psychiatry, 46,* 883–889.

Carr, R. A. (1988). The city-wide peer counselling program. *Children and Youth Services Review, 10,* 217–232.

Cash, T. F., & Janda, L. H. (1986, April). Body image survey report: The great American shape-up. *Psychology Today,* pp. 30–37.

Chaudhuri, A. (1994, October 13). Deadlier than the male. *Guardian,* p. 6.

Children's Legal Centre. (1996). *Bullying: A guide to the law* (Information Sheet 217). Essex, England: Author.

Clark, C. S. (1993, August). TV versus actual violence: Debate rises with crime. *Journal of the American Family Association, 11,* 6.

Clarke-McLean, J. G. (1996). Social networks among incarcerated juvenile offenders. *Social Development, 5,* 203–217.

Cloud, J., & Vaughan, G. M. (1970). Using balanced scales to control for acquiescence. *Sociometry, 33,* 193–202.

Cohen, S., & Wills, T. A. (1985). Stress, social support, and the buffering hypothesis. *Psychological Bulletin, 98,* 310–357.

Coie, J. D., & Christopoulos, C. (1989, November). *Types of aggressive relationships in boys' groups*. Paper presented at the biennial meeting of the Society for Research in Child Development, Kansas City, MO.

Colino, S. (1993, June/July). Fooling around or sexual harassment? *Parenting*, p. 30.

Collins, E. G. C., & Blodgett, T. B. (1981). Sexual harassment, some see it . . . some won't. *Harvard Business Review, 59*, 76–95.

Conley, F. K. (1998). *Walking out on the boys*. New York: Farrar, Straus, & Giroux.

Cook, P. J., & Ludwig, J. (2000). *Gun violence: The real costs*. New York: Oxford University Press.

Corson, D. (1992). Minority cultural values and discourse norms in majority culture classrooms. *Canadian Modern Language Review, 48*, 472–496.

Cottrell, N., & Epley, S. W. (1977). Affiliation, social comparison, and socially mediated stress reduction. In J. M. Suls & R. L. Miller (Eds.), *Social comparison processes: Theoretical and empirical perspectives* (pp. 43–68). Washington, DC: Hemisphere.

Coughlan, S. (1995, February 17). Screen violence in the firing line. *Times Educational Supplement*, Media Section, p. 23.

Cowen, E. L. (1994). The enhancement of psychological wellness: Challenges and opportunities. *American Journal of Community Psychology, 22*, 149–178.

Cowie, H. (1998). Perspectives of teachers and pupils on the experience of peer support against bullying. *Educational Research and Evaluation, 4*, 108–125.

Cowie, H. (1999). Peers helping peers: Interventions, initiatives and insights. *Journal of Adolescence, 22*, 433–436.

Cowie, H., Naylor, P., Talamelli, L., Chauhan, P., & Smith, P. K. (in press). Knowledge, use of and attitudes towards peer support: A two-year follow-up to the Prince's Trust survey. *Journal of Adolescence*.

Cowie, H., & Olafsson, R. (1999). The role of peer support against bullying. *School Psychology International, 20*, 96–105.

Cowie, H., & Sharp, S. (1992). Students themselves tackle the problem of bullying. *Pastoral Care in Education, 10*, 31–37.

Cowie, H., & Sharp, S. (1994). Tackling bullying through the curriculum. In P. K. Smith & S. Sharp (Eds.), *School bullying: Insights and perspectives* (pp. 84–107). New York: Routledge.

Craig, W., & Pepler, D. (1995). Peer processes in bullying and victimisation: An observational study. *Exceptionality Education Canada, 5*, 81–95.

Crary, D. (2001, April 20). Behavior problems found in day care. *Seattle Post-Intelligencer*, A. p. 14.

Crick, N. R. (1995). Relational aggression: The role of intent attributions, feelings of distress, and provocation type. *Development and Psychopathology, 7*, 313–322.

Crick, N. R., & Bigbee, M. A. (1998). Relational and overt forms of peer victimization: A multiinformant approach. *Journal of Consulting and Clinical Psychology, 66*, 337–347.

Crick, N. R., Casas, J. F., & Ku, H. C. (1999). Relational and physical forms of peer victimization in preschool. *Developmental Psychology, 35,* 376–385.

Crick, N. R., & Dodge, K. A. (1994). A review and reformulation of social information-processing mechanisms in children's social adjustment. *Psychological Bulletin, 115,* 74–101.

Crick, N. R., & Grotpeter, J. K. (1995). Relational aggression, gender, and social–psychological adjustment. *Child Development, 66,* 710–722.

Crick, N. R., & Grotpeter, J. K. (1996). Children's treatment by peers: Victims of relational and overt aggression. *Development and Psychopathology, 8,* 367–380.

Crick, N. R., Nelson, D. A., Morales, J. R., Cullerton-Sen, C., Casas, J. F., & Hickman, S. E. (2001). Relational victimization in childhood and adolescence: I hurt you through the grapevine. In J. Juvonen & S. Graham (Eds.), *Peer harassment in school: The plight of the vulnerable and victimized* (pp. 196–214). New York: Guilford Press.

Crime and Disorder Act 1998. London: Her Majesty's Stationery Office.

Crittenden, P. M., & DiLalla, D. L. (1988). Compulsive compliance: The development of an inhibitory coping strategy in infancy. *Journal of Abnormal Child Psychology, 16,* 585–599.

Dahl, D. (2001, October 1). Whatever happened to gun control? *In These Times,* pp. 15–17.

Dale, R. R. (1971). *Mixed or single-sex school* (3 vols.). London: Routledge.

Damon, W. (1999, October 3). The world of peace. *The New York Times,* p. A3.

Davey, A. G. (1983). *Learning to be prejudiced: Growing up in a multiethnic Britain.* London: Edward Arnold.

Dean, C. (1995, March 17). 4,000 staff say they are bullied. *Times Educational Supplement,* News, p. 6.

Debarbieux, E., & Blaya, C. (2001). *Violence in schools: Ten approaches in Europe.* Issy-les-Moulineaux, France: ESF.

Denn, R. (2001, August 14). White woman settles school reverse-bias suit. *Seattle Post-Intelligencer,* pp. 1, 7.

Department of Education and Employment. (1998). *Section 61(4)(B), School Standards and Framework Act, 1998.* London: Her Majesty's Stationery Office.

De Paulo, B. (1992). Nonverbal behavior and self-presentation. *Psychological Bulletin, 111,* 203–243.

Derbyshire, J. (2001, May 28). The problem with "zero." *National Review,* p. 46.

de Shazer, S. (1984). The death of resistance. *Family Process, 23,* 11–21.

de Shazer, S. (1988). *Keys to solution in brief therapy.* New York: Norton.

Deutsch, M. (1993). Educating for a peaceful world. *American Psychologist, 48,* 510–517.

Dibrell, L. L., & Yamamoto, K. (1988). In their own words: Concerns of young children. *Child Psychiatry and Human Development, 19,* 14–25.

Dickens, C. J. H. (1838, March). Oliver Twist: Or the parish boy's progress. *Bentley's Miscellany*. (Monthly serial beginning March 1938)

Dingwall, G., & Harding, C. (1998). Unofficial systems of discipline. In *Diversion in the Criminal Process*. London: Sweet & Maxwell.

Dodge, K. A., & Coie, J. D. (1989, November). *Bully–victim relationships in boys' play groups*. Paper presented at the biennial meeting of the Society for Research in Child Development, Kansas City, MO.

Dore, A. (1993, May 7). Dipping bullies in their well of guilt. *Times Educational Supplement*, p. 9.

Durrant, M. (1995). *Creative strategies for school problems*. New York: Norton.

Eden, R. E. (2001). Attorney General says start young to stop school violence. *Safe Schools Today*, *2*, 5.

Eder, D. (1991). The role of teasing in adolescent peer group culture. In S. Cahill (Ed.), *Sociological studies of child development* (Vol. 4, pp. 181–197). Greenwich, CT: JAI Press.

Eder, D. (1993). "Go get ya a french!": Romantic and sexual teasing among adolescent girls. In D. Tannen (Ed.), *Gender and conversational interaction: Oxford studies in sociolinguistics* (pp. 17–31). New York: Oxford University Press.

Eisenberg, A. R. (1986). Teasing: Verbal play in two Mexicano homes. In B. B. Schieffelin & E. Ochs (Eds.), *Language socialization across cultures* (pp. 182–198). Cambridge, England: Cambridge University Press.

Ekman, K. (1977). In Olweus, D. (1979). Stability of aggressive reaction patterns in males. A review. *Psychological Bulletin*, *86*, 852–875.

Elliott, M. (1986). *KIDSCAPE primary kit*. London: Kidscape.

Elliott, M. (Ed.). (1991). *Bullying: A practical guide to coping for schools*. Harlow, England: Longman.

Elliott, M. (1993). Bullies, victims, signs, solutions. In M. Elliott (Ed.), *Bullying: A practical guide to coping for schools* (pp. 8–14). Harlow, England: Longman.

Emery, R. E. (1992). Family conflicts and their developmental implications: A conceptual analysis of meanings for the structure of relationships. In C. U. Shantz & W. W. Hartup (Eds.), *Conflict in child and adolescent development* (pp. 270–299). Cambridge, England: Cambridge University Press.

Eron, L. D. (1986). Interventions to mitigate the psychological effects of media violence on aggressive behavior. *Journal of Social Issues*, *42*, 155–169.

Eron, L. D., & Huesmann, R. L. (1987). Aggression and its correlates over 22 years. In D. Crowell, I. M. Evans, & C. R. O'Donnell (Eds.), *Childhood aggression and violence* (pp. 249–262). New York: Plenum.

Eron, L. D., & Huesmann, R. L. (1990). The stability of aggressive behavior—Even unto the third generation. In M. Lewis & S. M. Miller (Eds.), *Handbook of developmental psychopathology* (pp. 147–156). New York: Plenum.

Evans, C., & Eder, D. (1993). "No exit": Processes of isolation in the middle school. *Journal of Contemporary Ethnography*, *22*, 139–170.

Fabian, L. J., & Thompson, J. K. (1989). Body image and disturbance in young females. *International Journal of Eating Disorders, 8*, 63–74.

Fagin, J. (1990). The social organization of drug use and drug dealing among urban gangs. *Criminology, 27*, 633–669.

Farrington, D. P. (1989). Early predictors of adolescent aggression and adult violence. *Violence Victim, 4*, 79–100.

Farrington, D. P. (1991). Childhood aggression and adult violence: Early precursors and later-life outcomes. In D. J. Pepler & K. H. Rubin (Eds.), *The development and treatment of childhood aggression* (pp. 5–29). Hillsdale, NJ: Erlbaum.

Farrington, D. P. (1993). Understanding and preventing bullying. In M. Tonry & N. Morris (Eds.), *Crime and justice: An annual review of research* (Vol. 17, pp. 387–458). Chicago: University of Chicago Press.

Featherstone, L., & Henwood, D. (2001, February 12). Economists vs. students. *The Nation*, pp. 6, 24.

Fennell, T. (1993, February 15). Fear in the hallways. *Maclean's, 106*, 19.

Feshbach, N. D. (1969). Sex differences in children's modes of aggressive responses towards outsiders. *Merrill-Palmer Quarterly, 15*, 249–258.

Fiennes, R. (1988). *Living dangerously*. New York: Atheneum.

Finkelhor, D. (1995). The victimization of children: A developmental perspective. *American Journal of Orthopsychiatry, 65*, 177–193.

Finkelhor, D., & Dziuba-Leatherman, J. (1994). Victimization of children. *American Psychologist, 49*, 173–183.

Finnegan, R. A., Hodges, E. V. E., & Perry, D. G. (1996). Preoccupied and avoiding coping during middle childhood. *Child Development, 67*, 1318–1328.

Finnegan, R. A., Hodges, E. V. E., & Perry, D. G. (1998). Victimization by peers: Associations with children's reports of mother–child interaction. *Journal of Personality and Social Psychology, 75*, 1076–1086.

Finnegan, R. A., & Perry, D. G. (1995). *Mother–child interaction and victimization by peers*. Unpublished manuscript, Florida Atlantic University.

Flavell, J. H. (1979). Metacognitive development and cognitive monitoring: A new area of cognitive development inquiry. *American Psychologist, 34*, 906–911.

Flavell, J. H., Fry, C., Wright, J., & Jarvis, P. (1968). *The development of role-taking and communication skills in children*. New York: Wiley.

Floyd, N. M. (1985). "Pick on somebody your own size!": Controlling victimization. *The Pointer, 29*, 9–17.

Floyd, N. M. (1987, Winter). Terrorism in the schools. *School Safety: National School Safety Center Newsjournal*, pp. 22–25.

Folkman, S. (1984). Personal control and stress and coping processes: A theoretical analysis. *Journal of Personality and Social Psychology, 46*, 839–852.

Folkman, S., & Moskowitz, J. T. (2000). Positive affect and the other side of coping. *American Psychologist, 55*, 647–654.

Forero, R., McLellan, L., Rissel, C., & Bauman, A. (1999). Bullying behavior and psychosocial health among school students: Cross sectional study. *British Medical Journal, 319*, 344–348.

Fortin, J. (1998). *Children's rights and developing law*. London: Butterworths.

Foster, S. L., DeLawyer, D. D., & Guevremont, D. C. (1986). A critical incident analysis of liked and disliked peer behaviors and their situation parameters in childhood and adolescence. *Behavioral Assessment, 8*, 115–133.

Fournier, R. (1994, November 25). First mom-in-law gathers no moss. *Seattle Post-Intelligencer*, p. A20.

Fox, M., Pratt, G., & Roberts, S. (1991). Developing the educational psychologist's work in the secondary school: A process model in change. *Educational Psychology in Practice, 6*, 163–164.

Fraczek, A. (1996). Violence and aggression in children and youth: A sociopsychological perspective. *European Review, 4*, 75–90.

Free to roam the streets in gangs. (1993, December 3). *Times Educational Supplement*, p. 12.

Frodi, A., Macaulay, J., & Thome, P. R. (1977). Are women always less aggressive than men? *Psychological Bulletin, 84*, 634–660.

Fry, D. P., & Björkqvist, K. (Eds.). (1997). *Cultural variation in conflict resolution: Alternatives to violence*. Mahwah, NJ: Erlbaum.

Furniss, C. (2000). Bullying in schools: It's not a crime—is it? *Education and the Law, 12*, 10–29.

Galen, B. R., & Underwood, M. K. (1997). A developmental investigation of social aggression among children. *Developmental Psychology, 33*, 589–600.

Galvin, R. M. (1992). The nature of shyness. *Harvard Magazine, 94*, 41–45.

Gaughan, E., Cerio, J. D., & Myers, R. A. (2001). *Lethal violence in schools*. Alfred, NY: Alfred University Press.

Gay, Lesbian, and Straight Education Network (GLSEN). (2000). *Hatred in the hallways: Report on gay students who did not feel safe at school*. Boston: Author.

Genta, M. L., Menesini, E., Fonzi, A., Costabile, A., & Smith, P. K. (1996). Bullies and victims in schools in central and southern Italy. *European Journal of Psychology of Education, 11*, 97–110.

Gillborn, D. (1992). Citizenship, "race" and the hidden curriculum. *International Studies in Sociology of Education, 2*, 57–73.

Gilligan, J. (1996). *Violence*. New York: Putnam.

Gilmartin, B. G. (1987). Peer group antecedents of severe love-shyness in males. *Journal of Personality, 55*, 467–489.

Ginsburg, H. J., Pollman, V. A., & Wauson, M. S. (1977). An ethological analysis of nonverbal inhibitors of aggressive behavior in male elementary school children. *Developmental Psychology, 13*, 417–418.

Glynn, A. (1970). *The British: Portrait of a people*. New York: Putnam's Sons.

Godwin, T. M. (1996). Teen courts: Empowering youth in community prevention and intervention efforts. *Perspectives, 20*, 20–24.

Godwin, T. M. (1998). Developing and using teen court programs. *Juvenile Justice Update, 4,* 1–2, 10–11.

Goffman, E. (1957). On face-work: An analysis of ritual elements in social interaction. *Psychiatry, 18,* 213–231.

Gougeon, C. (1989). Guidelines for special issues training sessions in secondary schools, peer counseling programs. *Canadian Journal of Counselling, 23,* 120–126.

Graham, P., Rutter, M., & George S. (1973). Temperamental characteristics as predictors of behaviour problems in children. *American Journal of Orthopsychiatry, 43,* 328–339.

Graham, S., & Juvonen, J. (1998). Self-blame and peer victimization in middle school: An attributional analysis. *Developmental Psychology, 34,* 587–599.

Graham, S., & Juvonen, J. (2001). An attributional approach to peer victimization. In J. Juvonen & S. Graham (Eds.), *Peer harassment in school: The plight of the vulnerable and victimized* (pp. 49–72). New York: Guilford Press.

Greenbaum, S. (1989). *Set straight on bullies.* Malibu, CA: Pepperdine University Press.

Greene, G. (1971). *A sort of life.* New York: Simon & Schuster.

Greenwood, P. W. (1995). Juvenile crime and juvenile justice. In J. Q. Wilson & J. Petersilia (Eds.), *Crime* (pp. 91–117). San Francisco: Institute for Contemporary Studies.

Greider, W. (2001, May 7). No to global sweatshops. *The Nation,* p. 26.

Gumperz, J. J. (1977). Sociocultural knowledge in conversational inference. In M. Saville-Troike (Ed.), *Linguistics and anthropology* (pp. 191–211). Washington, DC: Georgetown University Press.

Gutek, B. A. (1985). *Sex and the workplace: The impact of sexual behavior and harassment on women, men, and the organisation.* San Francisco: Jossey-Bass.

Gutek, B. A., Cohen, A. G., & Konrad, A. M. (1990). Predicting social–sexual behaviour at work: A contact hypothesis. *Academy of Management Journal, 33,* 560–577.

Haeselager, G. J. T., & van Lieshout, C. F. M. (1992, September). *Social and affective adjustment of self- and peer-reported victims and bullies.* Paper presented at the European Conference on Developmental Psychology, Seville, Spain.

Haigh, G. (1994, October 28). Blessed are the peacemakers. *Times Educational Supplement,* p. 6.

Hall, N. (1999, May 8). Reena Virk: A disposable kid to cruel attackers. *The Vancouver Sun,* pp. A1–A2.

Handgun Control, Inc. (1996). Washington, DC. (No longer accessible.)

Harachi, T. W., Catalano, R. F., & Hawkins, J. D. (1999a). Canada. In P. K. Smith, Y. Morita, J. Junger-Tas, D. Olweus, R. Catalano, & P. Slee (Eds.), *The nature of school bullying: A cross-national perspective* (pp. 296–306). London: Routledge.

Harachi, T. W., Catalano, R. F., & Hawkins, J. D. (1999b). United States. In P. K. Smith, Y. Morita, J. Junger-Tas, D. Olweus, R. Catalano, & P. Slee (Eds.),

The nature of school bullying: A cross-national perspective (pp. 279–295). London: Routledge.

Harrell, D. C. (2000, November 17). Classmates sexually harassed girl, 7, parents claim. *Seattle Post-Intelligencer*, p. B3.

Harris, J. R. (1995). Where is the child's environment? A group socialization theory of development. *Psychological Review, 102*, 458–489.

Hartup, W. W. (1996). The company they keep: Friendships and their developmental significance. *Child Development, 67*, 1–13.

Hawker, D. S. J., & Boulton, M. J. (2000). Twenty years of research on peer victimization and psychosocial maladjustment: A meta-analytic review of cross-sectional studies. *Journal of Child Psychology and Psychiatry, 41*, 441–455.

Hawkins, J. D., Herrenkohl, T., Farrington, D. P., Brewer, D., Catalano, R. F., Harachi, T. W., & Cothern, L. (1998). A review of predictors of youth violence. In R. Loeber & D. P. Farrington (Eds.), *Serious and violent juvenile offenders: Risk factors and successful interventions* (pp. 106–146). Thousand Oaks, CA: Sage.

Hawkins, J. D., Herrenkohl, T. I., Farrington, D. P., Brewer, D., Catalano, R. F., Harachi, T. W., & Cothern, L. (2000, April). *Predictors of youth violence: Juvenile Justice Bulletin*. Rockville, MD: Office of Juvenile Justice and Delinquency Prevention.

Hazler, R. J. (1996a). *Breaking the cycle of violence: Interventions for bullying and victimization*. Bristol, PA: Accelerated Development.

Hazler, R. J. (1996b). Bystanders: An overlooked factor in peer on peer abuse. *Journal for the Professional Counselor, 11*, 11–21.

Hazler, R. J., Carney, J. V., Green, S., Powell, R., & Jolly, L. S. (1997). Areas of expert agreement on identification of school bullies and victims. *School Psychology International, 18*, 3–12.

Hazler, R. J., Hoover, J. H., & Oliver, R. (1993). What do kids say about bullying? *Education Digest, 58*, 16–20.

Heinemann, P. P. (1973). *Mobbing-gruppvald blant barn och vuxna*. Stockholm: Natur och Kultur.

Herbert, B. (1997, March 7). The police bullies. *The New York Times*, Op. Ed., p. A17.

Hern, J., & Parkin, W. (1987). *Sex at work: The power and paradox of organisational sexuality*. New York: St. Martin's Press.

Herrenkohl, T. I., Maguin, E., Hill, K. G., Hawkins, J. D., & Abbott, R. D. (2000). Developmental risk factors for youth violence. *Journal of Adolescent Health, 26*, 176–186.

High power guns. (1998, June 14). *The New York Times*, p. A3.

Hirano, K. (1992, September). *Bullying and victimization in Japanese classrooms*. Paper presented at the European Conference on Developmental Psychology, Seville, Spain.

Hodges, E. V. E., Malone, M. J., & Perry, D. G. (1997). Individual risk and social risk as interacting determinants of victimization in the peer group. *Developmental Psychology, 33*, 1032–1039.

Hodges, E. V. E., & Perry, D. G. (1999a). Personal and interpersonal antecedents and consequences of victimization by peers. *Journal of Personality and Social Psychology, 76*, 677–685.

Hodges, E. V. E., & Perry, D. G. (1999b). Victims of peer abuse: An overview. *Journal of Emotional and Behavioral Problems, 5*, 23–28.

Home Office Police Research Group. (1996). *Preventing school bullying.* London: Author.

Hoover, J. H., Oliver, R., & Hazler, R. J. (1992). Bullying: Perceptions of adolescent victims in the midwestern USA. *School Psychology International, 13*, 5–16.

Hoover, J. H., & Olson, G. (2000a). Sticks and stones may break their bones: Teasing as bullying. *Reclaiming Children and Youth, 9*, 87–91.

Hoover, J. H., & Olson, G. W. (2000b). *Teasing and harassment: The frames and scripts approach for teachers and parents.* Bloomington, IN: National Educational Service.

Hoover, N. C., & Pollard, N. J. (2000). *Initiation rites in American high schools: A national survey.* Alfred, NY: Alfred University Press.

Horn, D. M. (Ed.). (2000, April). *Bruised inside: What our children say about youth violence, what causes it, and what we need to do about it.* Washington, DC: National Association of Attorneys General.

Horne, A. M., Glaser, B., & Sayger, T. V. (1994). Bullies. *Counseling and Human Development, 27*, 1112.

Hughes, T. (1857). *Tom Brown's schooldays.* New York: Harper.

Hutchison, K. (1993, December 29). Bus perils make an impression. *The Review*, p. A6.

International Association of Chiefs of Police. (1999). *Guide for preventing and responding to school violence—Bruised inside: What our children say about youth violence.* Washington, DC: Author.

Iwasaki, J. (1992, February 25). Contract law hits the playground: "Conflict managers" help keep peace. *Seattle Post-Intelligencer*, p. B3.

Jacobs, A. (2000, April). Violent rites. *The New York Times, 132*, pp. 9–13.

Jacobs, J. B., & Potter, K. A. (1999). Comprehensive handgun licensing and registration: An analysis and critique of Brady II, Gun Control's next (and last?) step. *Journal of Criminal Law and Criminology, 89*, 81–110.

James, O. (1994, May). Violent children. *Harpers & Queen*, 134, 136–137, 188–189.

Jarvie, G. J., Lahey, B., Graziano, W., & Framer, E. (1983). Childhood obesity and social stigma: What we know and what we don't know. *Developmental Review, 3*, 237–273.

Johnson, D. W., & Johnson, R. T. (1995). *Teaching students to be peacemakers* (3rd ed.). Edina, MN: Interaction Books.

Johnson, D. W., Johnson, R. T., Dudley, B., & Acikgoz, K. (1994). Effects of conflict resolution training on elementary school students. *Journal of Social Psychology, 134*, 803–817.

Johnston, L. D., O'Malley, P. M., & Bachman, J. G. (1993). *Monitoring the future study for Goal 6 of the national education goals: A special report for the National Education Goals Panel.* Ann Arbor: University of Michigan, Institute for Social Research.

Johnstone, M., Munn, P., & Edwards, L. (1991). *Action against bullying.* Edinburgh: Scottish Council Research in Education.

Jordan, M. (1994, December 18). Japanese trace bullying factor in student suicides. *The Washington Post,* p. 21.

Junger, M. (1990). Intergroup bullying and racial harassment in The Netherlands. *Sociology and Social Research, 74,* 65–72.

Juvonen, J., Nishina, A., & Graham, S. (2001). Self-views versus peer perceptions of victim status among early adolescents. In J. Juvonen & S. Graham (Eds.), *Peer harassment in school: The plight of the vulnerable and victimized* (pp. 105–124). New York: Guilford Press.

Kaltiala-Heino, R., Rimpelä, M., Marttunen, A. R., Rimpelä, A., & Rantanen, P. (1999). Bullying, depression, and suicidal ideation in Finnish adolescents: School survey. *British Medical Journal, 319,* 348–351.

Karr-Morse, R., & Wiley, M. S. (1997). *Ghosts from the nursery: Tracing the roots of violence.* New York: Atlantic Monthly Press.

Kashani, J. H., Reid, J. C., & Rosenberg, T. K. (1989). Levels of hopelessness in children and adolescents: A developmental perspective. *Journal of Consulting and Clinical Psychology, 57,* 496–499.

Katz, A. H. (1993). *Self-help in America: A social movement perspective.* New York: Twayne.

Kellerman, J. (1981). *Helping the fearful child.* New York: Norton.

Kelly, E., & Cohn, T. (1988). *Racism in schools: New research evidence.* Stoke-on-Trent, England: Trentham Books.

Keltner, D., Capps, L., Kring, A. M., Young, R. C., & Heerey, E. A. (2001). Just teasing: A conceptual analysis and empirical review. *Psychological Bulletin, 127,* 229–248.

Kirby, D. (2001, July 3). What makes a bully? *The Advocate,* pp. 31–34.

Klein, C. (1975). *The myth of the happy child.* New York: Harper & Row.

Klein, M. W. (1995). *The American street gang.* New York: Oxford University Press.

Klein, R. (1994, January 6). Where prejudice still flares into violence: Timetable of terror. *Times Educational Supplement,* Features, p. 9.

Knight, S. (1997, December 5). Let's get real about bullying. *Times Educational Supplement,* Talkback, p. 18.

Kochenderfer, B. J., & Ladd, G. W. (1996). Peer victimization: Cause or consequence of school maladjustment? *Child Development, 67,* 1305–1317.

Kochenderfer-Ladd, B., & Wardrop, J. L. (2001). Chronicity and instability of children's peer victimization experiences as predictors of loneliness and social satisfaction trajectories. *Child Development, 72,* 134–151.

Kumpulainen, K., Rasanen, E., Henttonen, I., Almqvist, F., Kresanov, K., Linna, S. L., et al. (1998). Bullying and psychiatric symptoms among elementary school-age children. *Child Abuse and Neglect, 22*, 705–717.

Kureishi, H. (1986). *My beautiful launderette and the rainbow sign.* London: Faber.

Kutner, L. (1981). *Parent and child: Getting through to each other.* New York: Morrow.

Labi, N. (2001, April 2). Let bullies beware. *Time*, p. 46.

Lacey, N. (1995). Contingency and criminalisation. In I. Loveland (Ed.), *Frontiers of Criminality.* London: Sweet & Maxwell.

Ladd, B. K., & Ladd, G. W. (2001). Variations in peer victimization: Relations to children's maladjustment. In J. Juvonen & S. Graham (Eds.), *Peer harassment in school: The plight of the vulnerable and victimized* (pp. 25–48). New York: Guilford Press.

La Fontaine, J. (1991). *Bullying, the child's view: An analysis of telephone calls to ChildLine about bullying.* London: Calouste Gulbenkian Foundation.

Lagerspetz, K. M. J., & Björkqvist, K. (1992). Indirect aggression in girls and boys. In L. R. Huesmann (Ed.), *Aggressive behavior: Current perspectives* (pp. 131–150). New York: Plenum.

Lagerspetz, K. M. J., Björkqvist, K., Berts, M., & King, E. (1982). Group aggression among school children in three schools. *Scandinavian Journal of Psychology, 23*, 45–52.

Lagerspetz, K. M. J., Björkqvist, K., & Peltonen, T. (1988). Is indirect aggression typical of females? Gender differences in aggressiveness in 11- to 12-year-old children. *Aggressive Behavior, 14*, 403–414.

Lambert, M. J. (1992). Implications of outcome research for psychotherapy integration. In J. C. Norcross & M. R. Goldfried (Eds.), *Handbook of psychotherapy integration* (pp. 94–129). New York: Basic Books.

Lane, D. A. (1989). Violent histories: Bullying and criminality. In D. P. Tattum & D. A. Lane (Eds.), *Bullying in schools* (pp. 95–104). Stoke-on-Trent, England: Trentham.

Latane, B., & Darley, J. M. (1970). *The unresponsive bystander: Why doesn't he help*? Englewood Cliffs, NJ: Prentice Hall.

Latane, B., & Nida, S. (1981). Ten years of research on group size and helping. *Psychological Bulletin, 89*, 308–324.

Lawrence, R. (1998). *School crime and juvenile justice.* New York: Oxford University Press.

Lazarus, R. S. (1966). *Psychological stress and the coping process.* New York: McGraw-Hill.

Lazarus, R. S., & Folkman, S. (1984). *Stress, appraisal, and coping.* New York: Springer.

Leach, E. (2001, May 11). Head uses mentors to fight racism. *Times Educational Supplement*, News, p. 21.

Leach, P. (1986). *Your growing child: From babyhood through adolescence.* New York: Knopf.

Leach, P. (1994). *Children first. What our society must do—and is not doing—for our children today.* New York: Knopf.

Lerner, M. J. (1980). *Belief in a just world: A fundamental delusion.* New York: Plenum Press.

Li, C. D. (2001, March 29). School bullying is rooted in a teenage caste system. *Seattle Post-Intelligencer,* p. B4.

Lipsey, M. W., & Derzon, J. H. (1998). Predictors of violent and serious delinquency in adolescence and early adulthood: A synthesis of longitudinal research. In R. Loeber & D. P. Farrington (Eds.), *Serious and violent juvenile offenders: Risk factors and successful interventions* (pp. 86–105). Thousand Oaks, CA: Sage.

Loach, B., & Bloor, C. (1995). Dropping the bully to find the racist. *Multicultural Teaching, 13,* 18–20.

Loeber, R., & Stouthamer-Loeber, M. (1998). Development of juvenile aggression and violence: Some misconceptions and controversies. *American Psychologist, 53,* 242–259.

Lucas, P. (1993). *A long-term follow-up study of the Pikas method of common concern.* Unpublished BA dissertation, University of Sheffield, Sheffield, England.

Lynch-Fraser, D. (1994). *Life's little miseries.* New York: Lexington Books, Macmillan.

Maccoby, E. E. (1980). *Social development: Psychological growth and the parent–child relationship.* New York: Harcourt Brace Jovanovich.

Maccoby, E. E., & Jacklin, C. N. (1974). *The psychology of sex differences.* Stanford, CA: Stanford University Press.

Mackey, R. (2000, March 19). Join the club. Expert opinion: Hazing. *The New York Times Magazine,* p. 11.

MacLeod, M., & Morris, S. (1996). *Why me? Children talking to ChildLine about bullying.* London: ChildLine.

Madsen, K., & Smith, P. K. (1993, August). *Age and gender differences in participants' perception of the concept of the term bullying.* Poster presentation at the Sixth European Conference on Developmental Psychology, Bonn, Germany.

Magnarelli, M. (2001, August). Saviors vs. snitch. *Seventeen,* 220–223.

Magnusson, D. (1996). The patterning of antisocial behavior and autonomic reactivity. In D. M. Stoff & R. B. Cairns (Eds.), *The neurobiology of clinical aggression* (pp. 291–308). Hillsdale, NJ: Erlbaum.

Maguin, E., & Loeber, R. (1996). Academic performance and delinquency. In M. Tonry (Ed.), *Crime and justice: A review of research* (Vol. 20, pp. 145–264). Chicago: University of Chicago Press.

Mahdavi, J., & Smith, P. K. (2002). The operation of a bully court and perceptions of its success. *School Psychology International, 23,* 327–341.

Mahoney, J. L. (2000). School extracurricular activity participation as a moderator in the development of antisocial patterns. *Child Development, 71,* 502–516.

Mahoney, J. L., & Cairns, R. B. (1997). Do extracurricular activities protect against early school dropout? *Developmental Psychology, 33,* 241–253.

Maines, B., & Robinson, G. (1992). *Stamp out bullying: Never mind the awareness, what can we do*? Portishead, England: Lame Duck Publishing.

Mannuzza, S., Klein, R. G., Konig, P. H., & Giampino, T. L. (1989). Hyperactive boys almost grown up: IV. Criminality and its relationship to psychiatric status. *Archives of General Psychiatry, 46,* 1073–1079.

Marano, H. E. (1995, September/October). Big. Bad. Bully. *Psychology Today, 28,* 50–57, 62, 64, 66, 68–70, 74, 76, 79, 82.

Maslow, A. (1970). *Motivation and personality* (2nd ed.). New York: Harper & Row.

Massachusetts Department of Education. (2000). *Report of gay and lesbian students threatened or injured in one school year*. Boston: Author.

McBurnett, K., Lahey, B. B., Rathouz, P. J., & Loeber, R. (2000). Low salivary cortisol and persistent aggression in boys referred for disruptive behavior. *Archives of General Psychiatry, 57,* 38–43.

McCarthy, S. (2001, May 14). To help kids deal with bullies, parents need to stay above the fray. *Liberal Opinion Week,* p. 23.

McCoy, E. (1992, November). Bully-proof your child. *Reader's Digest, 141,* 199–200, 203–205.

McEvoy, A. (1990). Combating gang activities in schools. *Education Digest, 56,* 31–34.

McGhee, P. E. (1989). The contribution of humor to children's social development. In P. E. McGhee (Ed.), *Humor and children's development: A guide to practical applications* (pp. 119–134). New York: Haworth Press.

Meichenbaum, D. H. (1971). Examination of model characteristics in reducing avoidance behavior. *Journal of Personality and Social Psychology, 17,* 298–307.

Mellor, A. (1991). Helping victims. In M. Elliott (Ed.), *Bullying: A practical guide to coping for schools* (pp. 90–102). Harlow, England: Longman.

Mellor Smith, H. (1992). *The effect of quality circles on bullying behaviour in schools*. Unpublished BA dissertation, University of Sheffield, Sheffield, England.

Menesini, E., & Smorti, A. (1997). Strategie di intervento scolastico contra il fenomeno delle prepotenze [Developing a positive school climate against bullying]. In P. K. Smith, Y. Morita, J. Junger-Tas, D. Olweus, R. Catalano, & P. Slee (Eds.). (1999). *The nature of school bullying: A cross-national perspective* (pp. 140–156). New York: Routledge.

Metropolitan Achievement Tests (7th ed.). (1993). San Antonio, TX: Harcourt, Psychological Corporation.

Miedzian, M. (1992). *Boys will be boys: Breaking the link between masculinity and violence*. New York: Doubleday.

Miller, P. (1986). Teasing as language socialization and verbal play in a White working-class community. In B. B. Schieffelin & E. Ochs (Eds.), *Language socialization across cultures* (pp. 199–212). Cambridge, England: Cambridge University Press.

Minton, L. (1994, February 20). Fresh voices: Have you ever been sexually harassed? *Seattle Post-Intelligencer*, Parade, p. 30.

Mirrlees-Black, C., Budd, T., Partridge, S., & Mayhew, P. (1998). *The 1998 British Crime Survey*. London: Home Office.

Moffit, T. E. (1993). Adolescence-limited and life-cycle-persistent antisocial behavior: A developmental taxonomy. *Psychological Review, 100*, 674–701.

Mooney, A., Creeser, R., & Blatchford, P. (1991). Children's views on teasing and fighting in junior schools. *Educational Research, 33*, 103–112.

Moore, D., Adair, V., Lysaght, K., & Kruiswijk, J. (1997). *Eliminating violence from Schools Evaluation project: Final report*. Wellington, New Zealand: Education Department, University of Auckland for the Ministry of Education.

Morgan, J., & Zedner, L. (1992). *Child victims: Crime, impact and criminal justice.* Oxford, England: Clarendon Press.

Morita, Y. (Ed.). (1985). *Sociological study on the structure of bullying group.* Osaka, Japan: Osaka City University, Department of Sociology.

Morita, Y., Soeda, H., Soeda, K., & Taki, M. (1999). Japan. In P. K. Smith, Y. Morita, J. Junger-Tas, D. Olweus, R. Catalano, & P. Slee (Eds.), *The nature of school bullying: A cross-national perspective* (pp. 309–323). London: Routledge.

Morrison, B. (1994, February 14). Letter from Liverpool—Children of circumstance. *The New Yorker*, pp. 48–60.

Moskos, C. C., Williams, J. A., & Segal, D. R. (Eds.). (2000). *The postmodern military*. New York: Oxford University Press.

Mrazek, P. J., & Haggerty, R. J. (Eds.). (1994). *Reducing risks for mental disorders: Frontiers for preventive intervention research.* Washington, DC: National Academy Press.

Muncie, J. (1999). *Youth and crime: A critical introduction.* London: Sage.

Munsch, J., & Kinchen, K. M. (1995). Adolescent sociometric status and social support. *Journal of Early Adolescence, 15*, 181–202.

Munthe, E. (1989). Bullying in Scandinavia. In E. Roland & E. Munthe (Eds.), *Bullying : An international perspective* (pp. 66–78). London: David Fulton.

Murano, H. E. (1995). When the bully is the boss. *Psychology Today, 28*, 58–61.

Murphy, J. J. (1997). *Solution-focused counseling in middle and high schools.* Alexandria, VA: American Counseling Association.

Naito, J. (2002, July 15). Bush shifts Head Start focus to the ABCs. *Seattle Post-Intelligencer*, pp. A1, A6.

Namie, G., & Namie, R. (2000). *The bully at work.* Naperville, IL: Sourcebooks.

Nansel, T. R., Overpeck, M., Pilla, R. S., Ruan, W. J., Simons-Morton, B., & Scheidt, P. (2001). Bullying behaviors among US youth. *Journal of the American Medical Association, 285*, 2094–2100.

Nash, I. (1989, October 20). True extent of bullying hidden. *Times Educational Supplement*, p. 5.

Nash, I. (1995, November 13). Bullying at the college level. *Times Educational Supplement*, p. 17.

Naylor, P., & Cowie, H. (1999). The effectiveness of peer support systems in challenging school bullying: The perspectives and experiences of teachers and pupils. *Journal of Adolescence, 22*, 467–479.

Naylor, P., Cowie, H., & del Rey, R. (2001). Coping strategies of secondary school children in response to being bullied. *Child Psychology and Psychiatry Review, 6*, 114–120.

Neary, A., & Joseph, S. (1994). Peer victimization and its relationship to self-concept and depression among schoolgirls. *Personality and Individual Differences, 16*, 183–186.

Needleman, H. L. (1973). Lead poisoning in children: Neurologic implications of widespread subclinical intoxication. *Seminars in Psychiatry, 5*, 47–53.

Needleman, H. L. (2000, May). *Report of the link between exposure to lead and antisocial behavior in delinquent boys*. Paper presented at the Joint Meeting of the American Academy of Pediatrics and the Pediatric Academic Society, Pittsburgh, PA.

Nelsen, J. (1985). *Positive discipline*. Fair Oaks, CA: Sunrise Press.

Nessel, P. A. (2000). Youth court: A national movement. In *Technical Assistance Bulletin* (No. 17, pp. 1–12). Chicago: American Bar Association Division for Public Education.

Neustatter, A. (1994, October 7). The hurt beneath a hard exterior. *Times Educational Supplement*, p. 6.

New Zealand Police. (1992). *Kia Kaha: Law related education program*. Wellington, New Zealand: Author.

Nicholls, J. (1984). Achievement motivation: Conceptions of ability, subjective experience, task choice, and performance. *Psychological Review, 91*, 328–346.

Nicolaides, S., Toda, Y., & Smith, P. K. (2002). Knowledge and attitudes about school bullying in trainee teachers. *British Journal of Educational Psychology*.

Nuutinen, T. (1999). Victim slide show. In P. K. Smith, Y. Morita, J. Junger-Tas, D. Olweus, R. Catalano, & P. Slee (Eds.), *The nature of school bullying: A cross-national perspective* (pp. 61–62). London: Routledge.

Nuwer, H. (1999). *Wrongs of passage: Fraternities, sororities, hazing, and binge drinking*. Bloomingdale: Indiana University Press.

Nyhan, D. (1999, May 10). School shootings. *Liberal Opinion Week*, p. 8.

O'Connell, P., Pepler, D., & Craig, W. (1999). Peer involvement in bullying: Insights and challenges for intervention. *Journal of Adolescence, 22*, 437–452.

O'Connor, M. (1995, April 14). Anxieties of our time addressed. *Times Educational Supplement*, p. 9.

Office of Juvenile Justice and Delinquency Prevention. (1999). *Fact sheet*. Washington, DC: U.S. Department of Justice.

Office of Juvenile Justice and Delinquency Prevention (OJJDP) Fact Sheet #118. (1999, October). *Teen courts in the United States: A profile of current programs.* Washington, DC: The Urban Institute, Program on Law & Behavior.

Ohbuchi, K. I., & Yamamoto, I. (1990). The power strategies of Japanese children in interpersonal conflict: Effects of age, gender, and target. *Journal of Genetic Psychology, 15,* 349–360.

Ohsako, T. (1999). The developing world. In P. K. Smith, Y. Morita, J. Junger-Tas, D. Olweus, R. Catalano, & P. Slee (Eds.), *The nature of school bullying: A cross-national perspective* (pp. 359–375). London: Routledge.

Olweus, D. (1978). *Aggression in the schools: Bullies and whipping boys.* Washington, DC: Hemisphere.

Olweus, D. (1979). Stability of aggressive reaction patterns in males: A review. *Psychological Bulletin, 86,* 852–875.

Olweus, D. (1980). Familial and temperamental determinants of aggressive behavior in adolescent boys: A causal analysis. *Developmental Psychology, 16,* 644–660.

Olweus, D. (1981). Bullying among school boys. In N. Cantwell (Ed.), *Children and violence* (pp. 97–131). Stockholm: Akademilitteratur.

Olweus, D. (1983). *Bully/Victim Questionnaire.* Unpublished manuscript, University of Bergen, Bergen, Norway.

Olweus, D. (1984). Aggressors and their victims: Bullying at school. In N. Frude & H. Gault (Eds.), *Disruptive behaviors in schools* (pp. 57–76). New York: Wiley.

Olweus, D. (1985). 80,000 pupils involved in bullying. *Norsk Skoleblad, 2,* 18–23.

Olweus, D. (1988). *Critical views on the Pikas method.* Unpublished manuscript, University of Bergen, Bergen, Norway.

Olweus, D. (1991). Bully/victim problems among school children: Basic facts and effects of a school-based intervention program. In D. Pepler & K. Rubin (Eds.), *The development and treatment of childhood aggression* (pp. 411–448). Hillsdale, NJ: Erlbaum.

Olweus, D. (1993a). *Bullying at school: What we know and what we can do.* Cambridge, MA: Blackwell.

Olweus, D. (1993b). Victimization by peers: Antecedents and long-term outcomes. In K. H. Rubin & J. B. Asendorpf (Eds.), *Social withdrawal, inhibition and shyness in childhood* (pp. 315–342). Hillsdale, NJ: Erlbaum.

Olweus, D. (1996). *The Revised Olweus Bully/Victim Questionnaire* [Mimeo]. Bergen, Norway: University of Bergen, Research Center for Health Promotion (HEMIL).

Olweus, D. (1997). Bully/victim problems in school: Facts and intervention. *European Journal of Psychology of Education, 12,* 495–510.

Olweus, D. (1999a). *Core Program Against Bullying and Antisocial Behavior: Part IV.* Bergen, Norway: University of Bergen, Research Center for Health Promotion.

Olweus, D. (1999b). Norway. In P. K. Smith, Y. Morita, J. Junger-Tas, D. Olweus, R. Catalano, & P. Slee (Eds.), *The nature of school bullying: A cross-national perspective* (pp. 28–48). London: Routledge.

Olweus, D. (1999c). Sweden. In P. K. Smith, Y. Morita, J. Junger-Tas, D. Olweus, R. Catalano, & P. Slee (Eds.), *The nature of school bullying: A cross-national perspective* (pp. 7–27). London: Routledge.

Olweus, D. (2001). Peer harassment: A critical analysis and some important issues. In J. Juvonen & S. Graham (Eds.), *Peer harassment in school: The plight of the vulnerable and victimized* (pp. 3–20). New York: Guilford Press.

Olweus, D., & Alsaker, F. D. (1991). Assessing change in a cohort longitudinal study with hierarchical data. In D. Magnusson, L. Bergman, G. Rudinger, & B. Törestad (Eds.), *Problems and methods in longitudinal research* (pp. 107–132). New York: Cambridge University Press.

Olweus, D., & Endresen, I. M. (1998). The importance of sex-of-stimulus object: Age trends and sex differences in empathic responsiveness. *Social Development, 7*, 370–388.

Olweus, D., & Limber, S. (1999). The Bullying Prevention Program. In D. S. Elliott (Series Ed.), *Blueprints for violence prevention*. Boulder: University of Colorado, Center for the Study and Prevention of Violence, Institute of Behavioral Science.

Olweus, D., & Smith, P. K. (1995). *Manual for the Olweus Bully/Victim Questionnaire*. Oxford, England: Blackwell.

O'Malley, B. (1993, June 18). Screening out the bullies. *Times Educational Supplement*, Resources, p. 15.

O'Moore, A. M. (1988). *Bullying in schools* (Council of Europe Report DECS-EGT [88] 5-E). Strasbourg, France: Council for Cultural Cooperation.

O'Moore, A. M., & Hillery, B. (1989). Bullying in Dublin schools. *Irish Journal of Psychology, 10*, 426–441.

O'Moore, A. M., Kirkham, C., & Smith, M. (1997). Bullying behaviour in Irish schools: A nationwide study. *Irish Journal of Psychology, 18*, 141–169.

Opie, I. (1993). *The people in the playground*. New York: Oxford University Press.

Opie, I., & Opie, P. (1959). *The lore and language of school children*. London: Oxford University Press.

Orlinsky, D. E., Grawe, K., & Parks, B. K. (1994). Process and outcome in psychotherapy. In A. E. Bergin & S. L. Garfield (Eds.), *Handbook of psychotherapy and behavior change* (pp. 270–376). New York: Wiley.

Osofsky, J. D. (1995). The effects of exposure to violence on young children. *American Psychologist, 50*, 782–788.

Österman, K., Björkqvist, K., Lagerspetz, K. M. J., Kaukiainen, A., Heusmann, R. L., & Fraczek, A. (1994). Peer and self estimated aggression in 8-year-old children from five ethnic groups. *Aggressive Behavior, 20*, 411–428.

Österman, K., Lagerspetz, K. M. J., Landau, S. F., Fraczek, A., & Pastorelli, C. (1997). Sex differences in styles of conflict resolution: A developmental and cross-cultural study with data from Finland, Israel, Italy, and Poland. In D. P. Fry & K. Björkqvist (Eds.), *Cultural variation in conflict resolution: Alternatives to violence* (pp. 185–197). Mahwah, NJ: Erlbaum.

Oswald, H., Krappman, L., Chowdhuri, I., & von Salisch, M. (1988). Gaps and bridges: Interactions between girls and boys in elementary school. In P. Adler & P. Adler (Eds.), *Sociological studies of child development* (Vol. 2, pp. 204–224). Greenwich, CT: JAI Press.

Owens, L. D. (1996). Sticks and stones and sugar and spice: Girls' and boys' aggression in schools. *Australian Journal of Guidance and Counselling, 6*, 45–55.

Owens, L. D. (1998). *Physical, verbal and indirect aggression amongst South Australian school students*. Unpublished doctoral dissertation, Flinders University of South Australia, Adelaide.

Owens, L., Shute, R., & Slee, P. (2000, April). "I'm in and you're out . . . ": Explanations for teenage girls' indirect aggression. *Psychology, Evolution and Gender*, pp. 19–46.

Owens, L., Slee, P., & Shute, R. (2000). "It hurts a hell of a lot . . .": The effects of indirect aggression on teenage girls. *School Psychology International, 21*, 359–376.

Owens, L., Slee, P., & Shute, R. (2001). Victimization among teenage girls: What can be done about indirect harassment? In J. Juvonen & S. Graham (Eds.), *Peer harassment in school: The plight of the vulnerable and victimized* (pp. 215–241). New York: Guilford Press.

Oxford English dictionary. (1993). Oxford, England: Oxford University Press.

Page, C. (1999, May 28). High court shows common sense about school sex harassment. *Seattle Post-Intelligencer*, p. A18.

Parke, R. D., & Slaby, R. G. (1983). The development of aggression. In P. H. Mussen (Series Ed.) & E. M. Hetherington (Vol. Ed.), *Handbook of child psychology: Vol. 4. Socialization, personality, and social development* (pp. 547–641). New York: Wiley.

Parker, J. G., & Asher, S. R. (1987). Peer relations and later personal adjustment: Are low-accepted children at risk? *Psychological Bulletin, 102*, 357–389.

Patterson, G. R., Littman, R. A., & Bricker, W. (1967). Assertive behavior in children: A step toward a theory of aggression. *Monographs of the Society for Research in Child Development, 32*(5, Serial No. 113).

Pawluk, C. J. (1989). Social construction of teasing. *Journal for the Theory of Social Behavior, 19*, 145–167.

Pearce, J. (1989). *Fighting, teasing, and bullying*. Wellingborough, England: Thorsons.

Pellegrini, A. D. (2001). Sampling instances of victimization in middle school: A methodological comparison. In J. Juvonen & S. Graham (Eds.), *Peer harassment in school: The plight of the vulnerable and victimized* (pp. 125–144). New York: Guilford Press.

Pellegrini, A. D., Bartini, M., & Brooks, F. (1999). School bullies, victims, and aggressive victims: Factors relating to group affiliation and victimization in early adolescence. *Journal of Educational Psychology, 91*, 216–224.

Perry, D. G., Hodges, E. V. E., & Egan, S. K. (2001). Determinants of chronic victimization by peers: A review and new model of family influence. In J. Juvonen & S. Graham (Eds.), *Peer harassment in school: The plight of the vulnerable and victimized* (pp. 73–104). New York: Guilford Press.

Perry, D. G., Kusel, S. J., & Perry, L. C. (1988). Victims of peer aggression. *Developmental Psychology, 24*, 807–814.

Perry, D. G., Perry, L. C., & Kennedy, E. (1992). Conflict and the development of anti-social behavior. In C. U. Shantz & W. W. Hartup (Eds.), *Conflict in child and adolescent development* (pp. 301–329). New York: Cambridge University Press.

Perry, D. G., Williard, J. C., & Perry, L. C. (1990). Peers' perceptions of the consequences that victimized children provide aggressors. *Child Development, 61*, 1310–1325.

Phillips, D. (1989). *How to give your child a great self-image*. New York: Random House.

Pierce, D. (Ed.). (2001, March). New video technique could make school pools safer. *Safe Schools Today*, pp. 1–2.

Pierce, K. A., & Cohen, R. (1995). Aggressors and their victims: Toward a contextual framework for understanding children's aggressor–victim relationships. *Developmental Review, 15*, 292–310.

Pikas, A. (1989). The common concern method for the treatment of mobbing. In E. Roland & E. Munthe (Eds.), *Bullying: An international perspective* (pp. 91–104). London: Fulton.

Pipher, M. (1994). *Reviving Ophelia: Saving the selves of adolescent girls*. New York: Ballantine Books.

Piquero, A., & Tibbets, S. (1999). The impact of pre/perinatal disturbances and disadvantaged familial environment in predicting criminal offending. *Studies on Crime and Crime Prevention, 8*, 52–70.

Pitfield, M. A. (1992). *An investigation into interest in, and effectiveness of bully courts*. Unpublished BA dissertation, University of Sheffield, Sheffield, England.

Pitts, J., & Smith, P. (1995). *Preventing school bullying*. London: Home Office Police Research Group.

Pollack, W. S. (2000). *Real boys' voices*. New York: Random House.

Pope, A. W., & Bierman, K. L. (1999). Predicting adolescent peer problems and antisocial activities: The relative roles of aggression and dysregulation. *Developmental Psychology, 35*, 335–346.

Powers, R. (2002, March). The apocalypse of adolescence. *The Atlantic Monthly, 289*, 58, 60–62, 64–65, 68–70, 72, 74.

Premack, D., & Woodruff, G. (1978). Does the chimpanzee have a theory of mind? *Behavioural and Brain Sci*ences, *1*, 515–526.

Prestage, M. (1994, December 2). How to beat bullies from the inside. *Times Educational Supplement*, p. 9.

Price, D. (2001, July 2). Love your neighbor. *Liberal Opinion Week*, p. 26.

Priest, D. (1987, May 20). Why bullies do it: "To really have fun": School violence being studied. *The Washington Post*, p. 24.

Prothrow-Stith, D. (1991). *Deadly consequences*. New York: HarperCollins.

Pulkkinen, L., & Tremblay, R. E. (1992). Patterns of boys' social adjustment in two cultures and at different ages: A longitudinal perspective. *International Journal of Behavioral Development, 15*, 527–553.

Pyke, N. (1994, May 20). Bullies lurk in every staffroom. *Times Educational Supplement*, p. 12.

Raine, A., Brennan, P., & Mednick, S. A. (1994). Birth complications combined with early maternal rejection at age 1 year predispose to violent crime at age 18 years. *Archives of General Psychiatry, 51*, 984–988.

Rakove, J. (2002, June 16). Contrary to Ashcroft's thinking, Second Amendment doesn't support an expansive right to bear arms. *Seattle Post-Intelligencer*, p. G-1.

Randall, P. E. (1997). *Adult bullying: Perpetrators and victims*. London: Routledge.

Ray, G. E., Cohen, R., Secrist, M. E., & Duncan, M. K. (1997). Relating aggressive and victimization behaviors to children's sociometric status and friendships. *Journal of Social and Personal Relationships, 14*, 95–108.

Reid, K. (1990). Bullying and persistent school absenteeism. In D. P. Tattum & D. A. Lane (Eds.), *Bullying in schools* (pp. 89–94). Stoke-on-Trent, England: Trentham Books.

Reiss, A. J., & Roth, J. A. (1993). *Understanding and preventing violence*. Washington, DC: National Academy Press.

Richman, N., Stevenson, J., & Graham, P. (1982). *Preschool to school: A behavioural study*. London: Academic Press.

Rigby, K. (1996). *Bullying in schools and what to do about it*. Melbourne: Australian Council for Educational Research.

Rigby, K. (1997). Attitudes and beliefs about bullying among Australian school children. *Irish Journal of Psychology, 18*, 202–220.

Rigby, K. (2001). Health consequences of bullying and its prevention in schools. In J. Juvonen & S. Graham (Eds.), *Peer harassment in school: The plight of the vulnerable and victimized* (pp. 310–331). New York: Guilford Press.

Rigby, K., & Slee, P. T. (1991). Bullying among Australian school children: Reported behavior and attitudes towards victims. *Journal of Social Psychology, 131*, 615–627.

Rigby, K., & Slee, P. (1993). Children's attitudes towards victims. In D. Tattum (Ed.), *Understanding and managing bullying* (pp. 119–135). Oxford, England: Heinemann Educational Books.

Riley, D. (1988). *Bullying: A study of victim and victimisers within one inner city secondary school* (In-service B.Ed. Inquiry Report). Sheffield, England: Crewe and Alsager College of Higher Education.

Rivers, I., & Smith, P. K. (1994). Types of bullying behaviour and their correlates. *Aggressive Behavior, 20,* 359–368.

Robinson, S. E., Morrow, S., Kigin, T., & Lindeman, M. (1991). Peer counselors in a high school setting: Evaluation and training impact on students. *School Counsellor, 39,* 35–40.

Robinson, T. N. (1999). Reducing children's television viewing to prevent obesity: A randomized controlled trial. *Journal of the American Medical Association, 282,* 1561–1567.

Robinson, T. N., Wilde, M. L., Navracruz, L. C., Haydel, K. F., & Varady, A. (2001). Effects of reducing children's television and video game use on aggressive behavior. *Archives of Pediatric Medicine, 155,* 17–23.

Rogers, W. S. (1993). Promoting, permitting and preventing bullying. In M. Elliott (Ed.), *Bullying: A practical guide to coping for schools* (pp. 50–58). Harlow, England: Longman.

Roland, E. (1989). Bullying: The Scandinavian research tradition. In D. P. Tattum & D. A. Lane (Eds.), *Bullying in schools* (pp. 21–32). Stoke-on-Trent, England: Trentham Books.

Rose, L. (1991). *The erosion of childhood: Child oppression in Britain, 1860–1918.* London: Routledge.

Ross, D. M. (1970). Incidental learning of number concepts in small group games. *American Journal of Mental Deficiency, 74,* 718–725.

Ross, D. M. (1973). *A teasing program for children.* Unpublished manuscript, University of California Medical Center, San Francisco.

Ross, D. M. (1977–1979). *Case studies.* San Francisco: University of California Medical School.

Ross, D. M. (1984). Thought-stopping: A coping strategy for impending feared events. *Issues in Comprehensive Pediatric Nursing, 7,* 83–89.

Ross, D. M. (1996). *Childhood bullying and teasing: What school personnel, other professionals, and parents can do.* Alexandria, VA: American Counseling Association.

Ross, D. M., & Ross, S. A. (1982). *Hyperactivity: Current issues, research and theory* (2nd ed.). New York: Wiley.

Ross, D. M., & Ross, S. A. (1984). Teaching the child with leukemia to cope with teasing. *Issues in Comprehensive Pediatric Nursing, 7,* 59–66.

Ross, D. M., & Ross, S. A. (1988). *Childhood pain: Current issues, research, and management.* Baltimore: Urban & Schwarzenburg.

Ross, S. A. (1969). Effects of intentional training in social behavior on retarded children. *American Journal of Mental Deficiency, 73,* 912–919.

Royal, G. P., & Roberts, M. C. (1987). Students' perceptions of and attitudes toward disabilities: A comparison of twenty conditions. *Journal of Clinical Child Psychology, 16,* 122–132.

Rutter, M. (1981). Stress, coping and development: Some issues and some questions. *Journal of Child Psychology and Psychiatry, 22,* 323–356.

Rutter, M. (1983). School effects on pupil progress: Research findings and policy implications. *Child Development, 54,* 1–19.

Rutter, M. (1987). Psychosocial resilience and protective mechanisms. *American Journal of Orthopsychiatry, 57,* 316–331.

Rutter, M., Maughan, B., Mortimore, P., & Ouston, J. (1979). *Fifteen thousand hours.* Shepton Mallet, England: Open Books.

Sales, N. J. (1996, December 16). Loaded and dangerous. *New York Magazine,* pp. 32–37.

Salinger, A. (1995). *In my room: Teenagers in their bedrooms.* San Francisco: Chronicle Books.

Salmivalli, C. (1992). *Kouluväkivalta ryhmäilmiönä* [Bullying as a group process]. Unpublished master's thesis, University of Turku, Department of Psychology, Turku, Finland.

Salmivalli, C. (1999). Participant role approach to school bullying: Implications for interventions. *Journal of Adolescence, 22,* 453–459.

Salmivalli, C. (2001). Group view on victimization: Empirical findings and their implications. In J. Juvonen & S. Graham (Eds.), *Peer harassment in school: The plight of the vulnerable and victimized* (pp. 398–419). New York: Guilford Press.

Salmivalli, C., Lagerspetz, K., Björkqvist, K., Österman, K., & Kaukiainen, A. (1996). Bullying as a group process: Participant roles and their relations to social status within the group. *Aggressive Behavior, 22,* 1–15.

Schulhofer, S. (1998). *Unwanted sex: The culture of intimidation and the failure of law.* Cambridge, MA: Harvard University Press.

Schwartz, D., Chang, L., & Farver, J. (2000). *Correlates of victimization in Chinese children's peer groups.* Manuscript submitted for publication.

Schwartz, D., Dodge, K. A., & Coie, J. D. (1993). The emergence of chronic peer victimization in boys' play groups. *Child Development, 64,* 1755–1793.

Schwartz, D., Dodge, K. A., Pettit, G. S., & Bates, J. E. (1997). The early socialization of aggressive victims of bullying. *Child Development, 68,* 665–675.

Schwartz, D., Proctor, L. J., & Chien, D. H. (2001). The aggressive victim of bullying: Emotional and behavioral dysregulation as a pathway to victimization by peers. In J. Juvonen & S. Graham (Eds.), *Peer harassment in school: The plight of the vulnerable and victimized* (pp. 147–174). New York: Guilford Press.

Scialli, J. (1991, November). When your child is picked on. *Parents Magazine, 66,* 47.

Seattle Post-Intelligencer. (1993, May 30). Navy harassment [Editorial], p. E2.

Seattle Post-Intelligencer. (1999, February 26). Violent video games should be reined in [Editorial], p. A18.

Seitz, V., Rosenbaum, L. K., & Apfel, N. H. (1985). Effects of family support intervention: A ten-year follow-up. *Child Development, 56,* 376–391.

Seligman, M. E. P. (1975). *Helplessness: On depression, development and death.* San Francisco: Freeman.

Selman, R. L. (1980). *The growth of interpersonal understanding: Developmental and clinical analyses.* New York: Academic Press.

Seville Statement on Violence. (1989). Reprinted in J. Groebel, J. Hinde, & R. Hinde (Eds.), *Aggression and war: Their biological and social bases.* New York: Cambridge University Press. (Original work published in 1986)

Shalala, D. E. (2001). Message from Donna E. Shalala. In *Youth violence: A report of the Surgeon General—Executive Summary.* Rockville, MD: U.S. Government Printing Office.

Shapiro, J. P., Baumeister, R. F., & Kessler, J. W. (1991). A three-component model of children's teasing: Aggression, humor, and ambiguity. *Journal of Social and Clinical Psychology, 10,* 459–472.

Sharp, S., Sellars, A., & Cowie, H. (1994). Time to listen: Setting up a peer counselling service to help tackle the problem of bullying in schools. *Pastoral Care in Education, 6,* 12–17.

Sharp, S., & Smith, P. K. (1993). Tackling bullying: The Sheffield Project. In D. Tattum (Ed.), *Understanding and managing bullying* (p. 128). London: Heinemann.

Sharp, S., & Smith, P. K. (Eds.). (1994). *Tackling bullying in your school: A practical handbook for teachers.* London: Routledge.

Sheed, F. J. (Trans.). (1993). *Augustine: Confessions, Books I–XIII.* Indianapolis, IN: Hackett.

Siann, G., Callaghan, M., Glissov, P., Lockhart, R., & Rawson, L. (1994). Who gets bullied? The effect of school, gender and ethnic group. *Educational Research, 36,* 123–134.

Siegel, B. S. (1986). *Love, medicine and miracles.* New York: Harper & Row.

Sigelman, C. K., & Begley, N. L. (1987). The early development of reactions to peers with controllable and uncontrollable problems. *Journal of Pediatric Psychology, 12,* 99–114.

Silver, R. L., & Wortman, C. B. (1980). Coping with undesirable life events. In J. Garber & M. E. P. Seligman (Eds.), *Human helplessness: Theory and applications* (pp. 279–340). New York: Academic Press.

Simmons, R. (2002). *Odd girl out.* New York: Harcourt Books.

Slaby, R. G. (1994, January 5). The role of scholars in combating "entertainment violence." *The Chronicle of Higher Education,* pp. B1, B2.

Slaby, R. G., Roedell, N. C., Arezzo, D., & Hendrix, K. (1995). *Early violence prevention: Tools for teachers of young children.* Washington, DC: National Association for the Education of Young Children.

Slee, P. T., & Rigby, K. (1993). The relationship of Eysenck's personality factors and self-esteem to bully/victim behaviour in Australian schoolboys. *Personality and Individual Differences, 14,* 371–373.

Smith, M. J. (1986). *Yes, I can say no.* New York: Arbor House.

Smith, P. K. (1991). The silent nightmare: Bullying and victimization in school peer groups. *The Psychologist, 4*, 243–248.

Smith, P. K. (1997). Bullying in life-span perspective: What can studies of school bullying and workplace bullying learn from each other? *Journal of Community and Applied Social Psychology, 7*, 249–255.

Smith, P. K. (2000). Bullying and harassment in schools and the rights of children. *Children & Society, 14*, 294–303.

Smith, P. K. (2001). [Comments about the failure to include coping with bullying in English teacher training courses, presented at the British Psychological Society Conference.] May, London: England.

Smith, P. K., & Brain, P. (2000). Bullying in schools: Lessons from two decades of research. *Aggressive Behavior, 26*, 1–9.

Smith, P. K., Cowie, H., Olafsson, R., & Liefooghe, A. P. D. (2002). Definitions of bullying: A comparison of terms used, and age and gender differences in a 14-country international comparison. *Child Development, 73*, 1119–1134.

Smith, P. K., & Levan, S. (1995). Perceptions and experiences of bullying in younger pupils. *British Journal of Educational Psychology, 65*, 489–500.

Smith, P. K., Madsen, K. C., & Moody, J. C. (1999). What causes the age decline in reports of being bullied at school? Towards a developmental analysis of risks of being bullied. *Educational Research, 41*, 267–285.

Smith, P. K., & Morita, Y. (1999). Introduction. In P. K. Smith, Y. Morita, J. Junger-Tas, D. Olweus, R. Catalano, & P. Slee (Eds.), *The nature of school bullying: A cross-national perspective* (p. 2). London: Routledge.

Smith, P. K., Morita, Y., Junger-Tas, J., Olweus, D., Catalano, R., & Slee, P. (Eds.). (1999). *The nature of school bullying: A cross-national perspective.* London: Routledge.

Smith, P. K., & Myron-Wilson, R. (1998). Parenting and school bullying. *Clinical Child Psychology and Psychiatry, 3*, 405–417.

Smith, P. K., & Sharp, S. (Eds.). (1994). *School bullying: Insights and perspectives.* London: Routledge.

Smith, P. K., & Shu, S. (2000). What good schools can do about bullying: Findings from a survey in English schools after a decade of research and action. *Childhood, 7*, 193–212.

Smith, P. K., & Thompson, D. A. (1991). Dealing with bully/victim problems in the U.K. In P. K. Smith & D. Thompson (Eds.), *Practical approaches to bullying* (pp. 1–12). London: David Fulton.

Sorensen, E. S. (1993). *Children's stress and coping*. New York: Guilford Press.

South Carolina Educational Television. (1996). *Bullying* (and accompanying lesson plans, appropriate for 3rd–8th grade students) [Videotape]. Available from South Carolina Educational Television, Marketing Department, P.O. Box 1100, Columbia, SC 29211.

Spock, B. (1986, August). How to tame a bully. *Redbook*, p. 36.

Spollen, C. (1994, March/April). Violence has a home address. *Psychology Today, 27*, p. 19.

Stein, N. (1993). No laughing matter: Sexual harassment in K–12 schools. In E. Buchwald, P. Fletcher, & M. Roth (Eds.), *Transforming a rape culture.* Minneapolis, MN: Milkweed Editions.

Stephens, R. D. (2000). Introduction. In D. M. Horn (Ed.), *Bruised inside: What our children say about youth violence, what causes it, and what we need to do about it* (p. 9). Washington, DC: National Association of Attorneys General Report.

Stephenson, P., & Smith, D. (1989). Bullying in the junior school. In D. P. Tattum & D. A. Lane (Eds.), *Bullying in schools* (pp. 45–57). Stoke-on-Trent, England: Trentham Books.

Stevahn, L., Johnson, D. W., Johnson, R. T., Green, K., & Laginski, A. M. (1997). Effects on high school students of conflict resolution integrated into English literature. *Journal of Social Psychology, 137*, 302–315.

Stevahn, L., Johnson, D. W., Johnson, R. T., Oberle, K., & Wahl, L. (2000). Effects of conflict resolution training integrated into a kindergarten curriculum. *Child Development, 71*, 772–784.

Strassberg, Z., Dodge, K. A., Pettit, G. S., & Bates, J. E. (1994). Spanking in the home and children's subsequent aggression toward kindergarten peers. *Development and Psychopathology, 6*, 445–461.

Strasser, T. (2000). *Give a boy a gun.* New York: Simon & Shuster.

Sullivan, K. (2000). Racist bullying: Creating understanding and strategies for teachers. In M. Leicester, C. Modgil, & S. Modgil (Eds.), *Institutional issues: Pupils, schools and teacher education* (Vol. II, pp. 80–99). London: Falmer Press.

Sutton, J., Smith, P. K., & Swettenham, J. (1999). Social cognition and bullying: Social inadequacy or skilled manipulation? *British Journal of Developmental Psychology, 17*, 435–450.

Tanner, L. (1996, February 7). Lead linked to anti-social behavior by kids. *Seattle Post-Intelligencer*, p. A3.

Tattum, D. P. (1989). Violence and aggression in schools. In D. P. Tattum & D. A. Lane (Eds.), *Bullying in schools* (pp. 7–19). Stoke-on-Trent, England: Trentham Books.

Taussig, H. N., & Litrownik, A. J. (1997). Self- and other-directed destructive behaviors: Assessment and relationship to type of abuse. *Child Maltreatment, 2*, 172–182.

Taylor, M. (1996). A theory of mind perspective on social cognitive development. In R. Gelman & T. Au (Eds.), *Handbook of perception and cognition: Vol. 13. Perceptual and cognitive development* (pp. 283–329). New York: Academic Press.

Teen Court Manual. (2000). Port Angeles, WA: Clallam County Juvenile Court Diversion Program.

Thelen, M. H., Fry, R. A., Fehrenbach, P. A., & Frautschi, N. M. (1979). Therapeutic videotape and film modeling: A review. *Psychological Bulletin, 86*, 701–720.

Thomas, A., & Chess, S. (1977). *Temperament and development*. New York: Brunner/Mazel.

Thompson, D. A., & Smith, P. K. (1991). Effective action against bullying: The key problems. In P. K. Smith & D. Thompson (Eds.), *Practical approaches to bullying* (pp. 140–152). London: David Fulton.

Thompson, M., & Grace, C. O. (2001). *Best friends, worst enemies: Understanding the social lives of children*. New York: Ballantine Books.

Thorne, B., & Luria, Z. (1986). Sexuality and gender in children's daily worlds. *Social Problems, 33*, 176–190.

Tremblay, R. E., Mâsse, B., Perron, D., Leblanc, M., Schwartzman, A. E., & Ledigham, J. E. (1992). Early disruptive behavior, poor school achievement, delinquent behavior, and delinquent personality: Longitudinal analyses. *Journal of Consulting and Clinical Psychology, 60*, 64–72.

Tremblay, R. E., Pagani-Kurtz, L., Mâsse, L. C., Vitaro, F., & Pihl, R. O. (1995). A bimodal preventive intervention for disruptive kindergarten boys: Its impact through mid-adolescence. *Journal of Consulting and Clinical Psychology, 63*, 560–568.

Tremblay, R. E., Pihl, R. O., Vitaro, F., & Dobkin, P. L. (1994). Predicting early onset of male antisocial behavior from preschool behavior. *Archives of General Psychiatry, 51*, 732–738.

Troy, M., & Sroufe, L. A. (1987). Victimization among preschoolers: Role of attachment relationship history. *Journal of the American Academy of Child and Adolescent Psychiatry, 26*, 166–172.

Twemlow, S. W. (2000). The roots of violence: Converging psychoanalytic explanatory models for power struggles and violence in schools. *Psychoanalytic Quarterly, 69*, 741–785.

Twemlow, S. W., Fonagy, P., & Sacco, F. C. (2001). An innovative psychodynamically influenced approach to reduce school violence. *Journal of the American Academy of Child and Adolescent Psychiatry, 40*, 377–379.

Twemlow, S. W., Fonagy, P., Sacco, F. C., Gies, M. L., Evans, R., & Ewbank, R. (2001). Creating a peaceful school learning environment: A controlled study of an elementary school intervention to reduce violence. *American Journal of Psychiatry, 158*, 808–810.

Twemlow, S. W., Sacco, F. C., & Twemlow, S. (2001). *Creating a peaceful school learning environment: A training program for elementary schools*. Agawam, Massachusetts: T & S Publishing Group.

U.S. Department of Health and Human Services. (2001). *Youth violence: A report of the Surgeon General Executive summary*. Rockville, MD: U.S. Government Printing Office.

Voss, L. S. (1997). Teasing, disputing, and playing: Cross-gender interactions and space utilization among first and third-graders. *Gender and Society, 11*, 238–256.

Wachtel, P. L. (1973). Psychodynamics, behaviour therapy and the implacable experimenter: An inquiry into the consistency of personality. *Journal of Abnormal Psychology, 83*, 324–334.

Wainwright, M. (1999, April 24). Gay pupil to sue school for negligence. *The Guardian*, p. 5.

Walker, H. (1996). In R. Karr-Morse & M. S. Wiley, *Ghosts from the nursery: Tracing the roots of violence* (p. 7). New York: Atlantic Monthly Press.

Warm, T. R. (1997). The role of teasing in development and vice versa. *Developmental and Behavioral Pediatrics, 18*, 97–101.

Watzlawick, P., Weakland, J., & Fisch, R. (1974). *Change: Principles of problem formation and problem resolution*. New York: Norton.

Wexler, D. B. (1991). *The adolescent self*. New York: Norton.

Whalen, C. K., & Henker, B. (1976). Psychostimulants and children: A review and analysis. *Psychological Bulletin, 83*, 1113–1130.

White, M. (1987). *The Japanese educational challenge*. London: Free Press/ Macmillan.

Whitney, I., & Smith, P. K. (1993). A survey of the nature and extent of bully/ victim problems in junior/middle and secondary schools. *Educational Research, 35*, 3–25.

Wiehe, V. R. (1991). *Perilous rivalry: When siblings become abusive*. Lexington, MA: Lexington Books.

Wiggins, J. S., & Winder, C. L. (1961). The Peer Nomination Inventory: An empirically derived sociometric measure of adjustment in preadolescent boys. *Psychological Reports, 9*, 643–677.

Williams, K., Chambers, M., Logan, S., & Robinson, D. (1996). Association of common health symptoms with bullying in primary school children. *British Medical Journal, 313*, 17–19.

Willis, P. (1977). *Learning to labour*. London: Saxon House.

Winfree, L. T., Esbensen, F.-A., & Osgood, D. W. (1995, April). *On becoming a youth gang member: Low self-control or learned behavior*? Paper presented at the annual meeting of the Academy of Criminal Justice Sciences, Boston.

Winn, M. (1987). *Unplugging the plug-in drug*. New York: Penguin Books.

Wolke, D. (1999, December 24). In S. Cassidy, Beware the "pure bully" who never takes time off. *Times Educational Supplement*, News Section, p. 3.

Wolpe, J., & Lazarus, A. A. (1966). *Behavior therapy techniques*. Pergamon Press.

Yamamoto, K. (1979). Children's ratings of the stressfulness of experiences. *Developmental Psychology, 15*, 581–582.

Yamamoto, K., & Byrnes, D. A. (1984). Classroom social status, ethnicity and ratings of stressful events. *Journal of Educational Research, 77*, 283–286.

Yamamoto, K., & Felsenthal, H. M. (1982). Stressful experiences of children: Professional judgments. *Psychological Reports, 50,* 1087–1093.

Yates, C., & Smith, P. K. (1989). Bullying in two English comprehensive schools. In E. Roland & E. Munthe (Eds.), *Bullying: An international perspective* (pp. 22–34). London: Fulton.

Yoshikawa-Cogley, L. (1995, February 8). Children talk out problems. *Seattle Post-Intelligencer,* pp. B1, B3.

Ziegler, S., & Rosenstein-Manner, M. (1991). *Bullying at school: Toronto in an international context* (Report No. 196). Toronto, Ontario, Canada: Toronto Board of Education, Research Services.

Zimbardo, P. G. (1982). *The shy child.* Garden City, NY: Doubleday.

Zimbardo, P. G. (1990). *Shyness: What it is. What to do about it.* New York: Addison-Wesley.

Zimbardo, P. G. (2001, December 30). The psychology of terrorism: Mind games and mind healing. *San Francisco Chronicle,* Insight, Year-end special edition, p. D6.

Zimmerman, J. (1995). *Tailspin: Women at war in the wake of Tailhook.* New York: Doubleday.

Zinn, H. (1995). *A people's history of the United States 1492–present.* New York: Harper Perennial.

Annotated Bibliography

BOOKS FOR PRIMARY-GRADE CHILDREN: FICTION

Alexander, M. (1983). *Move over, twerp*. New York: Dial Press.
Shows what happens when a child who is being pushed around by bigger boys takes a firm stand.

Berenstain, S., & Berenstain, J. (1993). *The Berenstain Bears and the bully*. New York: Random House.
When she gets beaten up by the class bully, Sister Bear learns an important lesson in self-defense and forgiveness. Discussion should stress that physical aggression is not a good strategy.

Bottner, B. (1980). *Mean Maxine*. New York: Pantheon.
Ralph is teased by Mean Maxine until he works up his courage for a confrontation with her. Note that he rehearses what he will say and how mean he will be.

Boyd, L. (1991). *Baily the big bully*. New York: Puffin Books.
Max, the new boy in school, uses assertiveness to tame Baily the bully, of whom everyone is afraid, and teaches Baily about teamwork and friendship.

Chapman, C. (1981). *Herbie's troubles*. New York: Dutton Children's Books.
After trying the advice of each of his friends on how to deal with a bully, Herbie solves his problem himself.

Cole, J. (1989). *Bully trouble*. New York: Random House.
Two small boys are bullied by a bigger boy until they strike back with a clever, simple plan.

Cushman, D. (1990). *Camp Big Paw*. New York: Harper & Row.
On Cyril's first day at camp he is picked on by Nigel, the camp tease. How Cyril manages Nigel with a clever strategy makes good reading.

Freschet, B. (1986). *Furlie Cat*. New York: Lothrop.
Furlie the fraidy cat mistakenly decides that being tough is the only way to overcome his fears. He becomes a bully overnight. When something happens that teaches him to be a friend to one of his victims, he gives up being a bully.

Henkes, K. (1991). *Chrysanthemum*. New York: Greenwillow Books.
A kindergarten-age mouse is teased because of her unusual name. The story shows empathy for the victim and the power of social support.

Kasza, K. (1993). *The rat and the tiger*. New York: Putnam's.
In his friendship with Rat, Tiger plays the bully because of his greater size, but one day Rat stands up for his rights. Tiger makes amends.

Kraus, R. (1977). *Noel the coward*. New York: Windmills Press.
Shows the effect that striking back has on bullies.

Passen, L. (1991). *Fat, fat Rose Marie*. New York: Holt.
Excellent on the importance of accepting others for who they are and for showing that if one child takes a stand against a bully, others will follow.

Petty, K., & Firmin, C. (1991). *Being bullied*. New York: Barron's Books.
A girl bully calls another girl names, teases, and scribbles on her papers. The victim seeks social support from her mother and also gets help from her teacher.

Wells, R. (1973). *Benjamin and Tulip*. New York: Dial Books.
An animal story in which the bully is a girl and the victim is a boy. When they encounter a bigger problem that affects them both, they team up and become friends.

Wilhelm, H. (1988). *Tyrone the horrible*. New York: Scholastic.
A little dinosaur tries several ways of dealing with Tyrone, the biggest bully in the swamp (avoidance, present/bribery, being cool, fighting him), and finally hits on a successful tactic.

BOOKS FOR PRIMARY-GRADE CHILDREN: NONFICTION

Berry, J. W. (1982). *Let's talk about teasing*. Newark, NJ: Peter Pan Industries.
Has some good ideas, but it suggests that the victim ignore the teasing and goes no further. If using this book in the teasing program, the adult

should suggest some other strategies that the child who is being teased could use if ignoring does not work.

Berry, J. W. (1985). *Let's talk about being bullied.* Chicago: Children's Press.
A simple book that helps the child who is being bullied. Strategies include facing up to the bullies, being kind, and staying away from them.

Carlson, N. (1988). *I like me.* New York: Viking.
A book about taking care of and valuing yourself. This book would be especially helpful for victimized children.

Guffe, T. (1991). *Bully for you.* New York: Child's Play.
Why it is not a good idea to be a bully. A book for overly aggressive young children tempted to bully others.

BOOKS FOR OLDER CHILDREN: FICTION

Bosch, C. (1988). *Bully on the bus.* Seattle, WA: Parenting Press.
"A Decision is Yours Book." When Nick Jones, the meanest kid in fifth grade, is waiting for you on the bus, you make the decision about how to deal with it. Several alternatives are presented, including talking it out and leaving anger behind.

Chambers, A. (1983). *The present takers.* New York: Harper & Row.
Lucy is tormented by a group of class bullies who demand gifts and money. When her classmates decide to take action against the bullies, a clever solution is found.

Coryell, S. (1989). *Eaglebait.* Orlando, FL: Harcourt, Brace, Jovanovich.
A shy, unpopular 14-year-old is taunted and bullied by his classmates first in a military school, then in a regular high school. Things change for the better when he starts to feel better about himself.

de Paola, T. (1979). *Oliver Button is a sissy.* New York: Harcourt, Brace, Jovanovich.
A sympathetic account of a boy who is teased because he is interested in dancing.

Duncan, L. (1988). *Wonder Kid meets the evil lunch snatcher.* Boston: Little, Brown.
Shows all the misery of being teased. Solution is very creative.

Gardner, R. A. (1972). *Dr. Gardner's stories about the real world*. Englewood Cliffs, NJ: Prentice-Hall.
The story, "Jerry and the bullies" (pp. 78–101), shows effects of passive withdrawal and of striking back.

Gifaldi, D. (1986). *One thing for sure*. Boston: Houghton Mifflin.
Dylan is teased when his father is imprisoned. He conquers the bullies with his strength, determination, nonviolent temperament, and positive outlook.

Kinsey-Warnock, N. (1991). *The night the bells rang*. New York: Cobblehill Books.
An excellent World War I story about a fifth-grade boy who learns a lot about bullying and in the process recognizes his own tendency to bully his younger brother.

Mauser, P. R. (1983). *A bundle of sticks*. New York: Atheneum.
At the mercy of the class bully, a fifth-grade boy is sent to a martial arts school where he learns techniques to defend himself as well as a philosophy that allows him not to fight.

Millman, D. (1991). *Secret of the peaceful warrior*. Tiburon, CA: Kramer.
An old man shows Danny the importance of looking brave, of not being afraid, because fear is the enemy of the victim. Good on extortion and striking back.

Needle, J. (1993). *The bully*. London: Hamish Hamilton.
An excellent account of school personnel's blindness to the misery of victims and the cunning behavior of bullies.

Robinson, N. K. (1980). *Wendy and the bullies*. New York: Scholastic Book Services.
Explains a lot about bullying. Good account of the strategies that victims use. Shows the effect of assertiveness. A good story.

Shreve, S. (1993). *Joshua T. Bates takes charge*. New York: Knopf.
Eleven-year-old Joshua, who is already worried about fitting in at school, suddenly has more problems when the new boy, Sean, whom he is supposed to be helping, becomes the target of the fifth-grade's biggest bully.

Sinykin, S. C. (1994). *The Shorty Society*. New York: Penguin Books.
Three seventh graders who are short and get teased band together to combat the teasers.

Zeier, J. T. (1993). *Stick boy*. New York: Atheneum.
A 7-inch growth spurt in the sixth grade makes skinny, self-conscious Eric a school misfit and the victim of the class bully.

BOOKS FOR OLDER CHILDREN: NONFICTION

Grunsell, A. (1990). *Bullying*. New York: Gloucester.
Discusses bullying, why it occurs, and how it can be handled. Excellent on importance of telling adults, not yielding to extortion or demands, why some children are bullies, and racist bullying.

Kaufman, G., & Raphael, L. (1990). *Stick up for yourself*. Minneapolis, MN: Free Spirit Publishing.
A guide to assertiveness and positive self-esteem that contains a wealth of ideas for victimized children.

Sanders, P. (1993). *What do you know about bullying?* New York: Gloucester Press.
An excellent general discussion about bullying including how children become bullies and how to stand up to them. A good section on racist bullying.

Webster-Doyle, T. (1991). *Why is everybody always picking on me? A guide to handling bullies*. Middlebury, VT: Atrium Society.
Uses stories and discussion to help children to understand bullies and to solve conflict in a nonviolent way. Shows how bullies can change their ways.

BOOKS FOR PARENTS

Lawson, S. (1994). *Helping children cope with bullying*. London: Sheldon.
An excellent book of practical advice on how parents can help the child who is bullied.

Pearce, J. (1989). *Fighting, teasing, and bullying*. Northamptonshire, England: Thorsons Publishers.
An excellent short book of advice on how parents can forestall or manage these problems. This book is out of print but should be available in many public libraries.

Zimbardo, P. G. (1982). *The shy child*. Garden City, NY: Doubleday.
Shyness often elicits teasing and other forms of bullying. This is an excellent book for parents of a child who seems to have a shyness problem.

VIDEOTAPES FOR SCHOOL PERSONNEL TO USE WITH STUDENTS

Bully. (1973). National Instructional Television Center, Box A, Bloomington, IN 47401.

A new boy who is very bright is resented by others, especially by a bully who harasses him continually. The video effectively shows how frightening it is to be singled out by a bully. Recommended for children in Grades 2 to 6.

Bully Smart. (1995). Street Smart, 105 North Virginia Avenue, Suite 305, Falls Church, VA 22042.

An excellent 20-minute video filled with practical suggestions about how to cope with bullies. Recommended for children in Grades K to 6.

Set Straight on Bullies. (1988). National School Safety Center, 4165 Thousand Oaks Boulevard, Suite 290, Westlake Village, CA 91362.

An 18-minute video about a young boy who is bullied by an older one. This video shows clearly that bullying affects everyone in the school environment and cannot be allowed. Recommended for children in Grades 4 and up.

Author Index

Subject Index

Subject Index